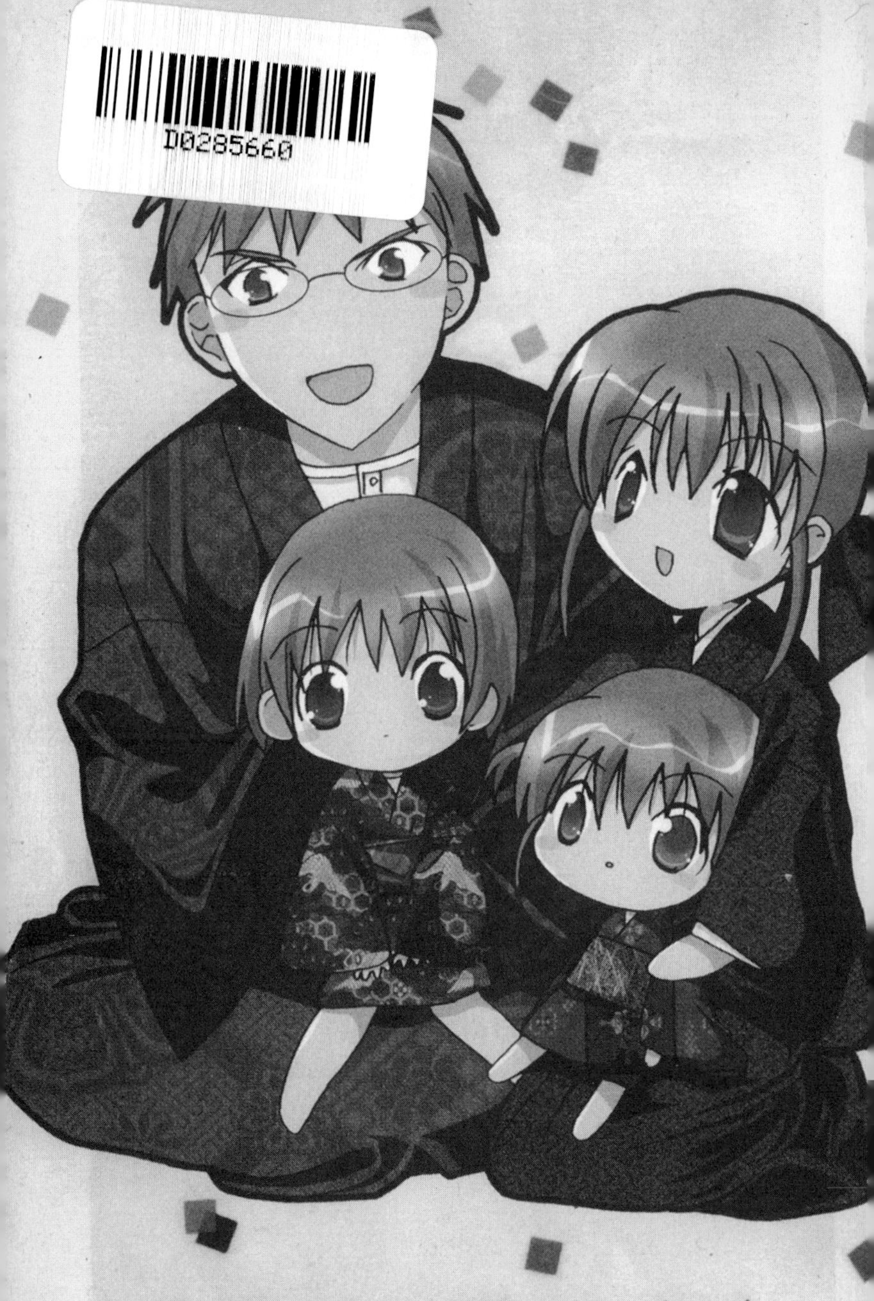

PITA-TEN

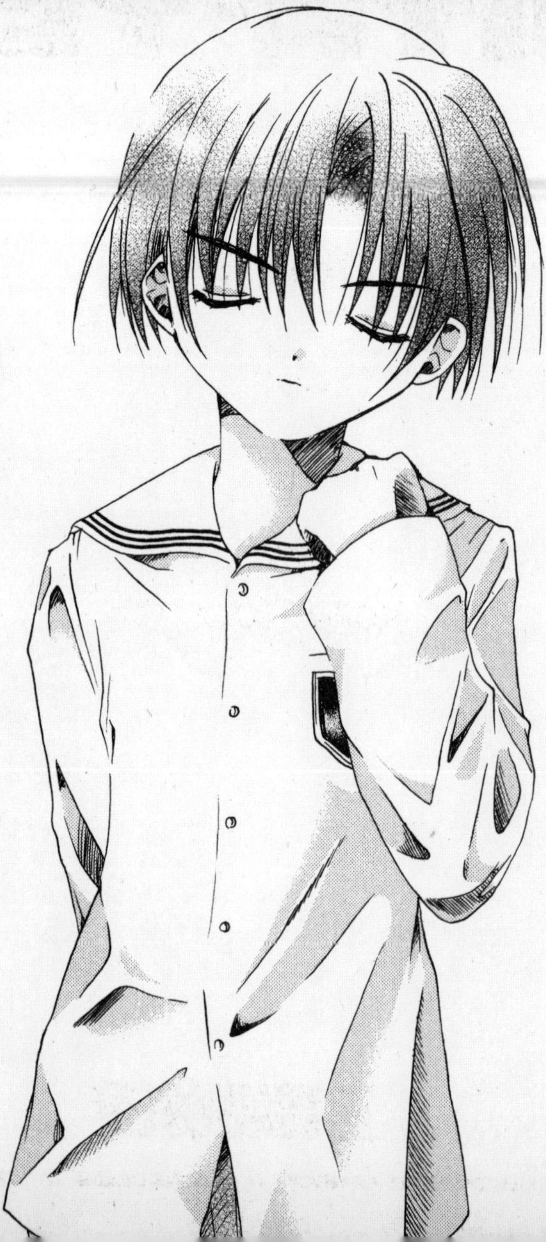

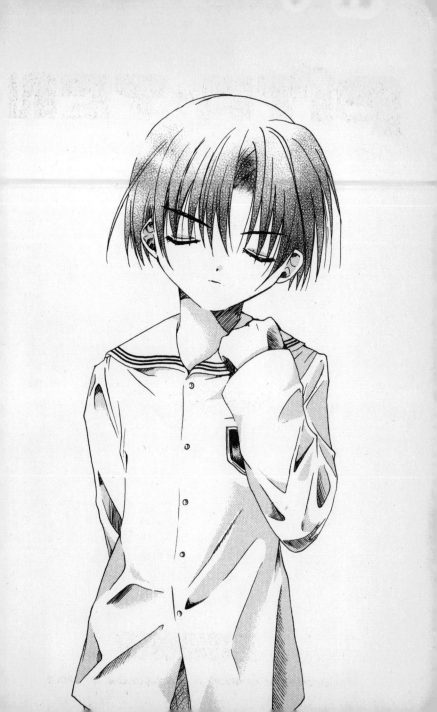

Volume 7

by
Koge-Donbo

HAMBURG // LONDON // LOS ANGELES // TOKYO

Pita-Ten Vol. 7
Created by Koge-Donbo

Translation - Nan Rymer
English Adaptation - Adam Arnold
Copy Editor - Peter Ahlstrom
Retouch and Lettering - Abolardo Biglng
Production Artist - James Dashiell
Cover Design - Raymond Makowski

Editor - Paul Morrissey
Digital Imaging Manager - Chris Buford
Pre-Press Manager - Antonio DePietro
Production Managers - Jennifer Miller and Mutsumi Miyazaki
Art Director - Matt Alford
Managing Editor - Jill Freshney
VP of Production - Ron Klamert
President and C.O.O. - John Parker
Publisher and C.E.O. - Stuart Levy

A **TOKYOPOP®** Manga

TOKYOPOP Inc.
5900 Wilshire Blvd. Suite 2000
Los Angeles, CA 90036

E-mail: info@TOKYOPOP.com
Come visit us online at www.TOKYOPOP.com

ISBN: 1-59532-016-4

First TOKYOPOP printing: January 2005
10 9 8 7 6 5 4 3 2 1
Printed in the USA

Contents

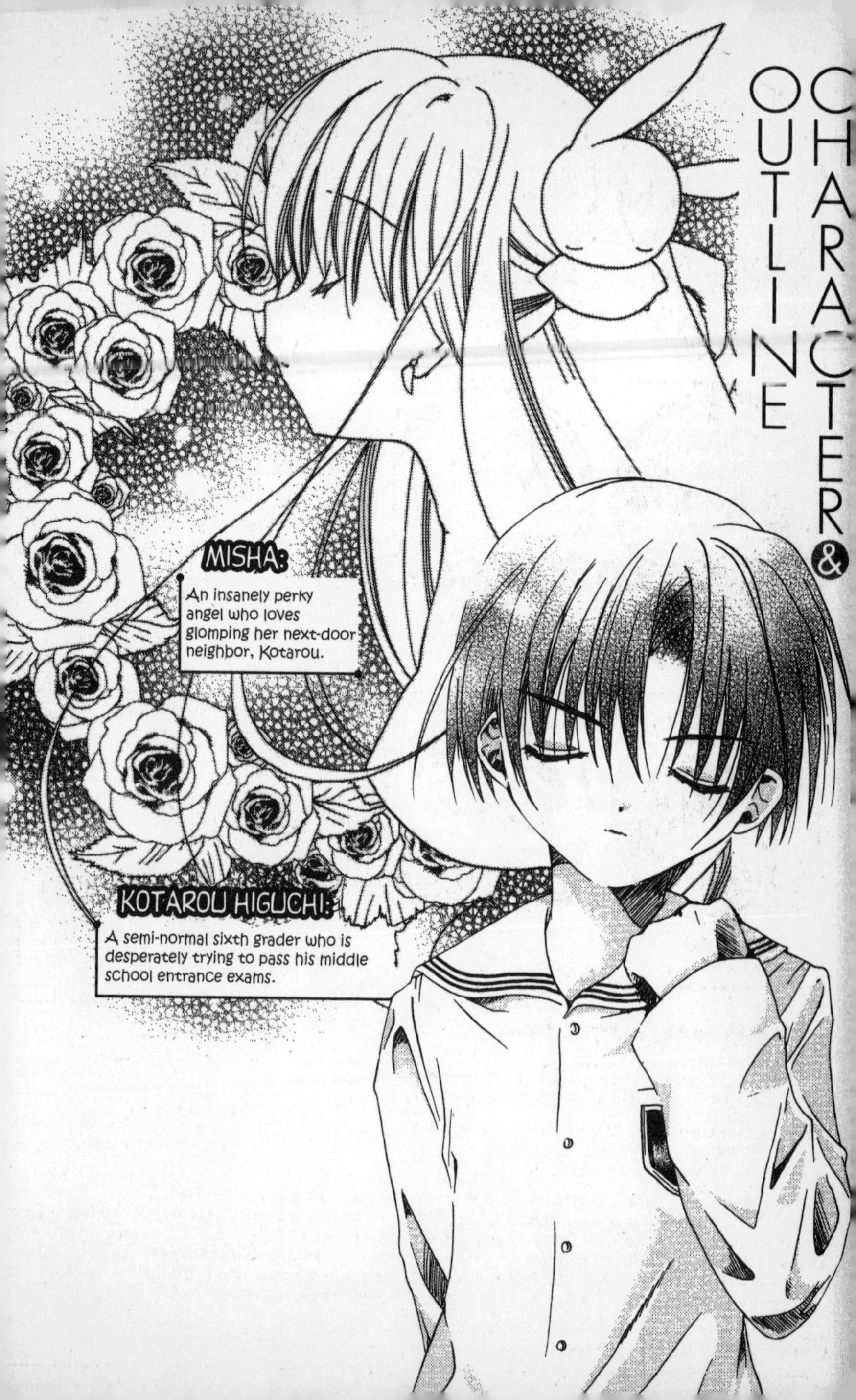
CHARACTER & OUTLINE
MISHA:
An insanely perky angel who loves glomping her next-door neighbor, Kotarou.
KOTAROU HIGUCHI:
A semi-normal sixth grader who is desperately trying to pass his middle school entrance exams.

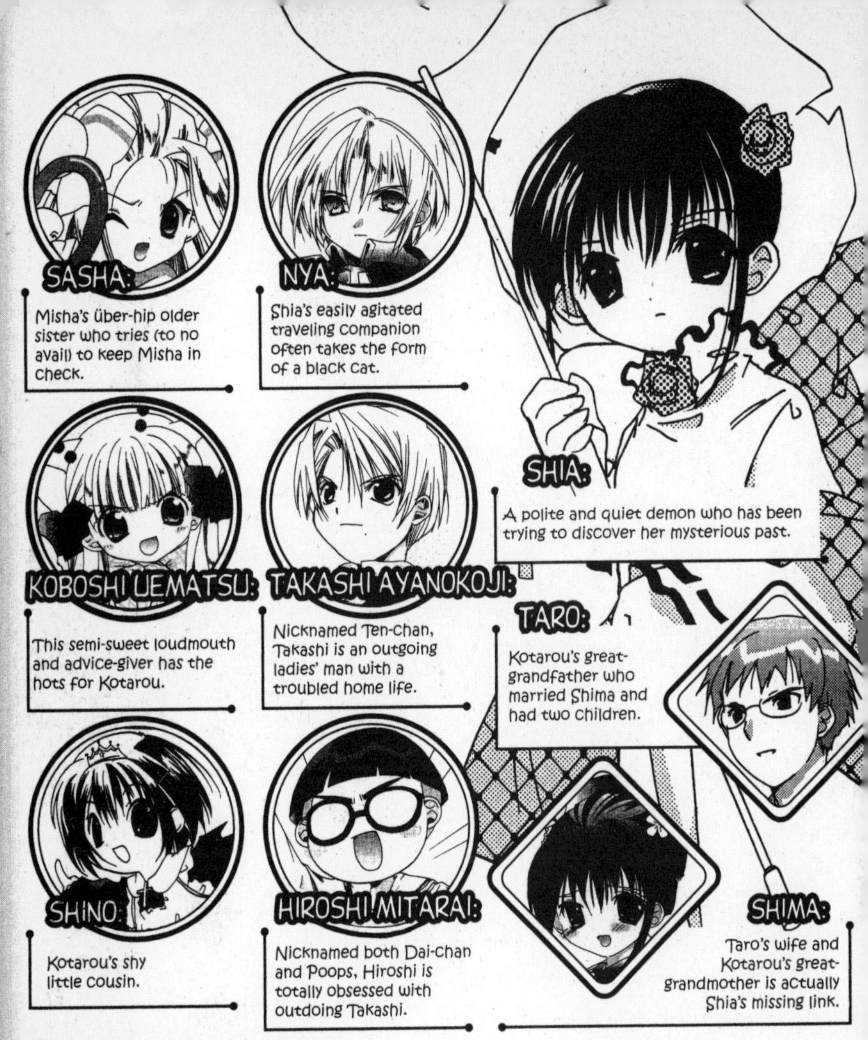
SASHA:
Misha's über-hip older sister who tries (to no avail) to keep Misha in check.
NYA:
Shia's easily agitated traveling companion often takes the form of a black cat.
SHIA:
A polite and quiet demon who has been trying to discover her mysterious past.
KOBOSHI UEMATSU:
This semi-sweet loudmouth and advice-giver has the hots for Kotarou.
TAKASHI AYANOKOJI:
Nicknamed Ten-chan, Takashi is an outgoing ladies' man with a troubled home life.
TARO:
Kotarou's great-grandfather who married Shima and had two children.
SHINO:
Kotarou's shy little cousin.
HIROSHI MITARAI:
Nicknamed both Dai-chan and Poops, Hiroshi is totally obsessed with outdoing Takashi.
SHIMA:
Taro's wife and Kotarou's great-grandmother is actually Shia's missing link.

The Story Until Now...

Quiet sixth grader Kotarou Higuchi was once your average student prepping for his middle school entrance exams, but when Misha, a spastic angel, and Shia, a kind-hearted demon, moved in next door, life became anything but ordinary!

Just as Kotarou manages to adjust to his topsy-turvy new life, he suffers a mysterious coma after Shia steals a kiss from him. By the time Misha manages to return Kotarou from the brink of an unending slumber, Shia has already fled, her wherebabouts unknown.

Shortly thereafter, Kotarou is informed of his maternal great-grandfather's degrading health and rushes to his mother's home. There he is miraculously reunited with Shia. Reality blurs and fate begins to reveal a tangled image of the past, where Kotarou, along with Misha, comes across a youthful version of his great-grandfather, Taro, and a spitting image of Shia named Shima. These two eventually marry and have two children; however, unable to suppress her natural demonic instincts, Shima bids Taro adieu. It is then that Kotarou learns that Shia had been searching for her family all this time. With this knowledge, Kotarou returns to the present, only to find that his great-grandfather has passed away.

On the day of his great-grandfather's funeral, Kotarou unites with Shia again in front of the temple and relays the painful news, and as her tears flow, so too do her long-lost memories...

Easy.
Suuu.

"((

Easy...

Lesson 38
How to Find What You're Looking For: Part 6

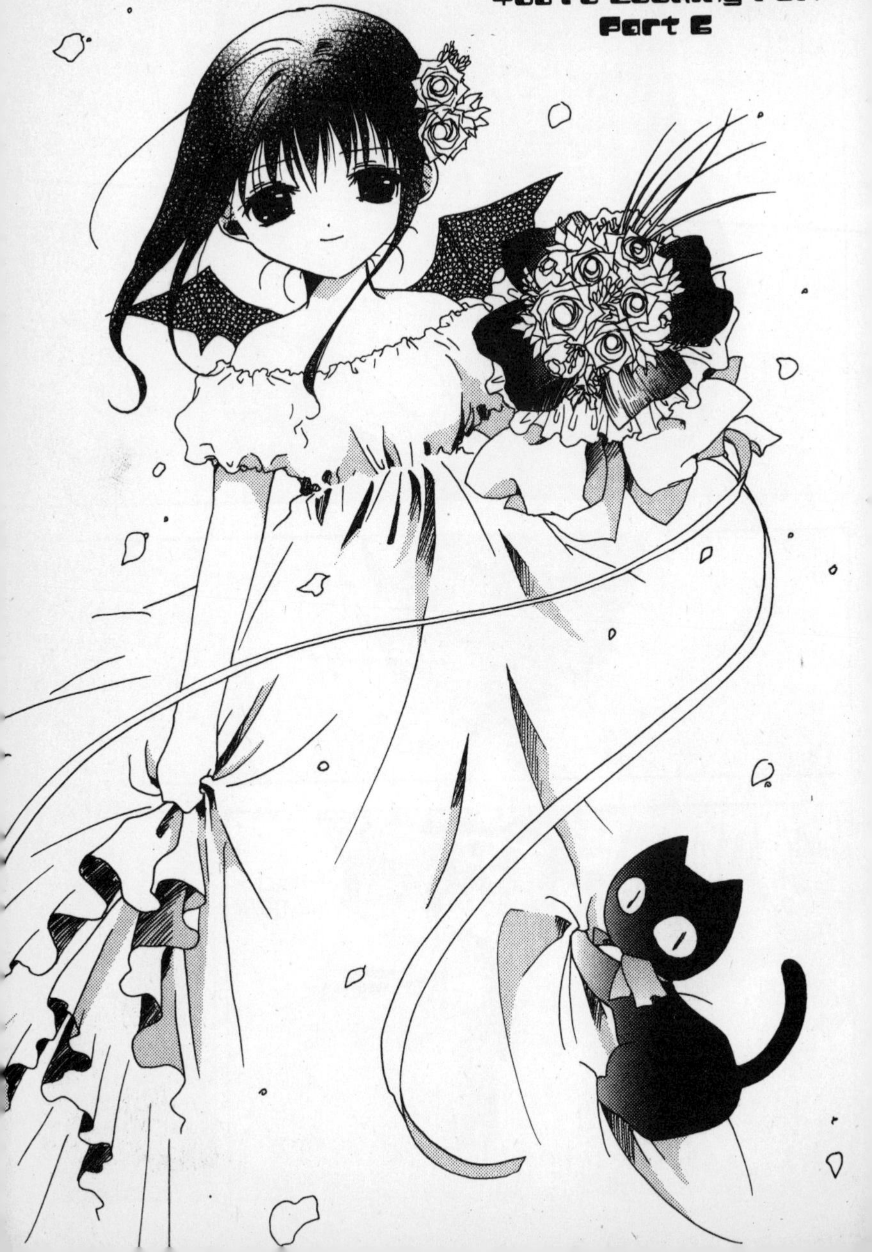

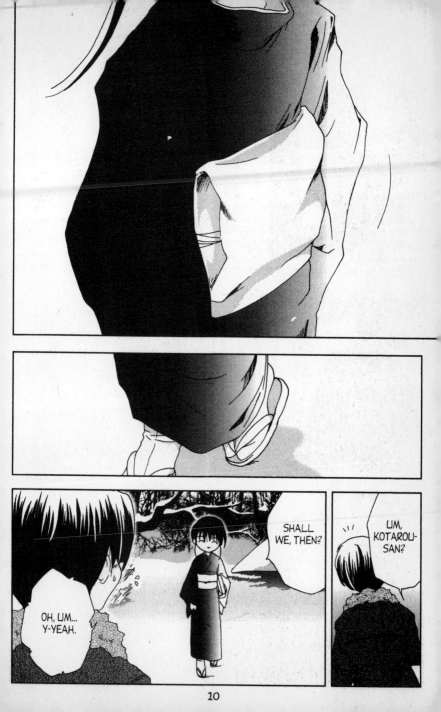

SHALL WE, THEN?

OH, UM... Y-YEAH.

UM, KOTAROU-SAN?

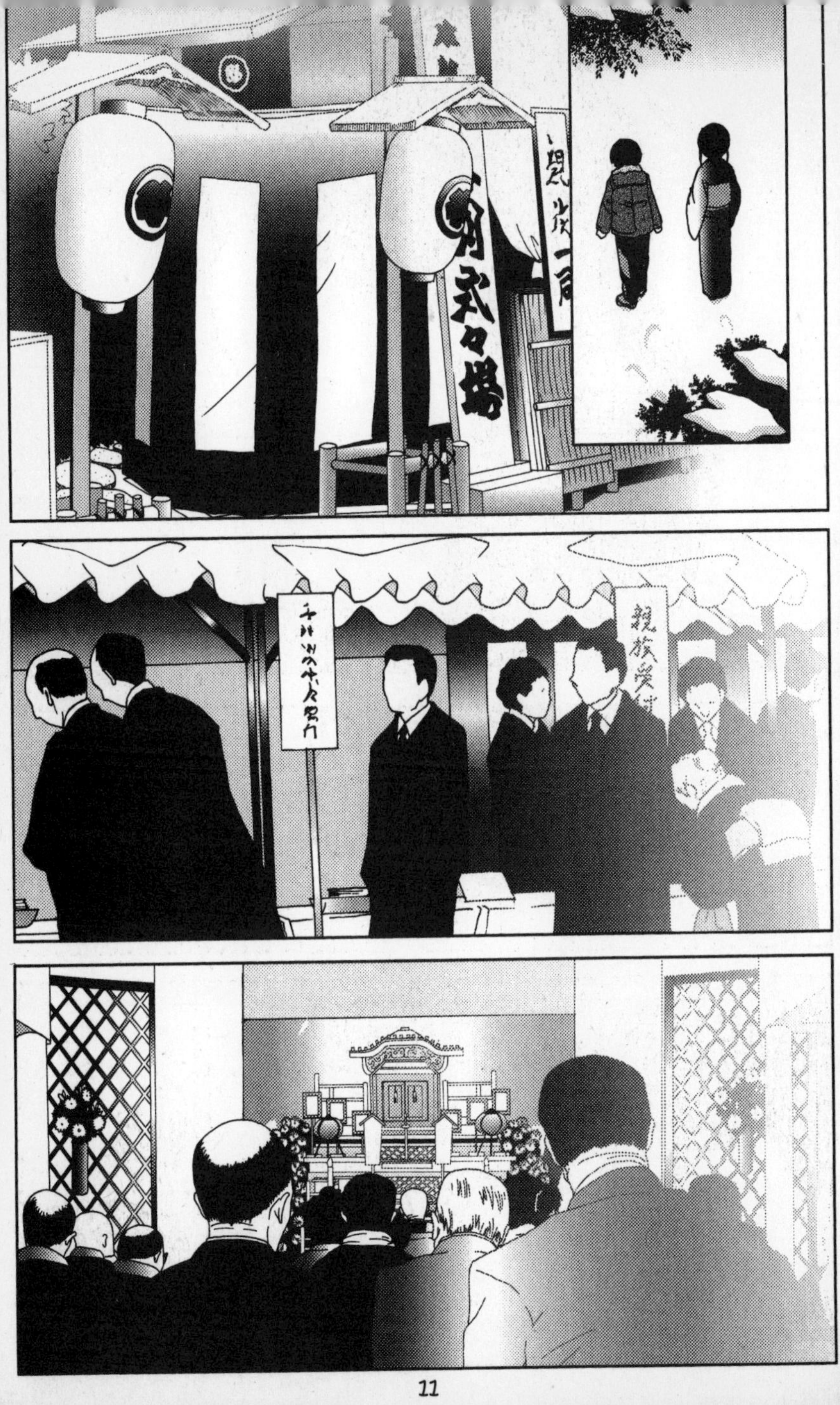

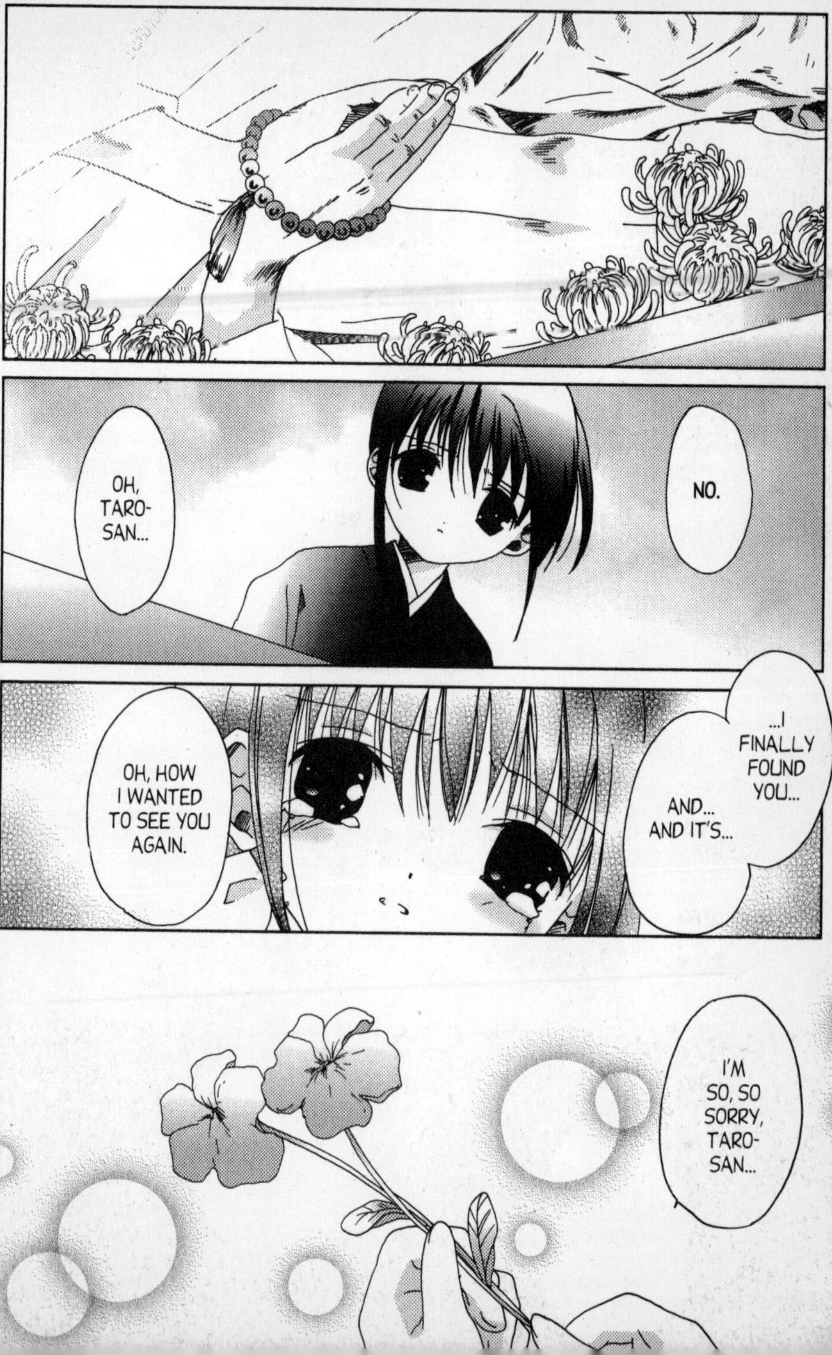
NO.
OH, TARO-SAN...
...I FINALLY FOUND YOU...
AND... AND IT'S...
OH, HOW I WANTED TO SEE YOU AGAIN.
I'M SO, SO SORRY, TARO-SAN...

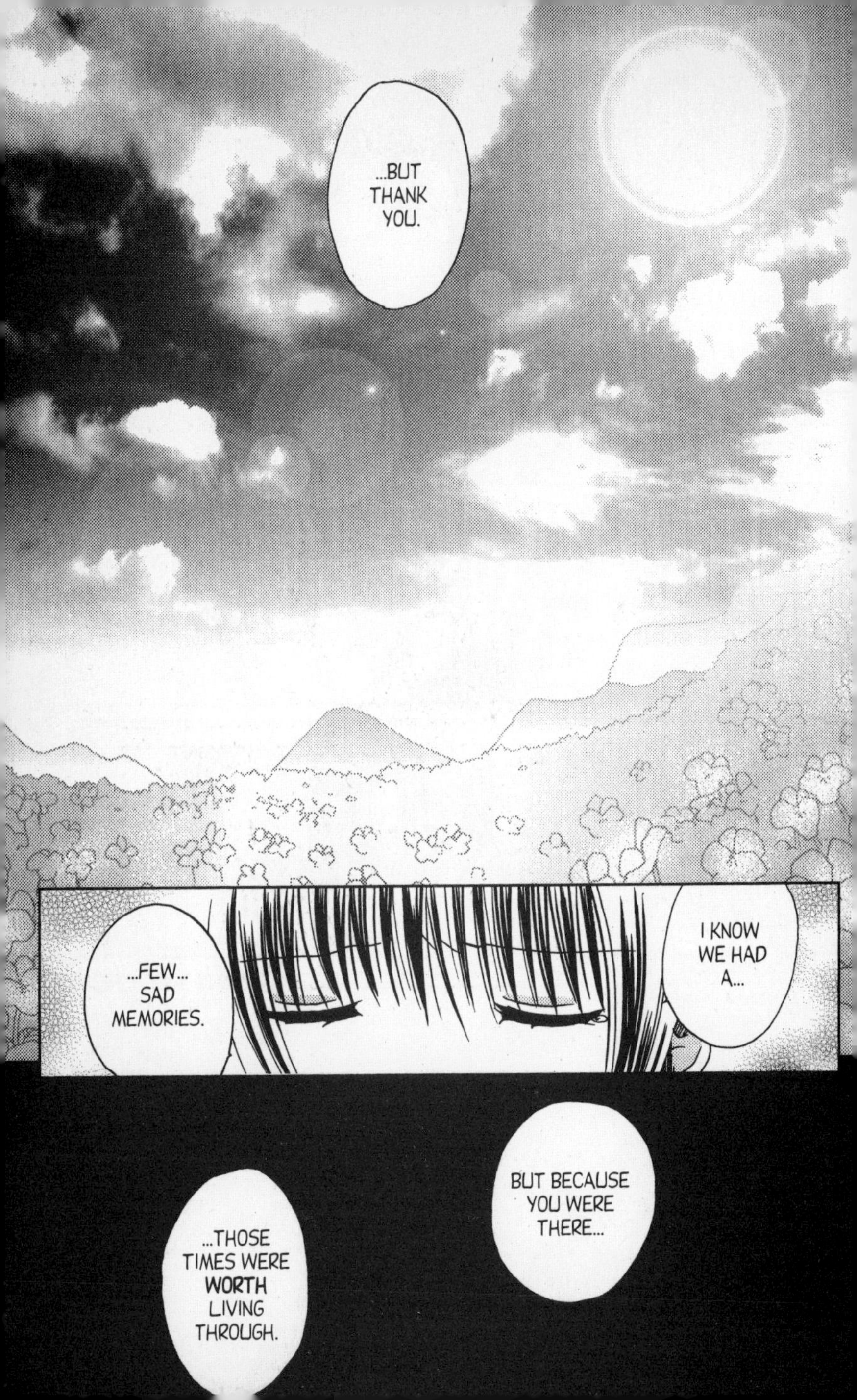
...BUT THANK YOU.
I KNOW WE HAD A...
...FEW... SAD MEMORIES.
BUT BECAUSE YOU WERE THERE...
...THOSE TIMES WERE **WORTH** LIVING THROUGH.

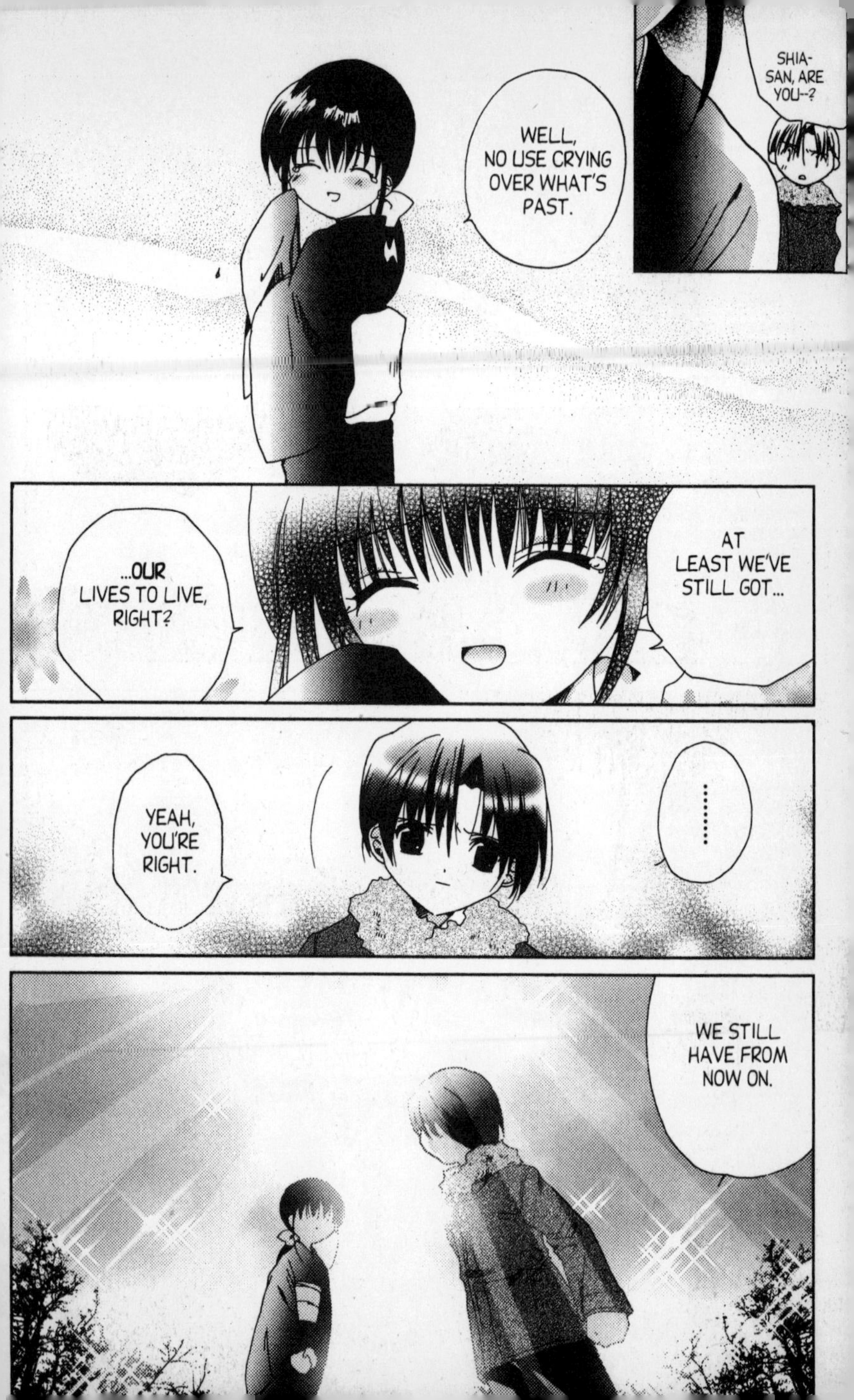
SHIA-SAN, ARE YOU--?
WELL, NO USE CRYING OVER WHAT'S PAST.
AT LEAST WE'VE STILL GOT...
...OUR LIVES TO LIVE, RIGHT?
....
YEAH, YOU'RE RIGHT.
WE STILL HAVE FROM NOW ON.

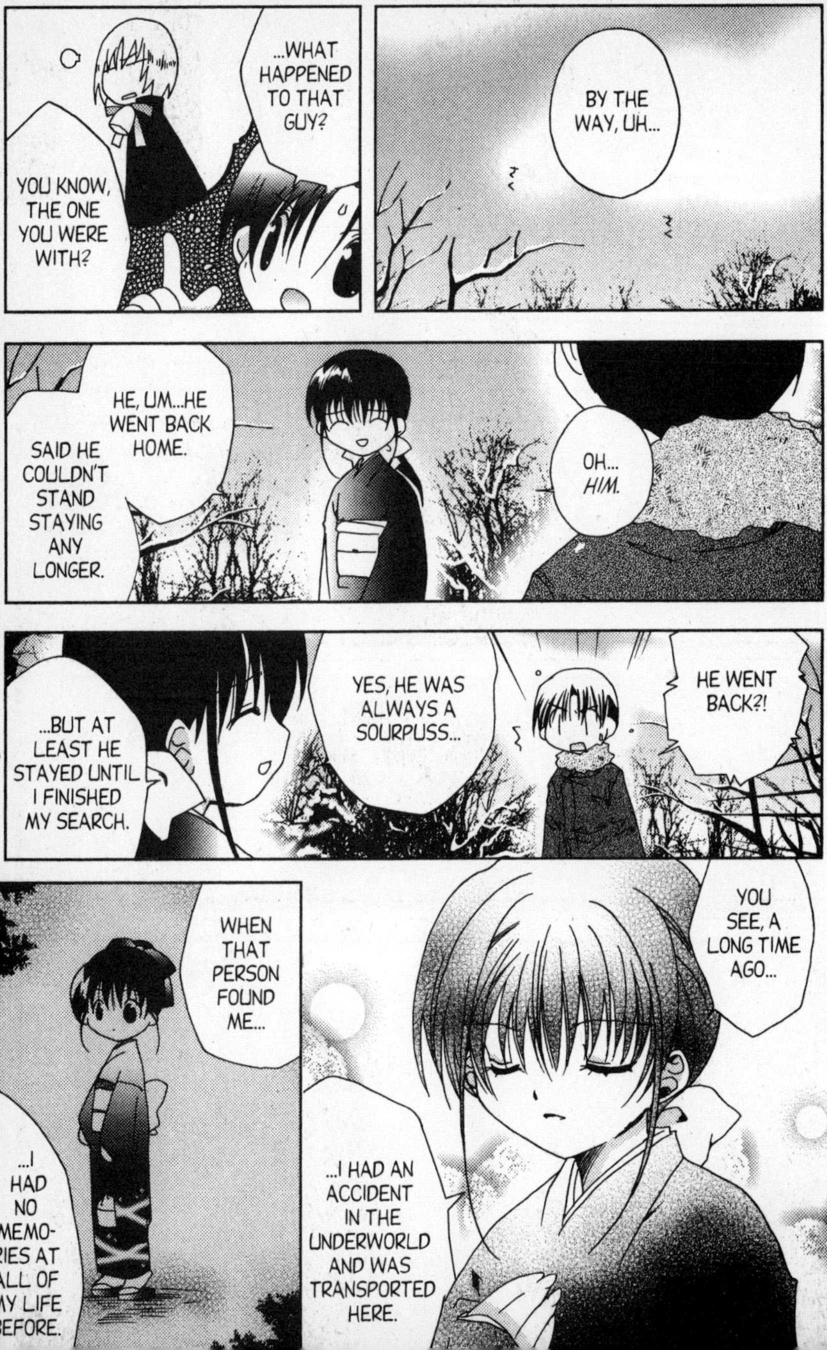
BY THE WAY, UH...
...WHAT HAPPENED TO THAT GUY?
YOU KNOW, THE ONE YOU WERE WITH?
OH... *HIM.*
HE, UM...HE WENT BACK HOME.
SAID HE COULDN'T STAND STAYING ANY LONGER.
HE WENT BACK?!
YES, HE WAS ALWAYS A SOURPUSS...
...BUT AT LEAST HE STAYED UNTIL I FINISHED MY SEARCH.
YOU SEE, A LONG TIME AGO...
...I HAD AN ACCIDENT IN THE UNDERWORLD AND WAS TRANSPORTED HERE.
WHEN THAT PERSON FOUND ME...
...I HAD NO MEMO-RIES AT ALL OF MY LIFE BEFORE.

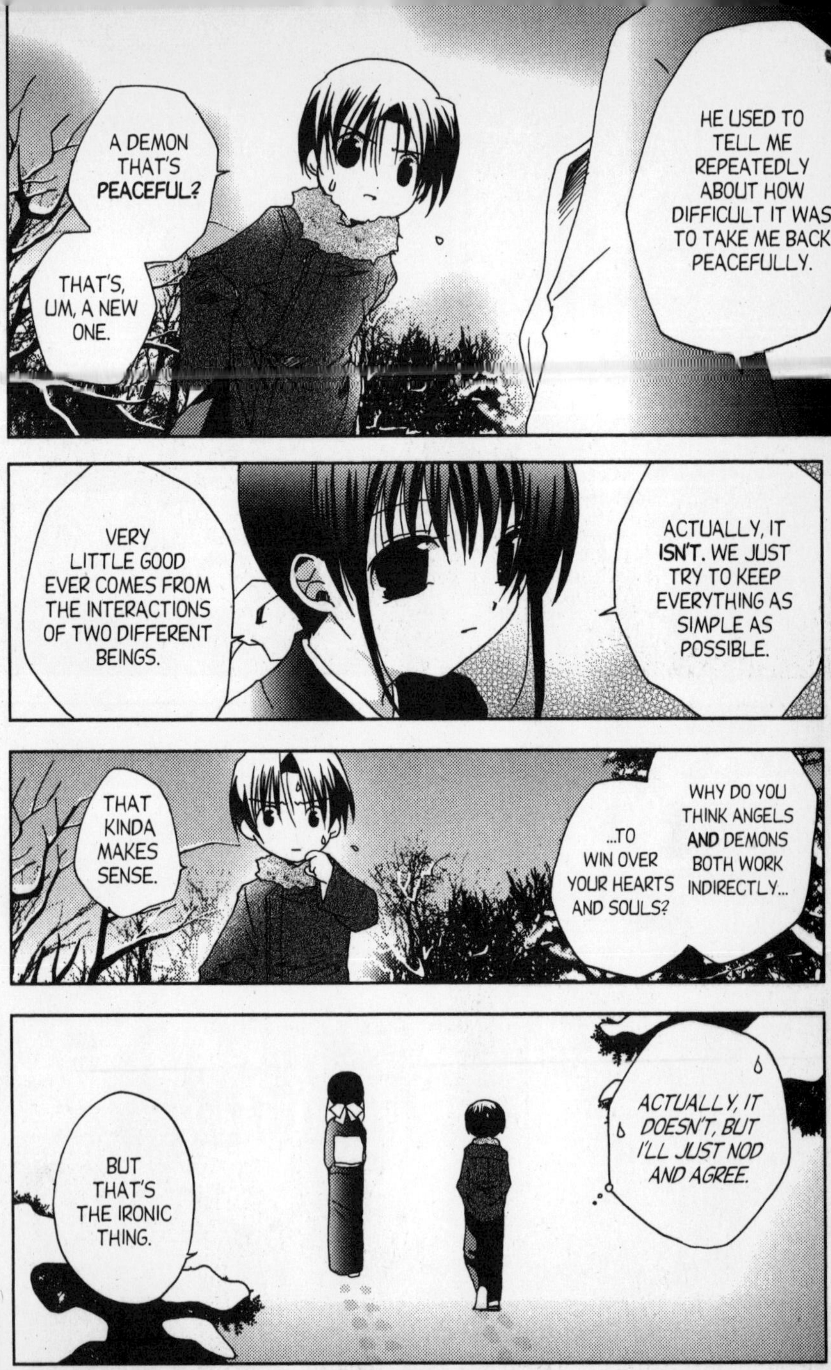
HE USED TO TELL ME REPEATEDLY ABOUT HOW DIFFICULT IT WAS TO TAKE ME BACK PEACEFULLY.
A DEMON THAT'S **PEACEFUL?**
THAT'S, UM, A NEW ONE.
ACTUALLY, IT **ISN'T.** WE JUST TRY TO KEEP EVERYTHING AS SIMPLE AS POSSIBLE.
VERY LITTLE GOOD EVER COMES FROM THE INTERACTIONS OF TWO DIFFERENT BEINGS.
WHY DO YOU THINK ANGELS **AND** DEMONS BOTH WORK INDIRECTLY...
...TO WIN OVER YOUR HEARTS AND SOULS?
THAT KINDA MAKES SENSE.
ACTUALLY, IT DOESN'T, BUT I'LL JUST NOD AND AGREE.
BUT THAT'S THE IRONIC THING.

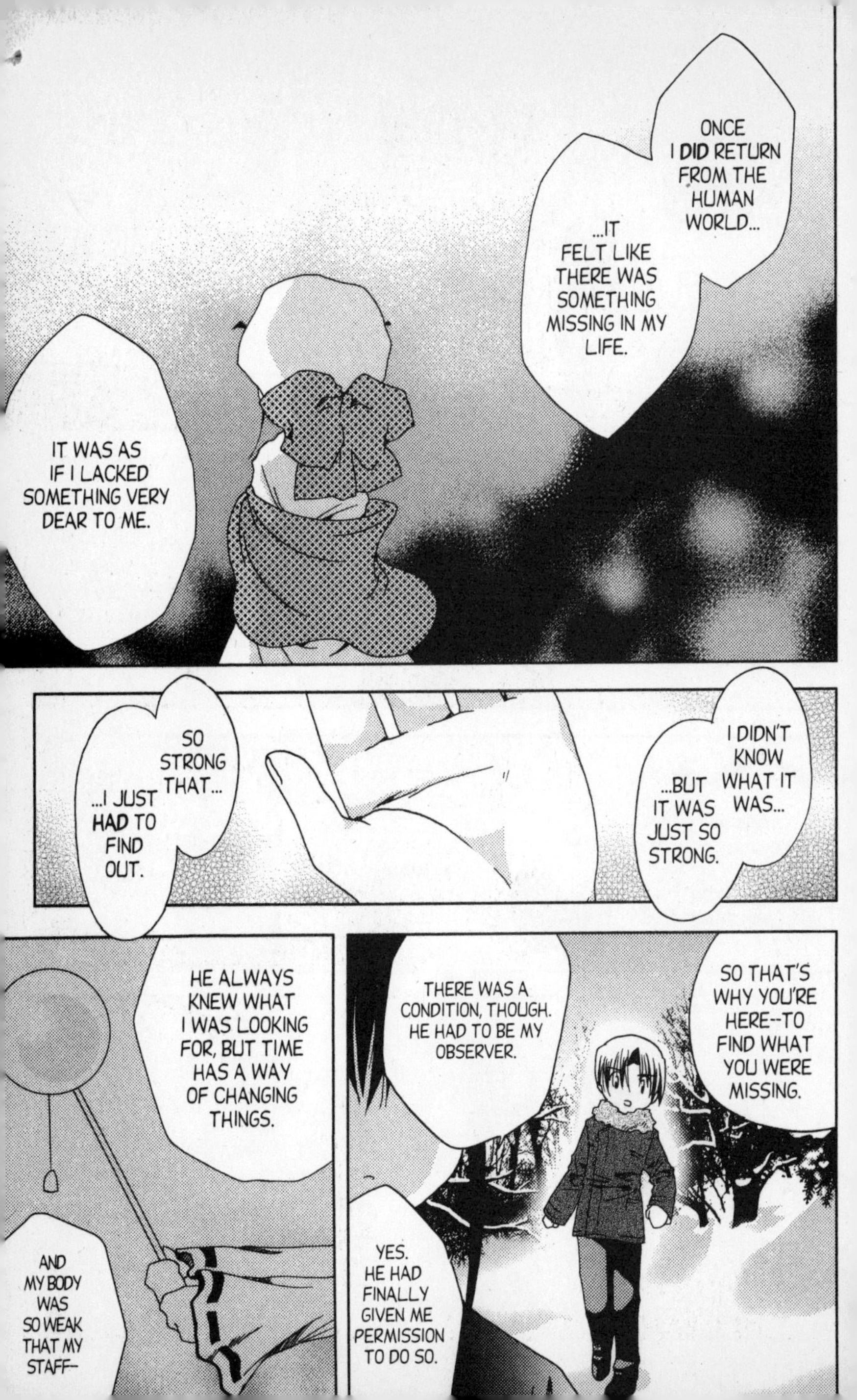
ONCE I **DID** RETURN FROM THE HUMAN WORLD...
...IT FELT LIKE THERE WAS SOMETHING MISSING IN MY LIFE.
IT WAS AS IF I LACKED SOMETHING VERY DEAR TO ME.
I DIDN'T KNOW WHAT IT WAS...
...BUT IT WAS JUST SO STRONG.
SO STRONG THAT...
...I JUST **HAD** TO FIND OUT.
SO THAT'S WHY YOU'RE HERE--TO FIND WHAT YOU WERE MISSING.
THERE WAS A CONDITION, THOUGH. HE HAD TO BE MY OBSERVER.
YES. HE HAD FINALLY GIVEN ME PERMISSION TO DO SO.
HE ALWAYS KNEW WHAT I WAS LOOKING FOR, BUT TIME HAS A WAY OF CHANGING THINGS.
AND MY BODY WAS SO WEAK THAT MY STAFF--

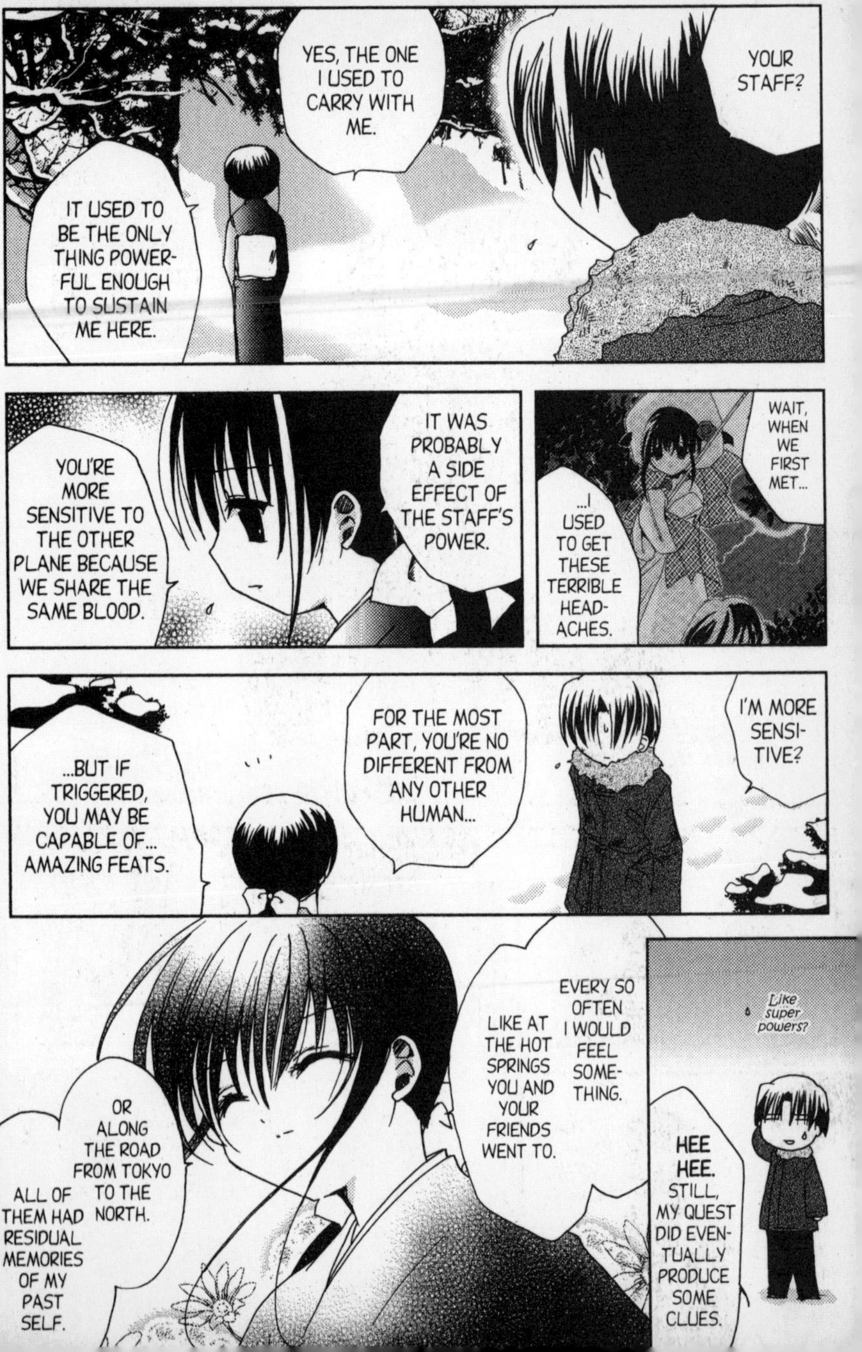
YOUR STAFF?
YES, THE ONE I USED TO CARRY WITH ME.
IT USED TO BE THE ONLY THING POWER-FUL ENOUGH TO SUSTAIN ME HERE.
WAIT, WHEN WE FIRST MET...
...I USED TO GET THESE TERRIBLE HEAD-ACHES.
IT WAS PROBABLY A SIDE EFFECT OF THE STAFF'S POWER.
YOU'RE MORE SENSITIVE TO THE OTHER PLANE BECAUSE WE SHARE THE SAME BLOOD.
I'M MORE SENSI-TIVE?
FOR THE MOST PART, YOU'RE NO DIFFERENT FROM ANY OTHER HUMAN...
...BUT IF TRIGGERED, YOU MAY BE CAPABLE OF... AMAZING FEATS.
Like super powers?
HEE HEE.
STILL, MY QUEST DID EVEN-TUALLY PRODUCE SOME CLUES.
EVERY SO OFTEN I WOULD FEEL SOME-THING.
LIKE AT THE HOT SPRINGS YOU AND YOUR FRIENDS WENT TO.
OR ALONG THE ROAD FROM TOKYO TO THE NORTH.
ALL OF THEM HAD RESIDUAL MEMORIES OF MY PAST SELF.

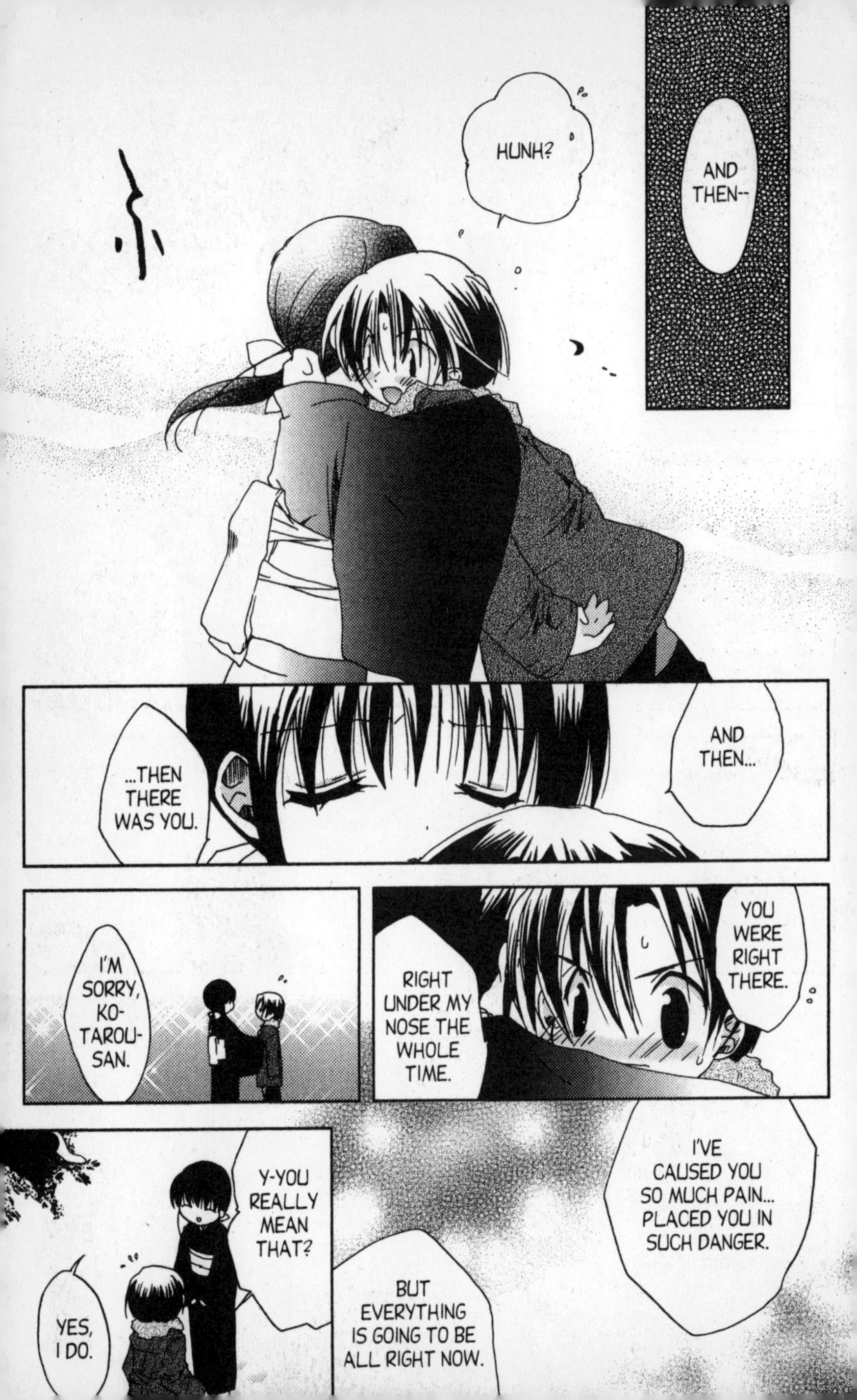
AND THEN--
HUNH?
ふ
AND THEN...
...THEN THERE WAS YOU.
YOU WERE RIGHT THERE.
RIGHT UNDER MY NOSE THE WHOLE TIME.
I'M SORRY, KO-TAROU-SAN.
I'VE CAUSED YOU SO MUCH PAIN... PLACED YOU IN SUCH DANGER.
BUT EVERYTHING IS GOING TO BE ALL RIGHT NOW.
Y-YOU REALLY MEAN THAT?
YES, I DO.

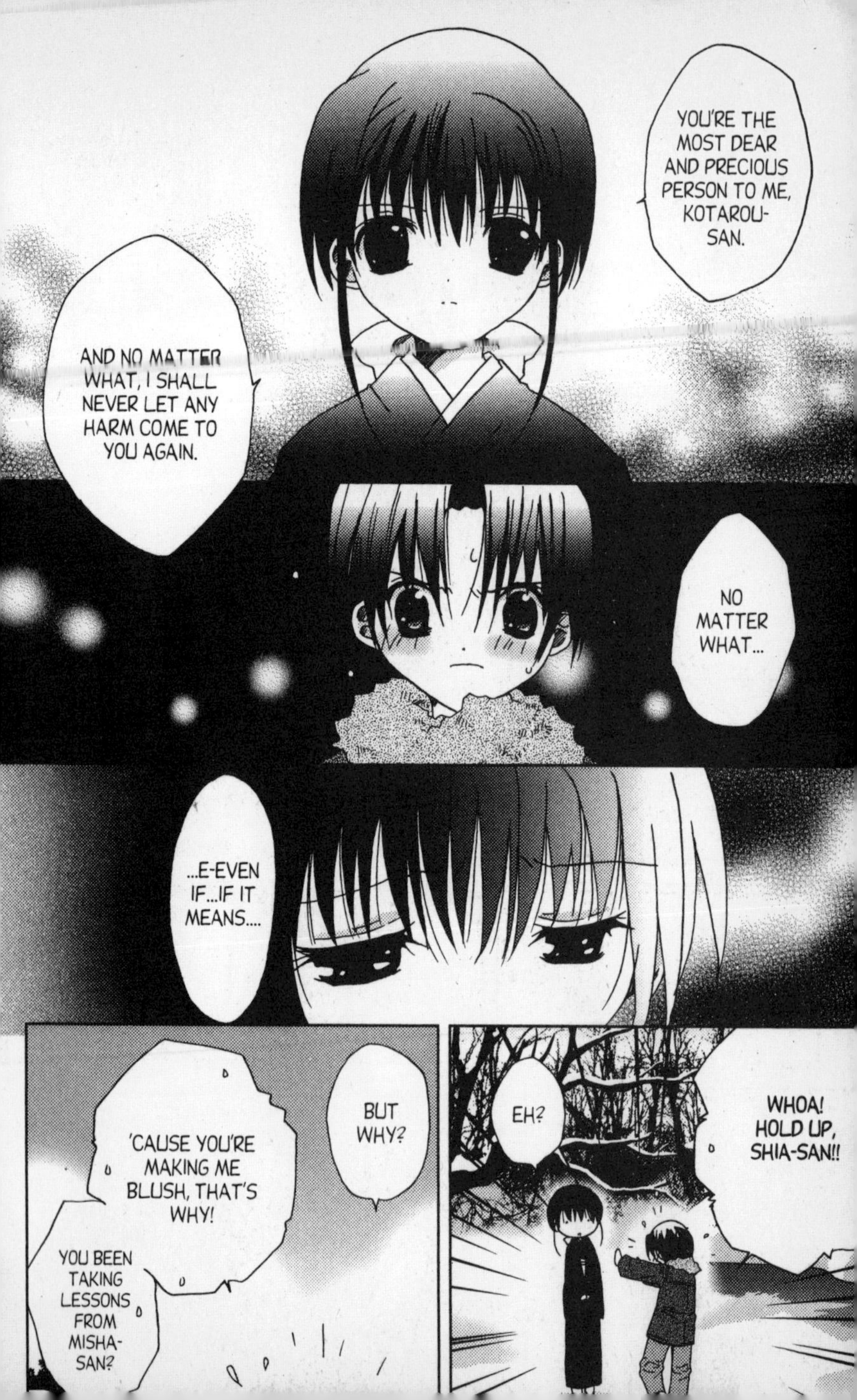
YOU'RE THE MOST DEAR AND PRECIOUS PERSON TO ME, KOTAROU-SAN.
AND NO MATTER WHAT, I SHALL NEVER LET ANY HARM COME TO YOU AGAIN.
NO MATTER WHAT...
...E-EVEN IF...IF IT MEANS....
WHOA! HOLD UP, SHIA-SAN!!
EH?
BUT WHY?
'CAUSE YOU'RE MAKING ME BLUSH, THAT'S WHY!
YOU BEEN TAKING LESSONS FROM MISHA-SAN?

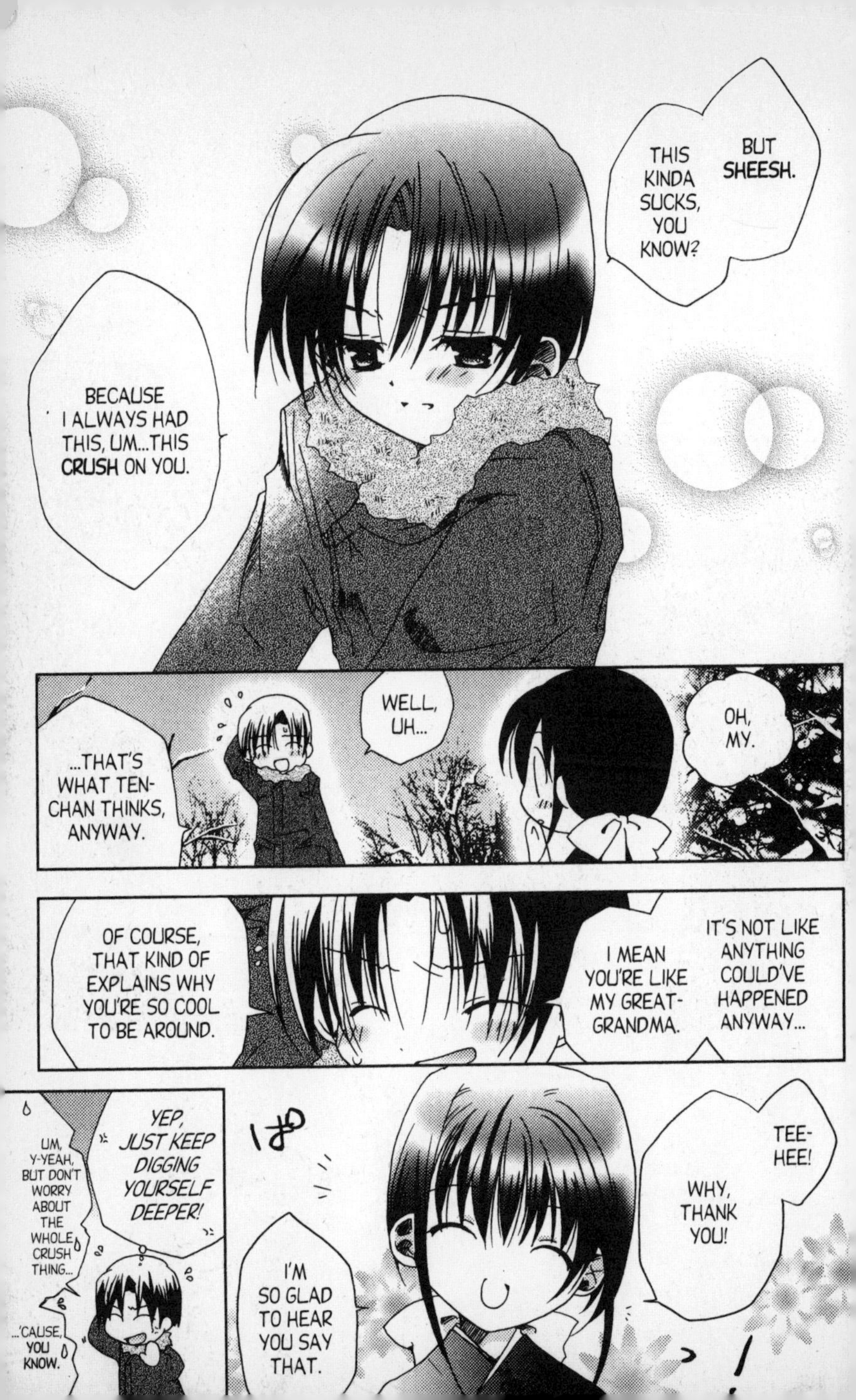
BUT SHEESH.
THIS KINDA SUCKS, YOU KNOW?
BECAUSE I ALWAYS HAD THIS, UM...THIS **CRUSH** ON YOU.
OH, MY.
WELL, UH...
...THAT'S WHAT TEN-CHAN THINKS, ANYWAY.
IT'S NOT LIKE ANYTHING COULD'VE HAPPENED ANYWAY...
I MEAN YOU'RE LIKE MY GREAT-GRANDMA.
OF COURSE, THAT KIND OF EXPLAINS WHY YOU'RE SO COOL TO BE AROUND.
TEE-HEE!
WHY, THANK YOU!
I'M SO GLAD TO HEAR YOU SAY THAT.
ぱ
YEP, JUST KEEP DIGGING YOURSELF DEEPER!
UM, Y-YEAH, BUT DON'T WORRY ABOUT THE WHOLE CRUSH THING...
...'CAUSE, YOU KNOW.

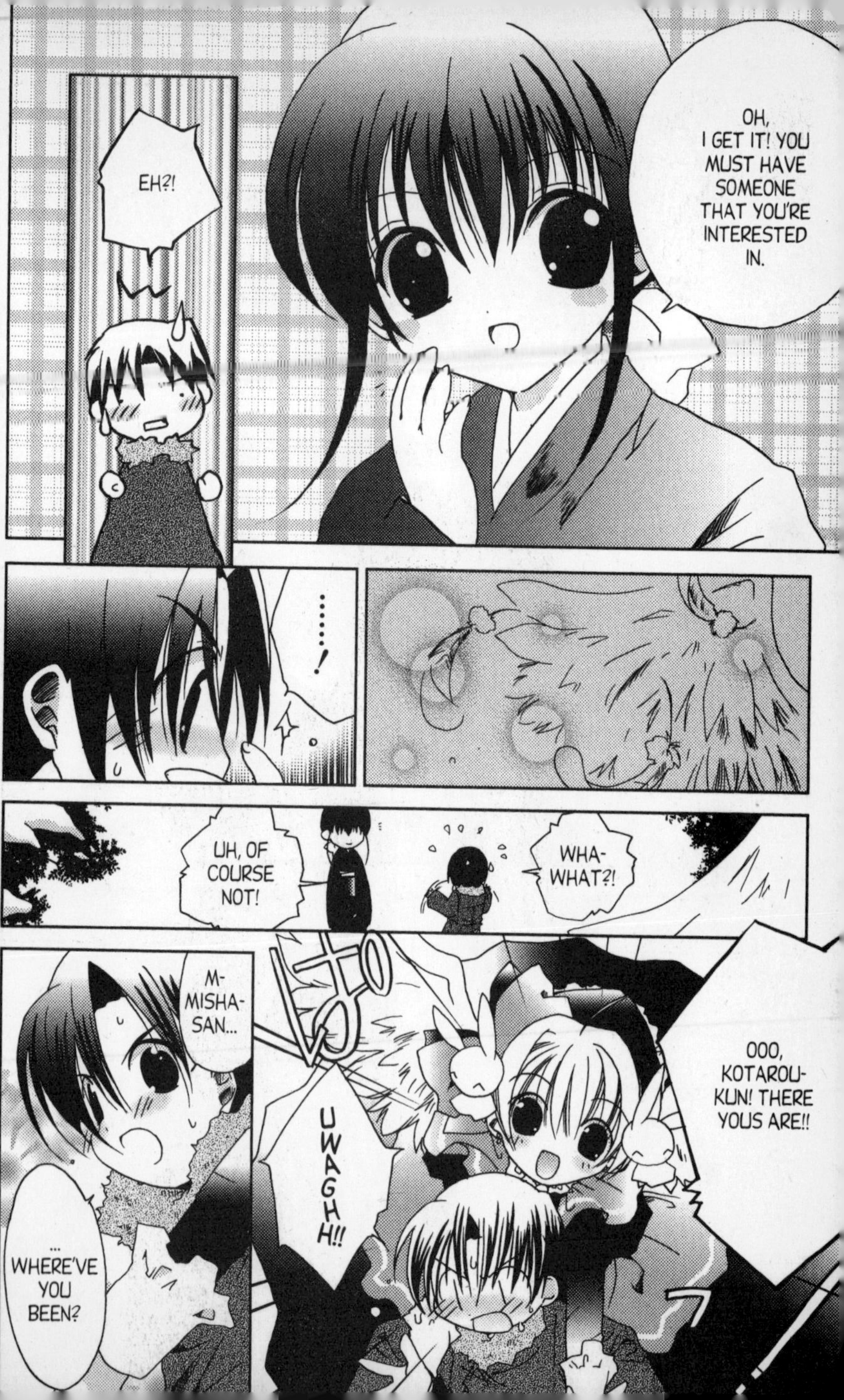
OH, I GET IT! YOU MUST HAVE SOMEONE THAT YOU'RE INTERESTED IN.
EH?!
......!
WHA-WHAT?!
UH, OF COURSE NOT!
OOO, KOTAROU-KUN! THERE YOUS ARE!!
UWAGHH!!
M-MISHA-SAN...
...WHERE'VE YOU BEEN?

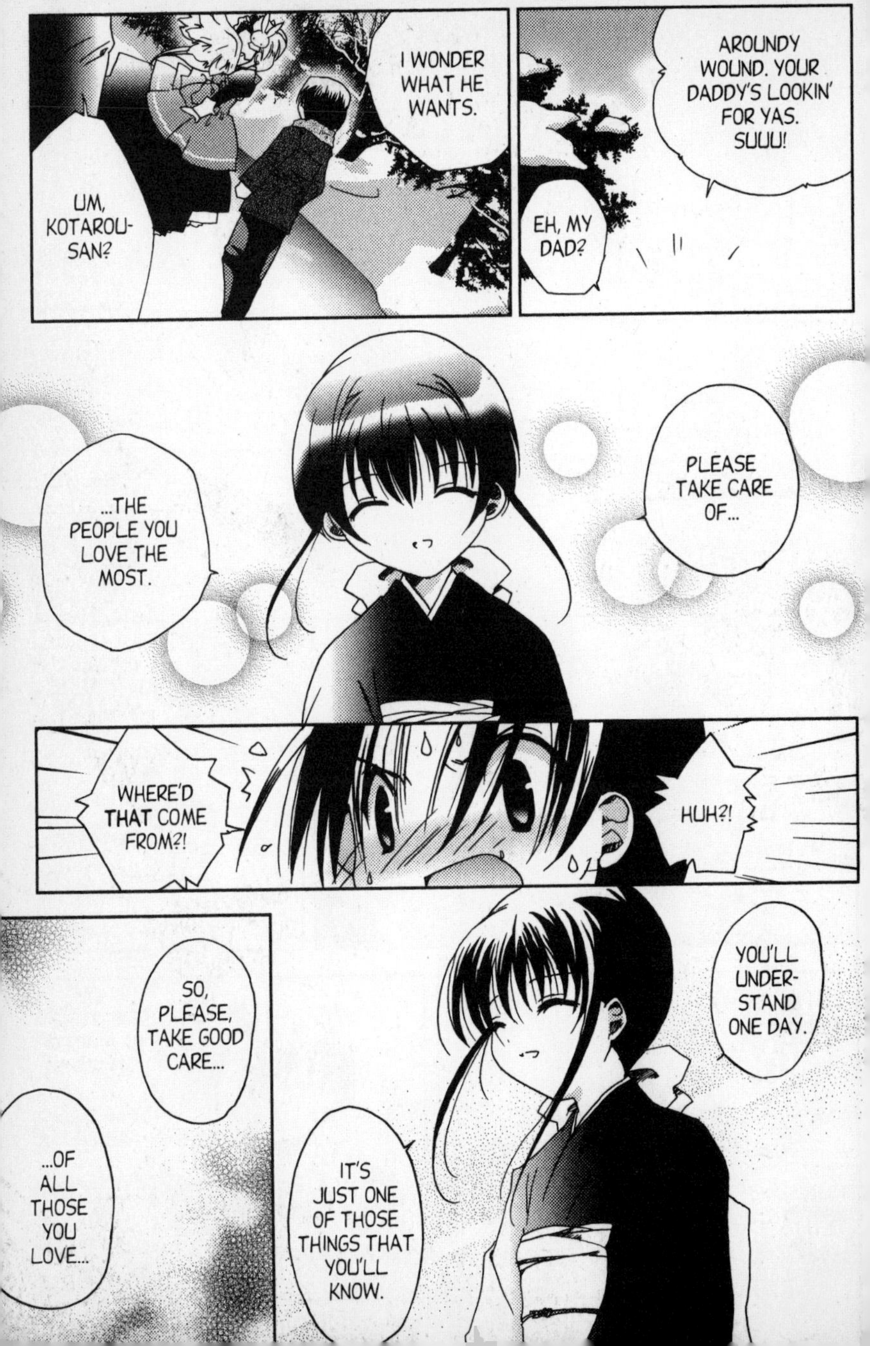
AROUNDY WOUND. YOUR DADDY'S LOOKIN' FOR YAS. SUUU!
EH, MY DAD?
I WONDER WHAT HE WANTS.
UM, KOTAROU-SAN?
PLEASE TAKE CARE OF...
...THE PEOPLE YOU LOVE THE MOST.
HUH?!
WHERE'D **THAT** COME FROM?!
YOU'LL UNDER-STAND ONE DAY.
IT'S JUST ONE OF THOSE THINGS THAT YOU'LL KNOW.
SO, PLEASE, TAKE GOOD CARE...
...OF ALL THOSE YOU LOVE...

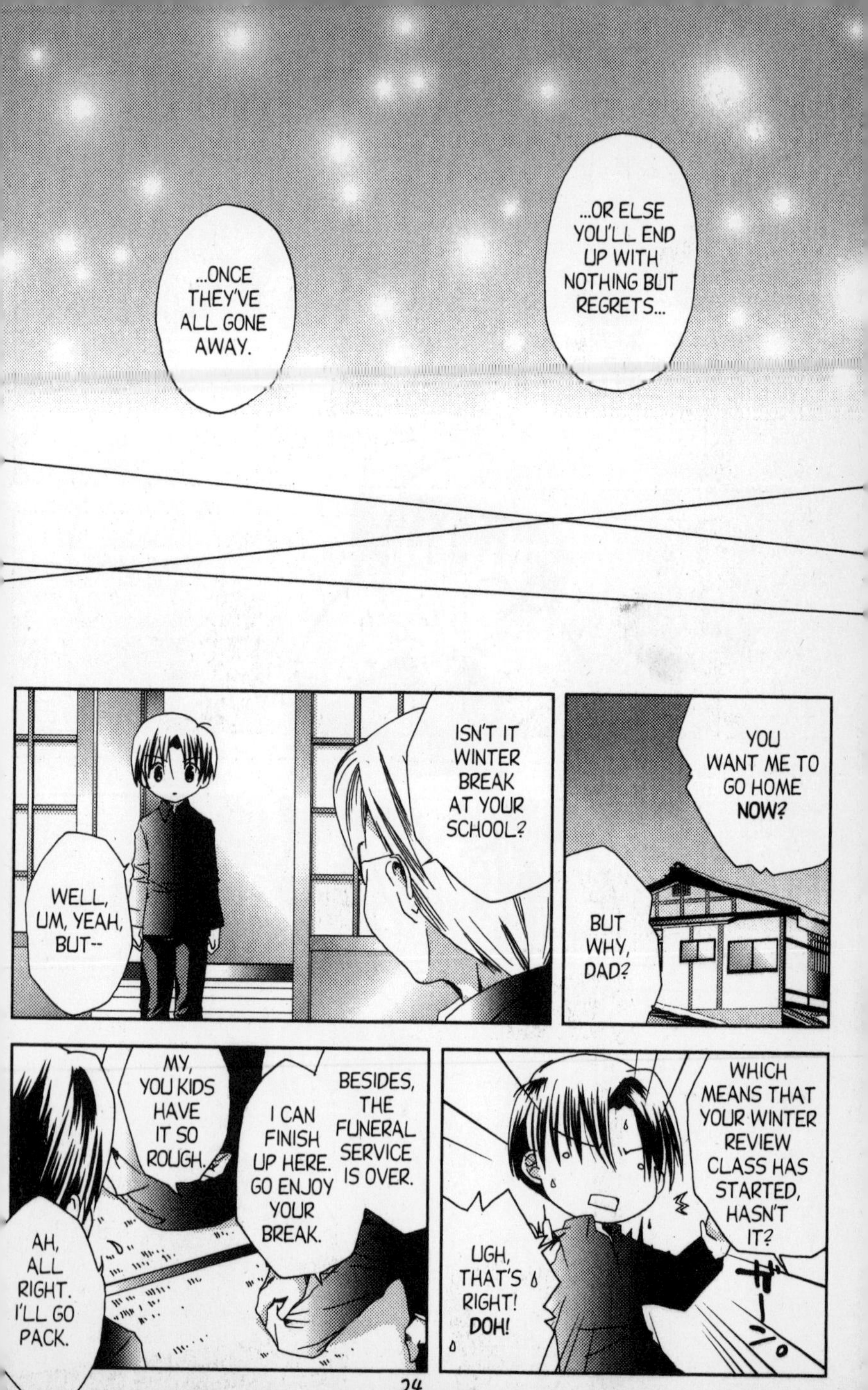
...OR ELSE YOU'LL END UP WITH NOTHING BUT REGRETS...
...ONCE THEY'VE ALL GONE AWAY.
YOU WANT ME TO GO HOME NOW?
BUT WHY, DAD?
ISN'T IT WINTER BREAK AT YOUR SCHOOL?
WELL, UM, YEAH, BUT--
WHICH MEANS THAT YOUR WINTER REVIEW CLASS HAS STARTED, HASN'T IT?
UGH, THAT'S RIGHT! DOH!
BESIDES, THE FUNERAL SERVICE IS OVER.
I CAN FINISH UP HERE. GO ENJOY YOUR BREAK.
MY, YOU KIDS HAVE IT SO ROUGH.
AH, ALL RIGHT. I'LL GO PACK.

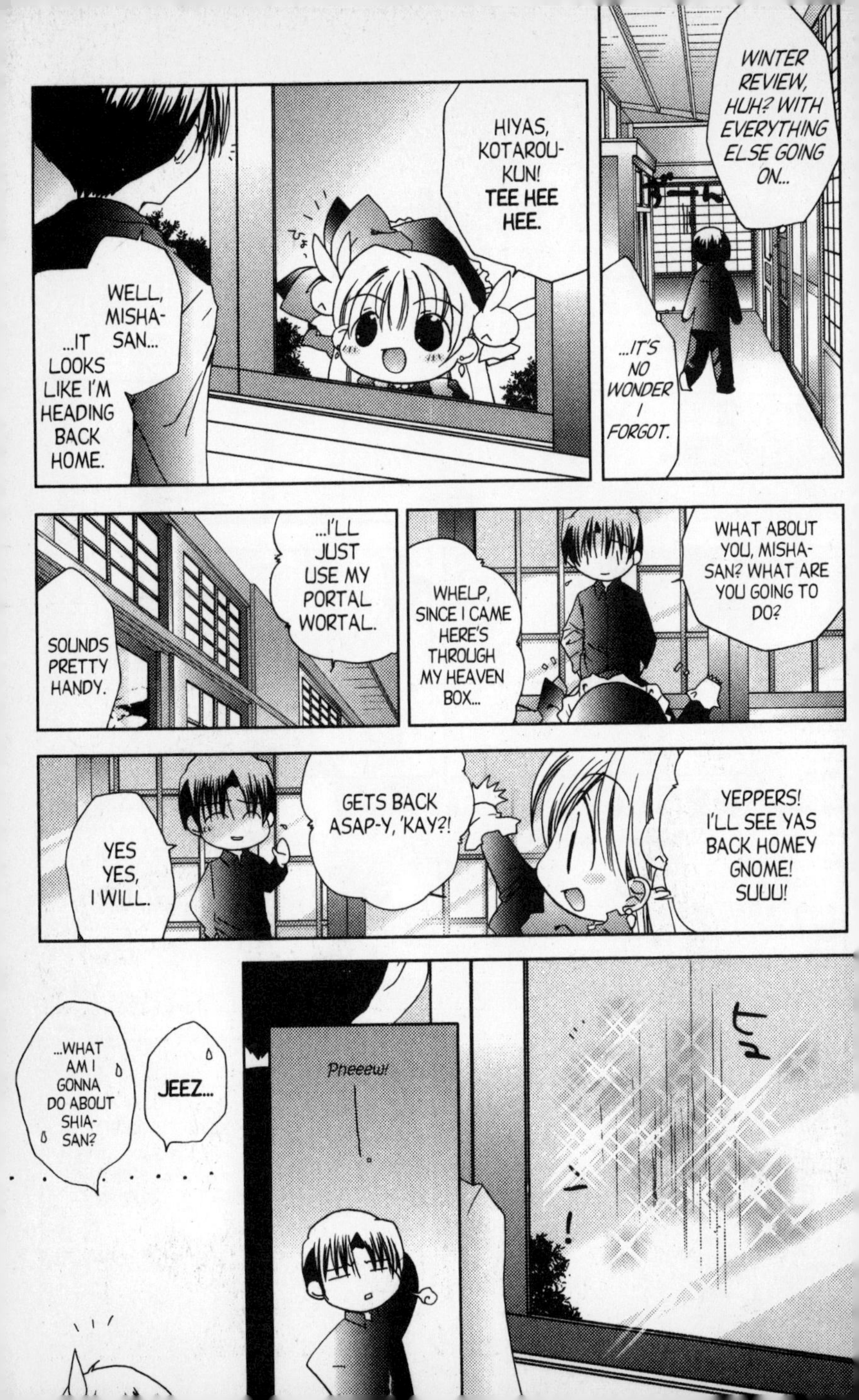
WINTER REVIEW, HUH? WITH EVERYTHING ELSE GOING ON...
...IT'S NO WONDER I FORGOT.
HIYAS, KOTAROU-KUN! TEE HEE HEE.
WELL, MISHA-SAN...
...IT LOOKS LIKE I'M HEADING BACK HOME.
WHAT ABOUT YOU, MISHA-SAN? WHAT ARE YOU GOING TO DO?
WHELP, SINCE I CAME HERE'S THROUGH MY HEAVEN BOX...
...I'LL JUST USE MY PORTAL WORTAL.
SOUNDS PRETTY HANDY.
YEPPERS! I'LL SEE YAS BACK HOMEY GNOME! SUUU!
GETS BACK ASAP-Y, 'KAY?!
YES YES, I WILL.
Pheeew!
JEEZ...
...WHAT AM I GONNA DO ABOUT SHIA-SAN?

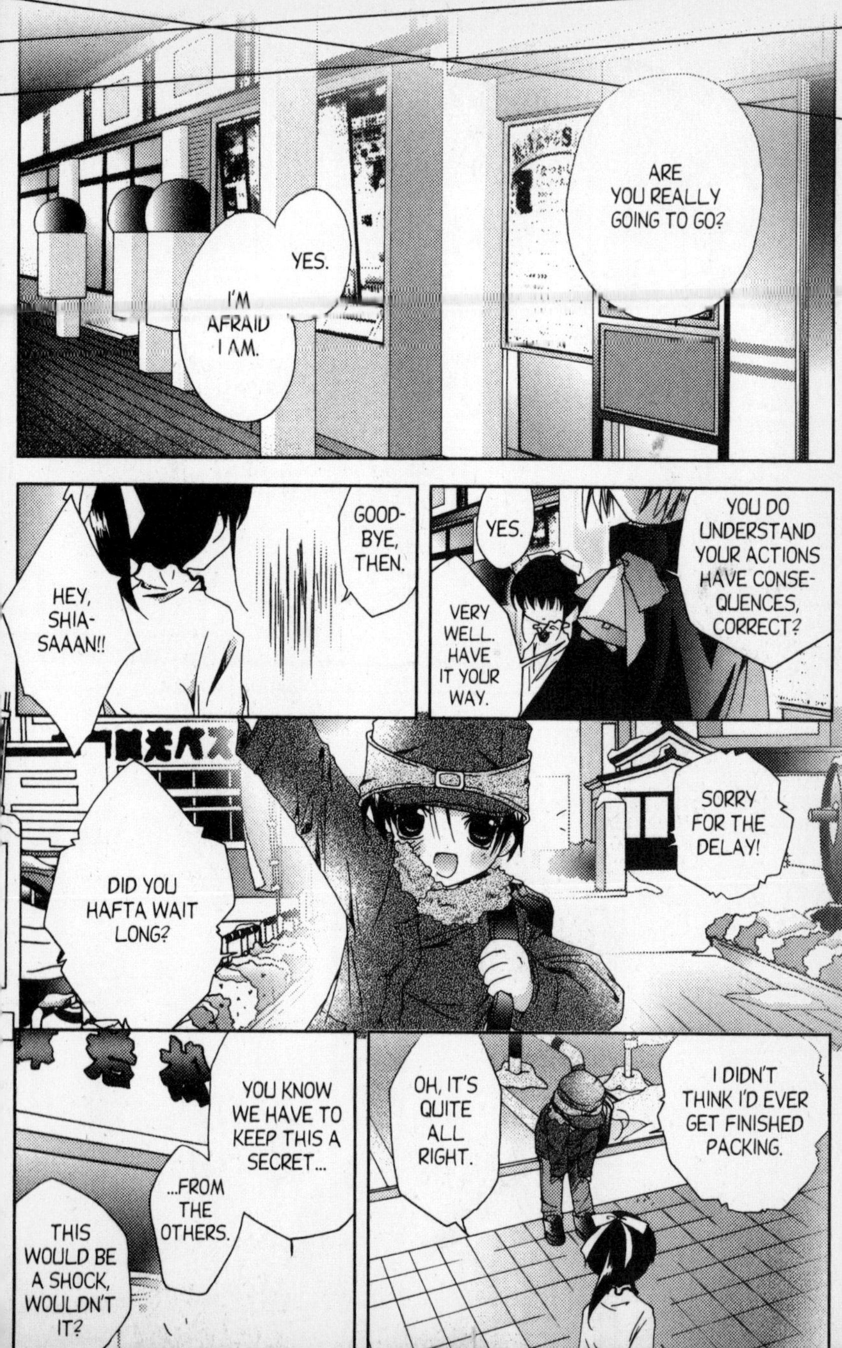
ARE YOU REALLY GOING TO GO?
YES. I'M AFRAID I AM.
YOU DO UNDERSTAND YOUR ACTIONS HAVE CONSE-QUENCES, CORRECT?
YES.
VERY WELL. HAVE IT YOUR WAY.
GOOD-BYE, THEN.
HEY, SHIA-SAAAN!!
SORRY FOR THE DELAY!
DID YOU HAFTA WAIT LONG?
I DIDN'T THINK I'D EVER GET FINISHED PACKING.
OH, IT'S QUITE ALL RIGHT.
YOU KNOW WE HAVE TO KEEP THIS A SECRET...
...FROM THE OTHERS.
THIS WOULD BE A SHOCK, WOULDN'T IT?

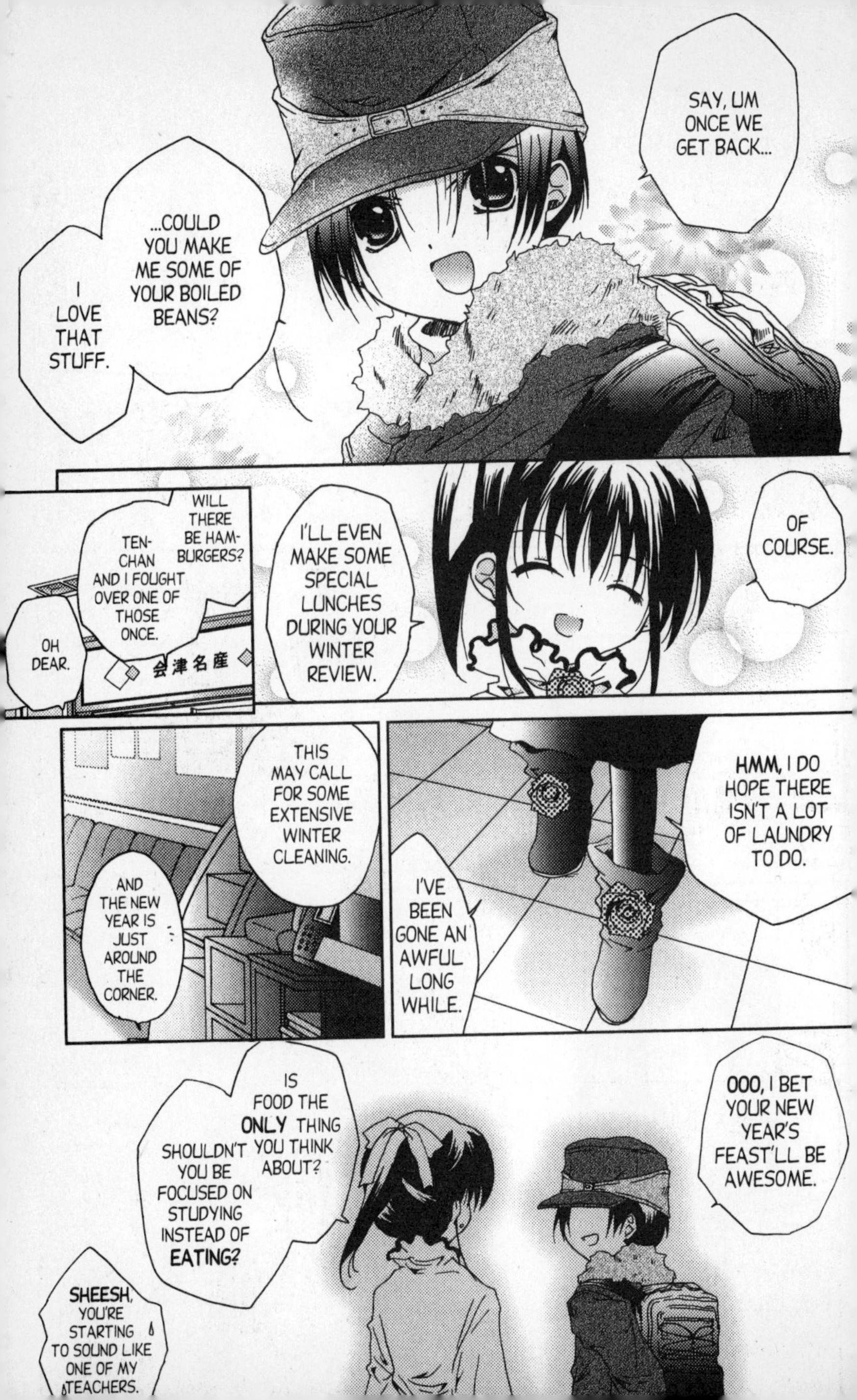
SAY, UM ONCE WE GET BACK...
...COULD YOU MAKE ME SOME OF YOUR BOILED BEANS?
I LOVE THAT STUFF.
OF COURSE.
I'LL EVEN MAKE SOME SPECIAL LUNCHES DURING YOUR WINTER REVIEW.
WILL THERE BE HAM-BURGERS?
TEN-CHAN AND I FOUGHT OVER ONE OF THOSE ONCE.
OH DEAR.
会津名産
HMM, I DO HOPE THERE ISN'T A LOT OF LAUNDRY TO DO.
I'VE BEEN GONE AN AWFUL LONG WHILE.
THIS MAY CALL FOR SOME EXTENSIVE WINTER CLEANING.
AND THE NEW YEAR IS JUST AROUND THE CORNER.
OOO, I BET YOUR NEW YEAR'S FEAST'LL BE AWESOME.
IS FOOD THE ONLY THING YOU THINK ABOUT?
SHOULDN'T YOU BE FOCUSED ON STUDYING INSTEAD OF EATING?
SHEESH, YOU'RE STARTING TO SOUND LIKE ONE OF MY TEACHERS.

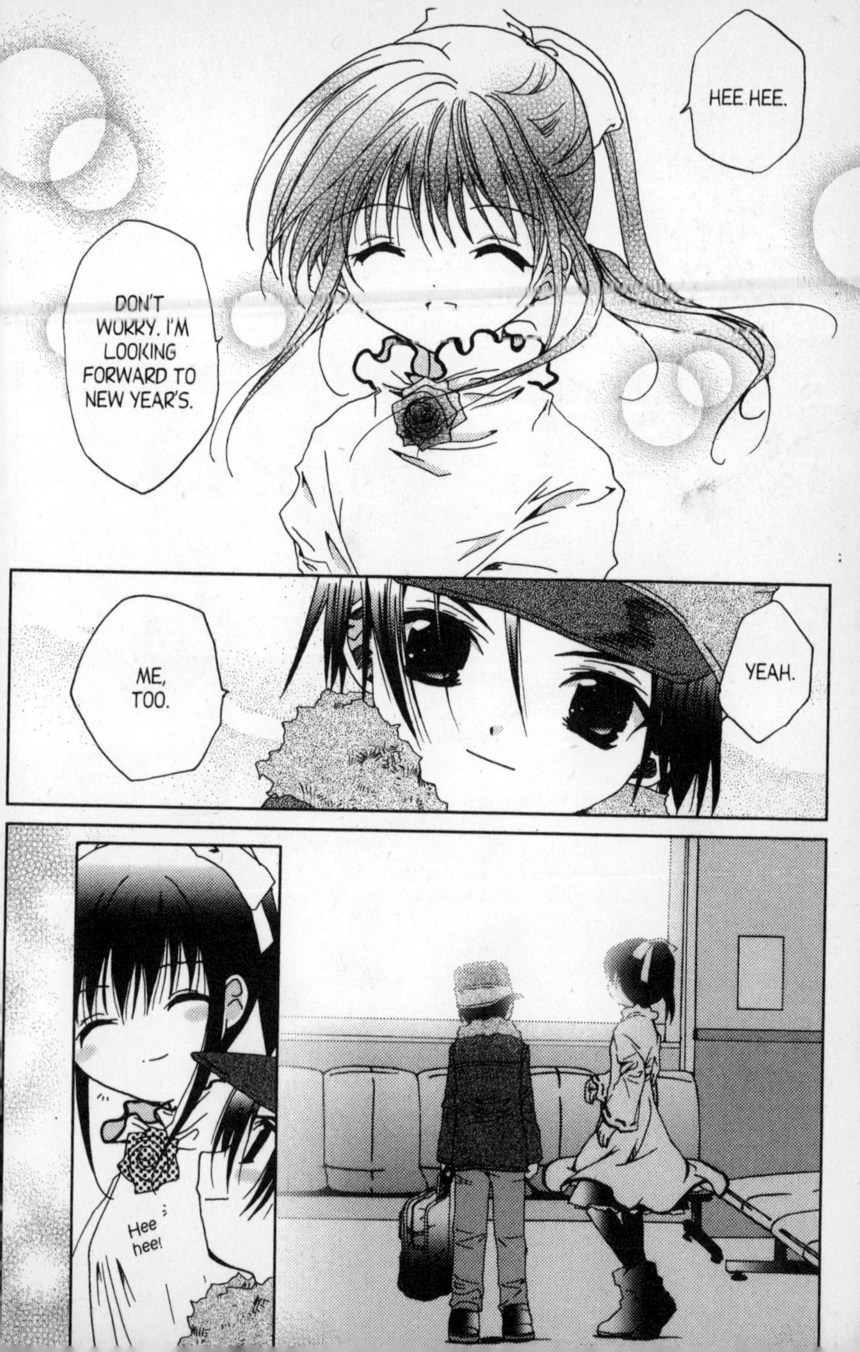
HEE HEE.
DON'T WORRY. I'M LOOKING FORWARD TO NEW YEAR'S.
YEAH.
ME, TOO.
Hee hee!

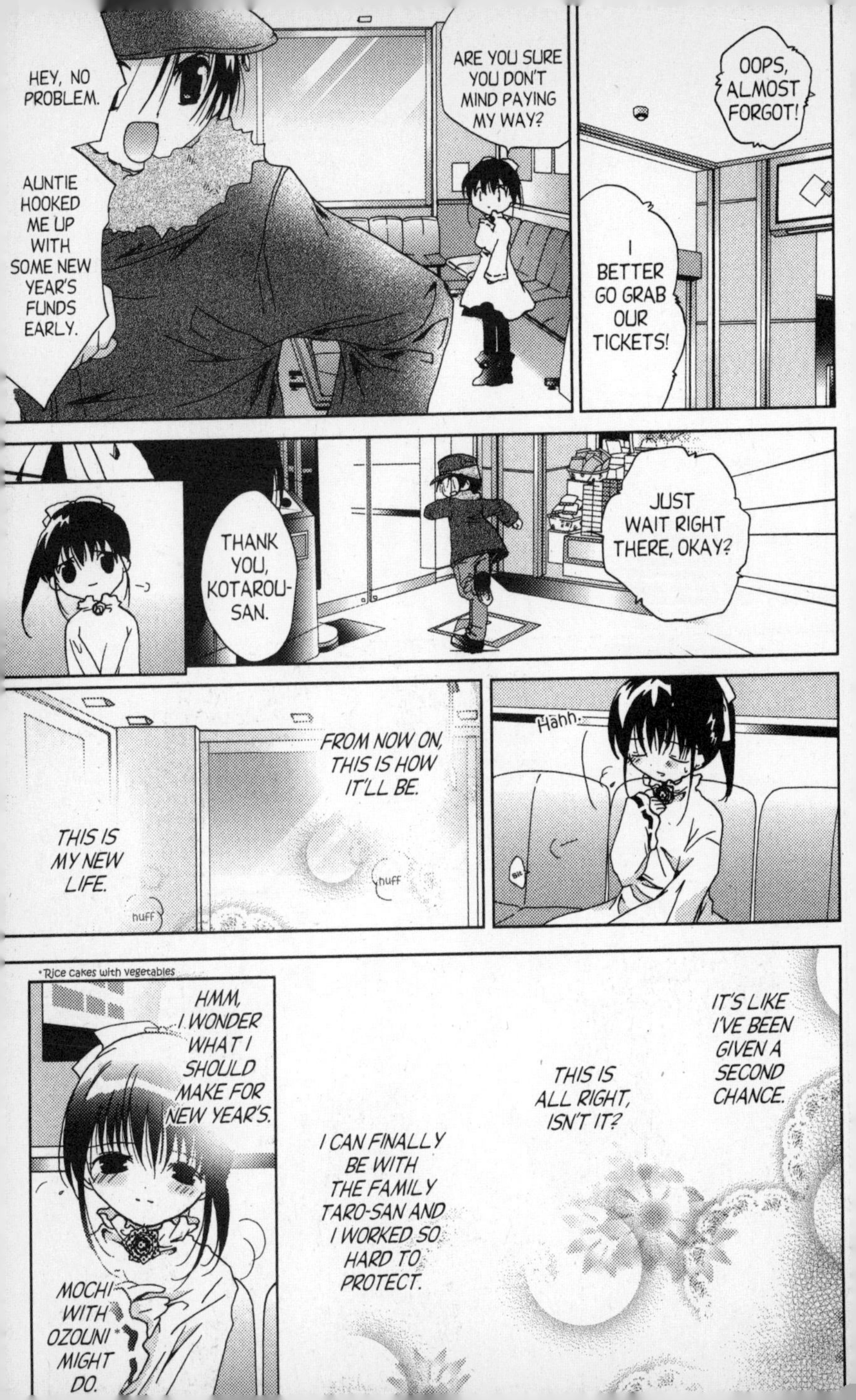
OOPS, ALMOST FORGOT!
I BETTER GO GRAB OUR TICKETS!
ARE YOU SURE YOU DON'T MIND PAYING MY WAY?
HEY, NO PROBLEM.
AUNTIE HOOKED ME UP WITH SOME NEW YEAR'S FUNDS EARLY.
JUST WAIT RIGHT THERE, OKAY?
THANK YOU, KOTAROU-SAN.
Hahh.
Sit
FROM NOW ON, THIS IS HOW IT'LL BE.
THIS IS MY NEW LIFE.
huff
huff
IT'S LIKE I'VE BEEN GIVEN A SECOND CHANCE.
THIS IS ALL RIGHT, ISN'T IT?
I CAN FINALLY BE WITH THE FAMILY TARO-SAN AND I WORKED SO HARD TO PROTECT.
HMM, I WONDER WHAT I SHOULD MAKE FOR NEW YEAR'S.
MOCHI WITH OZOUNI* MIGHT DO.

*Rice cakes with vegetables

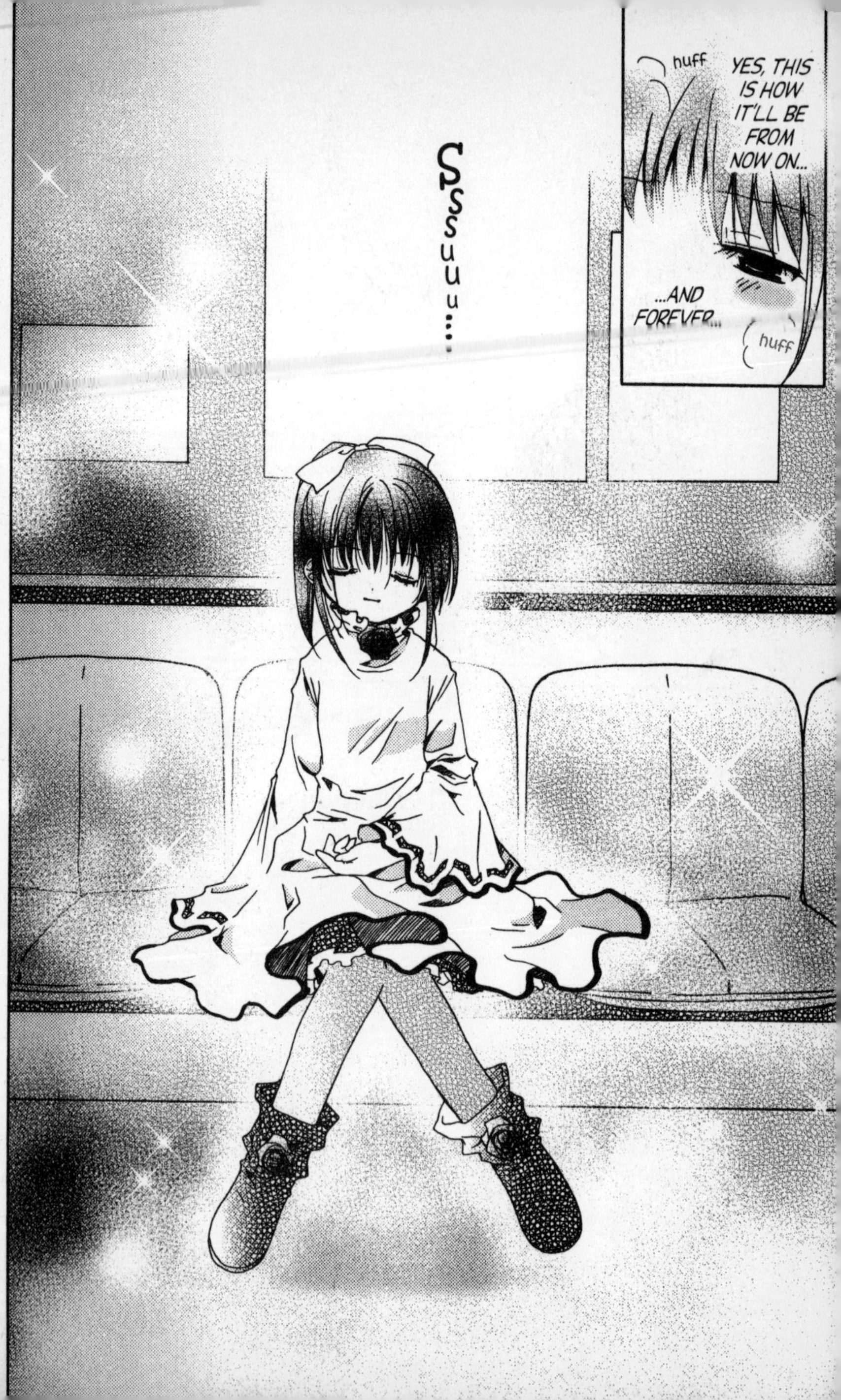
huff
YES, THIS IS HOW IT'LL BE FROM NOW ON...
...AND FOREVER...
huff
Sssuuu...

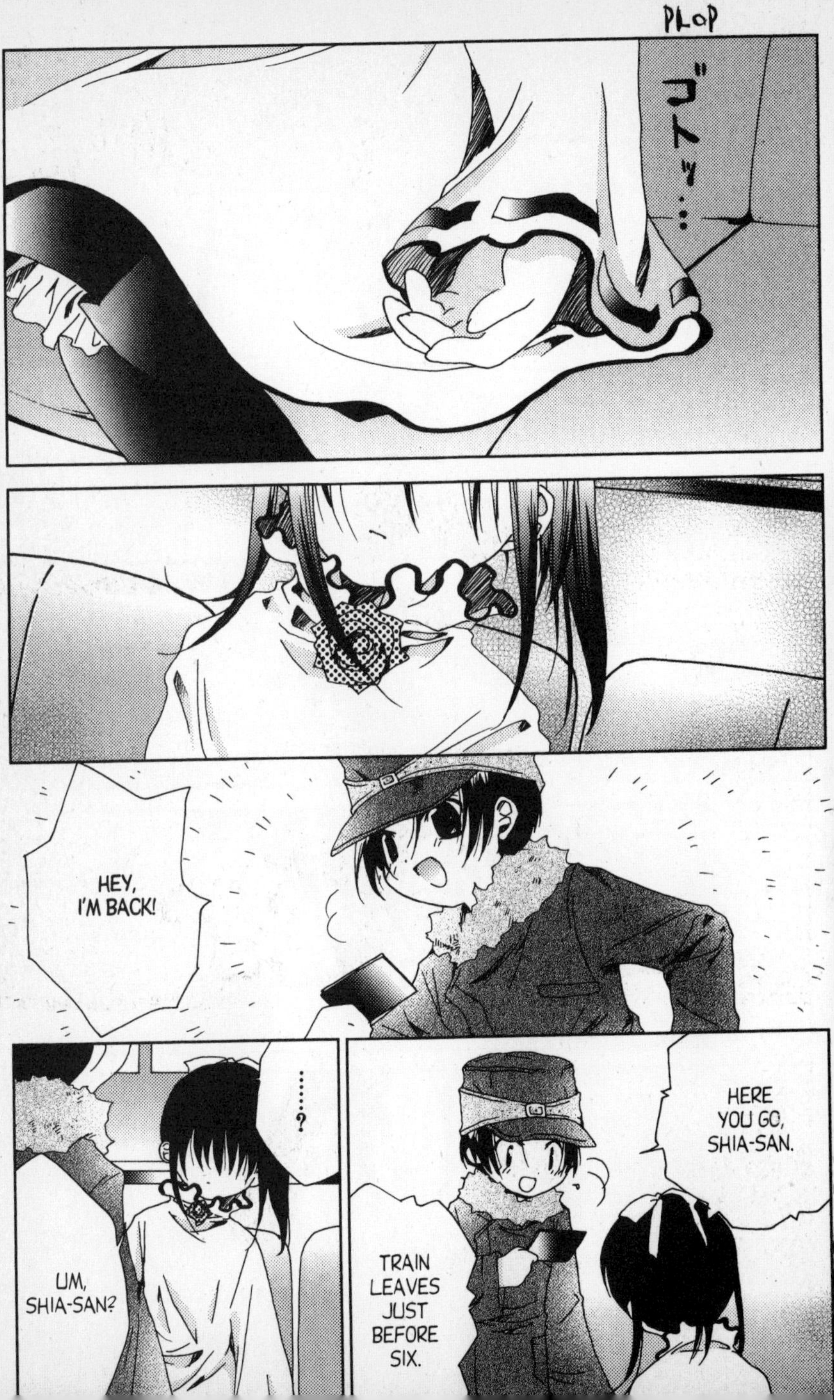
PLOP
ゴトッ…
HEY, I'M BACK!
HERE YOU GO, SHIA-SAN.
TRAIN LEAVES JUST BEFORE SIX.
……?
UM, SHIA-SAN?

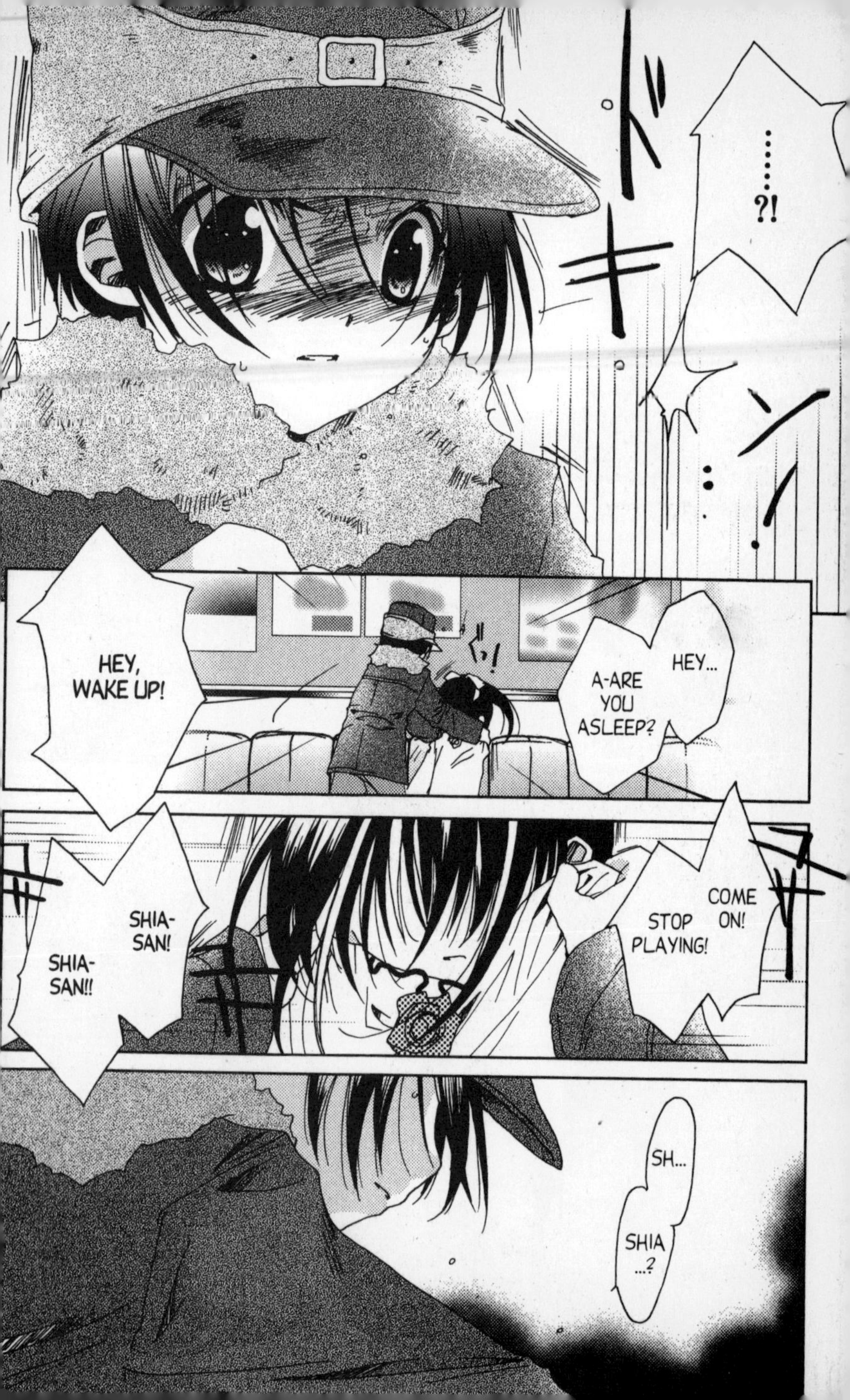
......?!
ドキン
HEY... A-ARE YOU ASLEEP?
HEY, WAKE UP!
COME ON! STOP PLAYING!
SHIA-SAN! SHIA-SAN!!
SH... SHIA ...?

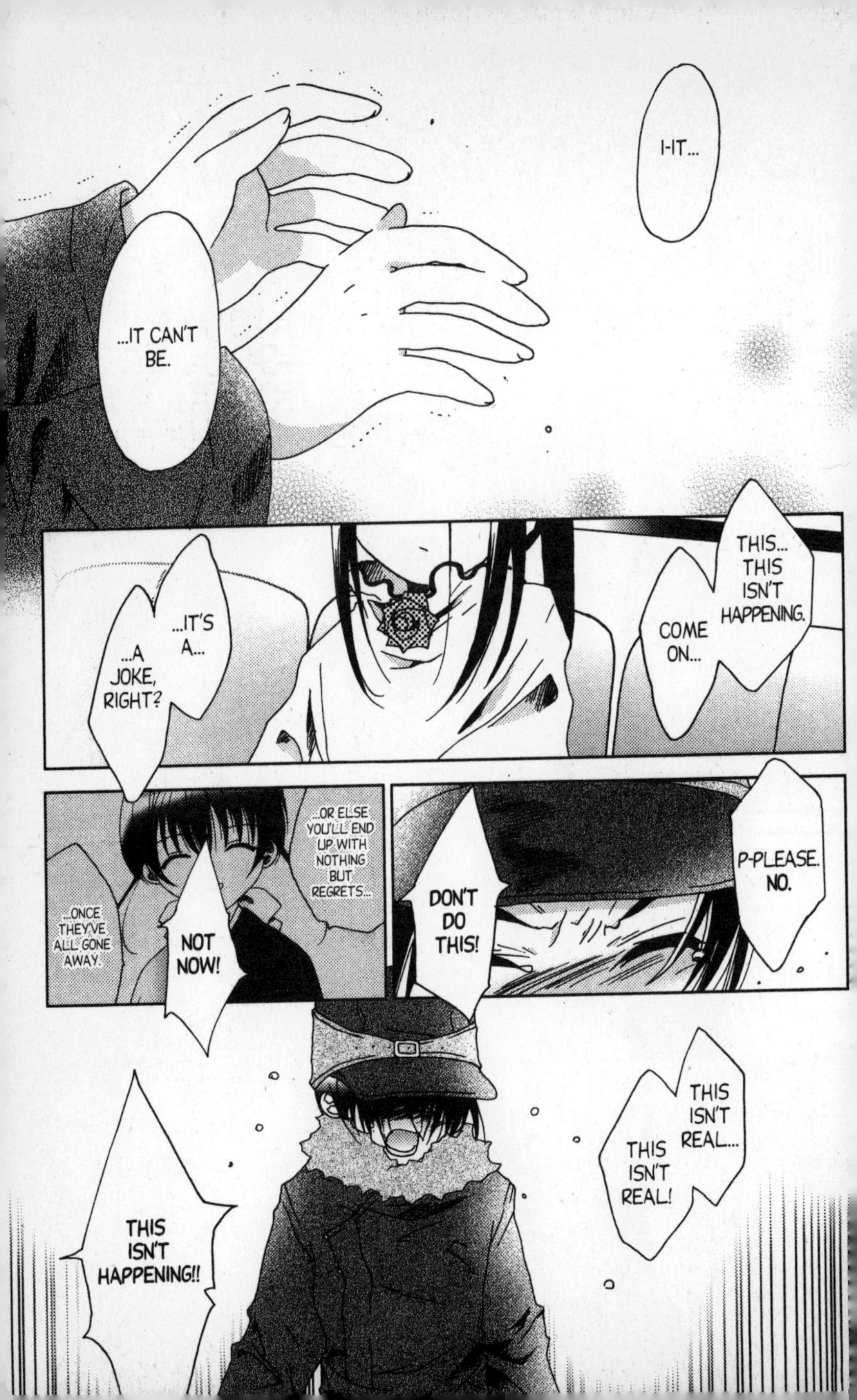
I-IT...
...IT CAN'T BE.
THIS... THIS ISN'T HAPPENING.
COME ON...
...IT'S A...
...A JOKE, RIGHT?
P-PLEASE. NO.
DON'T DO THIS!
...OR ELSE YOU'LL END UP WITH NOTHING BUT REGRETS...
NOT NOW!
...ONCE THEY'VE ALL GONE AWAY.
THIS ISN'T REAL...
THIS ISN'T REAL!
THIS ISN'T HAPPENING!!

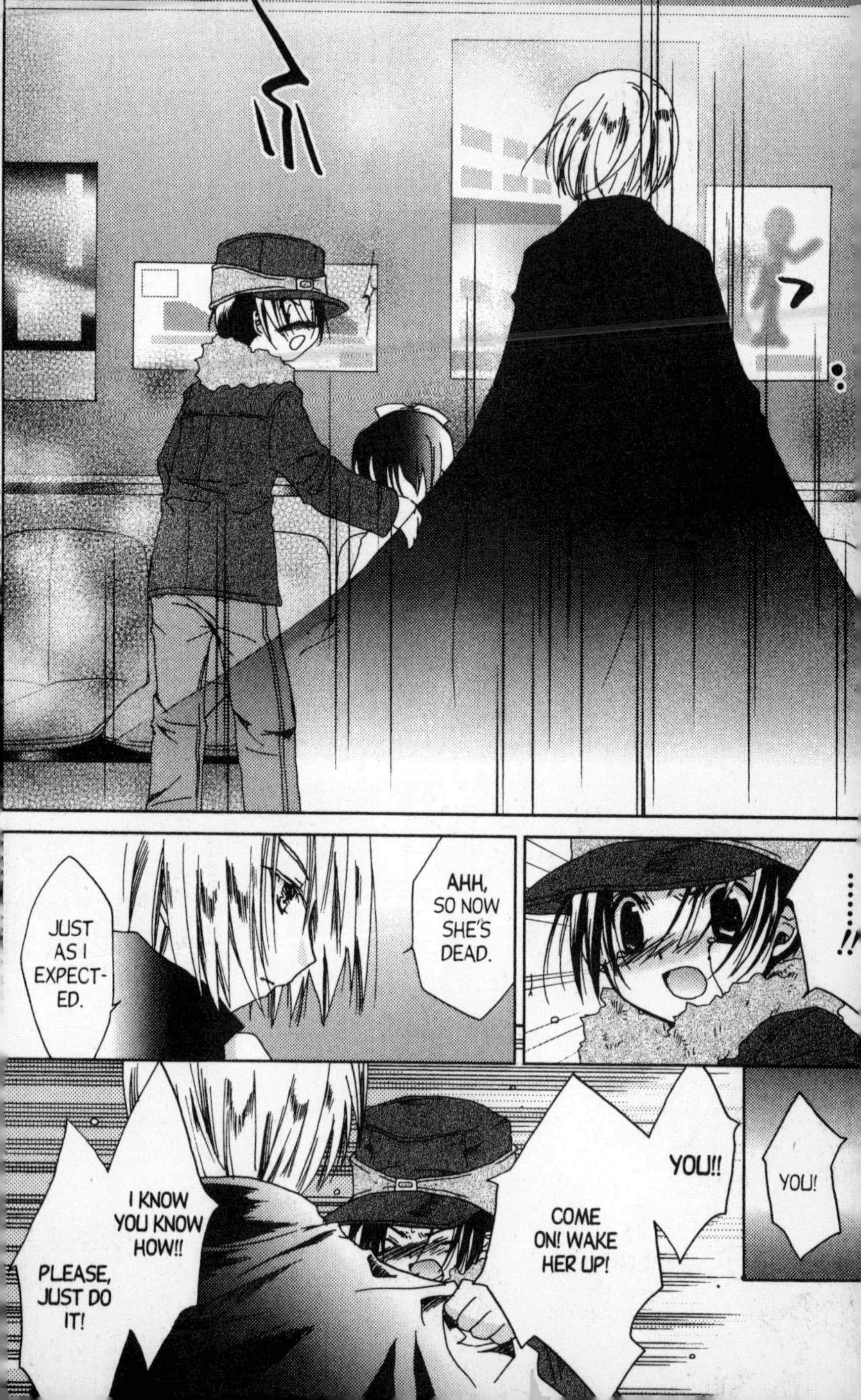

......!!
AHH, SO NOW SHE'S DEAD.
JUST AS I EXPECTED.
YOU!
YOU!!
COME ON! WAKE HER UP!
I KNOW YOU KNOW HOW!!
PLEASE, JUST DO IT!

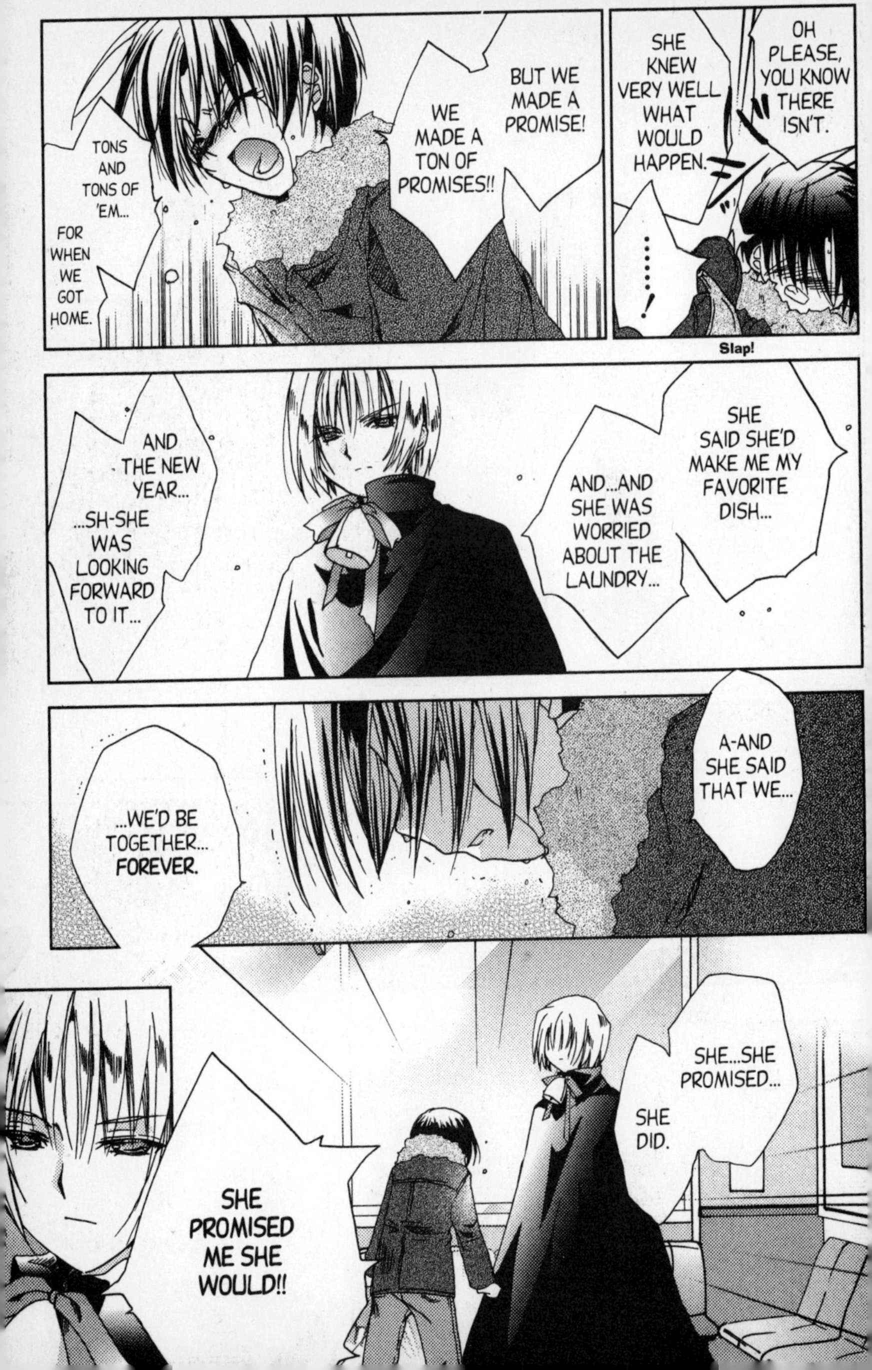
OH PLEASE, YOU KNOW THERE ISN'T.
SHE KNEW VERY WELL WHAT WOULD HAPPEN.
......!
Slap!
BUT WE MADE A PROMISE!
WE MADE A TON OF PROMISES!!
TONS AND TONS OF 'EM...
FOR WHEN WE GOT HOME.
SHE SAID SHE'D MAKE ME MY FAVORITE DISH...
AND...AND SHE WAS WORRIED ABOUT THE LAUNDRY...
AND THE NEW YEAR...
...SH-SHE WAS LOOKING FORWARD TO IT...
A-AND SHE SAID THAT WE...
...WE'D BE TOGETHER... FOREVER.
SHE...SHE PROMISED...
SHE DID.
SHE PROMISED ME SHE WOULD!!

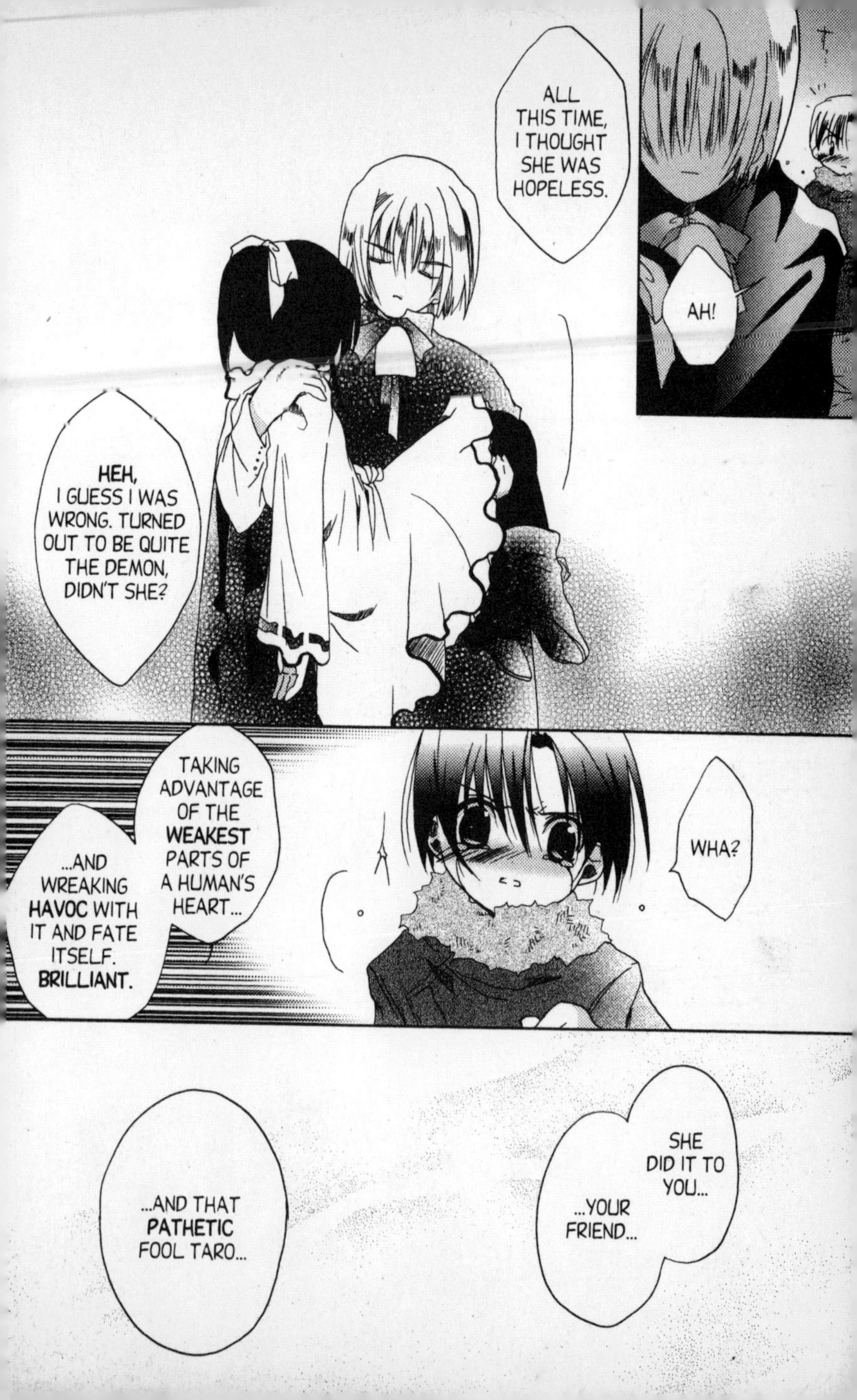
AH!
ALL THIS TIME, I THOUGHT SHE WAS HOPELESS.
HEH, I GUESS I WAS WRONG. TURNED OUT TO BE QUITE THE DEMON, DIDN'T SHE?
WHA?
TAKING ADVANTAGE OF THE WEAKEST PARTS OF A HUMAN'S HEART...
...AND WREAKING HAVOC WITH IT AND FATE ITSELF. BRILLIANT.
SHE DID IT TO YOU...
...YOUR FRIEND...
...AND THAT PATHETIC FOOL TARO...

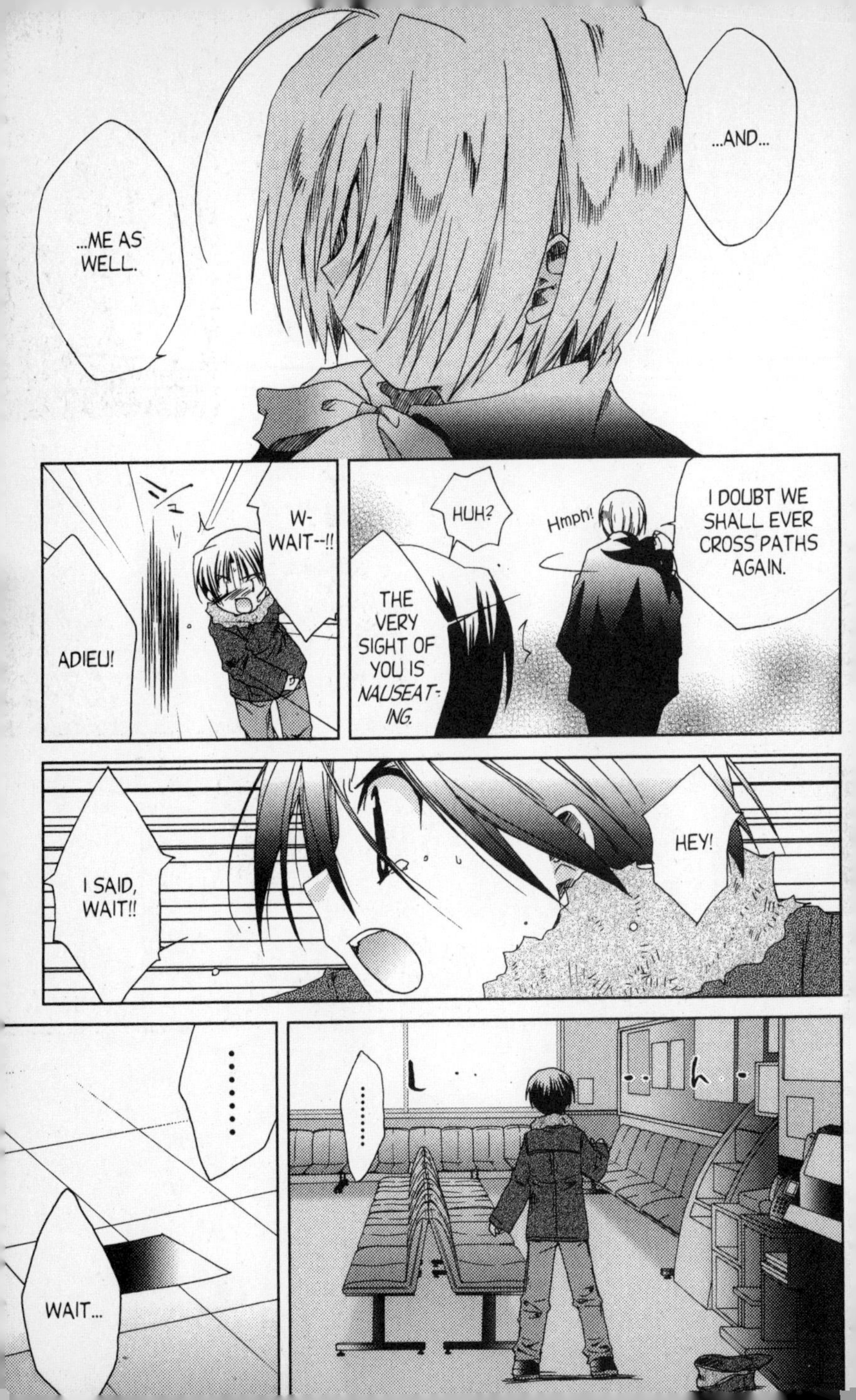
...AND...
...ME AS WELL.
I DOUBT WE SHALL EVER CROSS PATHS AGAIN.
Hmph!
HUH?
THE VERY SIGHT OF YOU IS NAUSEAT-ING.
W- WAIT--!!
ADIEU!
HEY!
I SAID, WAIT!!
......
......
WAIT...

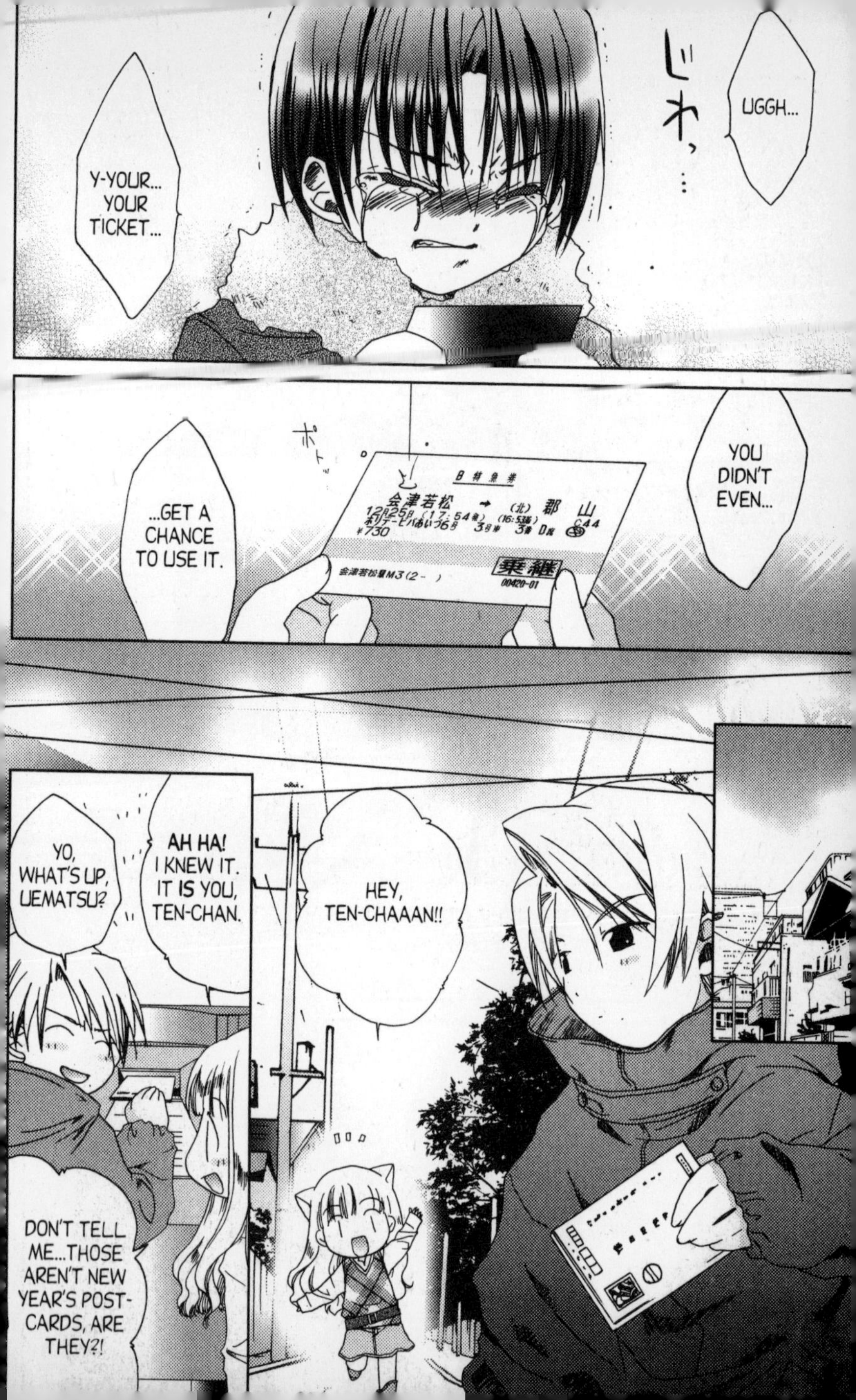
UGGH...
じわっ...
Y-YOUR... YOUR TICKET...
YOU DIDN'T EVEN...
ポトッ
会津若松 → (北) 郡山
¥730
乗継
...GET A CHANCE TO USE IT.
HEY, TEN-CHAAAN!!
AH HA! I KNEW IT. IT IS YOU, TEN-CHAN.
YO, WHAT'S UP, UEMATSU?
DON'T TELL ME...THOSE AREN'T NEW YEAR'S POST-CARDS, ARE THEY?!

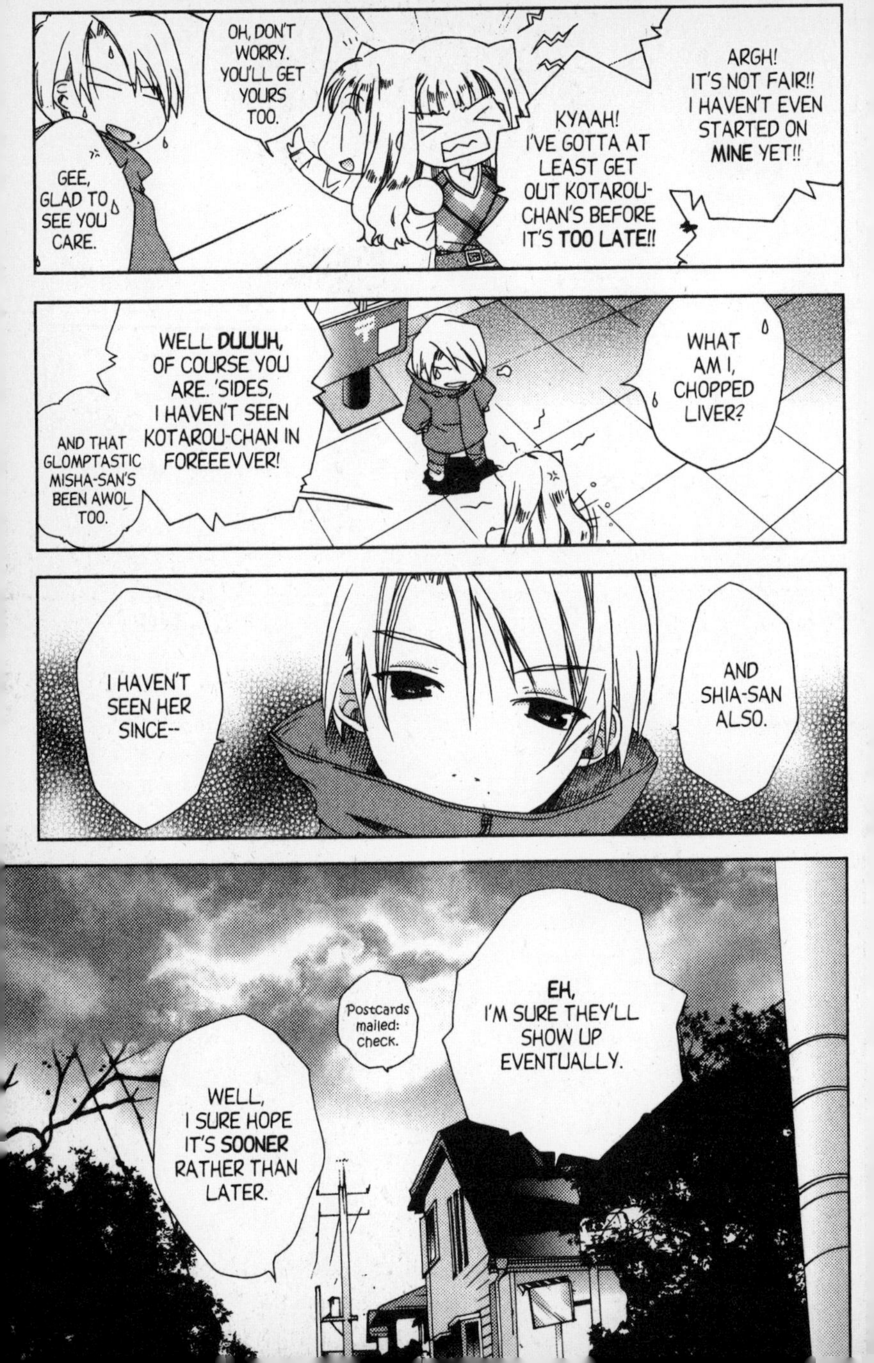
ARGH! IT'S NOT FAIR!! I HAVEN'T EVEN STARTED ON MINE YET!!
KYAAH! I'VE GOTTA AT LEAST GET OUT KOTAROU-CHAN'S BEFORE IT'S TOO LATE!!
OH, DON'T WORRY. YOU'LL GET YOURS TOO.
GEE, GLAD TO SEE YOU CARE.
WHAT AM I, CHOPPED LIVER?
WELL DUUUH, OF COURSE YOU ARE. 'SIDES, I HAVEN'T SEEN KOTAROU-CHAN IN FOREEEVVER!
AND THAT GLOMPTASTIC MISHA-SAN'S BEEN AWOL TOO.
AND SHIA-SAN ALSO.
I HAVEN'T SEEN HER SINCE--
EH, I'M SURE THEY'LL SHOW UP EVENTUALLY.
Postcards mailed: check.
WELL, I SURE HOPE IT'S SOONER RATHER THAN LATER.

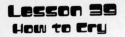

Lesson 39
How to Cry

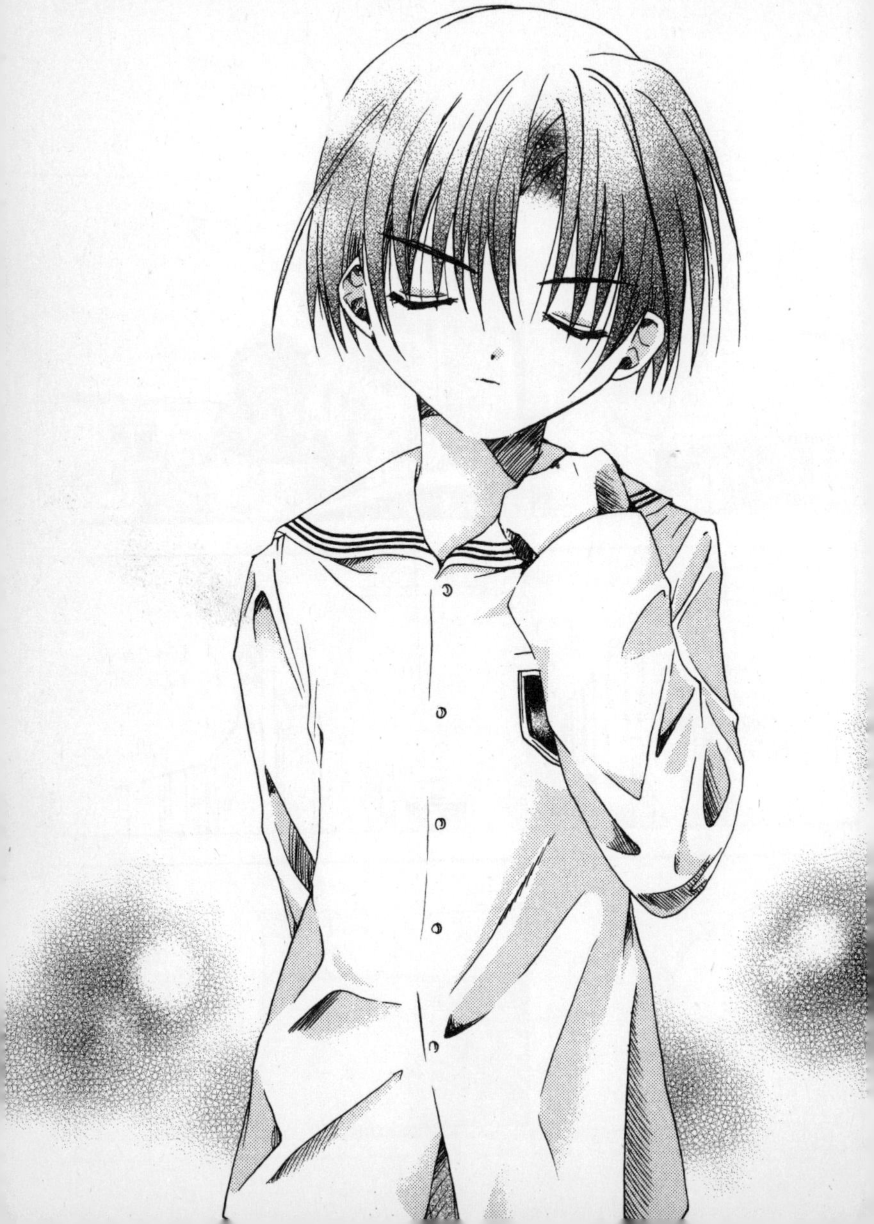

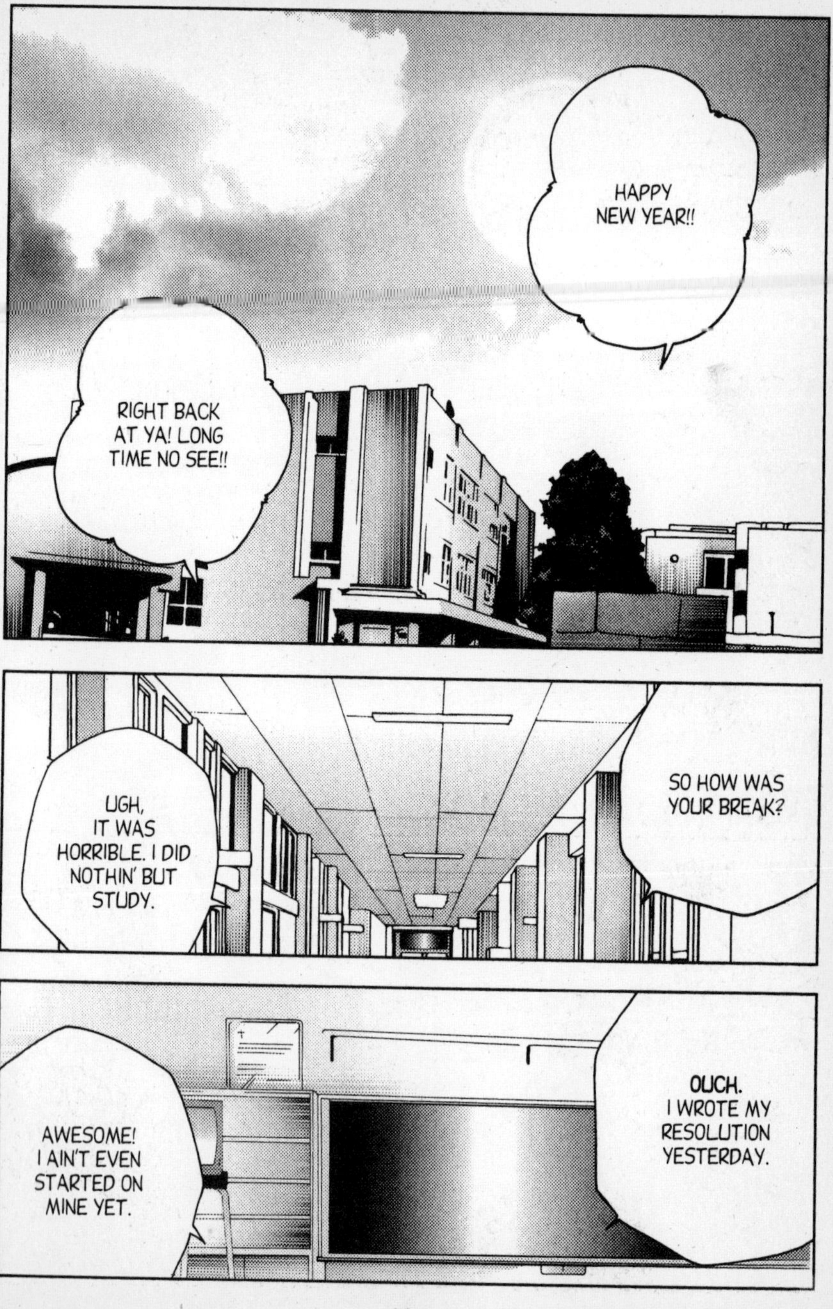
HAPPY NEW YEAR!!
RIGHT BACK AT YA! LONG TIME NO SEE!!
SO HOW WAS YOUR BREAK?
UGH, IT WAS HORRIBLE. I DID NOTHIN' BUT STUDY.
OUCH. I WROTE MY RESOLUTION YESTERDAY.
AWESOME! I AIN'T EVEN STARTED ON MINE YET.

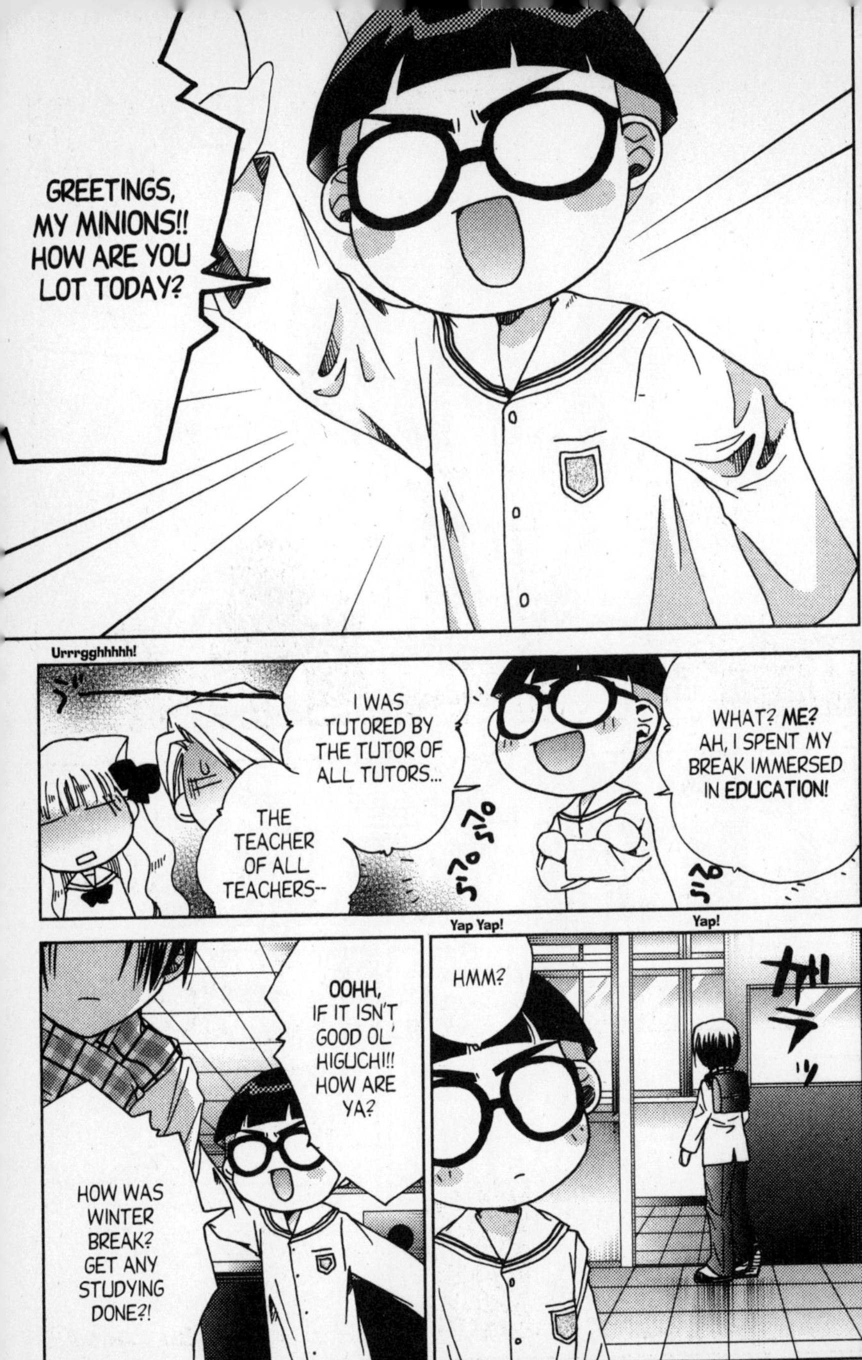
GREETINGS, MY MINIONS!! HOW ARE YOU LOT TODAY?
WHAT? ME? AH, I SPENT MY BREAK IMMERSED IN EDUCATION!
Yap!
I WAS TUTORED BY THE TUTOR OF ALL TUTORS...
THE TEACHER OF ALL TEACHERS--
Yap Yap!
Urrrgghhhhh!
ガラッ
HMM?
OOHH, IF IT ISN'T GOOD OL' HIGUCHI!!! HOW ARE YA?
HOW WAS WINTER BREAK? GET ANY STUDYING DONE?!

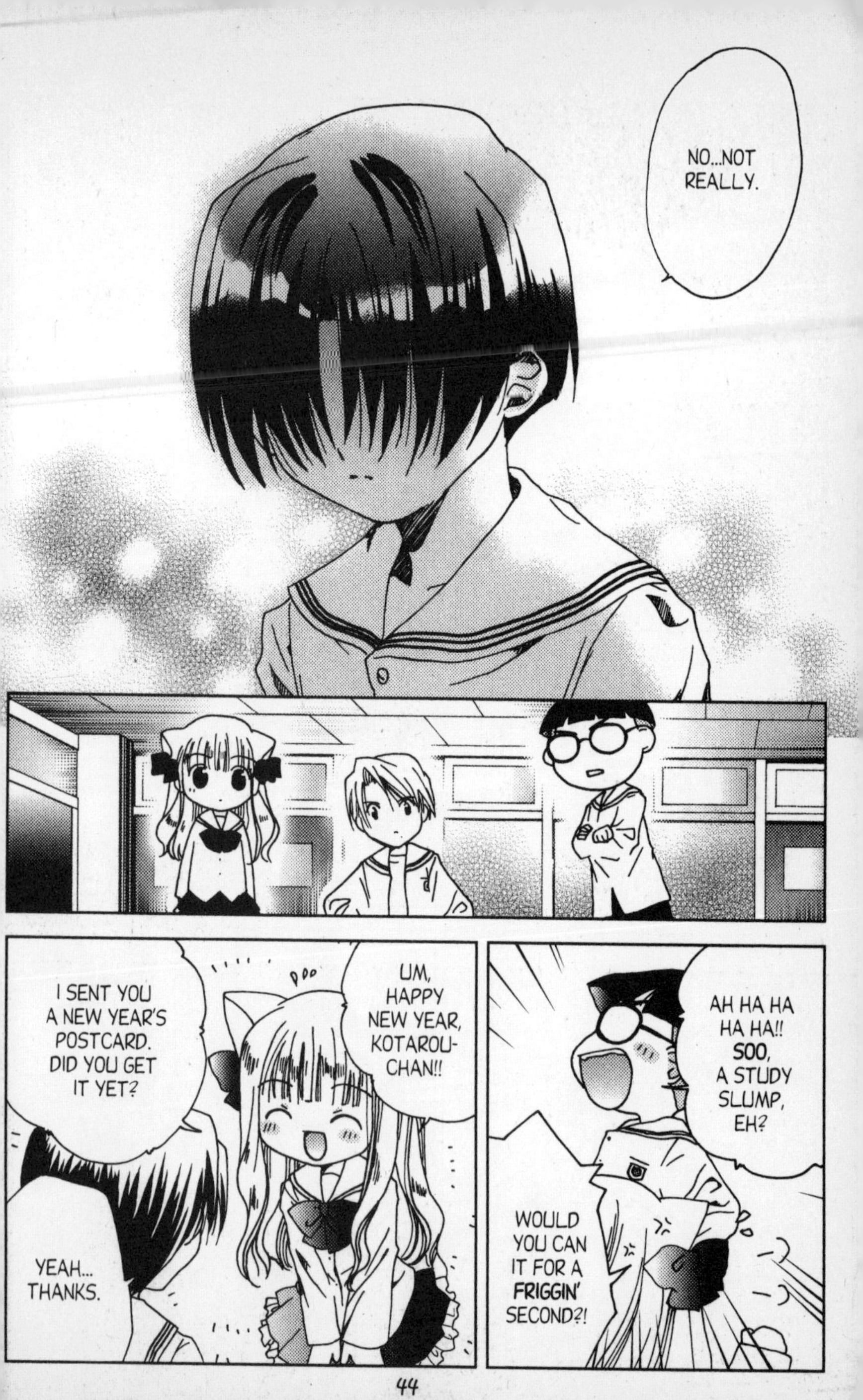
NO...NOT REALLY.
AH HA HA HA HA!! **SOO,** A STUDY SLUMP, EH?
WOULD YOU CAN IT FOR A **FRIGGIN'** SECOND?!
UM, HAPPY NEW YEAR, KOTAROU-CHAN!!
I SENT YOU A NEW YEAR'S POSTCARD. DID YOU GET IT YET?
YEAH... THANKS.

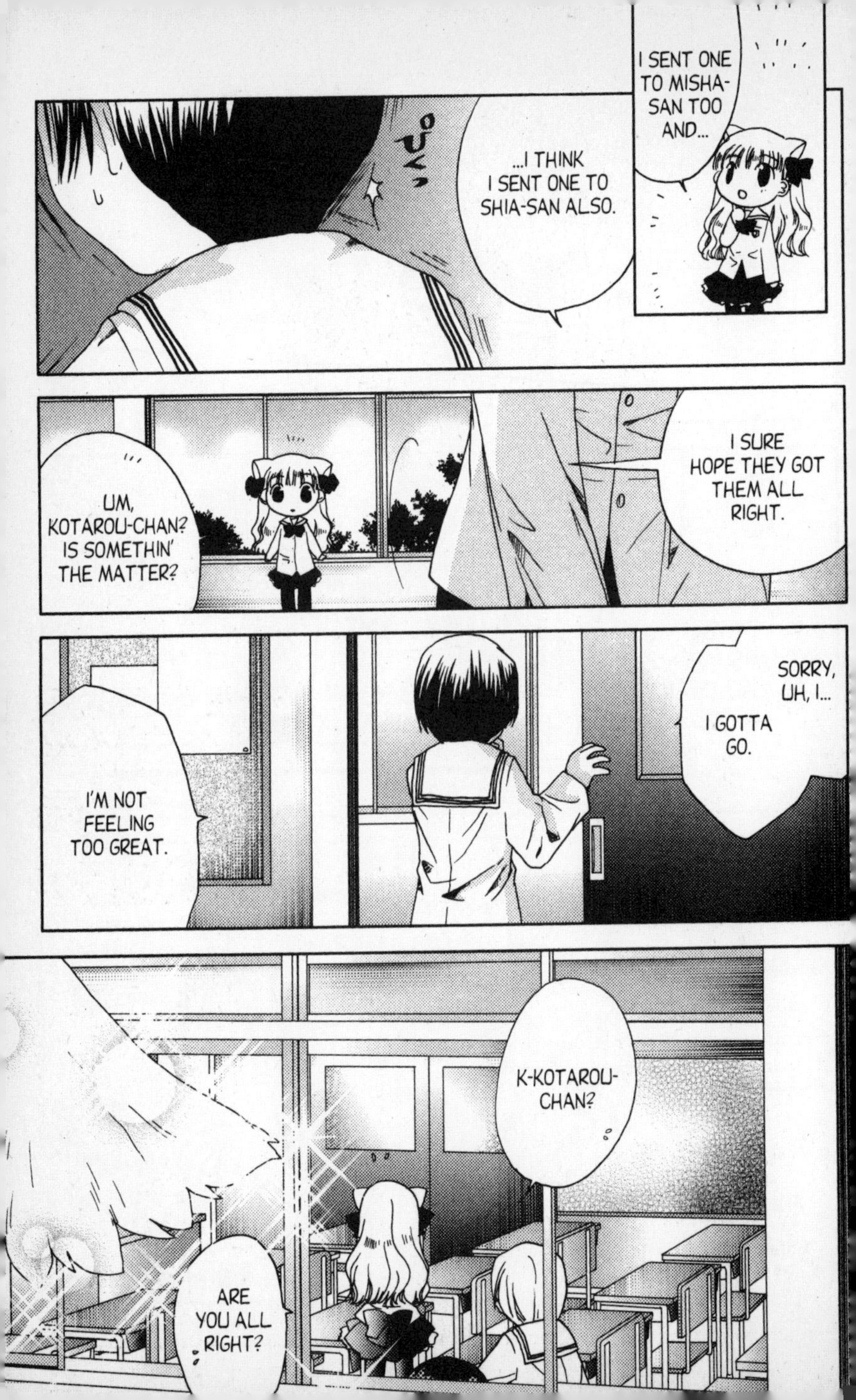
I SENT ONE TO MISHA-SAN TOO AND...
...I THINK I SENT ONE TO SHIA-SAN ALSO.
I SURE HOPE THEY GOT THEM ALL RIGHT.
UM, KOTAROU-CHAN? IS SOMETHIN' THE MATTER?
SORRY, UH, I...
I GOTTA GO.
I'M NOT FEELING TOO GREAT.
K-KOTAROU-CHAN?
ARE YOU ALL RIGHT?

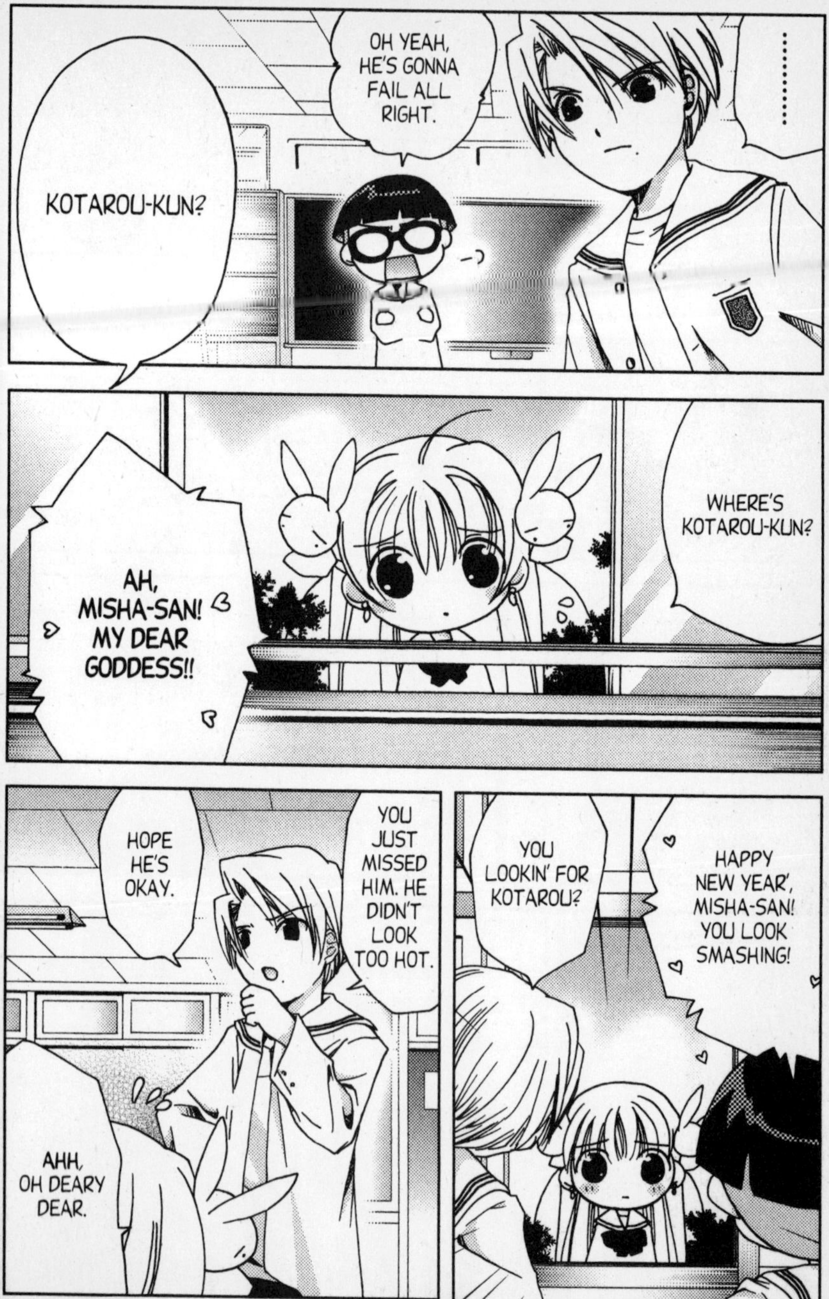
......
OH YEAH, HE'S GONNA FAIL ALL RIGHT.
KOTAROU-KUN?
WHERE'S KOTAROU-KUN?
AH, MISHA-SAN! MY DEAR GODDESS!!
HAPPY NEW YEAR', MISHA-SAN! YOU LOOK SMASHING!
YOU LOOKIN' FOR KOTAROU?
YOU JUST MISSED HIM. HE DIDN'T LOOK TOO HOT.
HOPE HE'S OKAY.
AHH, OH DEARY DEAR.

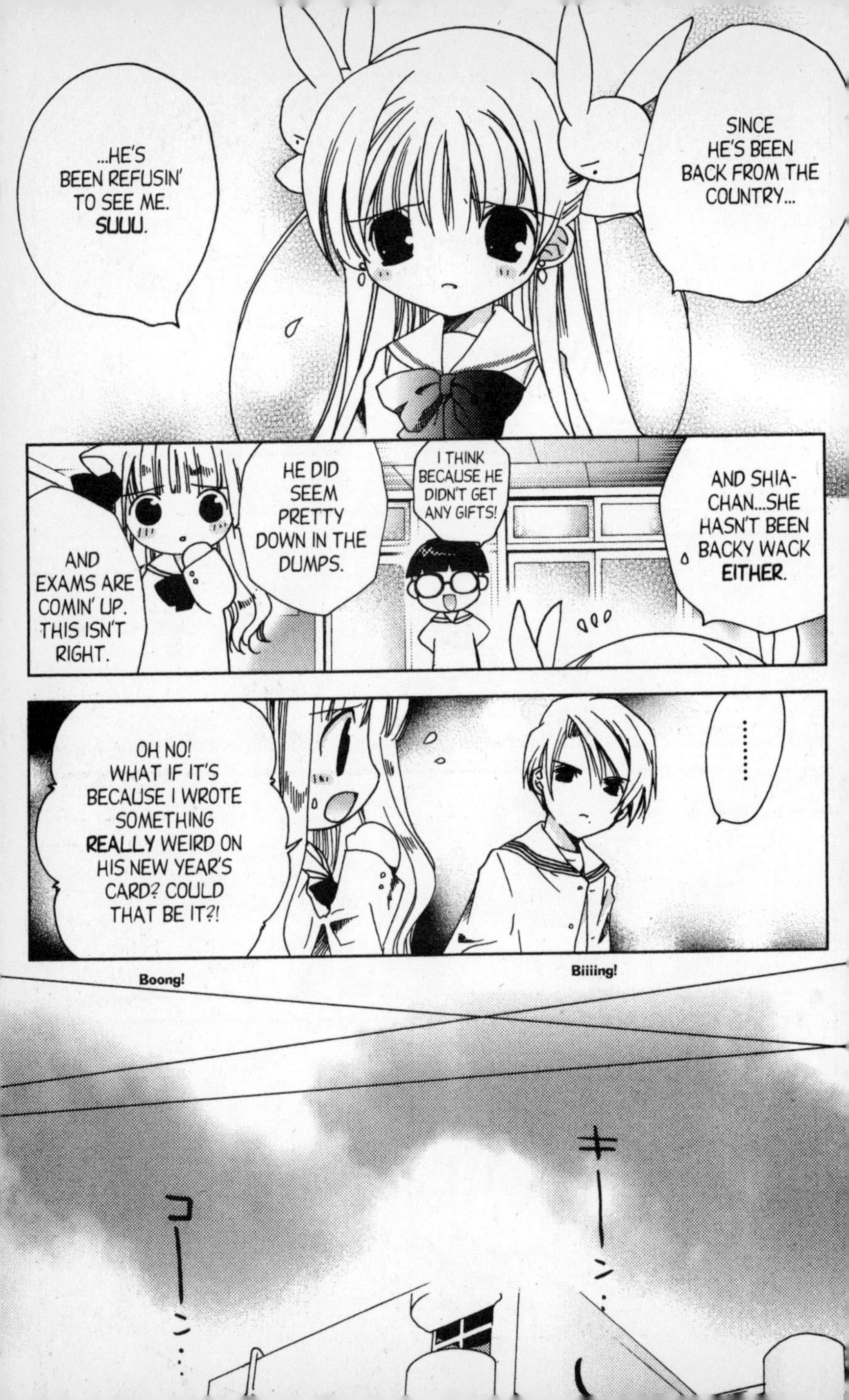

SINCE HE'S BEEN BACK FROM THE COUNTRY...
...HE'S BEEN REFUSIN' TO SEE ME. SUUU.
AND SHIA-CHAN...SHE HASN'T BEEN BACKY WACK EITHER.
I THINK BECAUSE HE DIDN'T GET ANY GIFTS!
HE DID SEEM PRETTY DOWN IN THE DUMPS.
AND EXAMS ARE COMIN' UP. THIS ISN'T RIGHT.
....
OH NO! WHAT IF IT'S BECAUSE I WROTE SOMETHING REALLY WEIRD ON HIS NEW YEAR'S CARD? COULD THAT BE IT?!
Biiiing!
Boong!
キーン…
コーン…

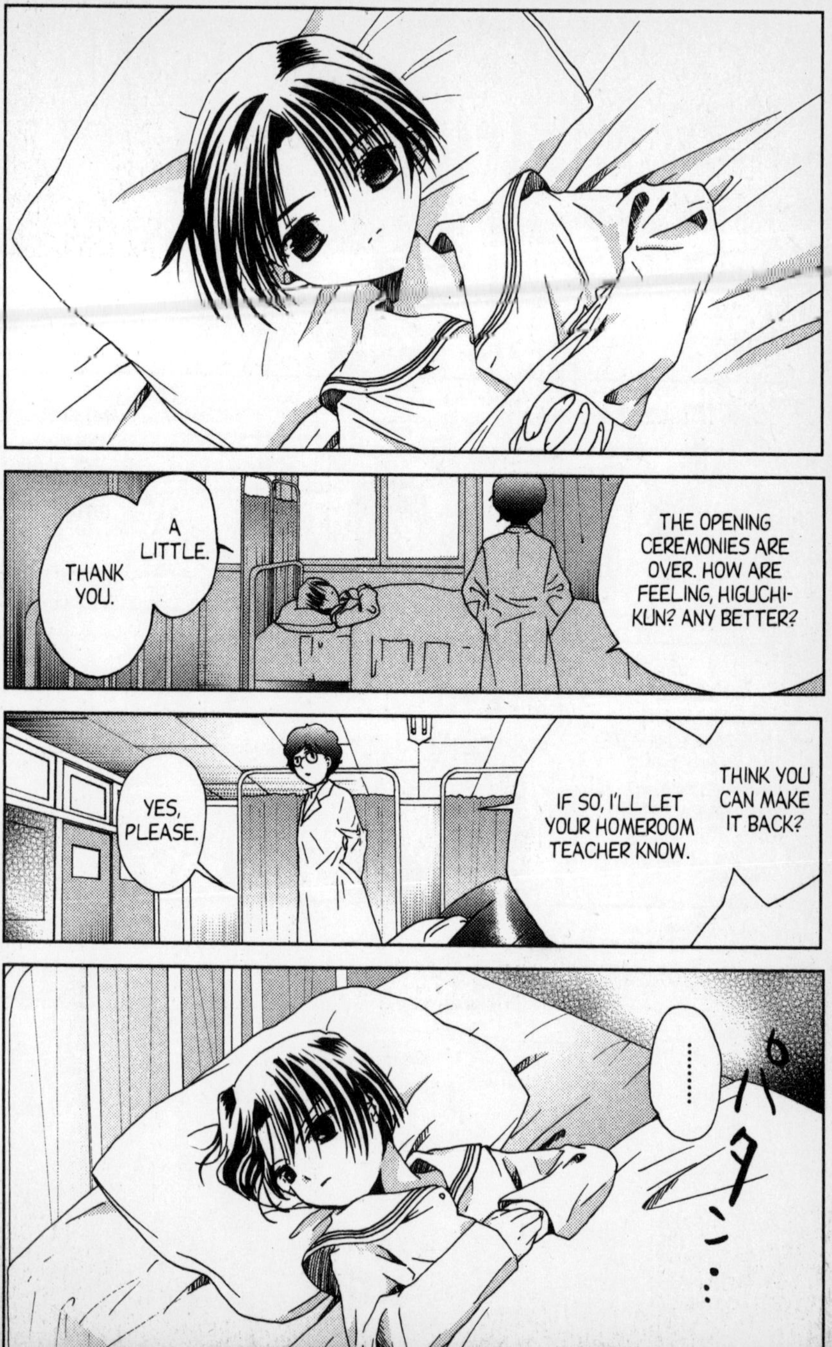
THE OPENING CEREMONIES ARE OVER. HOW ARE FEELING, HIGUCHI-KUN? ANY BETTER?
A LITTLE.
THANK YOU.
THINK YOU CAN MAKE IT BACK?
IF SO, I'LL LET YOUR HOMEROOM TEACHER KNOW.
YES, PLEASE.
……
パタン…

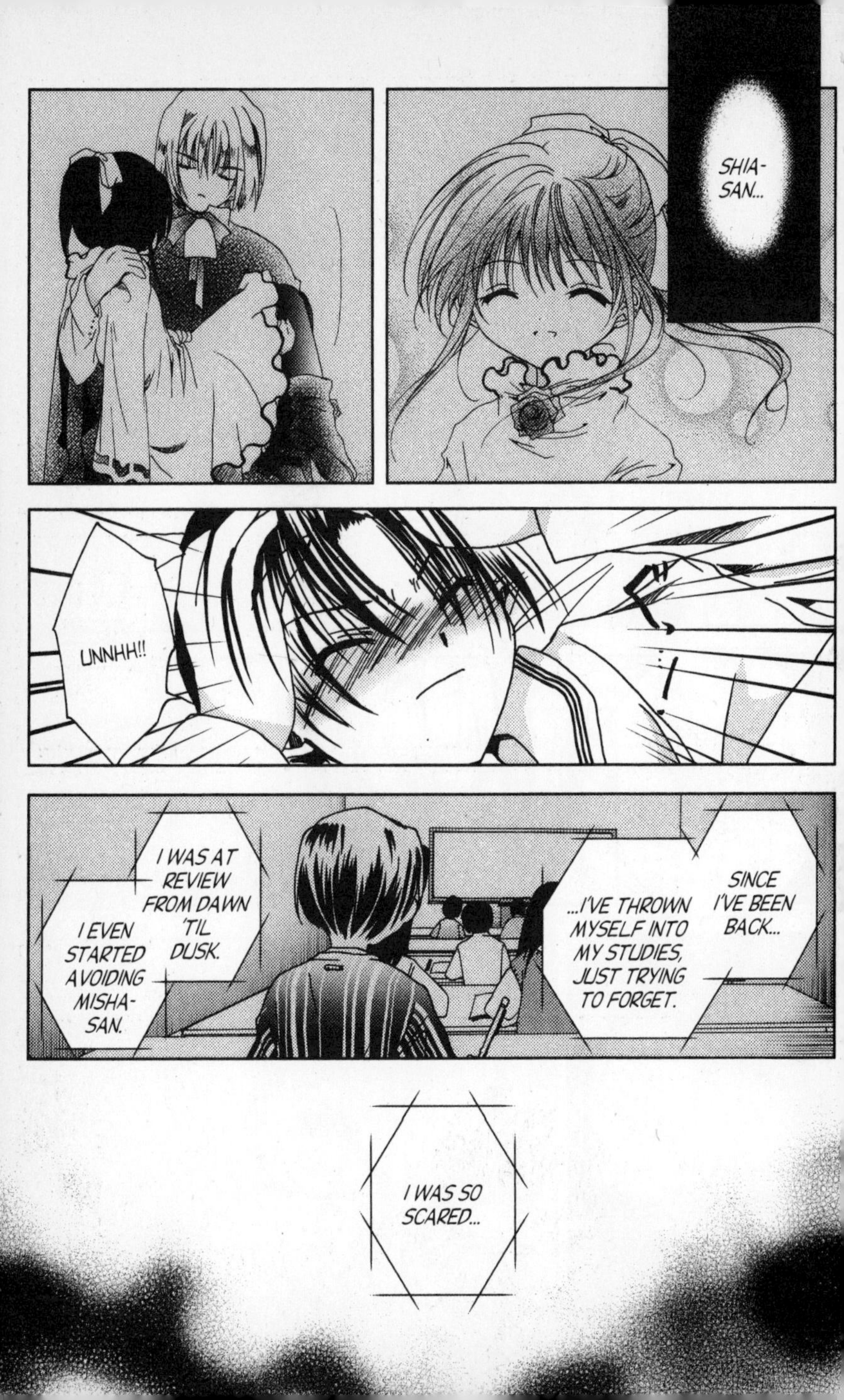
SHIA-SAN...
UNNHH!!
SINCE I'VE BEEN BACK...
...I'VE THROWN MYSELF INTO MY STUDIES, JUST TRYING TO FORGET.
I WAS AT REVIEW FROM DAWN 'TIL DUSK.
I EVEN STARTED AVOIDING MISHA-SAN.
I WAS SO SCARED...

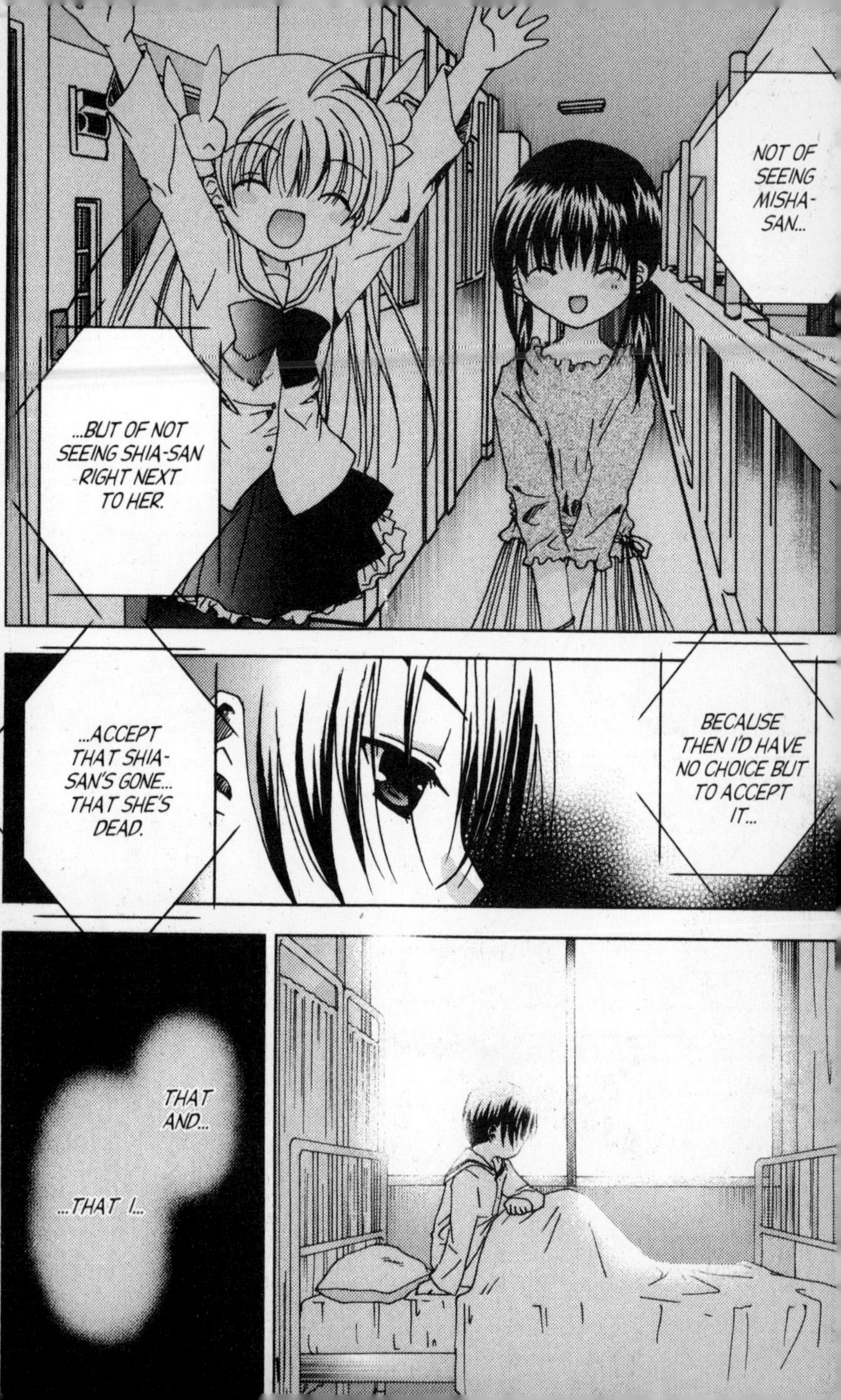
NOT OF SEEING MISHA-SAN...
...BUT OF NOT SEEING SHIA-SAN RIGHT NEXT TO HER.
BECAUSE THEN I'D HAVE NO CHOICE BUT TO ACCEPT IT...
...ACCEPT THAT SHIA-SAN'S GONE... THAT SHE'S DEAD.
THAT AND...
...THAT I...

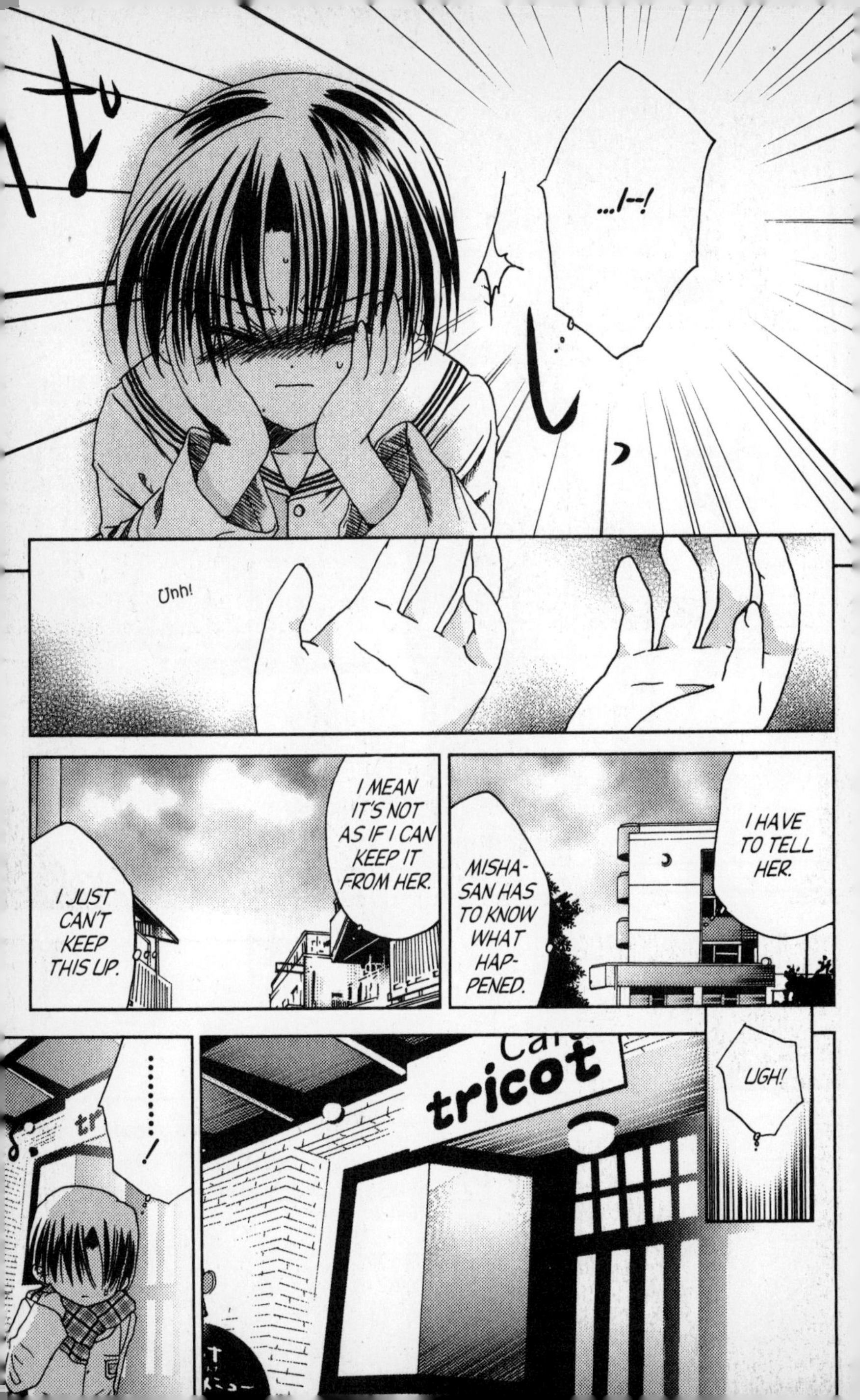
...I--!
Unh!
I HAVE TO TELL HER.
MISHA-SAN HAS TO KNOW WHAT HAPPENED.
I MEAN IT'S NOT AS IF I CAN KEEP IT FROM HER.
I JUST CAN'T KEEP THIS UP.
UGH!
tricot
......!

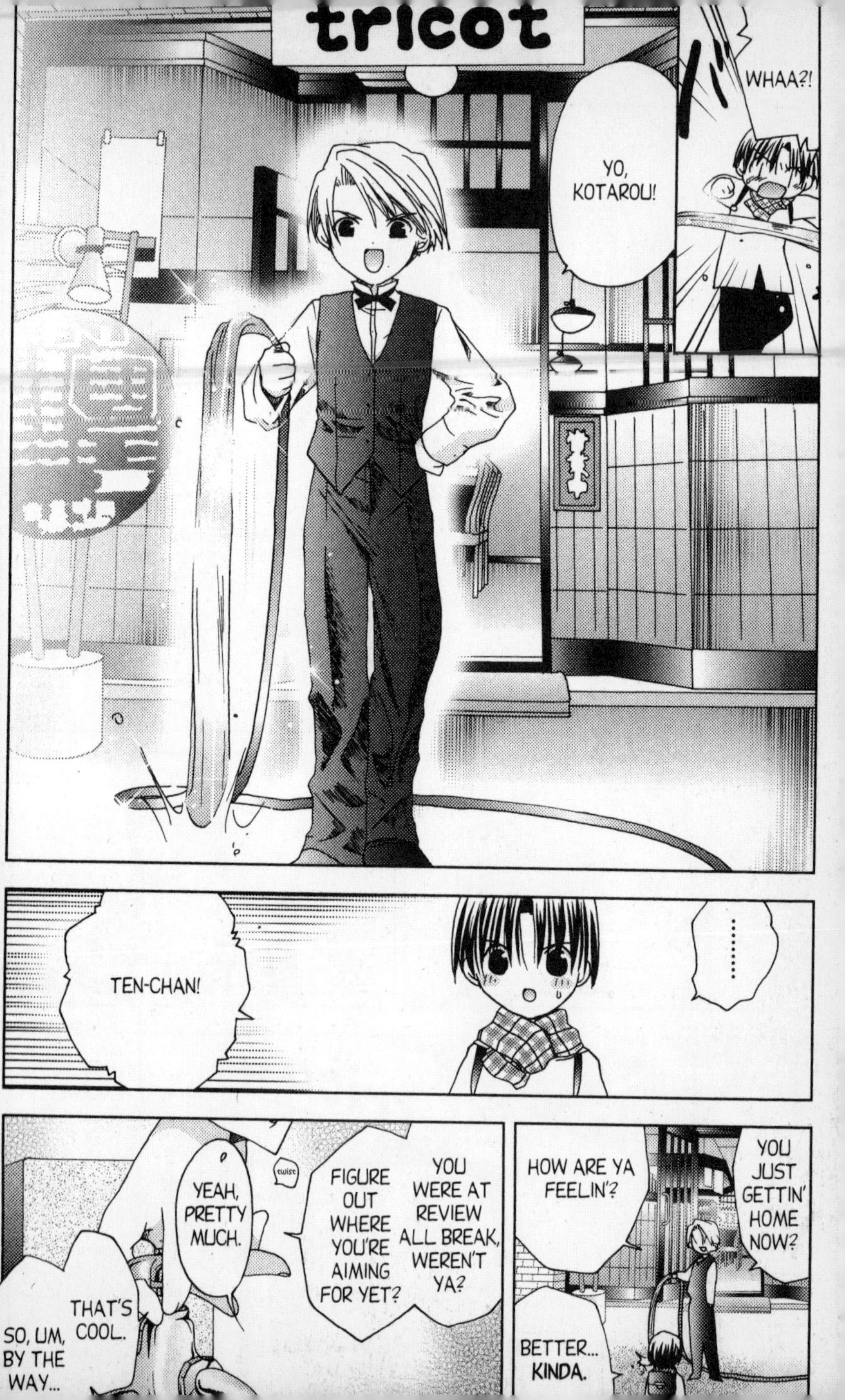
tricot
WHAA?!
YO, KOTAROU!
......
TEN-CHAN!
YOU JUST GETTIN' HOME NOW?
HOW ARE YA FEELIN'?
BETTER... KINDA.
YOU WERE AT REVIEW ALL BREAK, WEREN'T YA?
FIGURE OUT WHERE YOU'RE AIMING FOR YET?
twist
YEAH, PRETTY MUCH.
THAT'S COOL.
SO, UM, BY THE WAY...

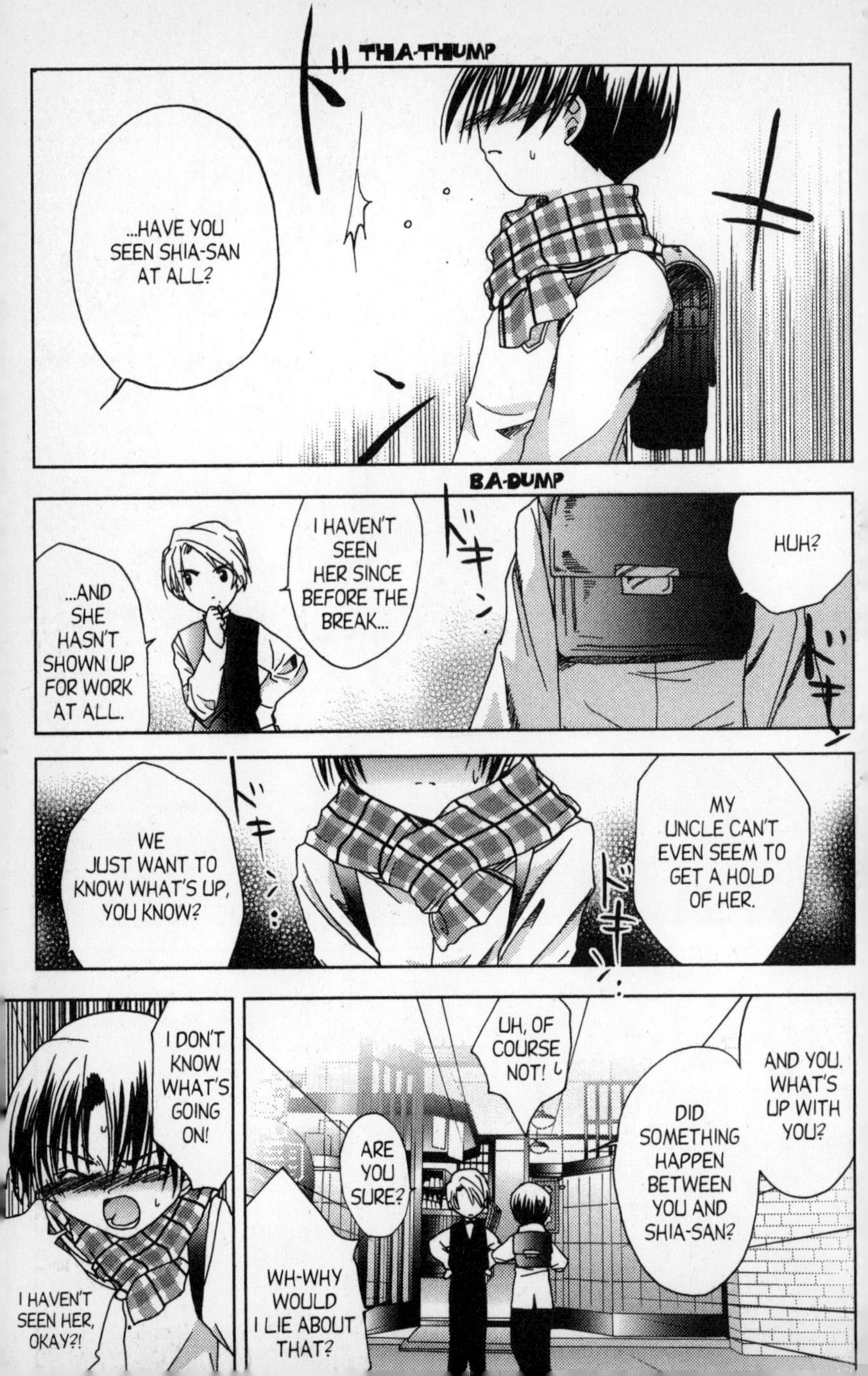
THA-THUMP
...HAVE YOU SEEN SHIA-SAN AT ALL?
BA-DUMP
HUH?
I HAVEN'T SEEN HER SINCE BEFORE THE BREAK...
...AND SHE HASN'T SHOWN UP FOR WORK AT ALL.
MY UNCLE CAN'T EVEN SEEM TO GET A HOLD OF HER.
WE JUST WANT TO KNOW WHAT'S UP, YOU KNOW?
AND YOU. WHAT'S UP WITH YOU?
DID SOMETHING HAPPEN BETWEEN YOU AND SHIA-SAN?
UH, OF COURSE NOT!
ARE YOU SURE?
WH-WHY WOULD I LIE ABOUT THAT?
I DON'T KNOW WHAT'S GOING ON!
I HAVEN'T SEEN HER, OKAY?!

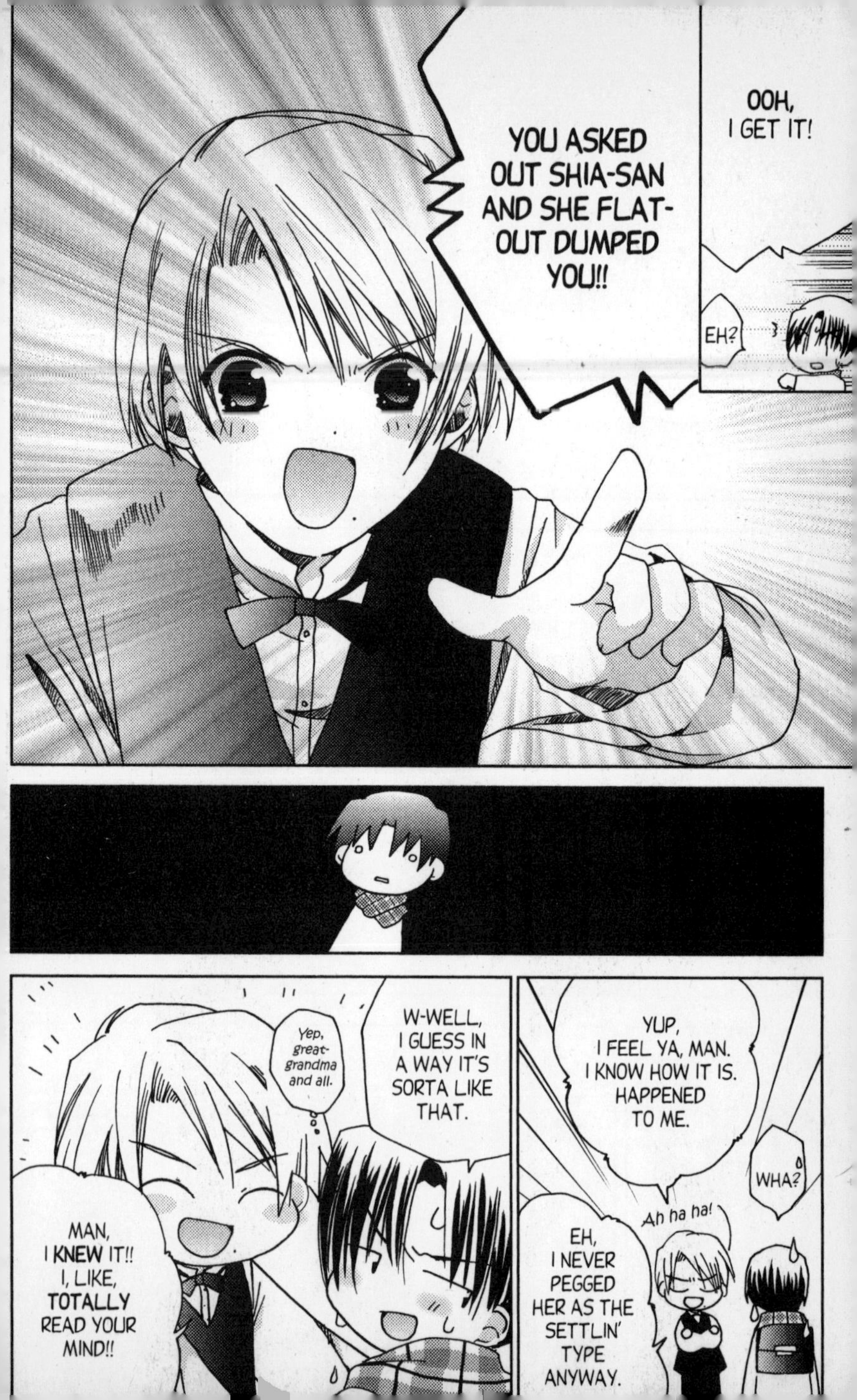
OOH, I GET IT!
EH?
YOU ASKED OUT SHIA-SAN AND SHE FLAT-OUT DUMPED YOU!!
YUP, I FEEL YA, MAN. I KNOW HOW IT IS. HAPPENED TO ME.
WHA?
Ah ha ha!
EH, I NEVER PEGGED HER AS THE SETTLIN' TYPE ANYWAY.
W-WELL, I GUESS IN A WAY IT'S SORTA LIKE THAT.
Yep, great-grandma and all.
MAN, I KNEW IT!! I, LIKE, TOTALLY READ YOUR MIND!!

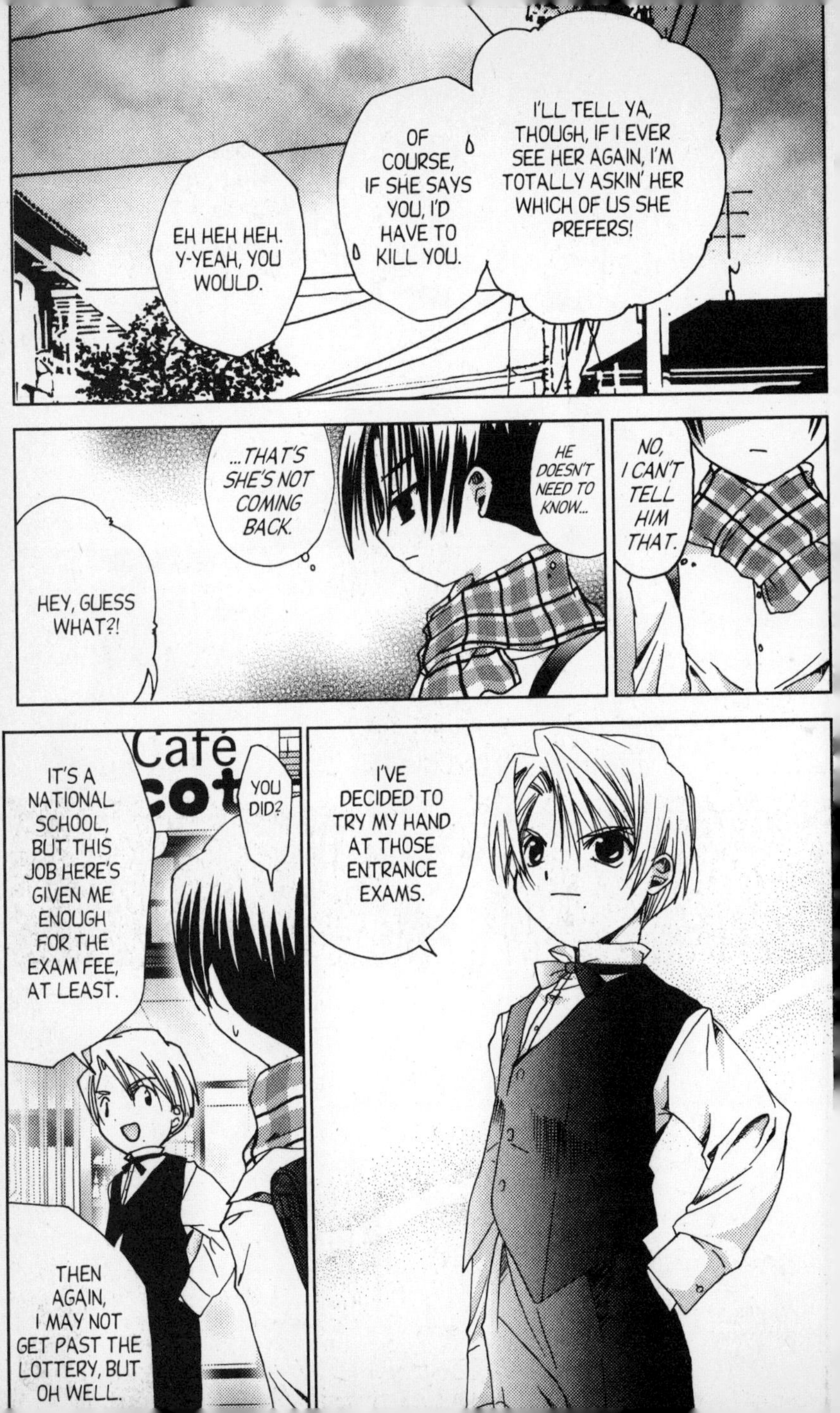
I'LL TELL YA, THOUGH, IF I EVER SEE HER AGAIN, I'M TOTALLY ASKIN' HER WHICH OF US SHE PREFERS!
OF COURSE, IF SHE SAYS YOU, I'D HAVE TO KILL YOU.
EH HEH HEH. Y-YEAH, YOU WOULD.
NO, I CAN'T TELL HIM THAT.
HE DOESN'T NEED TO KNOW...
...THAT'S SHE'S NOT COMING BACK.
HEY, GUESS WHAT?!
I'VE DECIDED TO TRY MY HAND AT THOSE ENTRANCE EXAMS.
YOU DID?
Café
IT'S A NATIONAL SCHOOL, BUT THIS JOB HERE'S GIVEN ME ENOUGH FOR THE EXAM FEE, AT LEAST.
THEN AGAIN, I MAY NOT GET PAST THE LOTTERY, BUT OH WELL.

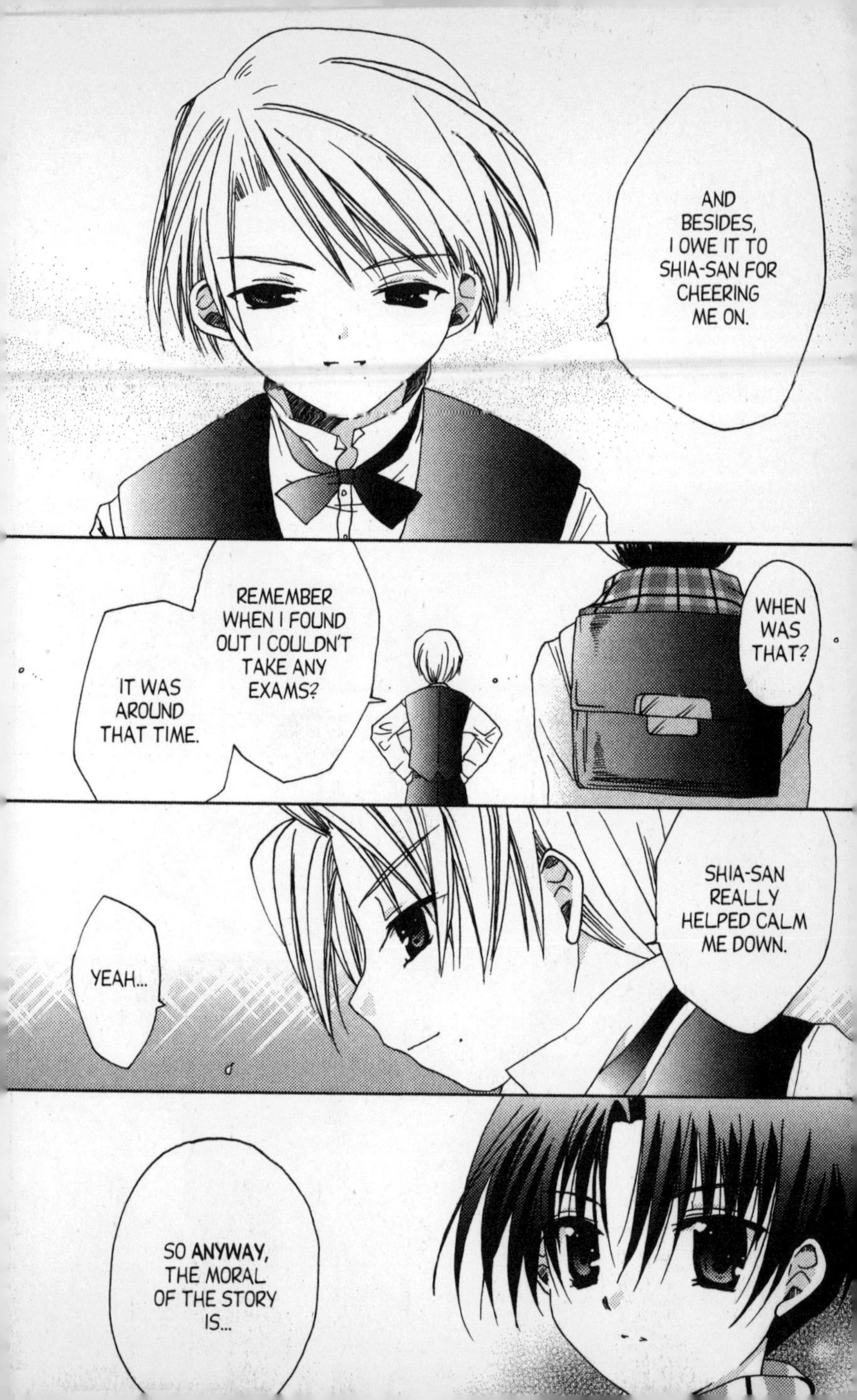
AND BESIDES, I OWE IT TO SHIA-SAN FOR CHEERING ME ON.
WHEN WAS THAT?
REMEMBER WHEN I FOUND OUT I COULDN'T TAKE ANY EXAMS?
IT WAS AROUND THAT TIME.
SHIA-SAN REALLY HELPED CALM ME DOWN.
YEAH...
SO ANYWAY, THE MORAL OF THE STORY IS...

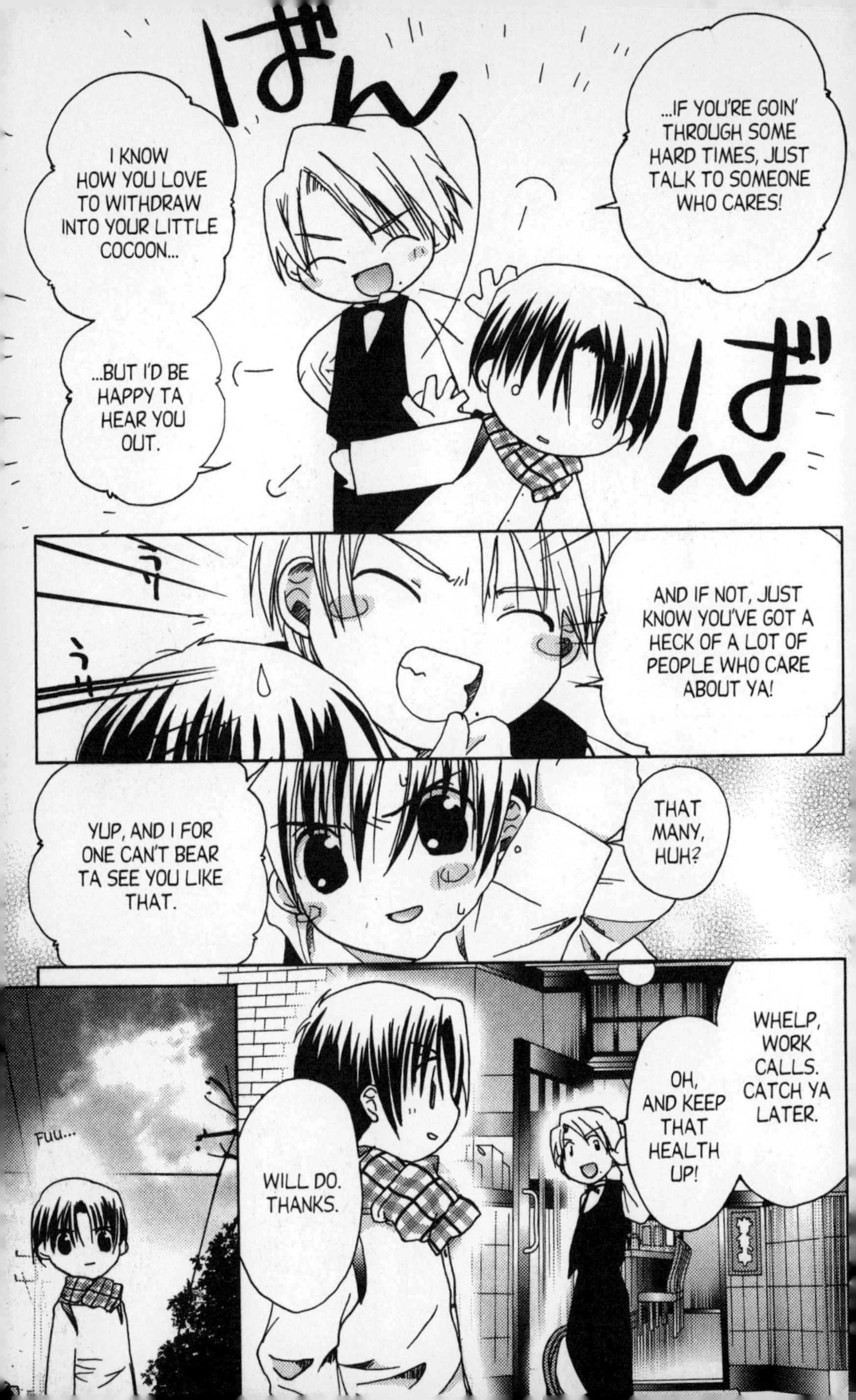
...IF YOU'RE GOIN' THROUGH SOME HARD TIMES, JUST TALK TO SOMEONE WHO CARES!
ぽん
ぽん
I KNOW HOW YOU LOVE TO WITHDRAW INTO YOUR LITTLE COCOON...
...BUT I'D BE HAPPY TA HEAR YOU OUT.
AND IF NOT, JUST KNOW YOU'VE GOT A HECK OF A LOT OF PEOPLE WHO CARE ABOUT YA!
THAT MANY, HUH?
YUP, AND I FOR ONE CAN'T BEAR TA SEE YOU LIKE THAT.
WHELP, WORK CALLS. CATCH YA LATER.
OH, AND KEEP THAT HEALTH UP!
WILL DO. THANKS.
Fuu...

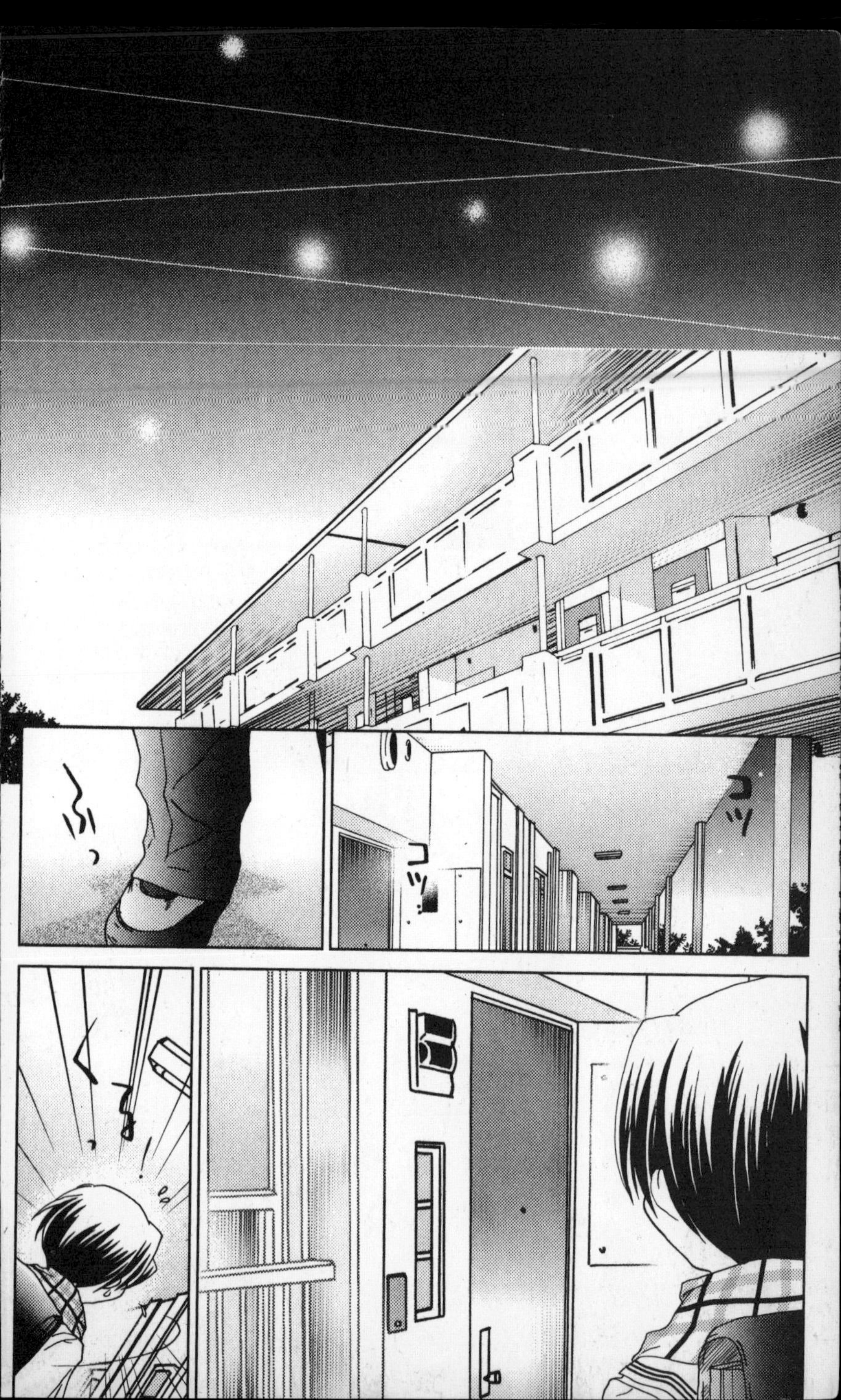
コッ
コッ
ふっ
くるっ!

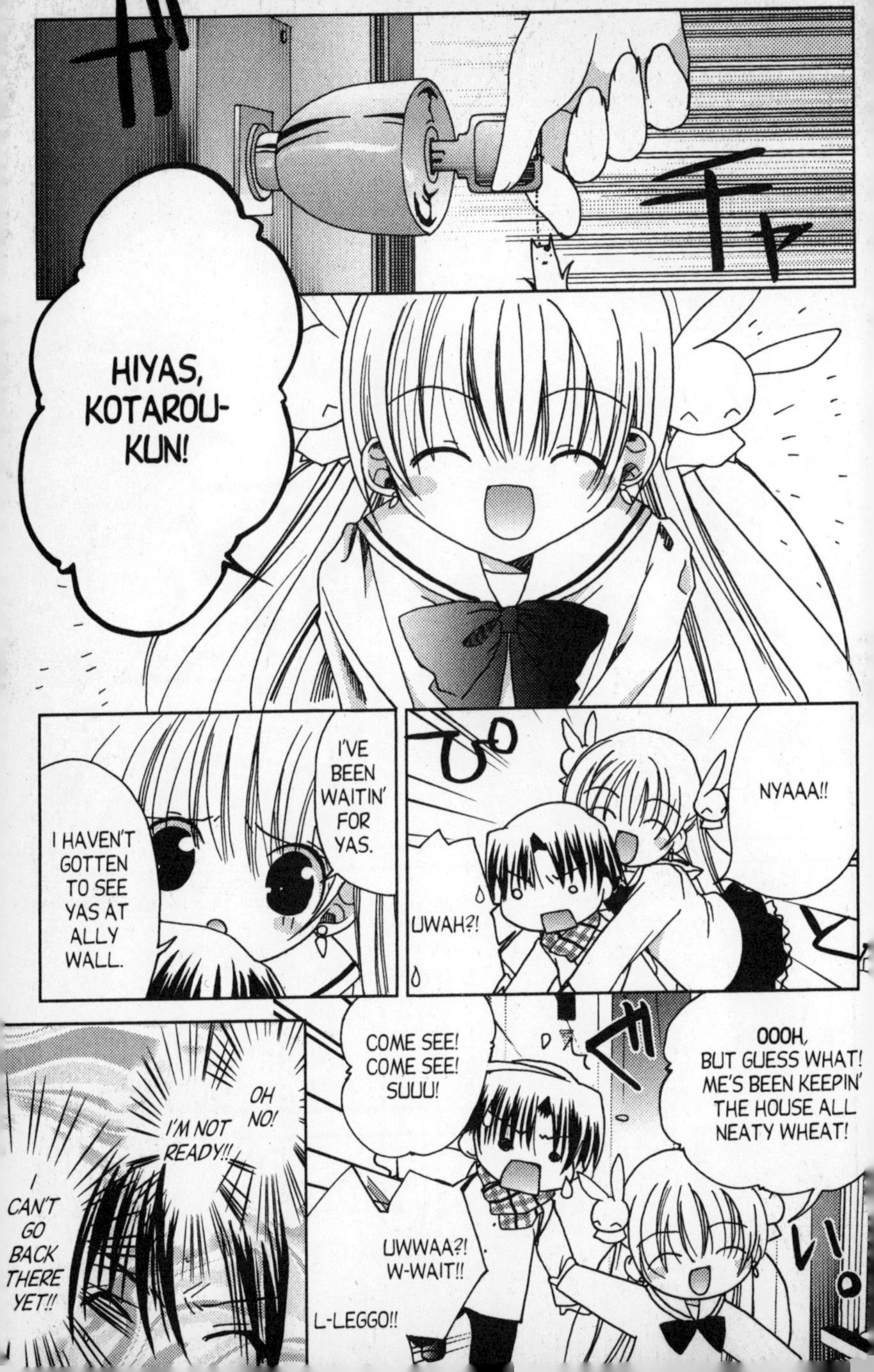
ガチャ
HIYAS, KOTAROU-KUN!
NYAAA!!
UWAH?!
I'VE BEEN WAITIN' FOR YAS.
I HAVEN'T GOTTEN TO SEE YAS AT ALLY WALL.
OOOH, BUT GUESS WHAT! ME'S BEEN KEEPIN' THE HOUSE ALL NEATY WHEAT!
COME SEE! COME SEE! SUUU!
UWWAA?! W-WAIT!!
L-LEGGO!!
OH NO!
I'M NOT READY!!
I CAN'T GO BACK THERE YET!!

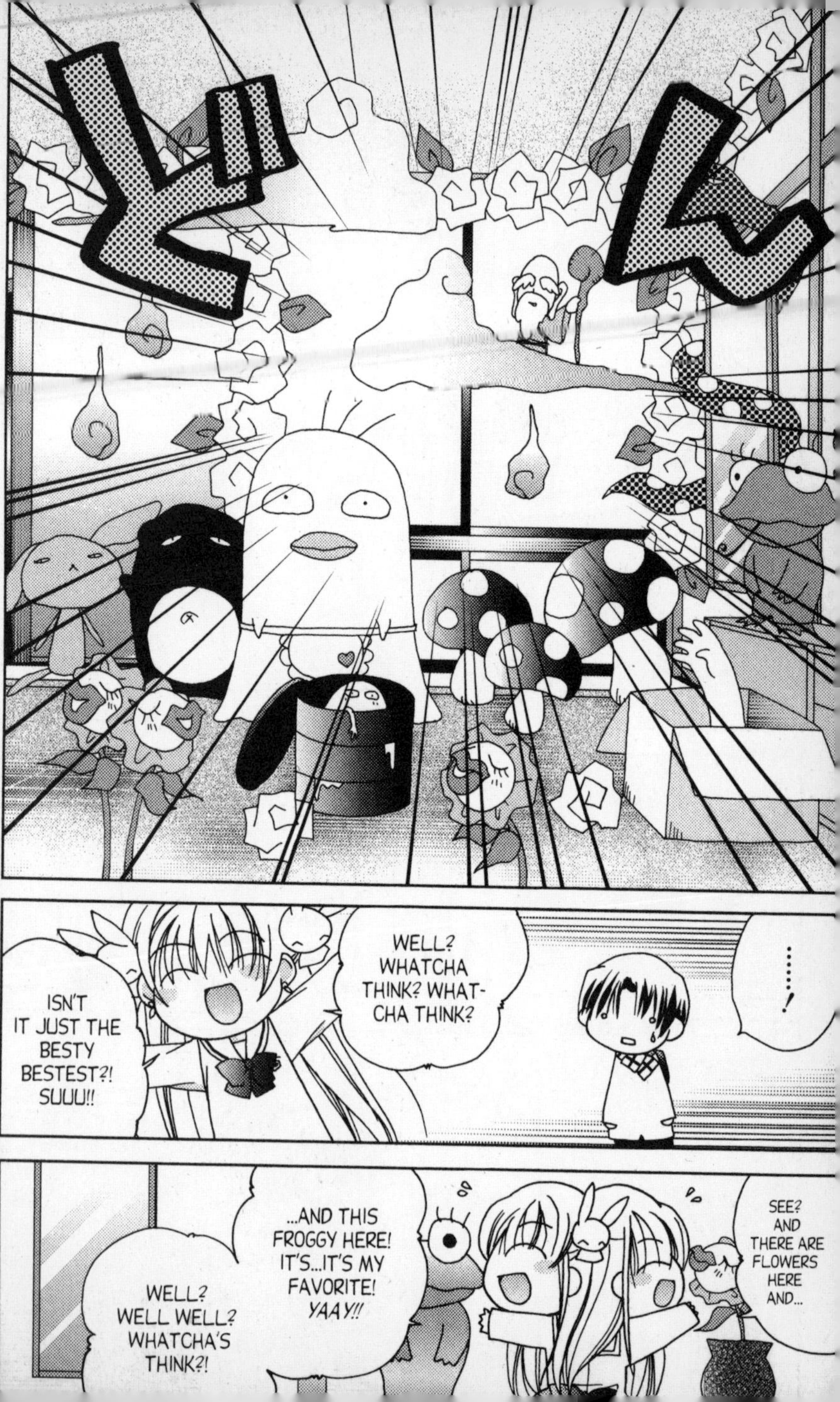
......!
WELL? WHATCHA THINK? WHAT-CHA THINK?
ISN'T IT JUST THE BESTY BESTEST?! SUUU!!
SEE? AND THERE ARE FLOWERS HERE AND...
...AND THIS FROGGY HERE! IT'S...IT'S MY FAVORITE! YAAY!!
WELL? WELL WELL? WHATCHA'S THINK?!

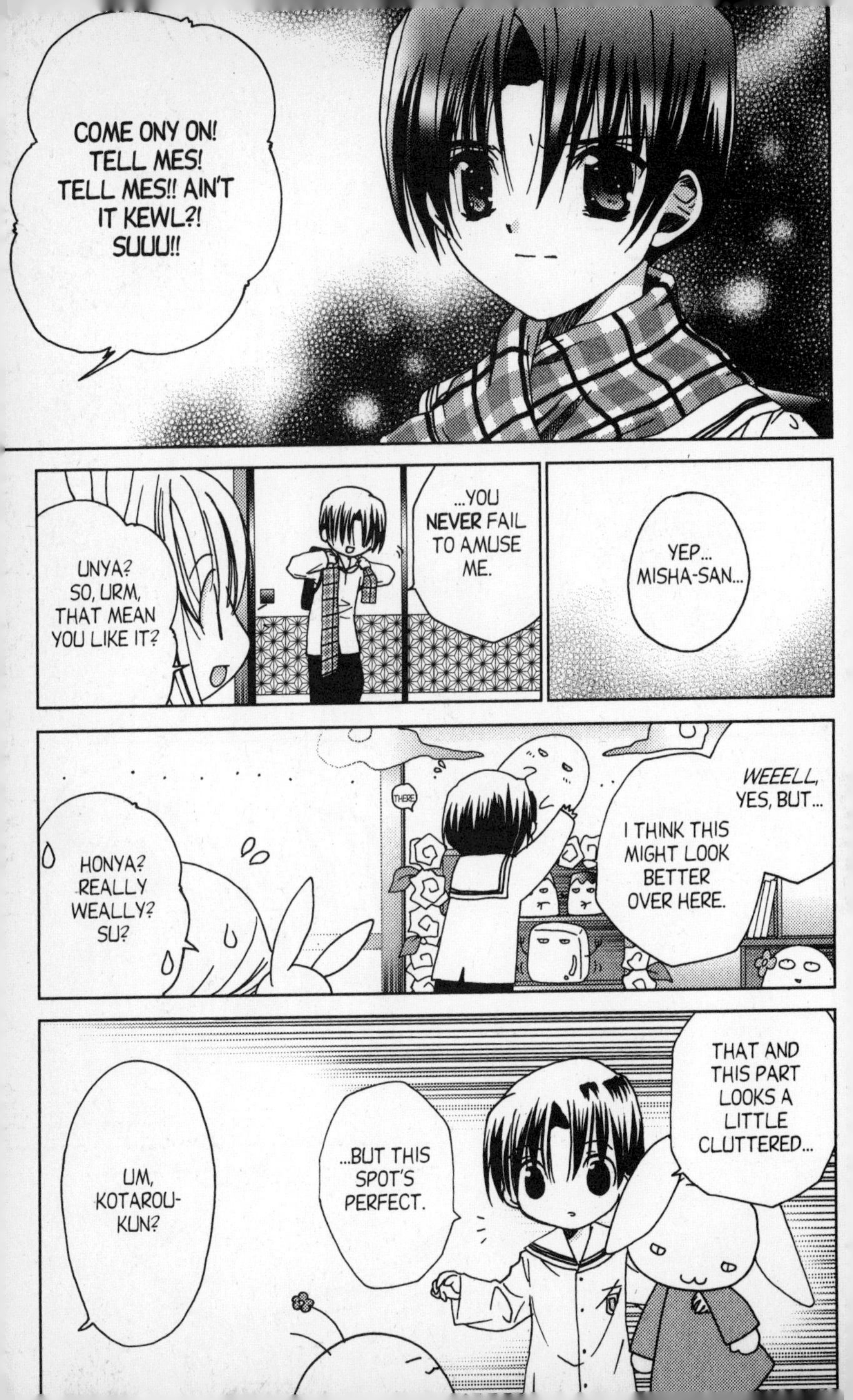
COME ONY ON! TELL MES! TELL MES!! AIN'T IT KEWL?! SUUU!!
YEP... MISHA-SAN...
...YOU NEVER FAIL TO AMUSE ME.
UNYA? SO, URM, THAT MEAN YOU LIKE IT?
WEEELL, YES, BUT...
I THINK THIS MIGHT LOOK BETTER OVER HERE.
THERE
......
HONYA? REALLY WEALLY? SU?
THAT AND THIS PART LOOKS A LITTLE CLUTTERED...
...BUT THIS SPOT'S PERFECT.
UM, KOTAROU-KUN?

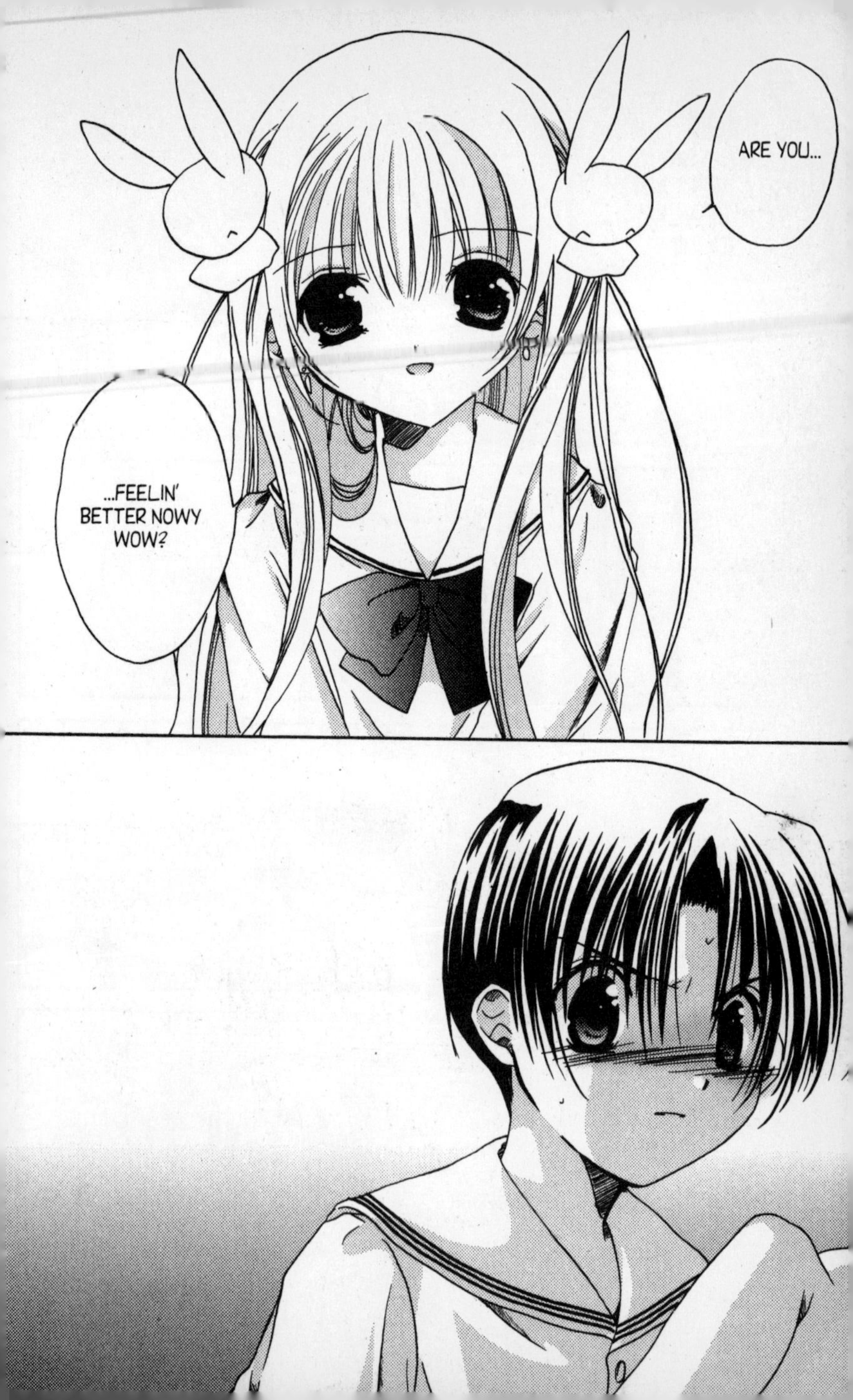
ARE YOU...
...FEELIN' BETTER NOWY WOW?

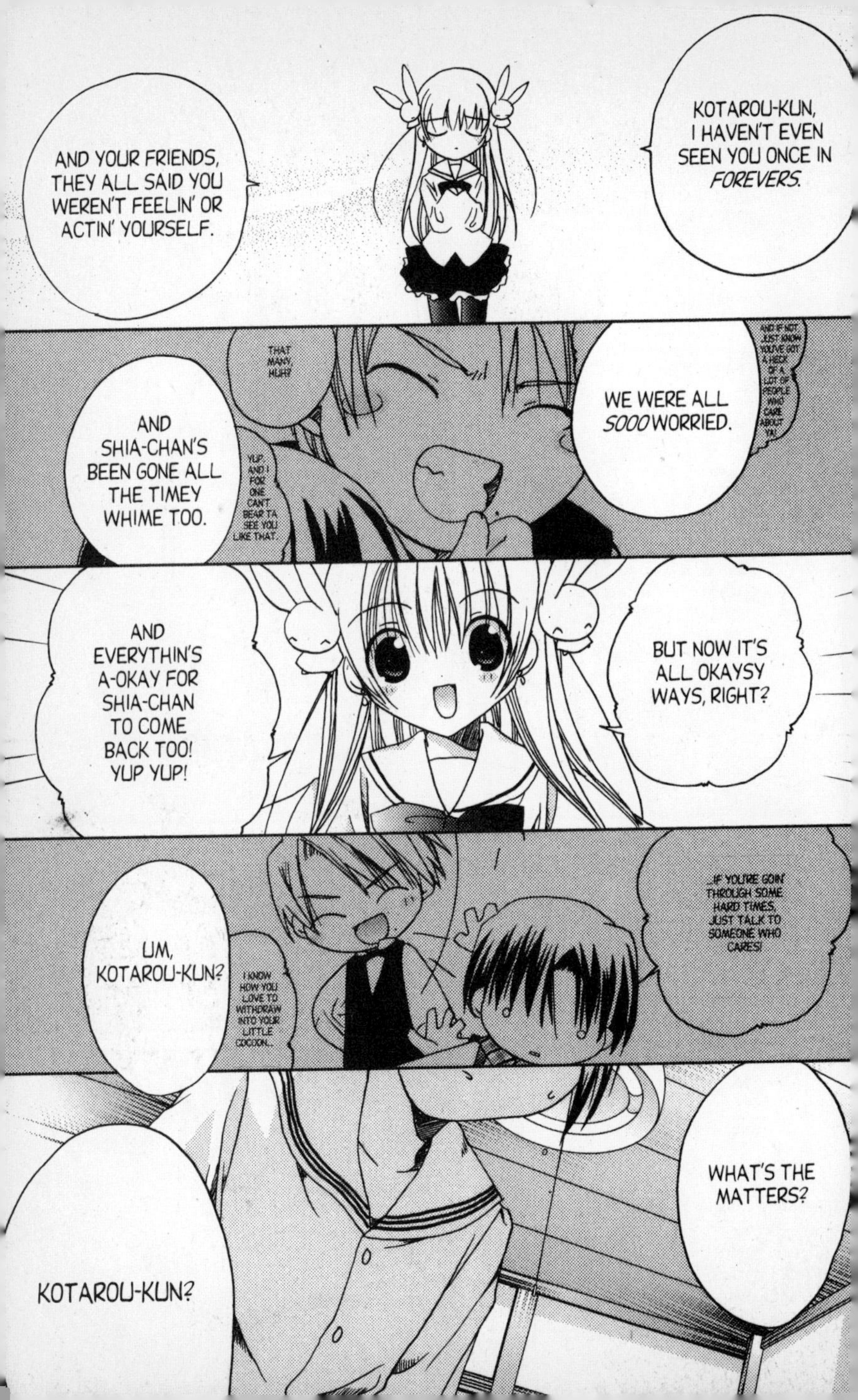
KOTAROU-KUN, I HAVEN'T EVEN SEEN YOU ONCE IN *FOREVERS.*
AND YOUR FRIENDS, THEY ALL SAID YOU WEREN'T FEELIN' OR ACTIN' YOURSELF.
AND IF NOT, JUST KNOW YOU'VE GOT A HECK OF A LOT OF PEOPLE WHO CARE ABOUT YA!
WE WERE ALL *SOOO* WORRIED.
THAT MANY, HUH?
YUP, AND I FOR ONE CAN'T BEAR TA SEE YOU LIKE THAT.
AND SHIA-CHAN'S BEEN GONE ALL THE TIMEY WHIME TOO.
BUT NOW IT'S ALL OKAYSY WAYS, RIGHT?
AND EVERYTHIN'S A-OKAY FOR SHIA-CHAN TO COME BACK TOO! YUP YUP!
...IF YOU'RE GOIN' THROUGH SOME HARD TIMES, JUST TALK TO SOMEONE WHO CARES!
I KNOW HOW YOU LOVE TO WITHDRAW INTO YOUR LITTLE COCOON...
UM, KOTAROU-KUN?
WHAT'S THE MATTERS?
KOTAROU-KUN?

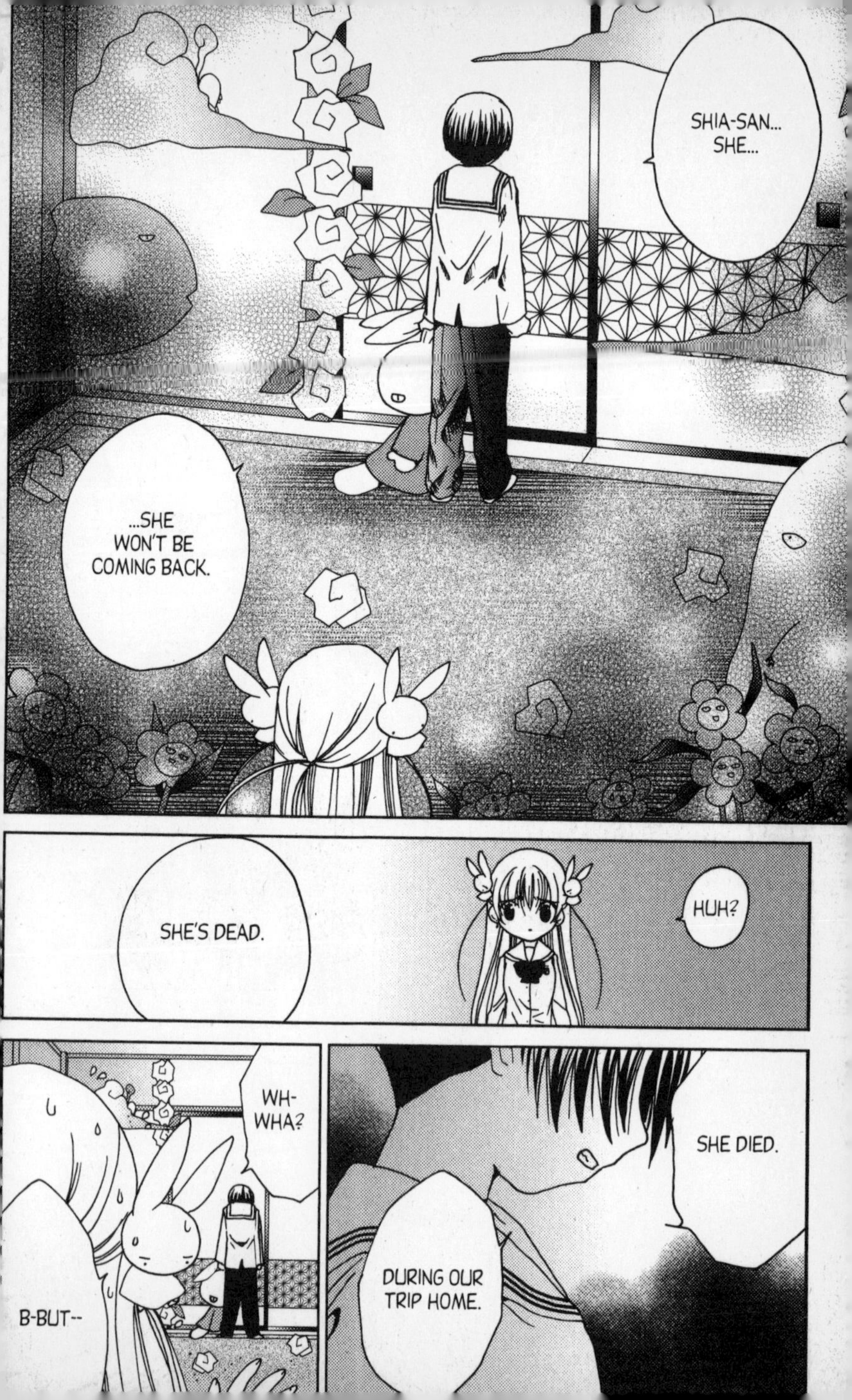
SHIA-SAN... SHE...
...SHE WON'T BE COMING BACK.
HUH?
SHE'S DEAD.
SHE DIED.
DURING OUR TRIP HOME.
WH- WHA?
B-BUT--

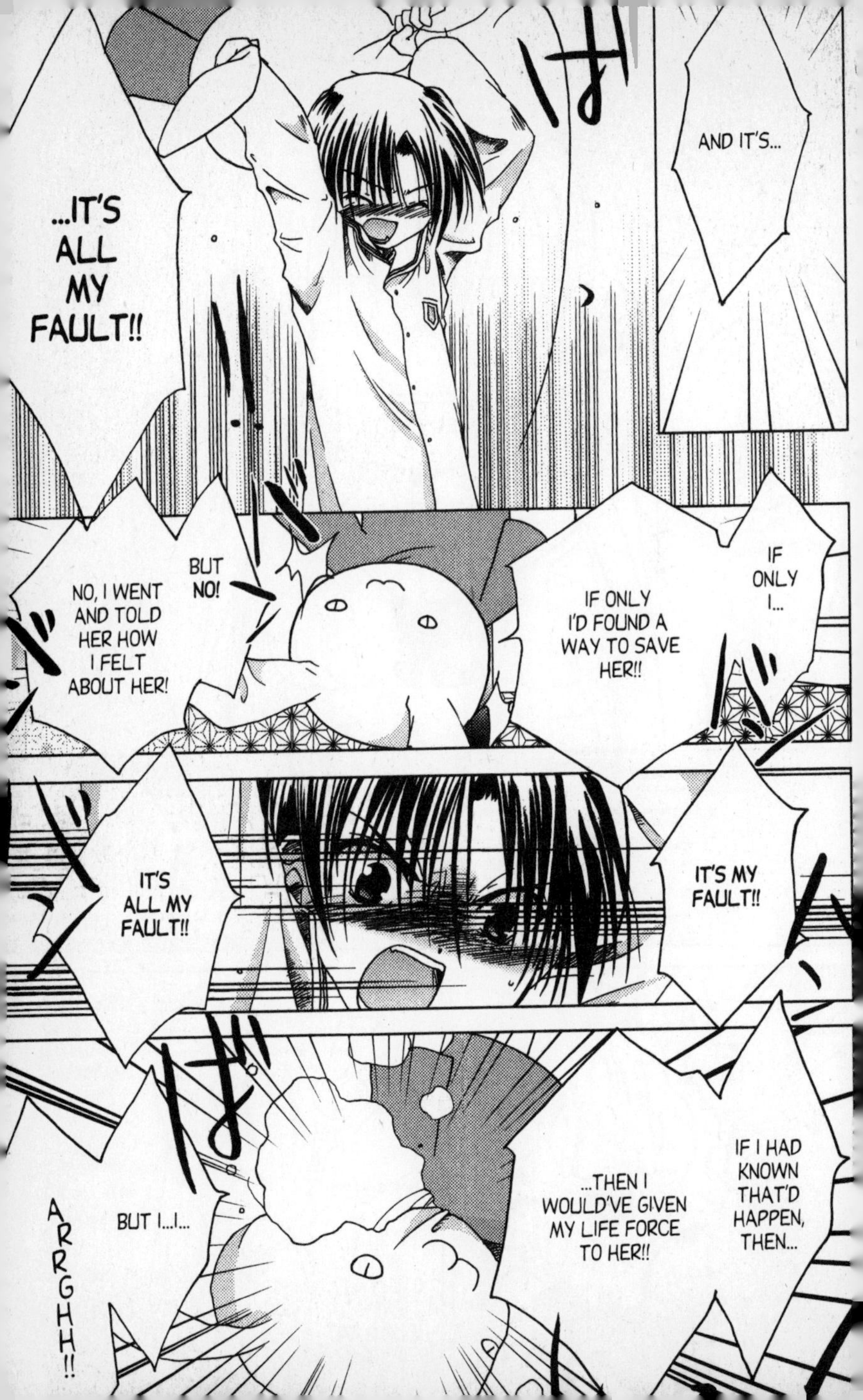
AND IT'S...
...IT'S ALL MY FAULT!!
IF ONLY I...
IF ONLY I'D FOUND A WAY TO SAVE HER!!
BUT NO!
NO, I WENT AND TOLD HER HOW I FELT ABOUT HER!
IT'S MY FAULT!!
IT'S ALL MY FAULT!!
IF I HAD KNOWN THAT'D HAPPEN, THEN...
...THEN I WOULD'VE GIVEN MY LIFE FORCE TO HER!!
BUT I...I...
ARRGHH!!

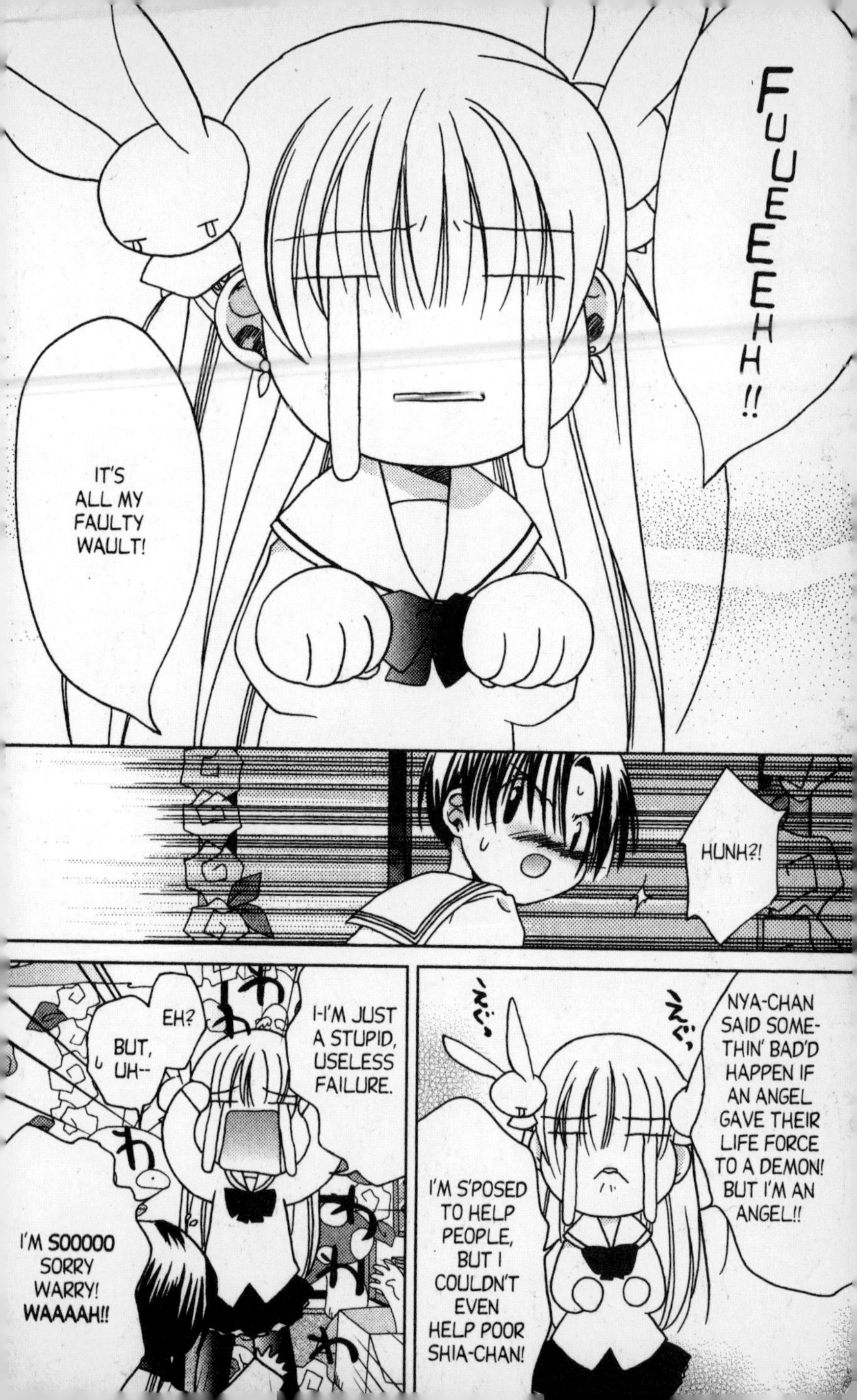
FUUEEEHH!!
IT'S ALL MY FAULTY WAULT!
HUNH?!
NYA-CHAN SAID SOME-THIN' BAD'D HAPPEN IF AN ANGEL GAVE THEIR LIFE FORCE TO A DEMON! BUT I'M AN ANGEL!!
I'M S'POSED TO HELP PEOPLE, BUT I COULDN'T EVEN HELP POOR SHIA-CHAN!
I-I'M JUST A STUPID, USELESS FAILURE.
EH?
BUT, UH--
I'M SOOOOO SORRY WARRY! WAAAAH!!

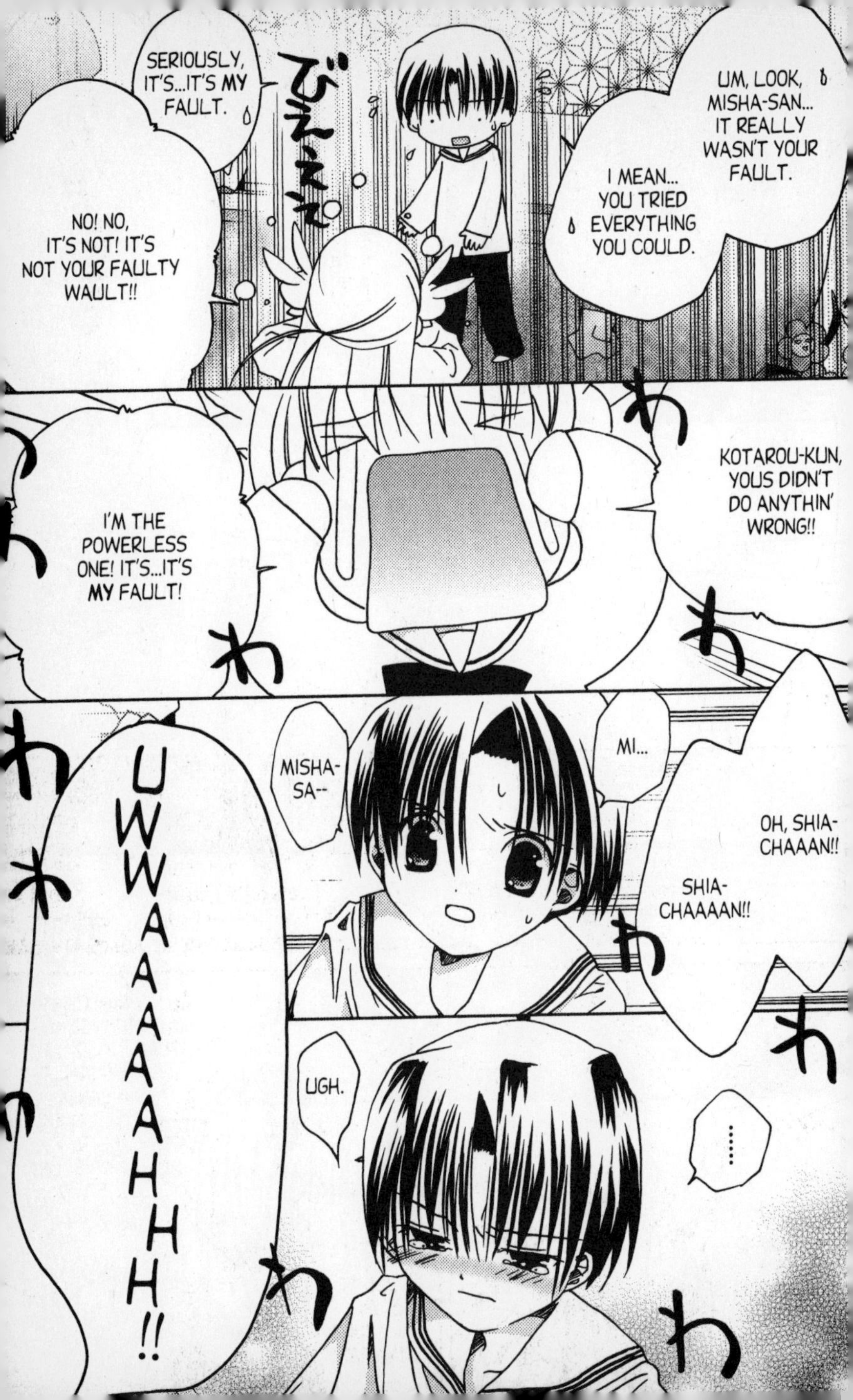
UM, LOOK, MISHA-SAN... IT REALLY WASN'T YOUR FAULT.
I MEAN... YOU TRIED EVERYTHING YOU COULD.
びえええ
SERIOUSLY, IT'S...IT'S MY FAULT.
NO! NO, IT'S NOT! IT'S NOT YOUR FAULTY WAULT!!
わ
KOTAROU-KUN, YOUS DIDN'T DO ANYTHIN' WRONG!!
わ
わ
I'M THE POWERLESS ONE! IT'S...IT'S MY FAULT!
わ
OH, SHIA-CHAAAN!!
SHIA-CHAAAAN!!
わ
MI...
MISHA-SA--
わ
わ
UWWAAAAAHHH!!
わ
......
UGH.
わ
わ

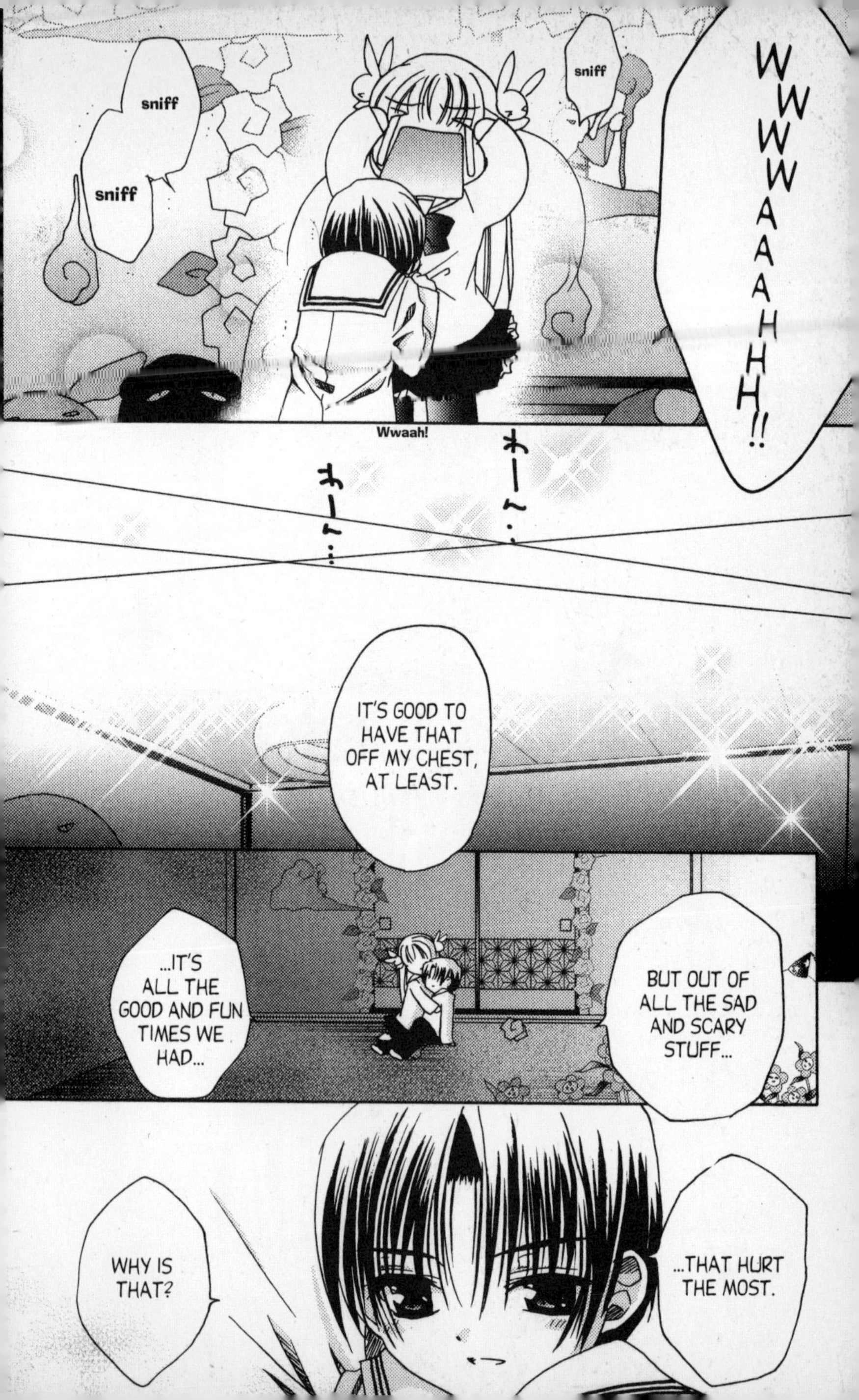
WWWWAAAHHH!!
sniff
sniff
sniff
Wwaah!
わーん‥
わーん‥
IT'S GOOD TO HAVE THAT OFF MY CHEST, AT LEAST.
BUT OUT OF ALL THE SAD AND SCARY STUFF...
...IT'S ALL THE GOOD AND FUN TIMES WE HAD...
...THAT HURT THE MOST.
WHY IS THAT?

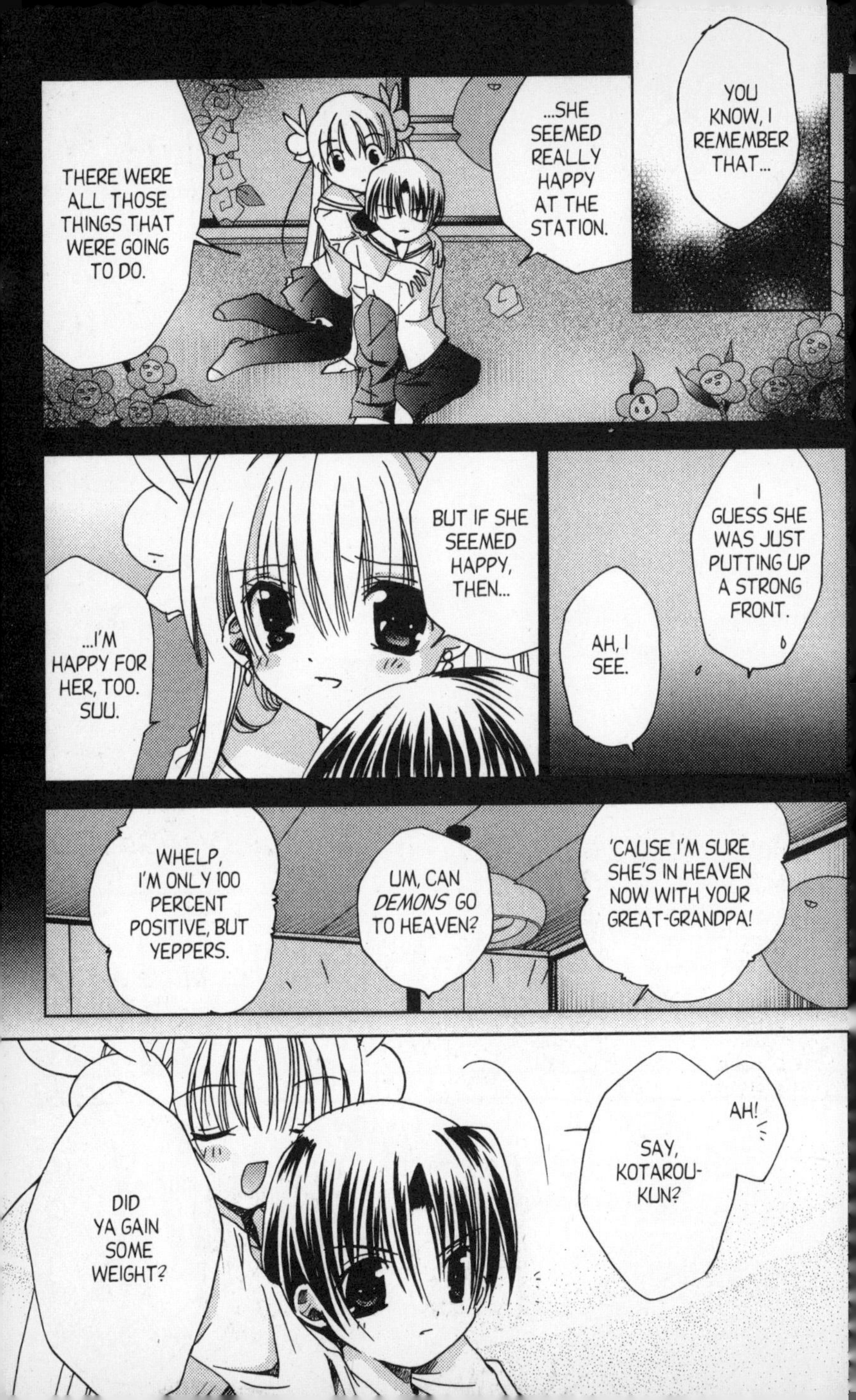
YOU KNOW, I REMEMBER THAT...
...SHE SEEMED REALLY HAPPY AT THE STATION.
THERE WERE ALL THOSE THINGS THAT WERE GOING TO DO.
I GUESS SHE WAS JUST PUTTING UP A STRONG FRONT.
AH, I SEE.
BUT IF SHE SEEMED HAPPY, THEN...
...I'M HAPPY FOR HER, TOO. SUU.
'CAUSE I'M SURE SHE'S IN HEAVEN NOW WITH YOUR GREAT-GRANDPA!
UM, CAN *DEMONS* GO TO HEAVEN?
WHELP, I'M ONLY 100 PERCENT POSITIVE, BUT YEPPERS.
AH!
SAY, KOTAROU-KUN?
DID YA GAIN SOME WEIGHT?

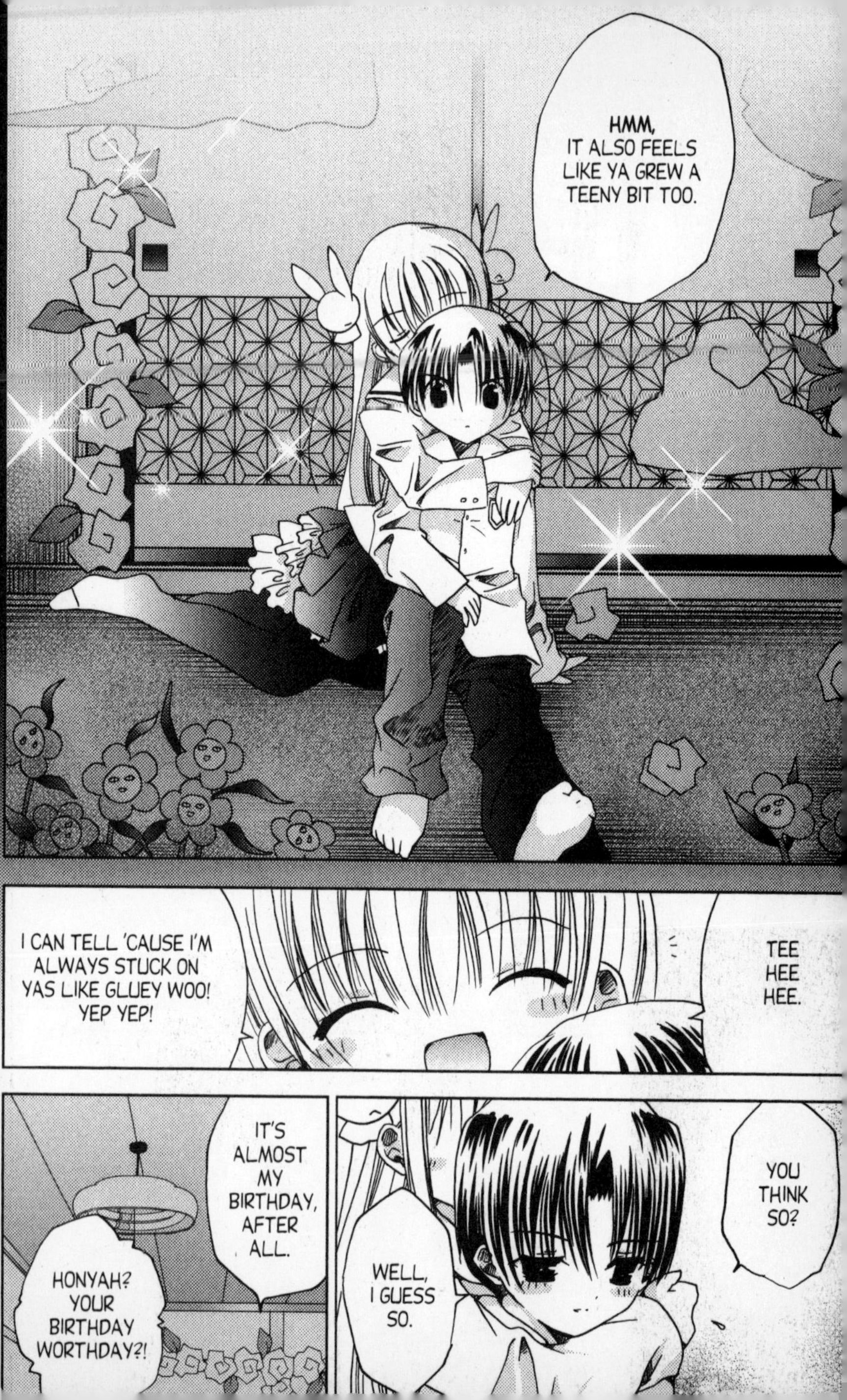
HMM, IT ALSO FEELS LIKE YA GREW A TEENY BIT TOO.
TEE HEE HEE.
I CAN TELL 'CAUSE I'M ALWAYS STUCK ON YAS LIKE GLUEY WOO! YEP YEP!
YOU THINK SO?
WELL, I GUESS SO.
IT'S ALMOST MY BIRTHDAY, AFTER ALL.
HONYAH? YOUR BIRTHDAY WORTHDAY?!

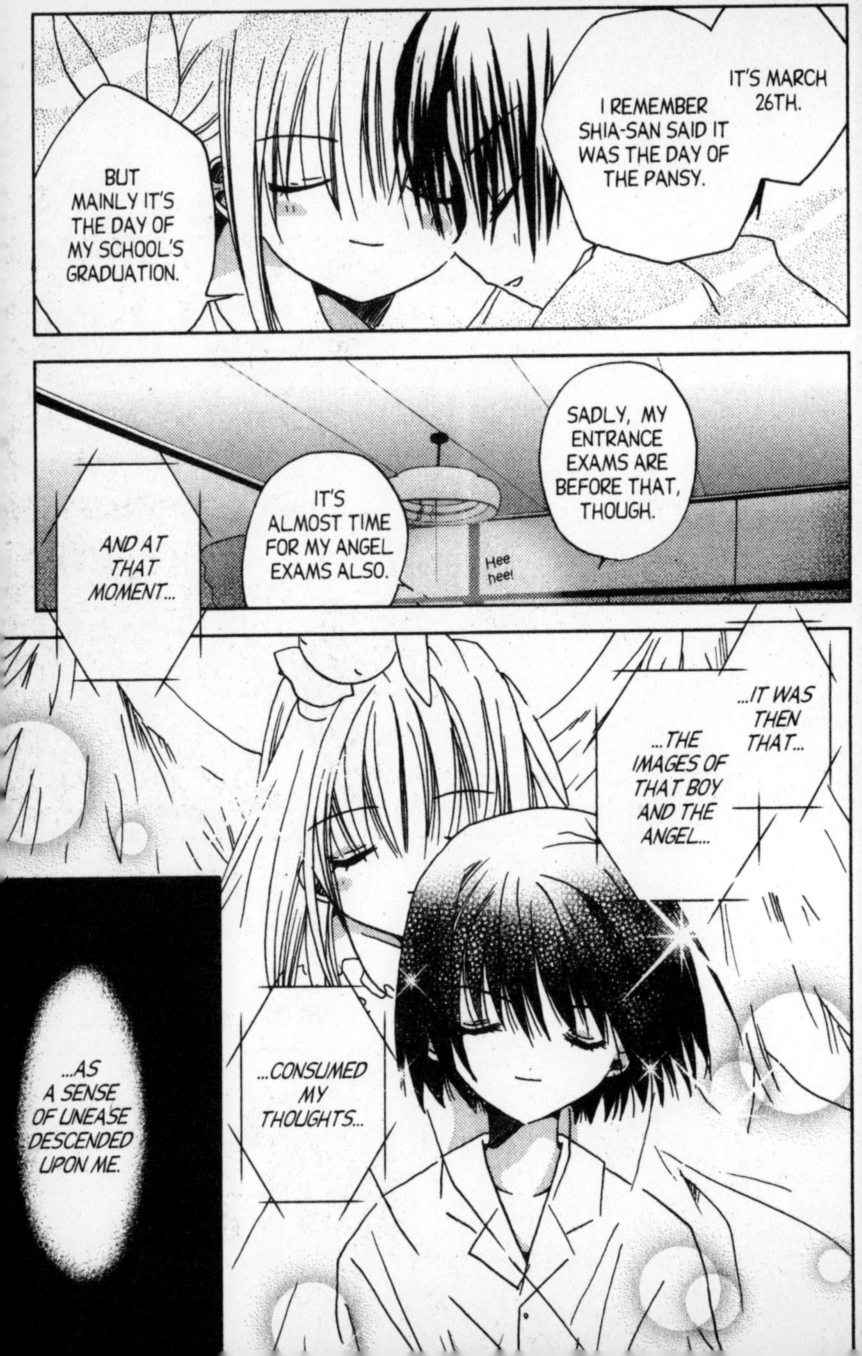
IT'S MARCH 26TH.
I REMEMBER SHIA-SAN SAID IT WAS THE DAY OF THE PANSY.
BUT MAINLY IT'S THE DAY OF MY SCHOOL'S GRADUATION.
SADLY, MY ENTRANCE EXAMS ARE BEFORE THAT, THOUGH.
Hee hee!
IT'S ALMOST TIME FOR MY ANGEL EXAMS ALSO.
AND AT THAT MOMENT...
...IT WAS THEN THAT...
...THE IMAGES OF THAT BOY AND THE ANGEL...
...CONSUMED MY THOUGHTS...
...AS A SENSE OF UNEASE DESCENDED UPON ME.

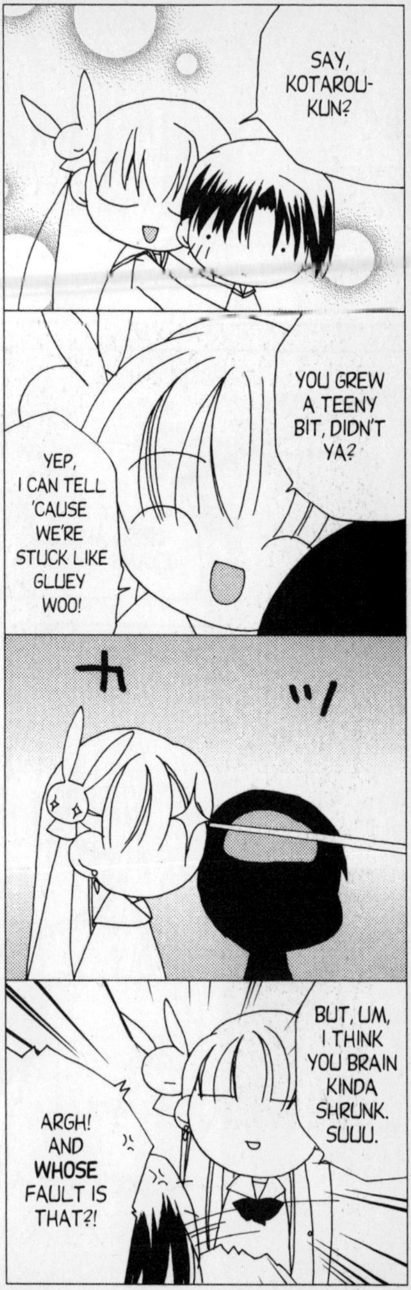

SAY, KOTAROU-KUN?
YOU GREW A TEENY BIT, DIDN'T YA?
YEP, I CAN TELL 'CAUSE WE'RE STUCK LIKE GLUEY WOO!
カッ
BUT, UM, I THINK YOU BRAIN KINDA SHRUNK. SUUU.
ARGH! AND **WHOSE** FAULT IS THAT?!

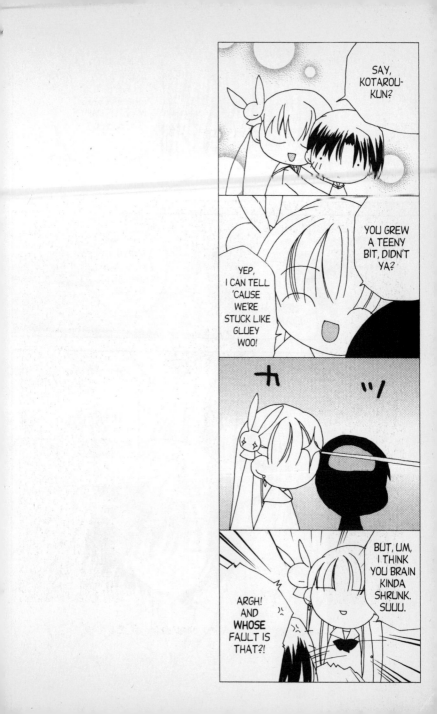

Lesson 40

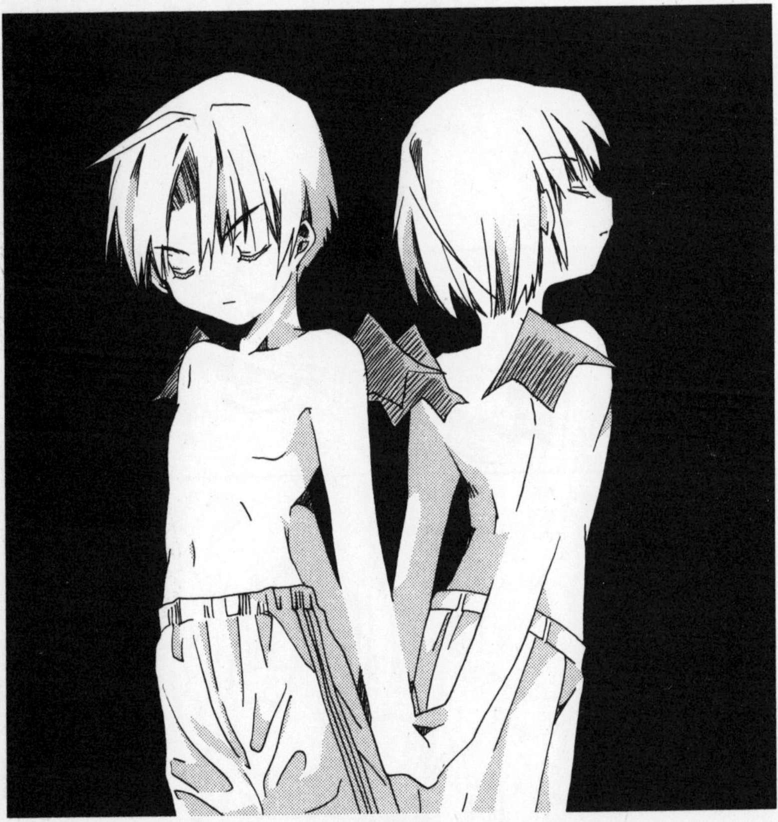

How to Find Yourself: Part 1

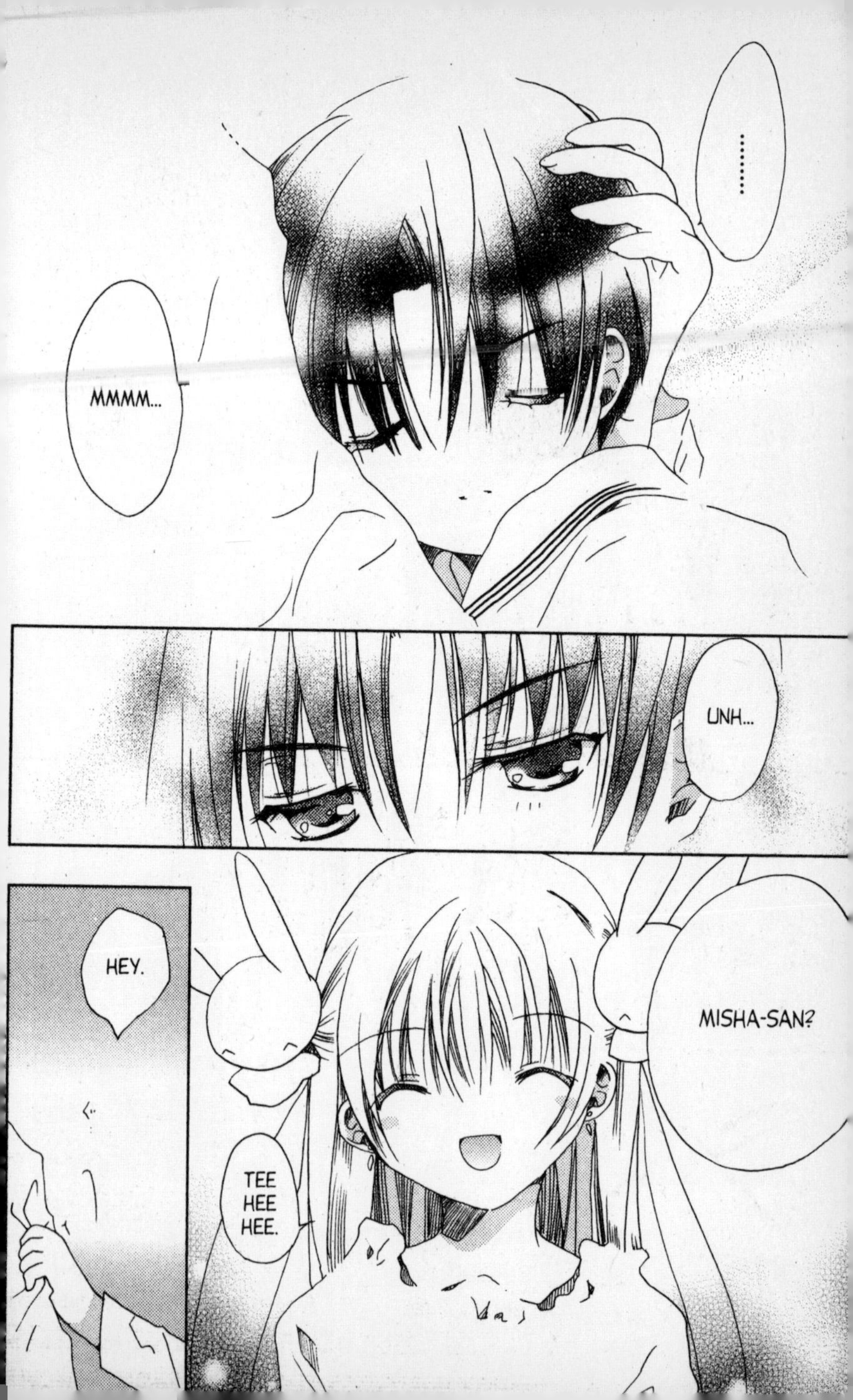
......
MMMM...
UNH...
MISHA-SAN?
HEY.
TEE HEE HEE.

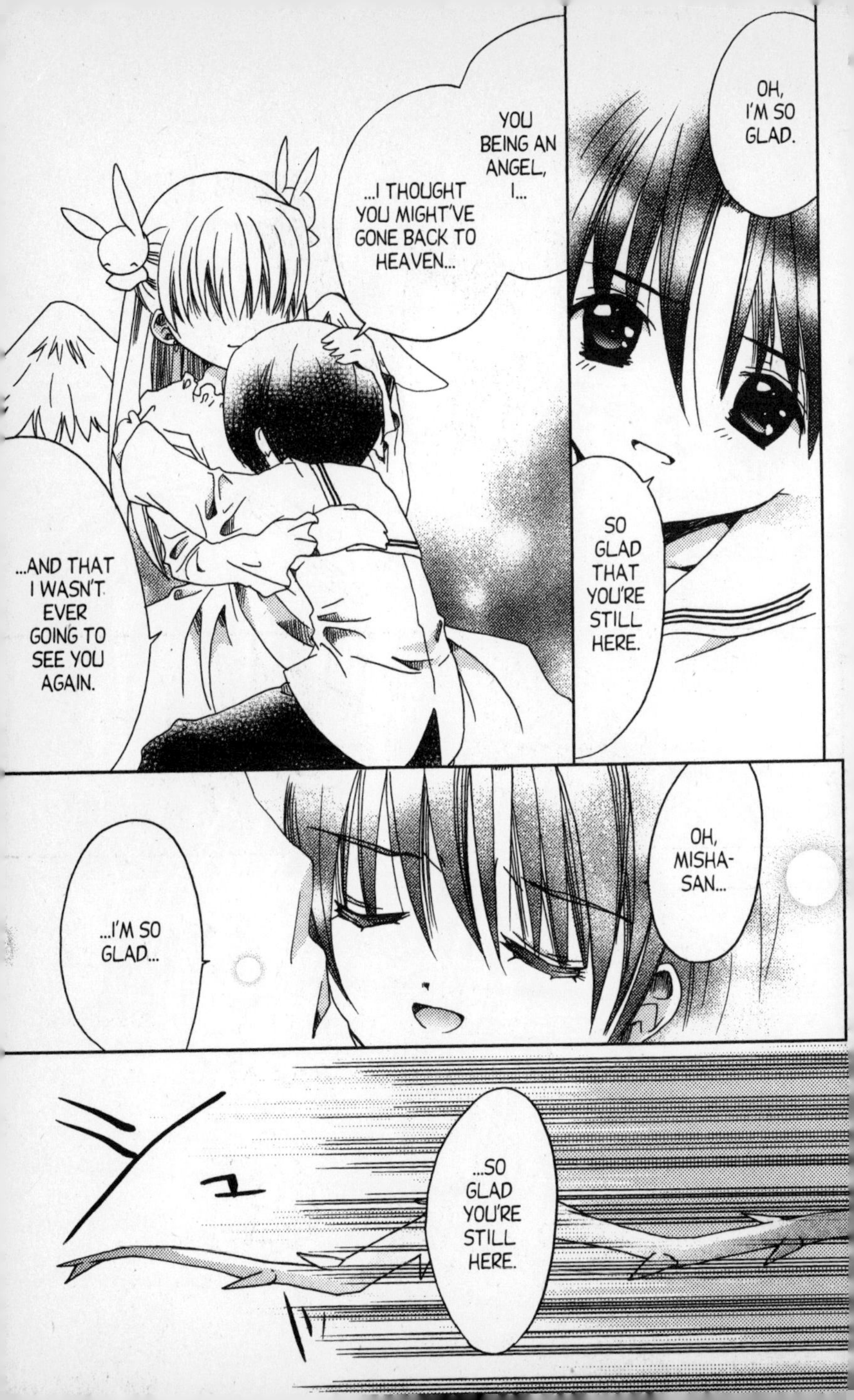
OH, I'M SO GLAD.
SO GLAD THAT YOU'RE STILL HERE.
YOU BEING AN ANGEL, I...
...I THOUGHT YOU MIGHT'VE GONE BACK TO HEAVEN...
...AND THAT I WASN'T EVER GOING TO SEE YOU AGAIN.
OH, MISHA-SAN...
...I'M SO GLAD...
...SO GLAD YOU'RE STILL HERE.

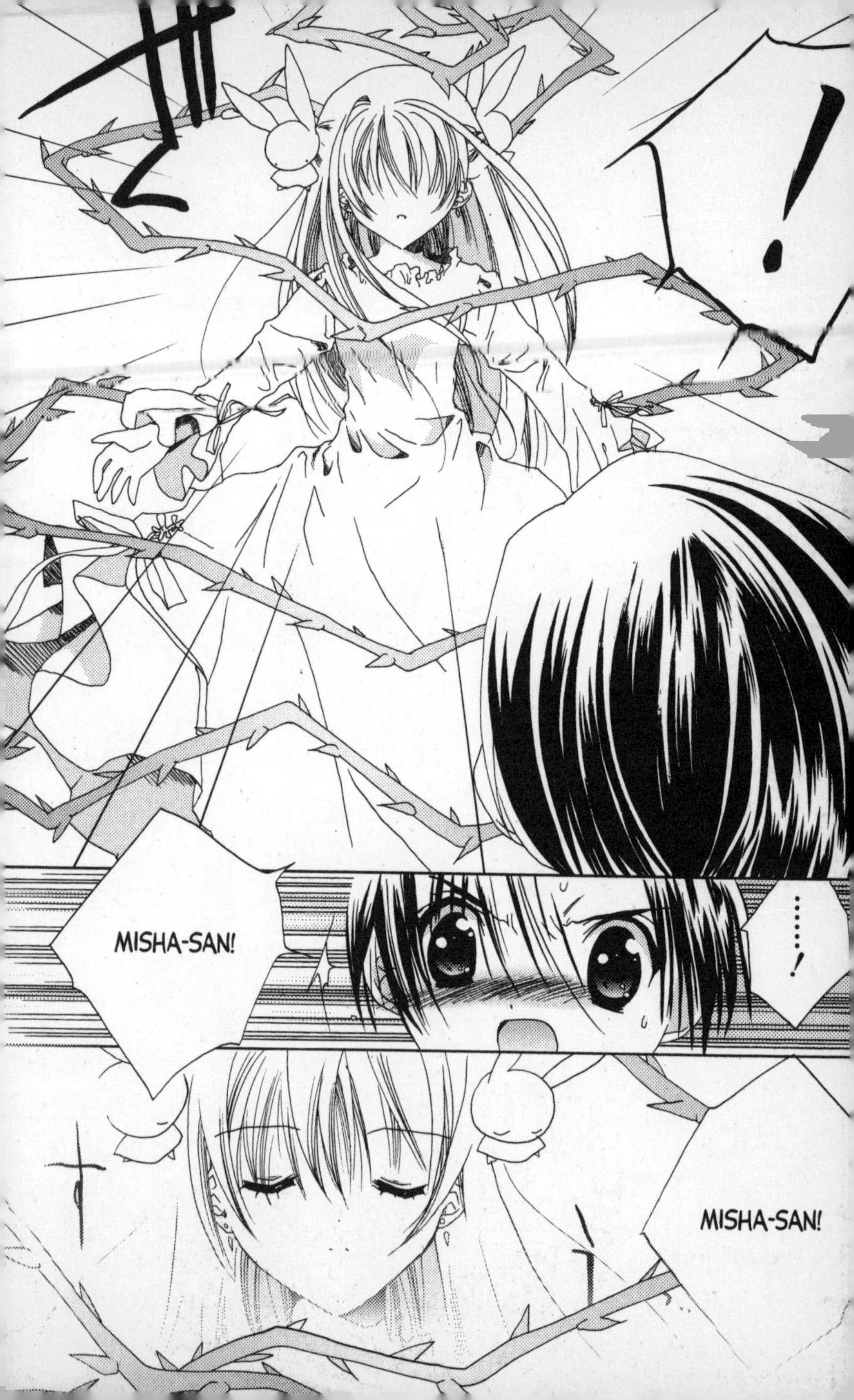
!
......!
MISHA-SAN!
MISHA-SAN!

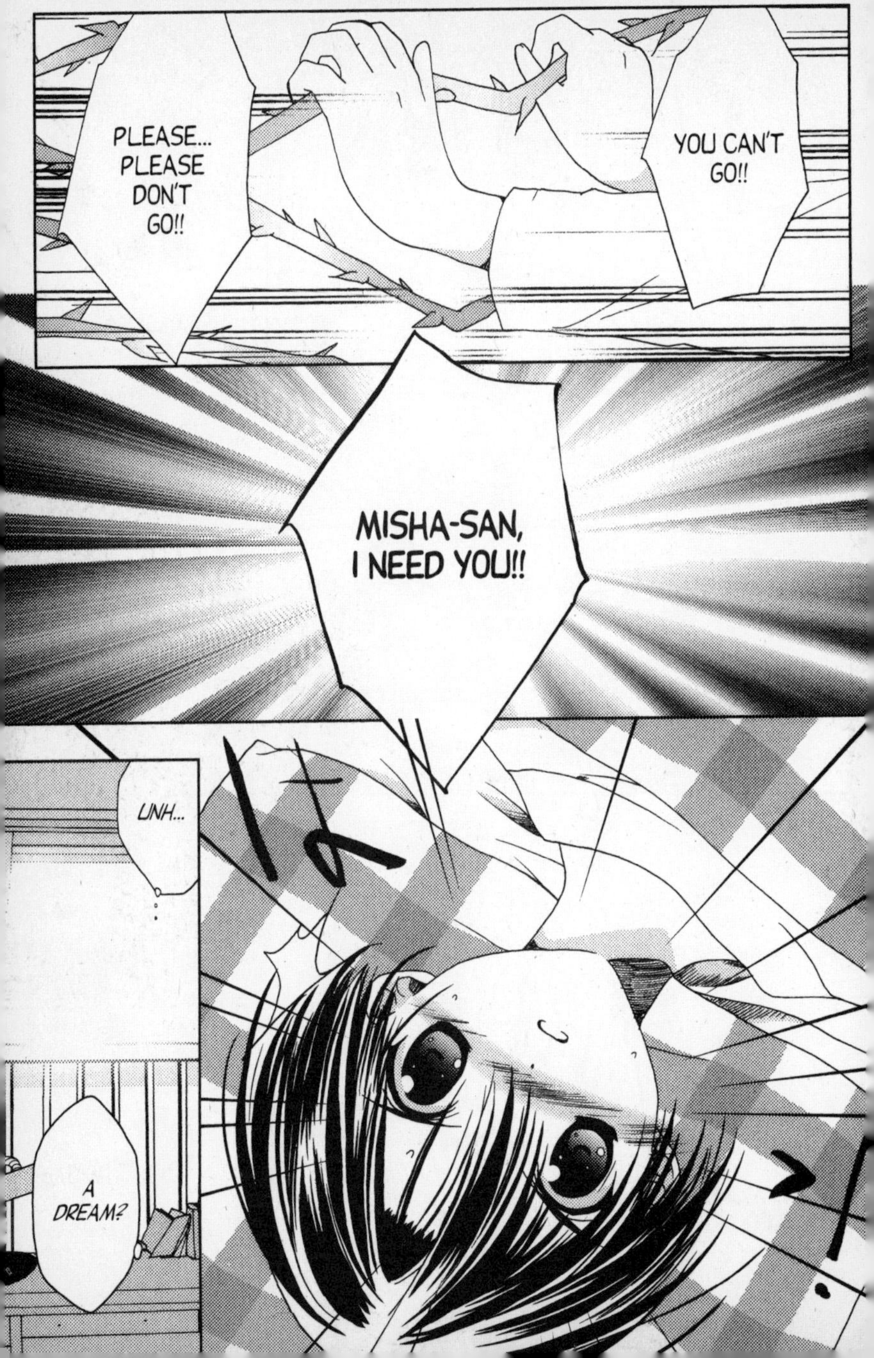
YOU CAN'T GO!!
PLEASE... PLEASE DON'T GO!!
MISHA-SAN, I NEED YOU!!
UNH...
A DREAM?

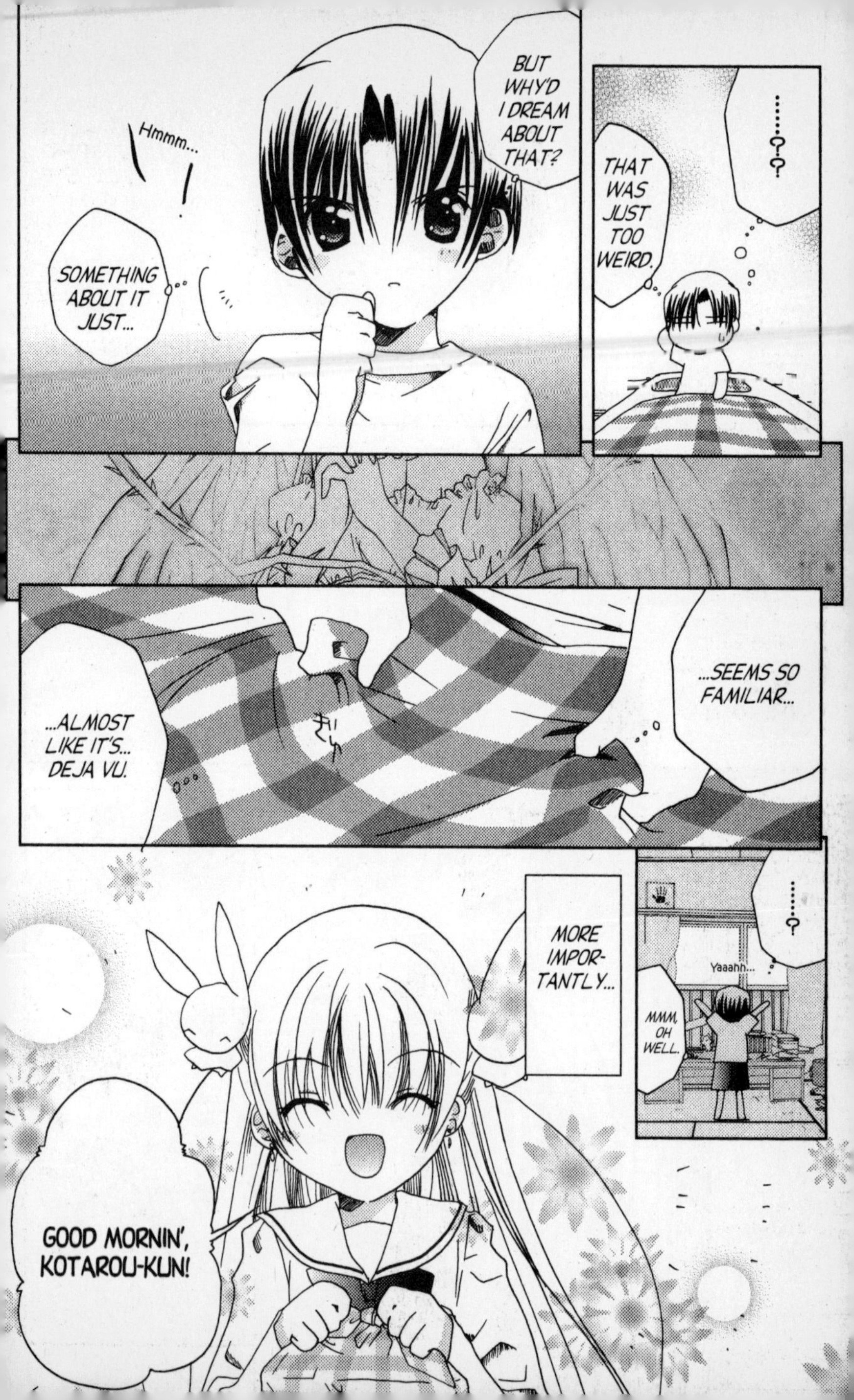
......??
THAT WAS JUST TOO WEIRD.
BUT WHY'D I DREAM ABOUT THAT?
Hmmm...
SOMETHING ABOUT IT JUST...
...SEEMS SO FAMILIAR...
...ALMOST LIKE IT'S... DEJA VU.
......?
Yaaahh...
MMM, OH WELL.
MORE IMPORTANTLY...
GOOD MORNIN', KOTAROU-KUN!

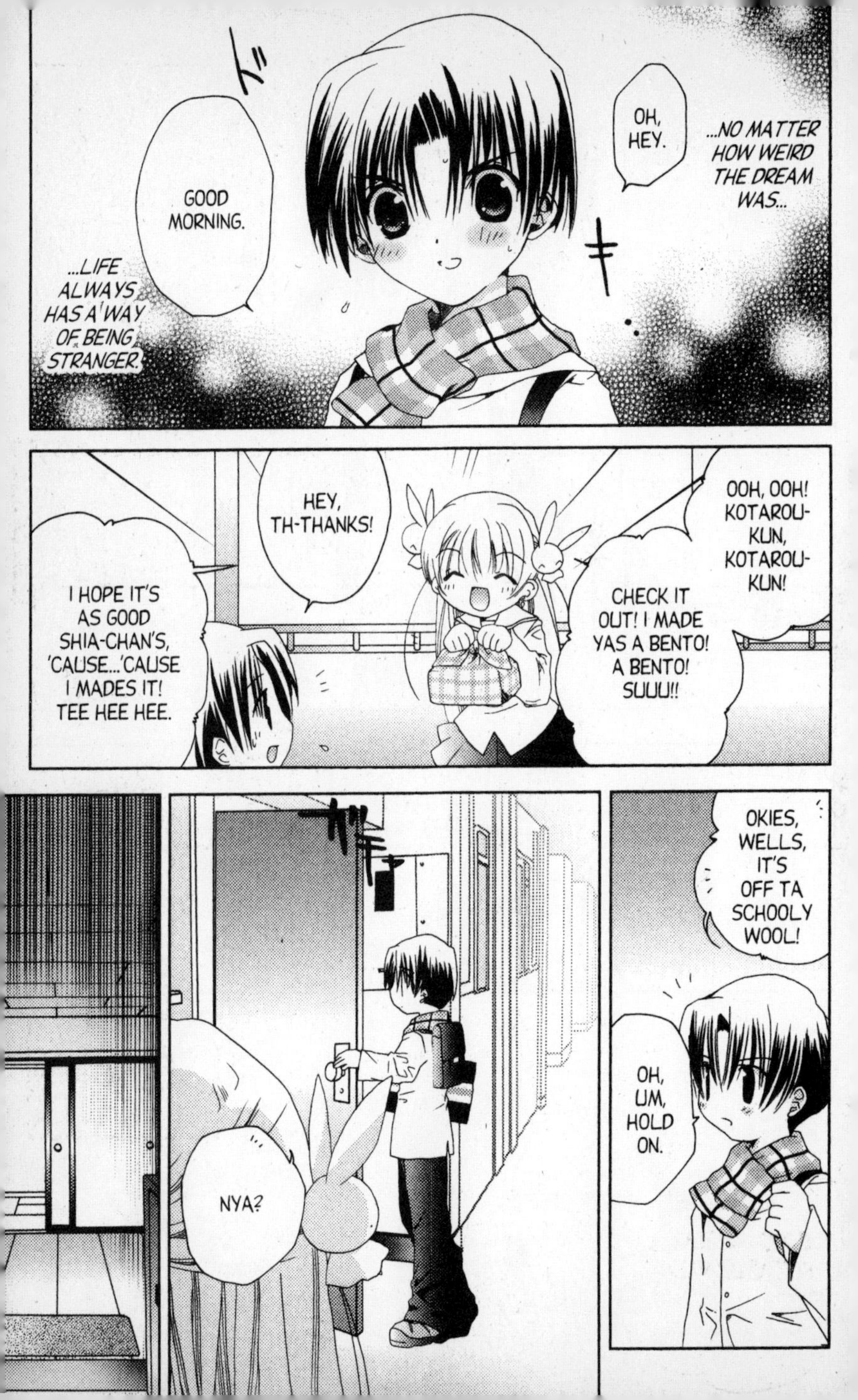
...NO MATTER HOW WEIRD THE DREAM WAS...
OH, HEY.
GOOD MORNING.
...LIFE ALWAYS HAS A WAY OF BEING STRANGER.
OOH, OOH! KOTAROU-KUN, KOTAROU-KUN!
CHECK IT OUT! I MADE YAS A BENTO! A BENTO! SUUU!!
HEY, TH-THANKS!
I HOPE IT'S AS GOOD SHIA-CHAN'S, 'CAUSE...'CAUSE I MADES IT! TEE HEE HEE.
OKIES, WELLS, IT'S OFF TA SCHOOLY WOOL!
OH, UM, HOLD ON.
NYA?

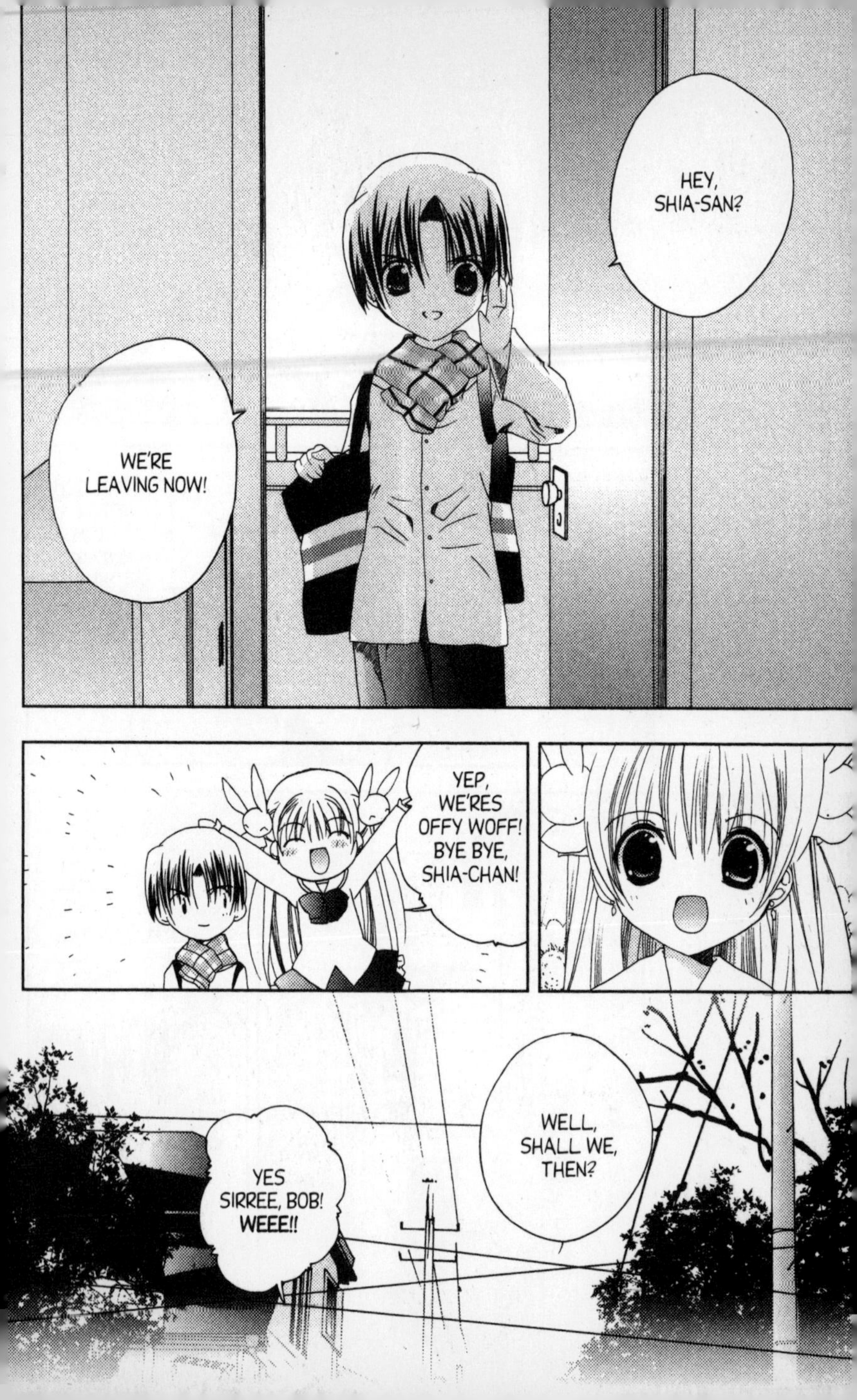
HEY, SHIA-SAN?
WE'RE LEAVING NOW!
YEP, WE'RES OFFY WOFF! BYE BYE, SHIA-CHAN!
WELL, SHALL WE, THEN?
YES SIRREE, BOB! WEEE!!

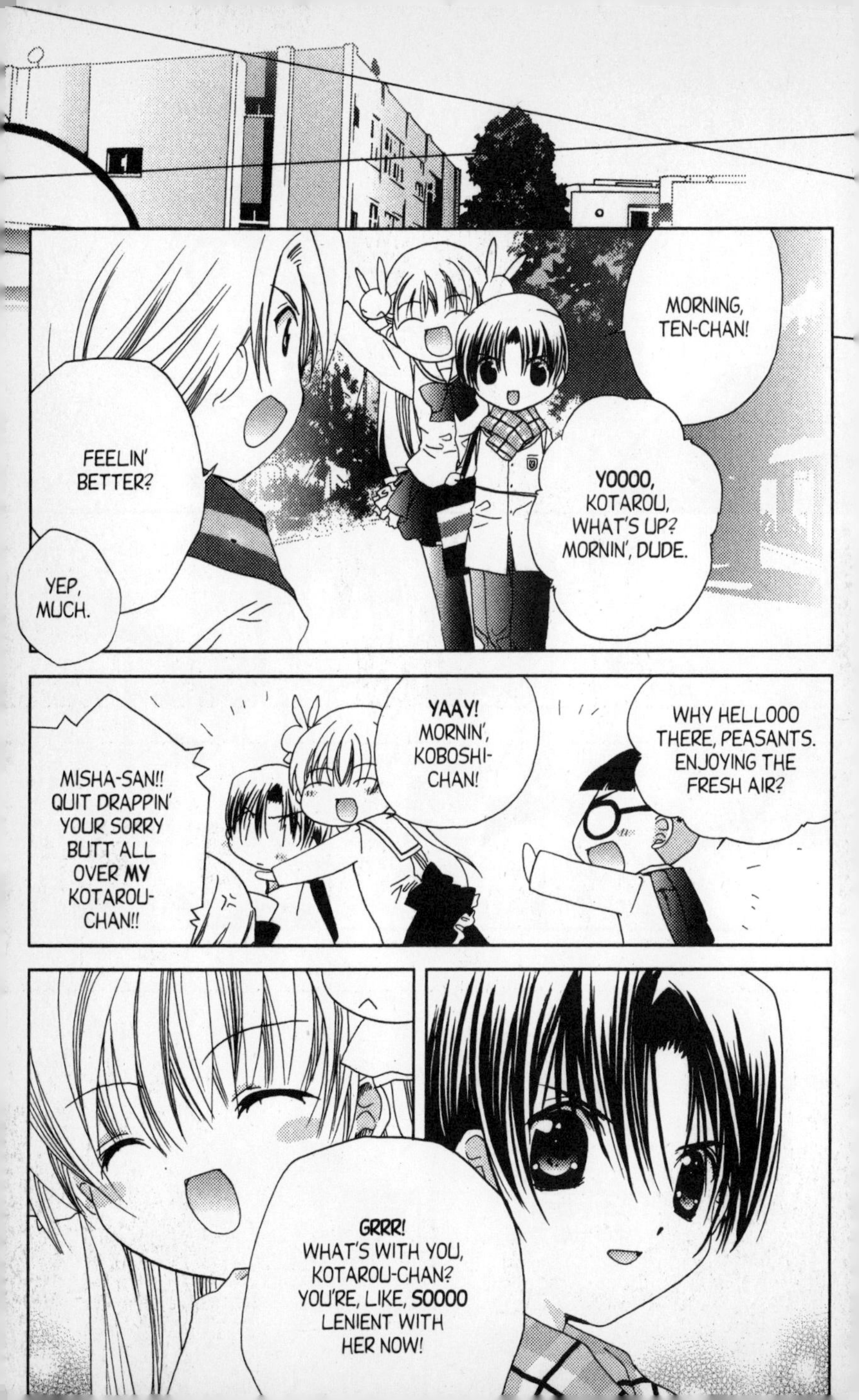
MORNING, TEN-CHAN!
YOOOO, KOTAROU, WHAT'S UP? MORNIN', DUDE.
FEELIN' BETTER?
YEP, MUCH.
WHY HELLOOO THERE, PEASANTS. ENJOYING THE FRESH AIR?
YAAY! MORNIN', KOBOSHI-CHAN!
MISHA-SAN!! QUIT DRAPPIN' YOUR SORRY BUTT ALL OVER MY KOTAROU-CHAN!!
GRRR! WHAT'S WITH YOU, KOTAROU-CHAN? YOU'RE, LIKE, SOOOO LENIENT WITH HER NOW!

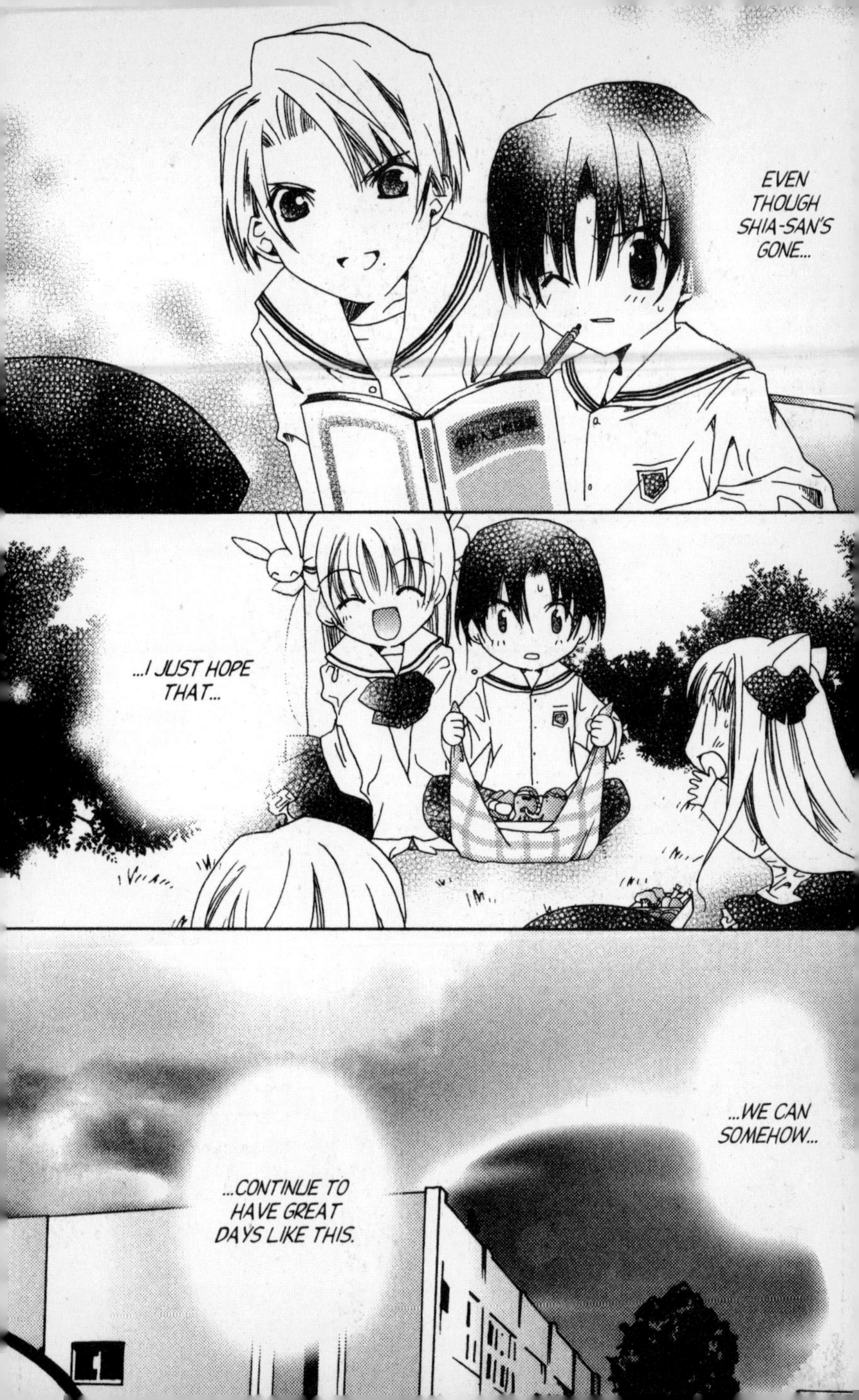
EVEN THOUGH SHIA-SAN'S GONE...
...I JUST HOPE THAT...
...WE CAN SOMEHOW...
...CONTINUE TO HAVE GREAT DAYS LIKE THIS.

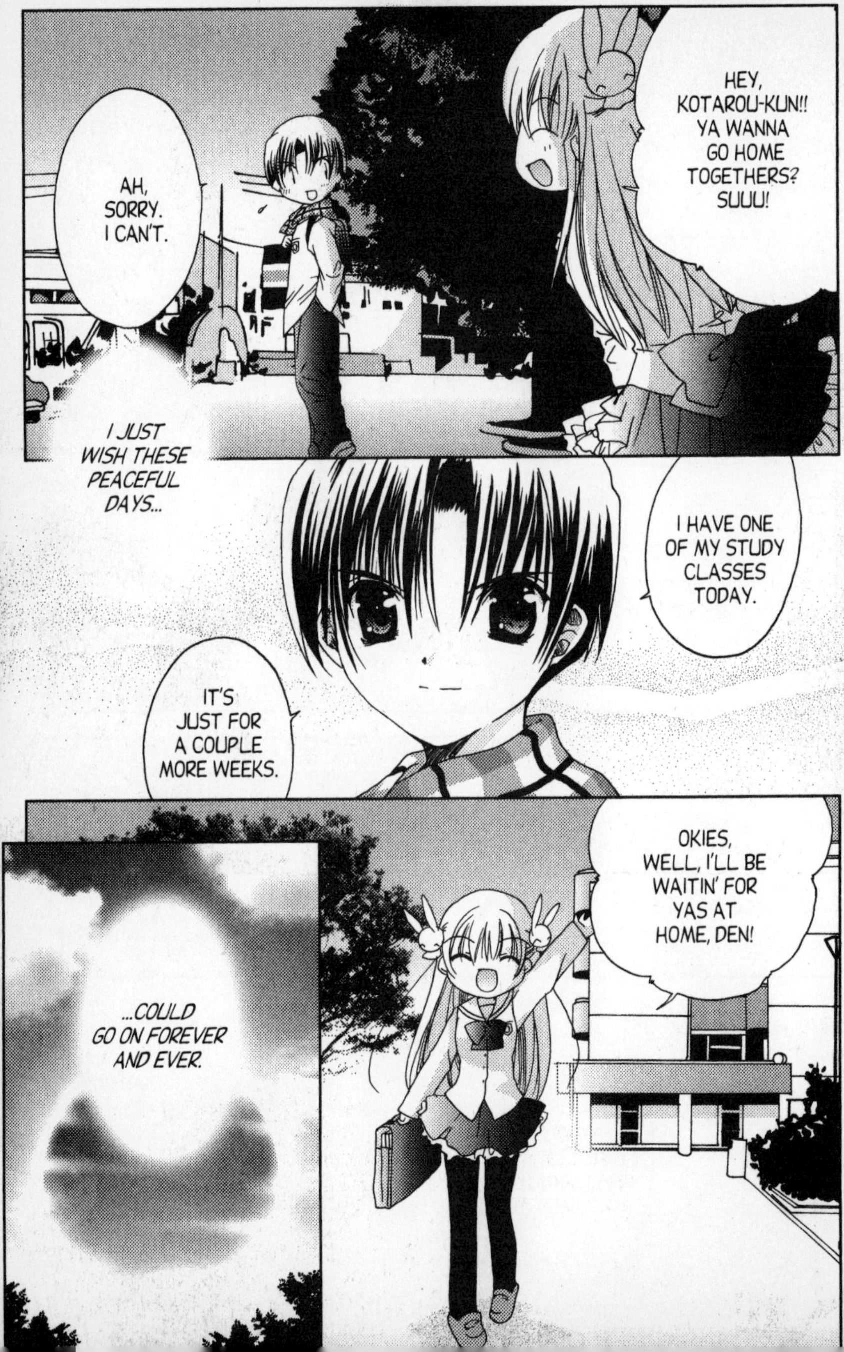
HEY, KOTAROU-KUN!! YA WANNA GO HOME TOGETHERS? SUUU!
AH, SORRY. I CAN'T.
I JUST WISH THESE PEACEFUL DAYS...
I HAVE ONE OF MY STUDY CLASSES TODAY.
IT'S JUST FOR A COUPLE MORE WEEKS.
OKIES, WELL, I'LL BE WAITIN' FOR YAS AT HOME, DEN!
...COULD GO ON FOREVER AND EVER.

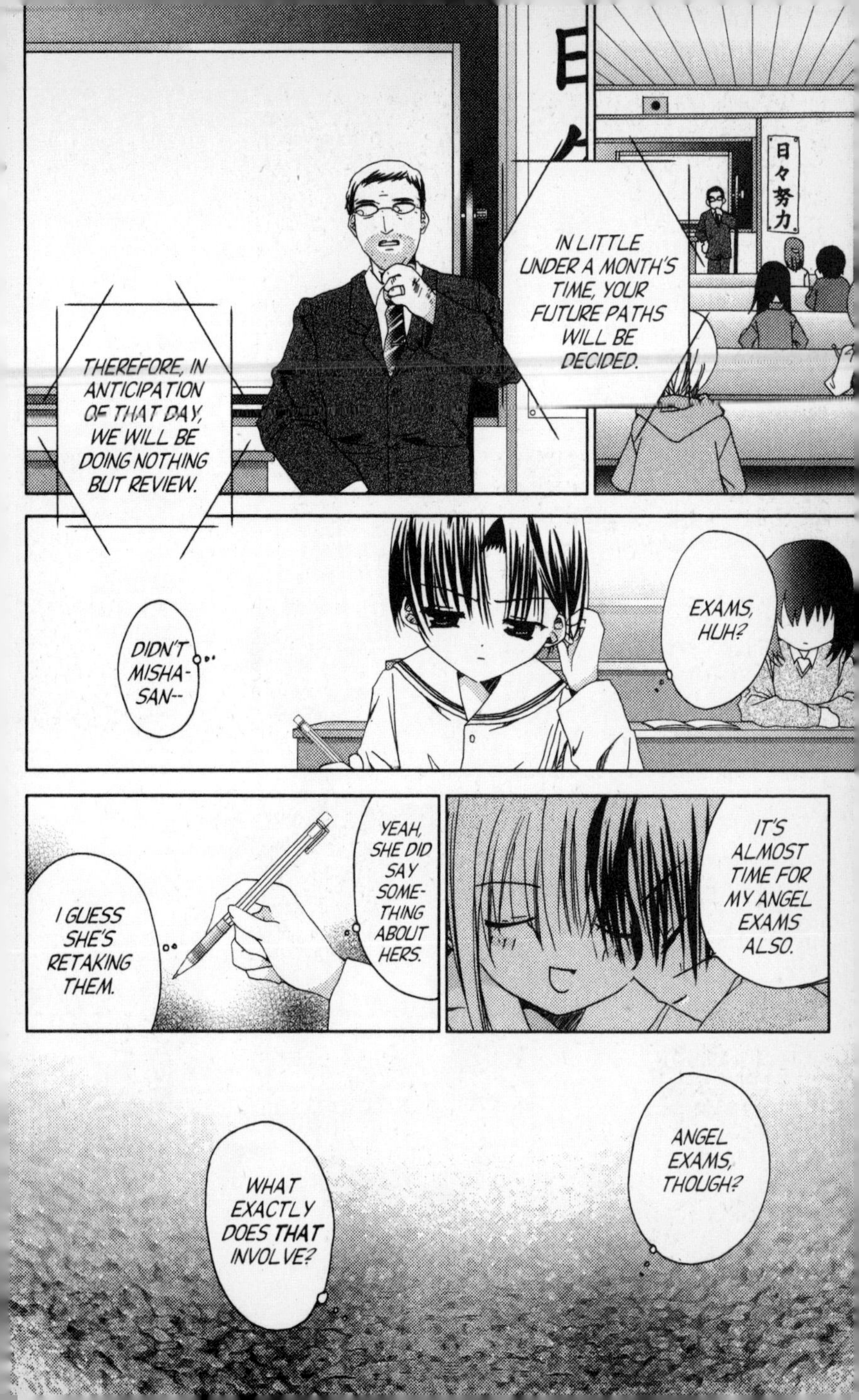
日々努力
IN LITTLE UNDER A MONTH'S TIME, YOUR FUTURE PATHS WILL BE DECIDED.
THEREFORE, IN ANTICIPATION OF THAT DAY, WE WILL BE DOING NOTHING BUT REVIEW.
EXAMS, HUH?
DIDN'T MISHA-SAN--
IT'S ALMOST TIME FOR MY ANGEL EXAMS ALSO.
YEAH, SHE DID SAY SOMETHING ABOUT HERS.
I GUESS SHE'S RETAKING THEM.
ANGEL EXAMS, THOUGH?
WHAT EXACTLY DOES THAT INVOLVE?

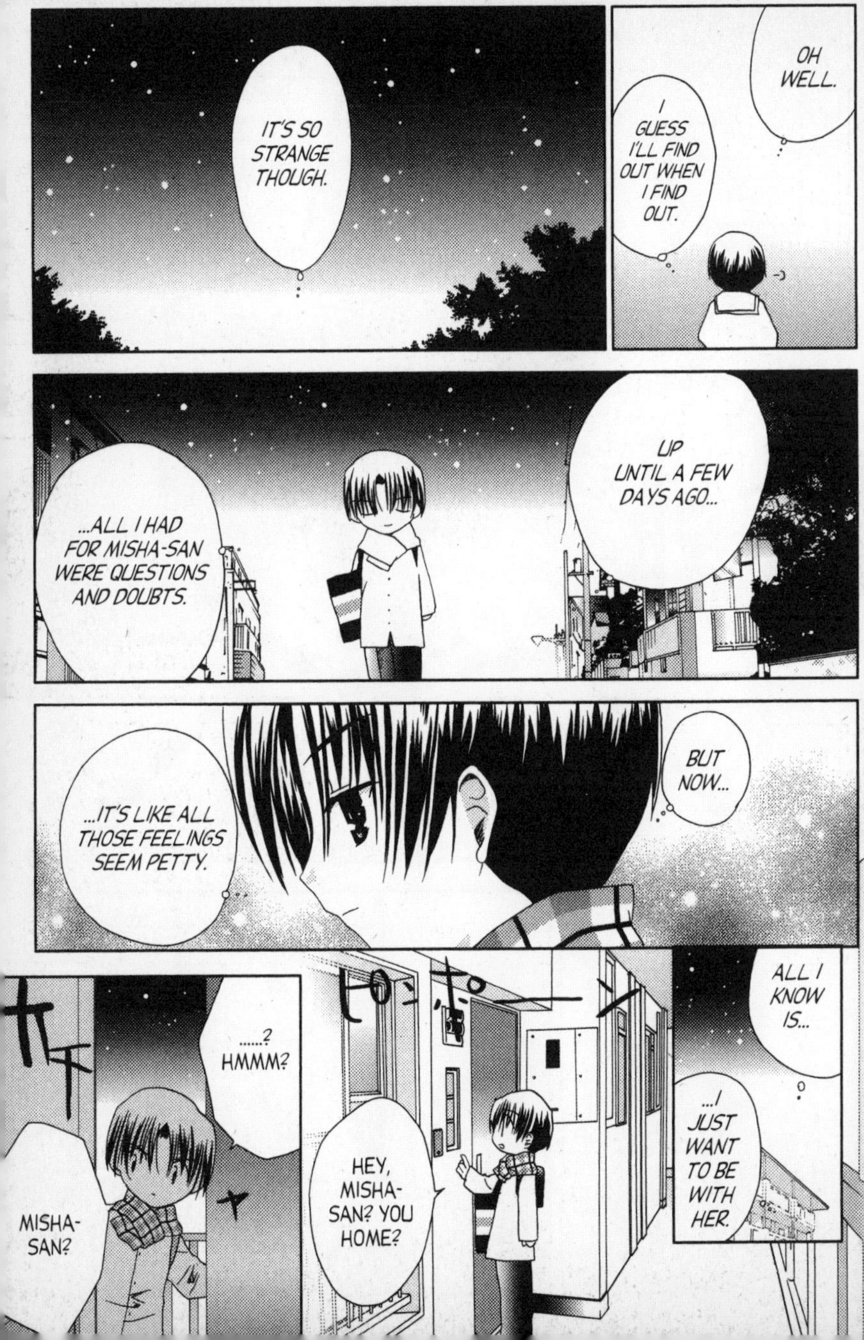
OH WELL.
I GUESS I'LL FIND OUT WHEN I FIND OUT.
IT'S SO STRANGE THOUGH.
UP UNTIL A FEW DAYS AGO...
...ALL I HAD FOR MISHA-SAN WERE QUESTIONS AND DOUBTS.
BUT NOW...
...IT'S LIKE ALL THOSE FEELINGS SEEM PETTY.
ALL I KNOW IS...
...I JUST WANT TO BE WITH HER.
ピンポーン
HEY, MISHA-SAN? YOU HOME?
......? HMMM?
MISHA-SAN?

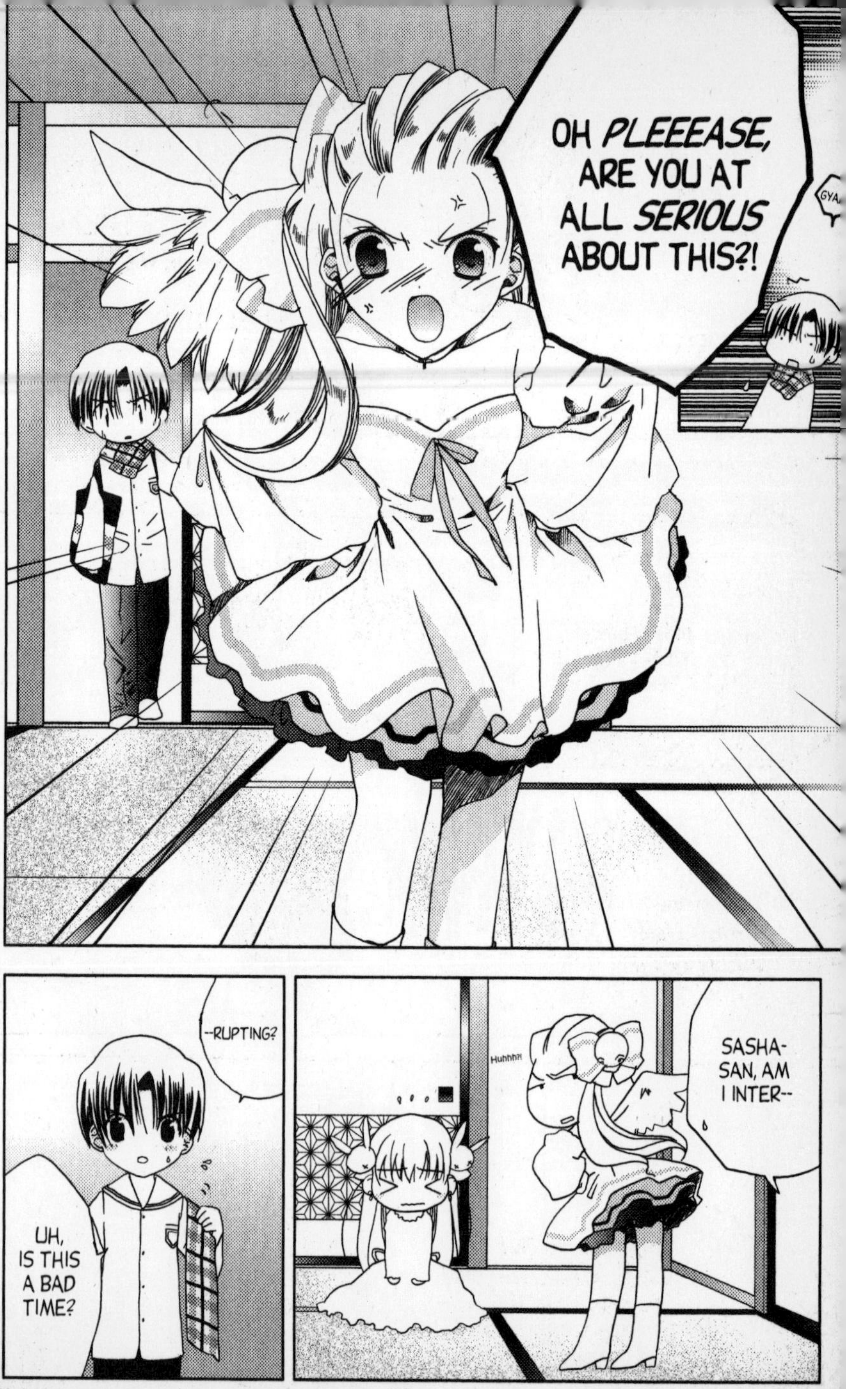
GYA
OH *PLEEEASE,* ARE YOU AT ALL *SERIOUS* ABOUT THIS?!
SASHA-SAN, AM I INTER--
Huhhh?!
--RUPTING?
UH, IS THIS A BAD TIME?

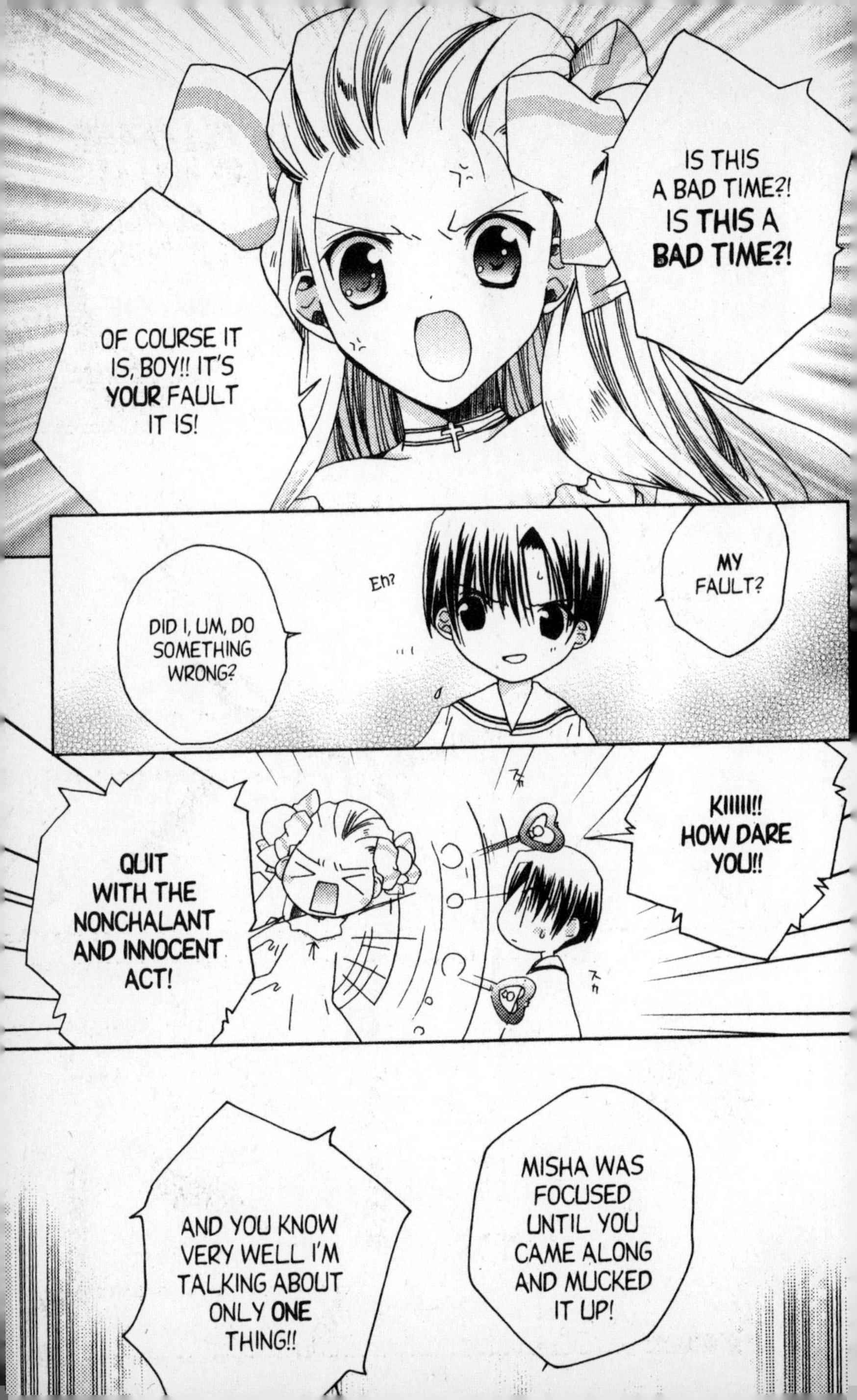

IS THIS A BAD TIME?! IS THIS A BAD TIME?!
OF COURSE IT IS, BOY!! IT'S YOUR FAULT IT IS!
MY FAULT?
Eh?
DID I, UM, DO SOMETHING WRONG?
KIIIII!! HOW DARE YOU!!
QUIT WITH THE NONCHALANT AND INNOCENT ACT!
MISHA WAS FOCUSED UNTIL YOU CAME ALONG AND MUCKED IT UP!
AND YOU KNOW VERY WELL I'M TALKING ABOUT ONLY ONE THING!!

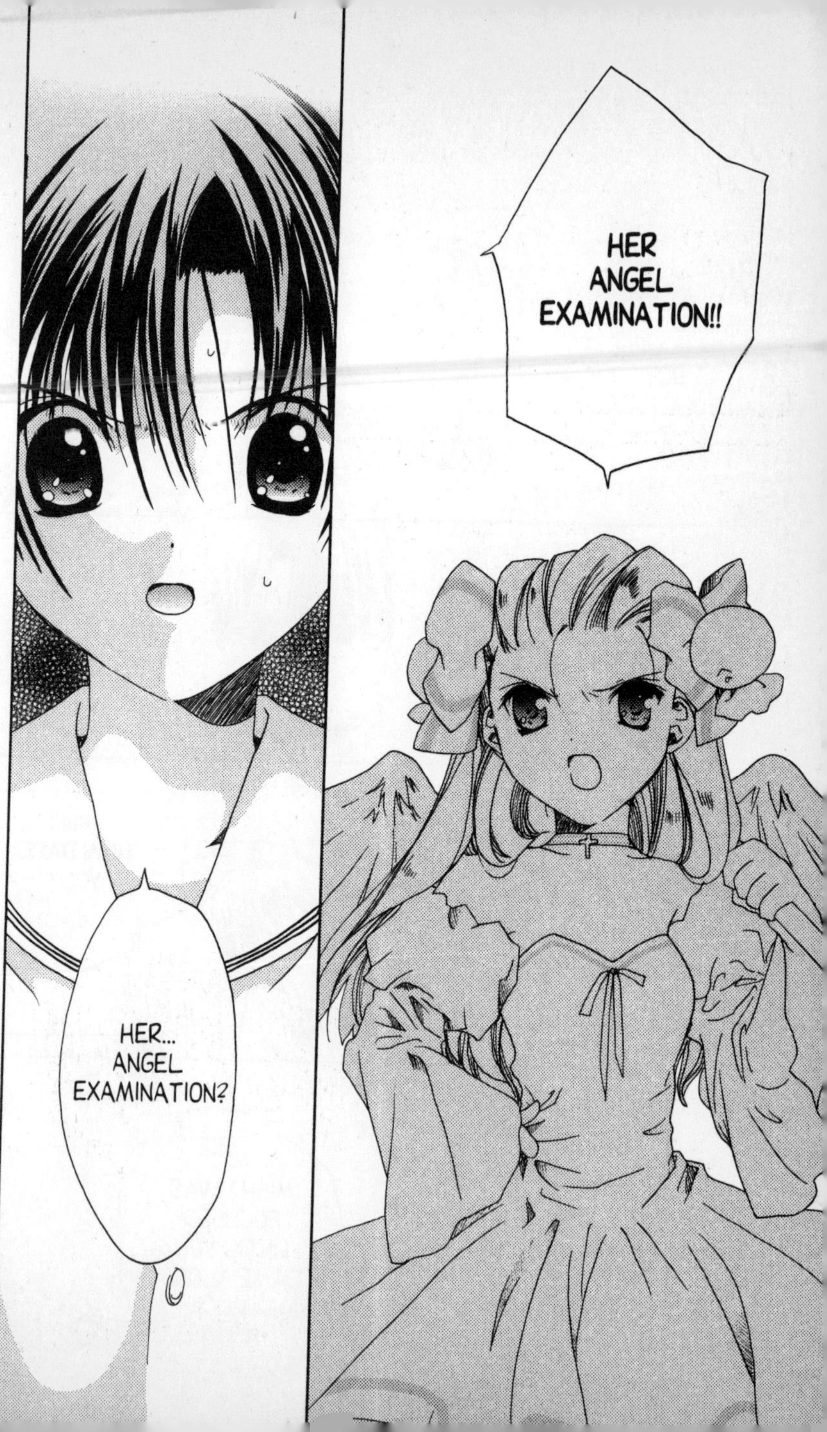
HER ANGEL EXAMINATION!!
HER... ANGEL EXAMINATION?

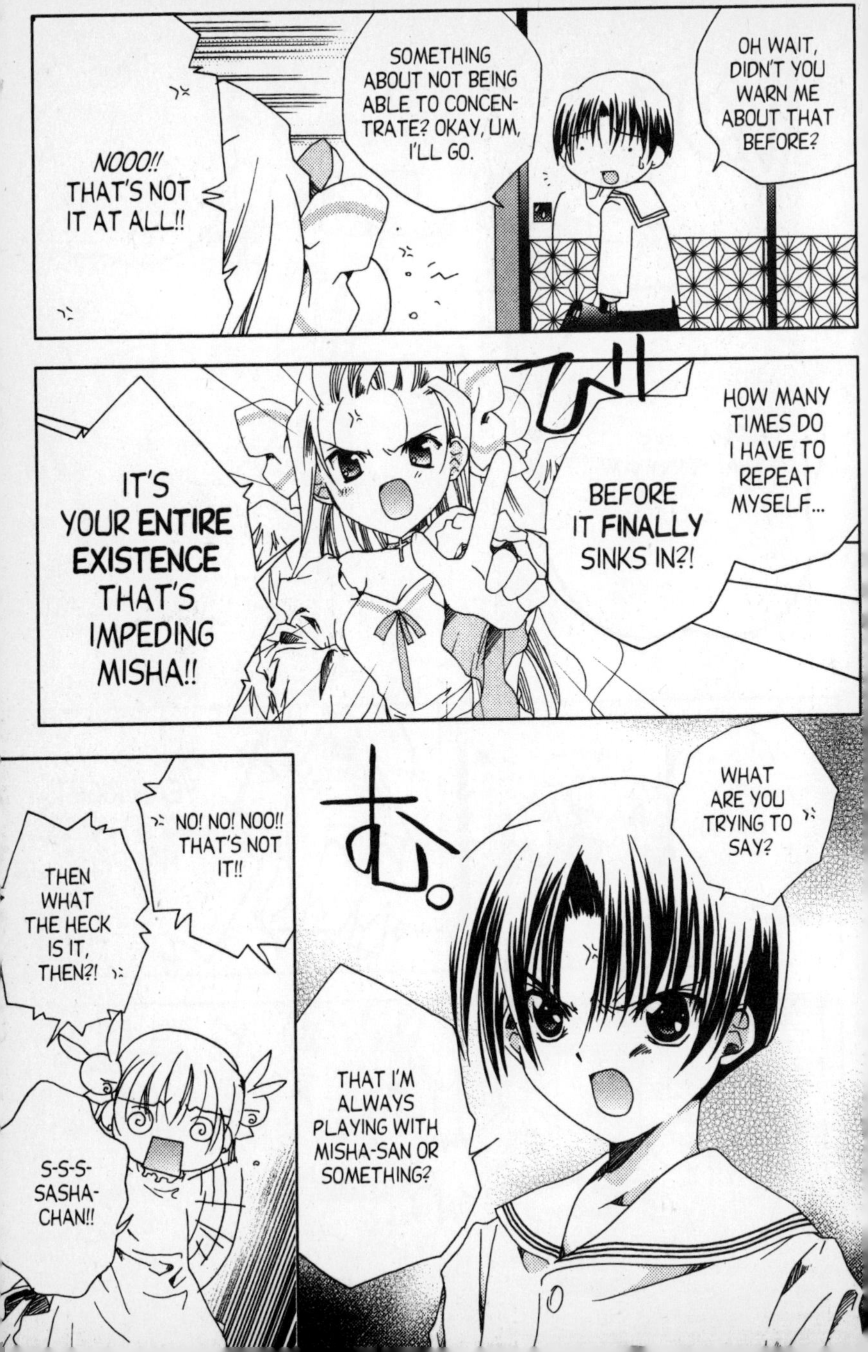
OH WAIT, DIDN'T YOU WARN ME ABOUT THAT BEFORE?
SOMETHING ABOUT NOT BEING ABLE TO CONCENTRATE? OKAY, UM, I'LL GO.
NOOO!! THAT'S NOT IT AT ALL!!
HOW MANY TIMES DO I HAVE TO REPEAT MYSELF...
BEFORE IT FINALLY SINKS IN?!
IT'S YOUR ENTIRE EXISTENCE THAT'S IMPEDING MISHA!!
WHAT ARE YOU TRYING TO SAY?
む。
THAT I'M ALWAYS PLAYING WITH MISHA-SAN OR SOMETHING?
NO! NO! NOO!! THAT'S NOT IT!!
THEN WHAT THE HECK IS IT, THEN?!
S-S-S-SASHA-CHAN!!

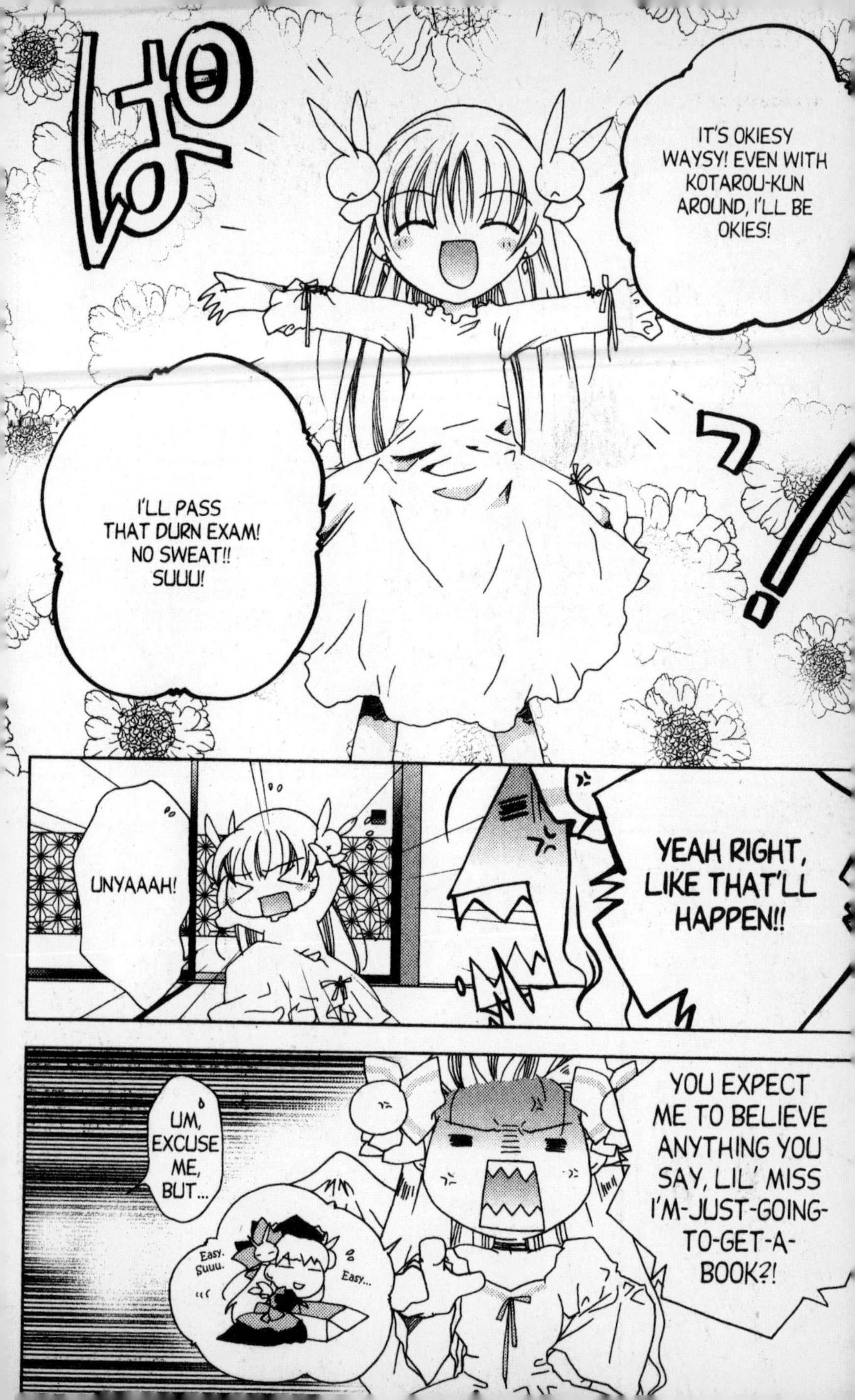
IT'S OKIESY WAYSY! EVEN WITH KOTAROU-KUN AROUND, I'LL BE OKIES!
ぱっ!
I'LL PASS THAT DURN EXAM! NO SWEAT!! SUUU!
YEAH RIGHT, LIKE THAT'LL HAPPEN!!
UNYAAAH!
YOU EXPECT ME TO BELIEVE ANYTHING YOU SAY, LIL' MISS I'M-JUST-GOING-TO-GET-A-BOOK?!
UM, EXCUSE ME, BUT...
Easy. Suuu.
Easy...

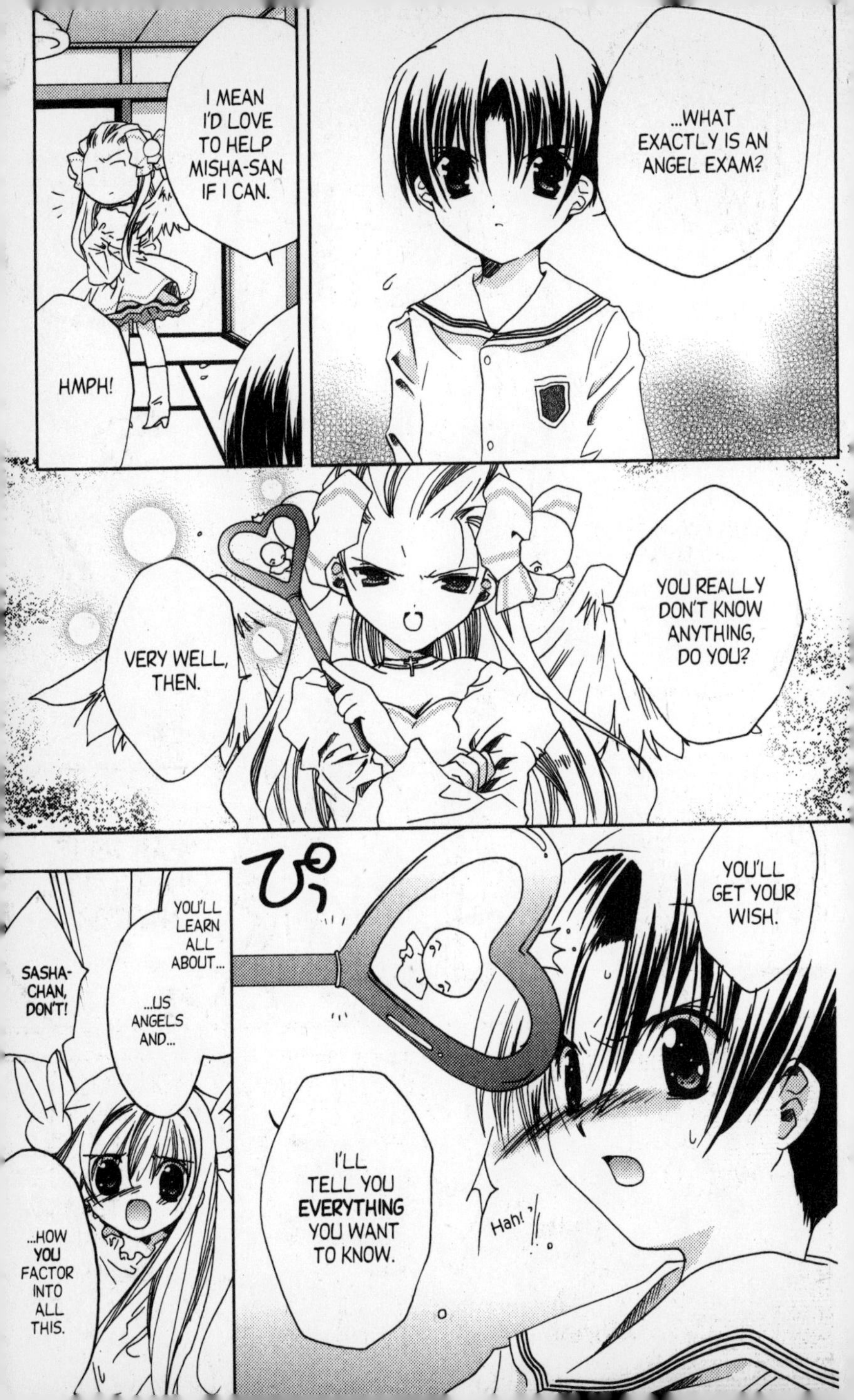

...WHAT EXACTLY IS AN ANGEL EXAM?
I MEAN I'D LOVE TO HELP MISHA-SAN IF I CAN.
HMPH!
YOU REALLY DON'T KNOW ANYTHING, DO YOU?
VERY WELL, THEN.
YOU'LL GET YOUR WISH.
ぴっ
I'LL TELL YOU **EVERYTHING** YOU WANT TO KNOW.
Hah!
YOU'LL LEARN ALL ABOUT...
...US ANGELS AND...
SASHA-CHAN, DON'T!
...HOW **YOU** FACTOR INTO ALL THIS.

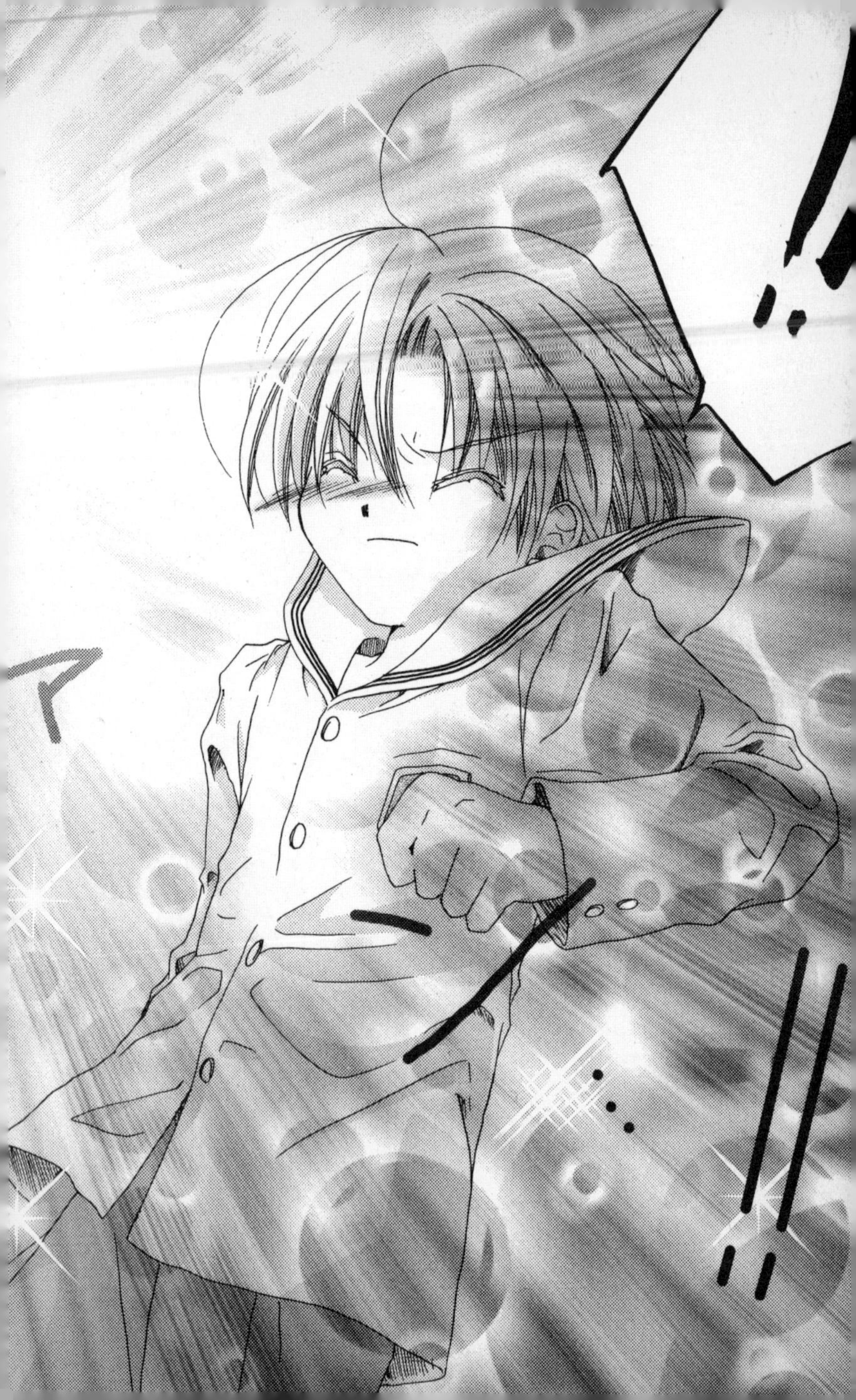

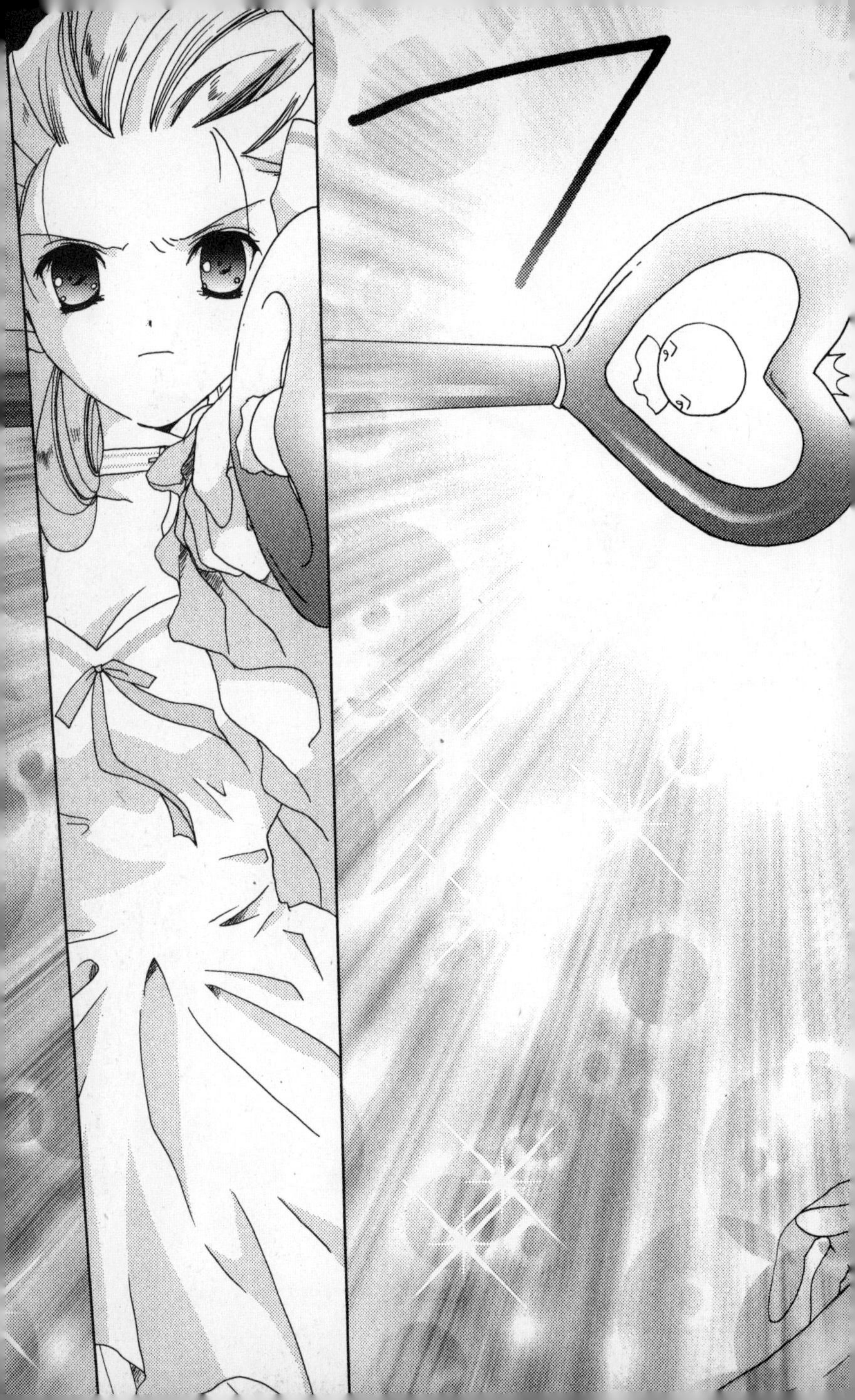

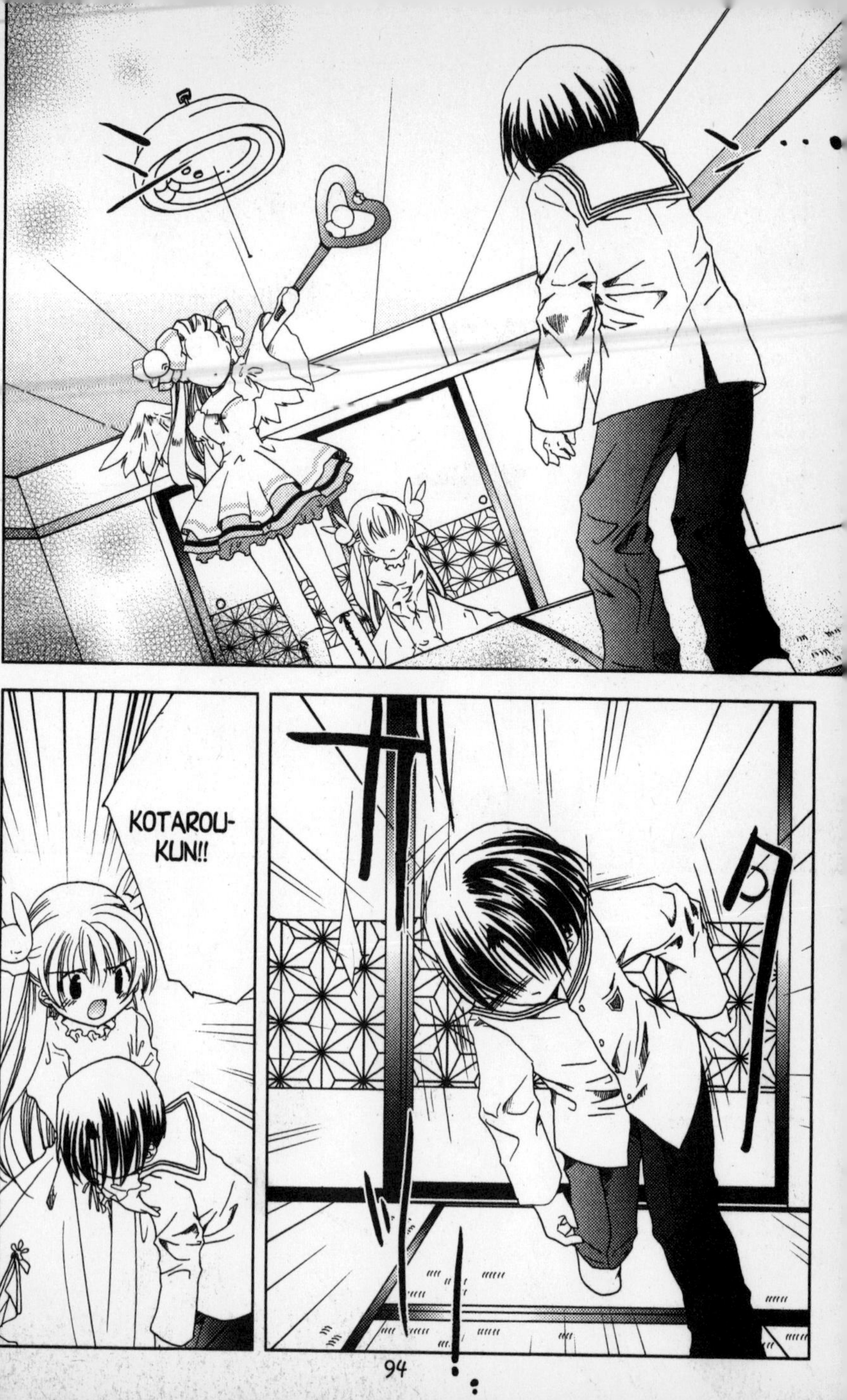
KOTAROU-KUN!!

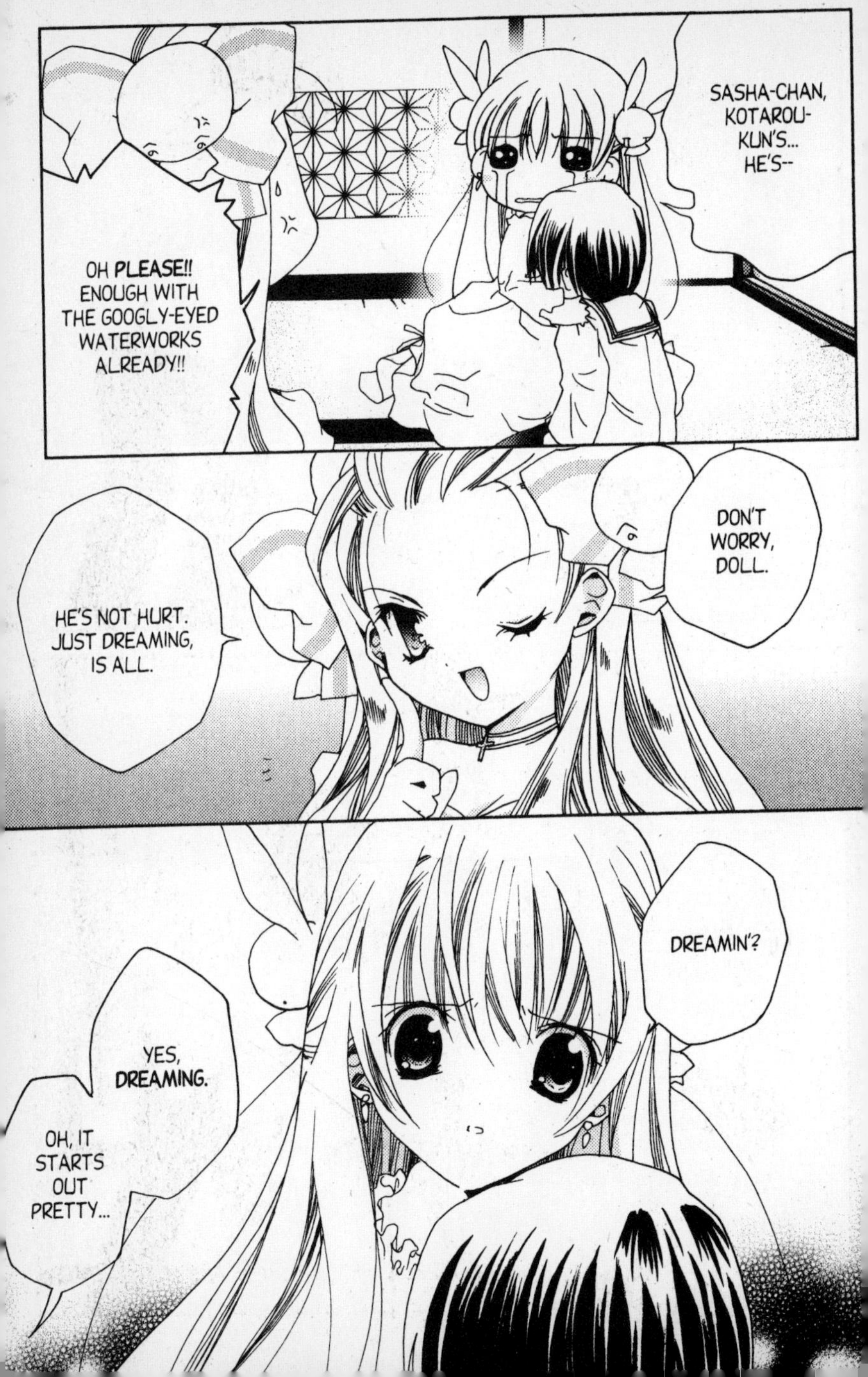
SASHA-CHAN, KOTAROU-KUN'S... HE'S--
OH **PLEASE!!** ENOUGH WITH THE GOOGLY-EYED WATERWORKS ALREADY!!
DON'T WORRY, DOLL.
HE'S NOT HURT. JUST DREAMING, IS ALL.
DREAMIN'?
YES, **DREAMING.**
OH, IT STARTS OUT PRETTY...

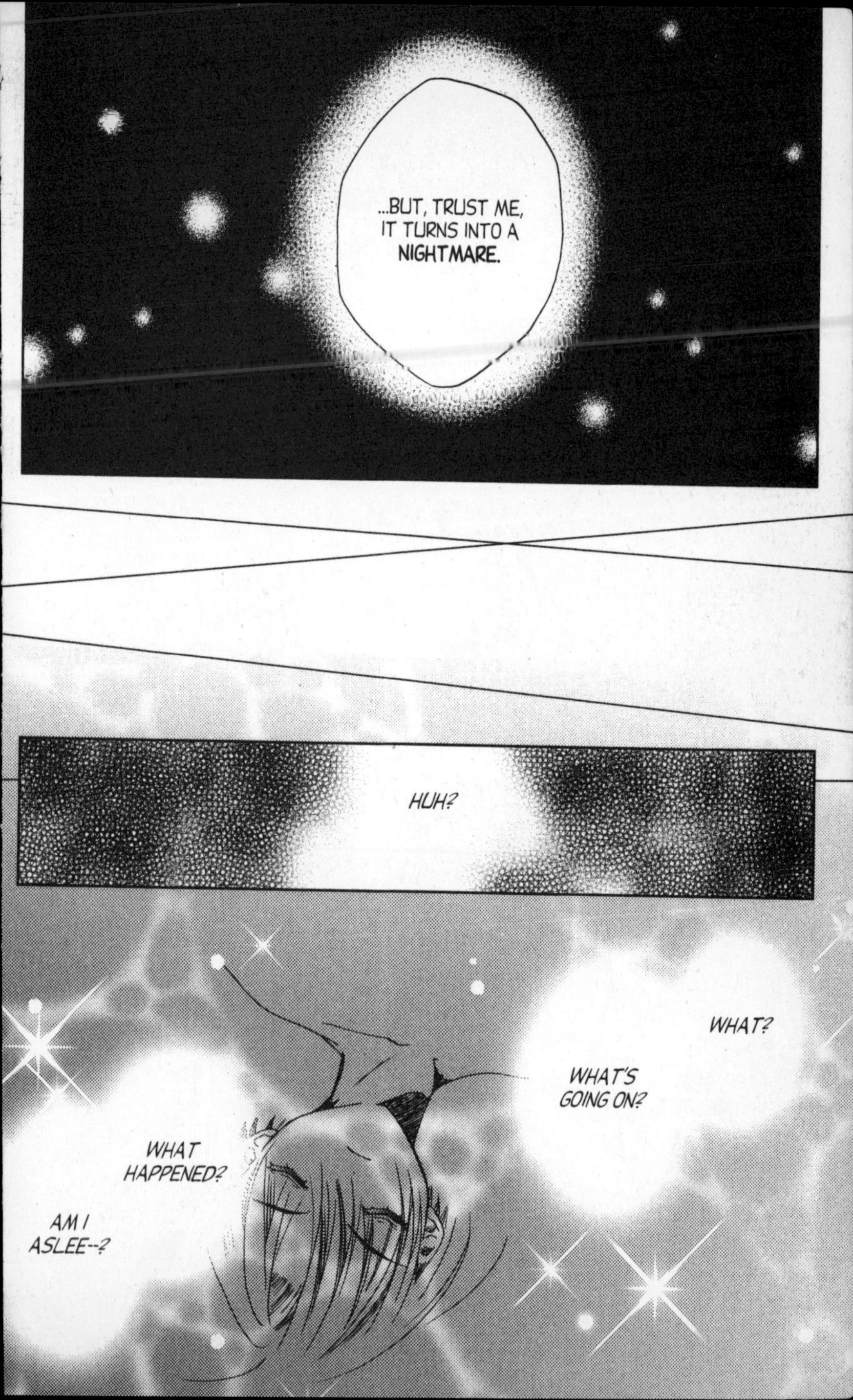
...BUT, TRUST ME, IT TURNS INTO A NIGHTMARE.
HUH?
WHAT?
WHAT'S GOING ON?
WHAT HAPPENED?
AM I ASLEE--?

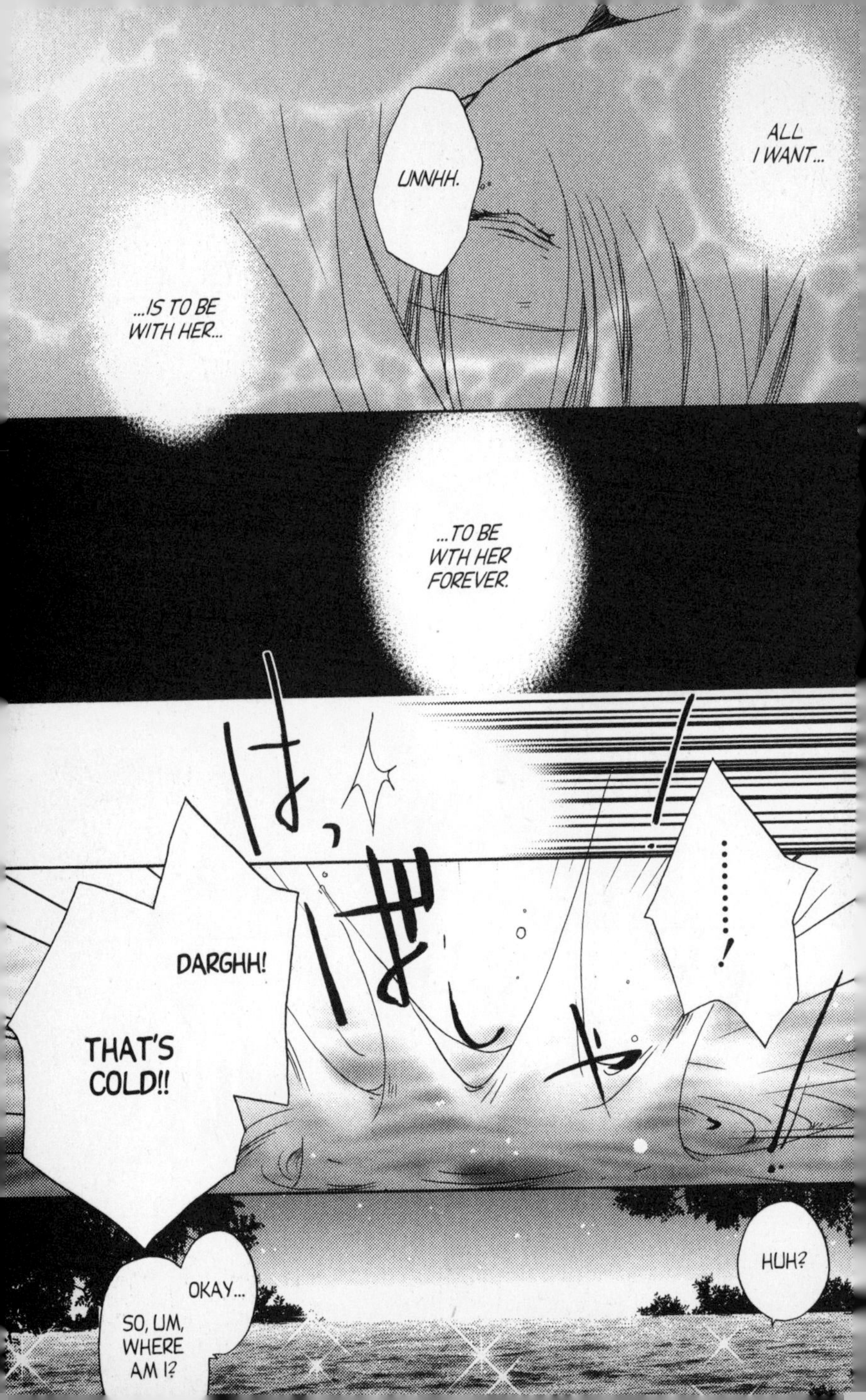
ALL I WANT...
UNNHH.
...IS TO BE WITH HER...
...TO BE WTH HER FOREVER.
......!
DARGHH! THAT'S COLD!!
HUH?
OKAY... SO, UM, WHERE AM I?

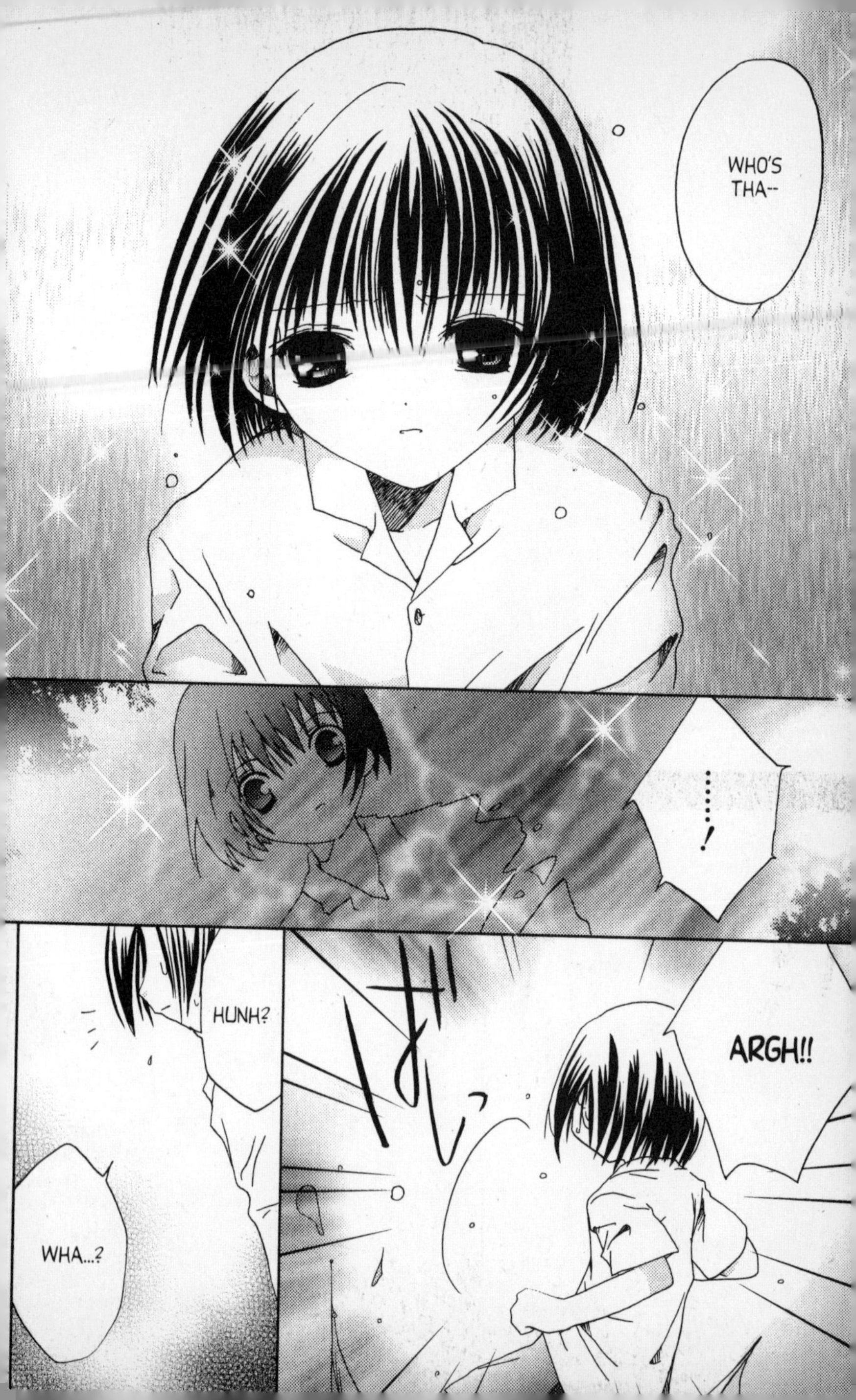
WHO'S THA--
......!
ARGH!!
HUNH?
WHA...?

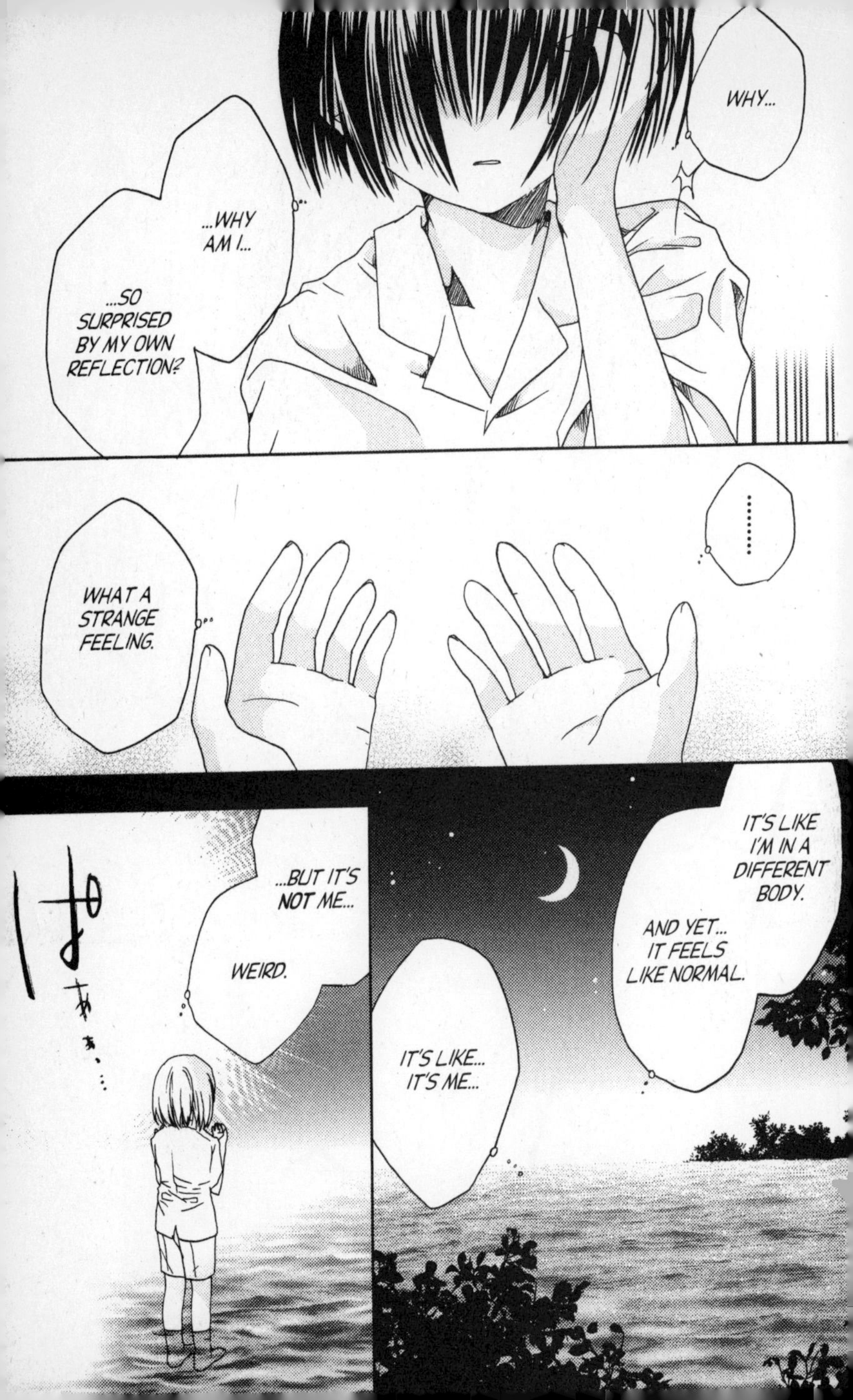
WHY...
...WHY AM I...
...SO SURPRISED BY MY OWN REFLECTION?
....
WHAT A STRANGE FEELING.
IT'S LIKE I'M IN A DIFFERENT BODY.
AND YET... IT FEELS LIKE NORMAL.
IT'S LIKE... IT'S ME...
...BUT IT'S NOT ME...
WEIRD.
はぁぁ…

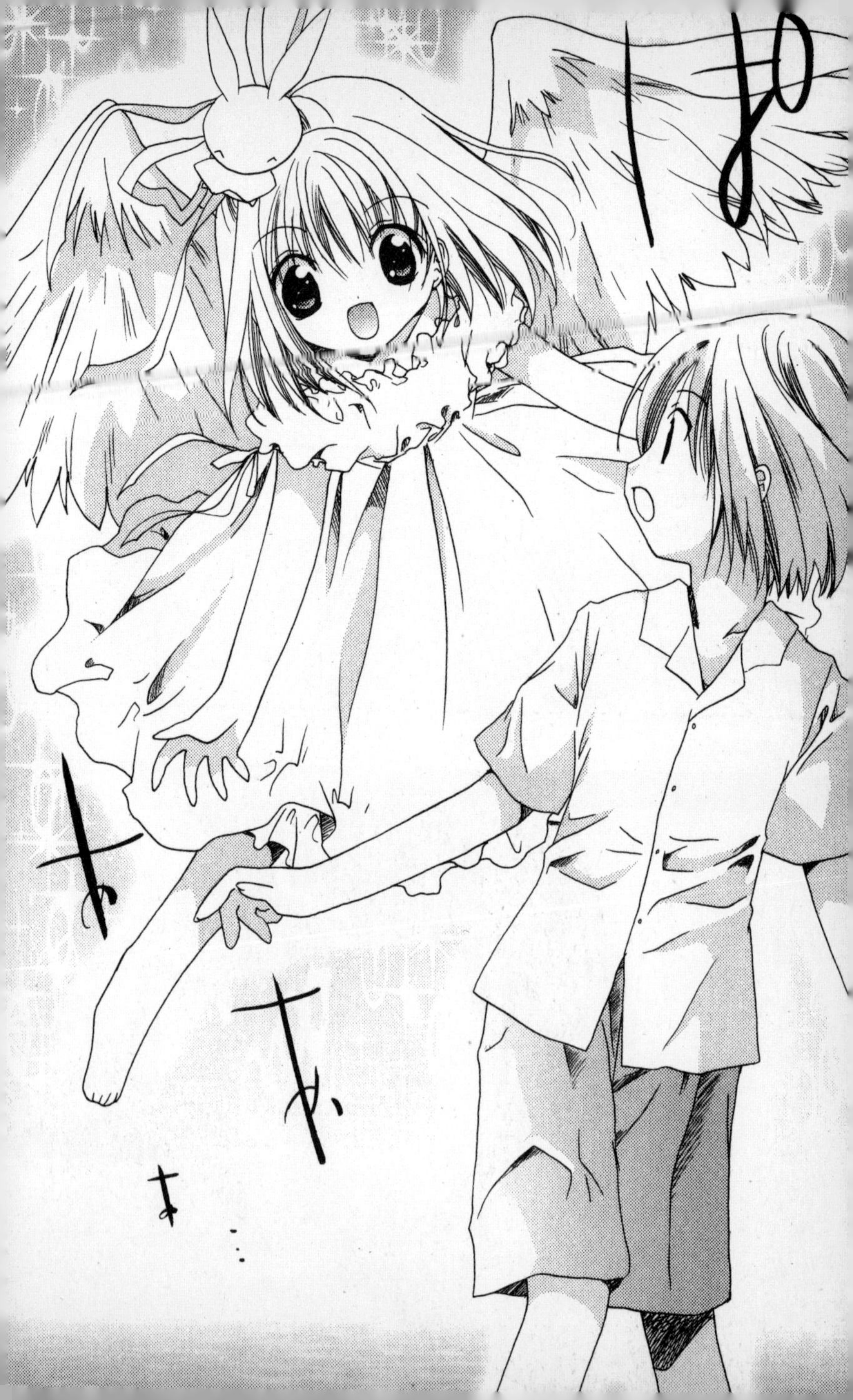

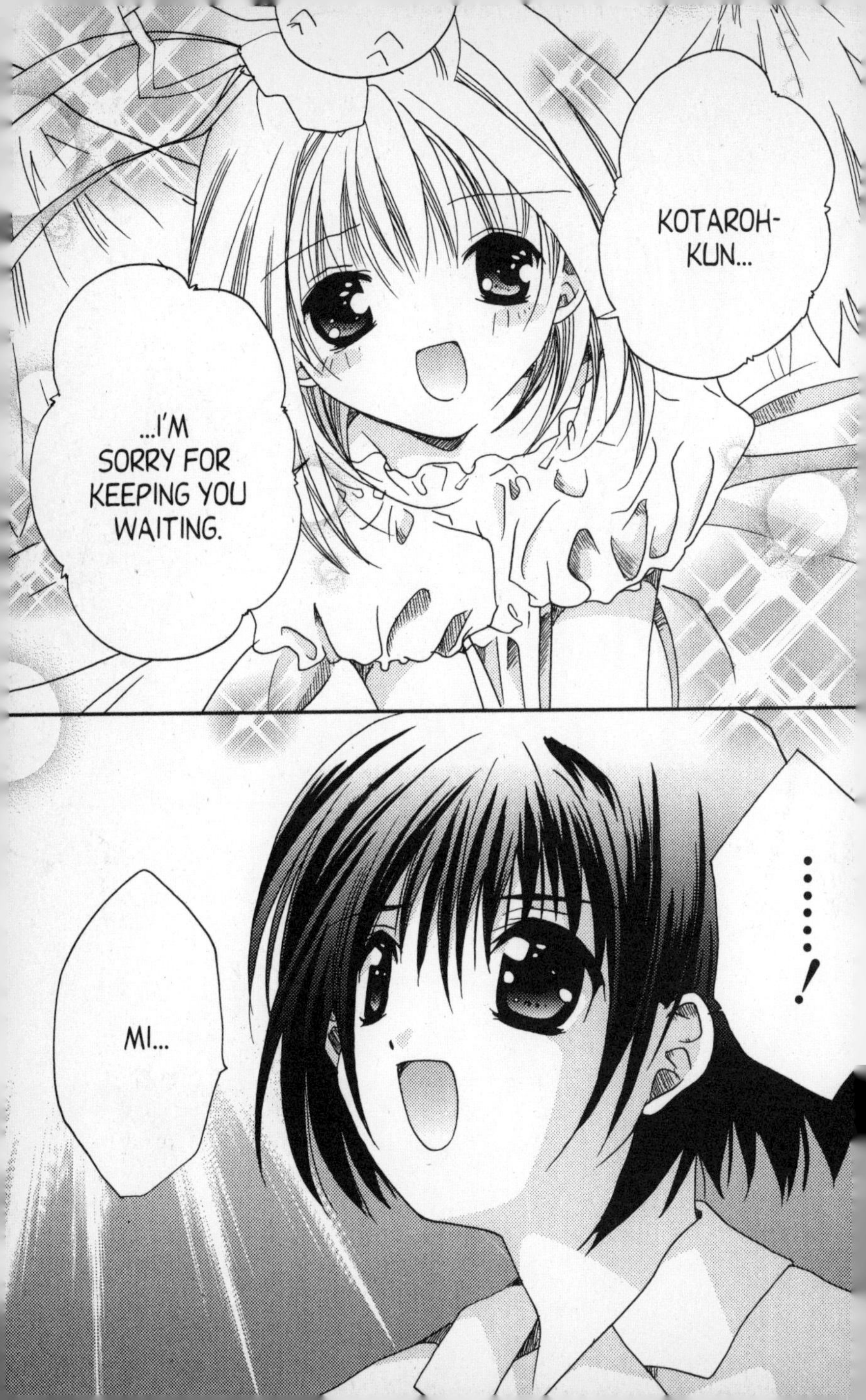
KOTAROH-KUN...
...I'M SORRY FOR KEEPING YOU WAITING.
......!
MI...

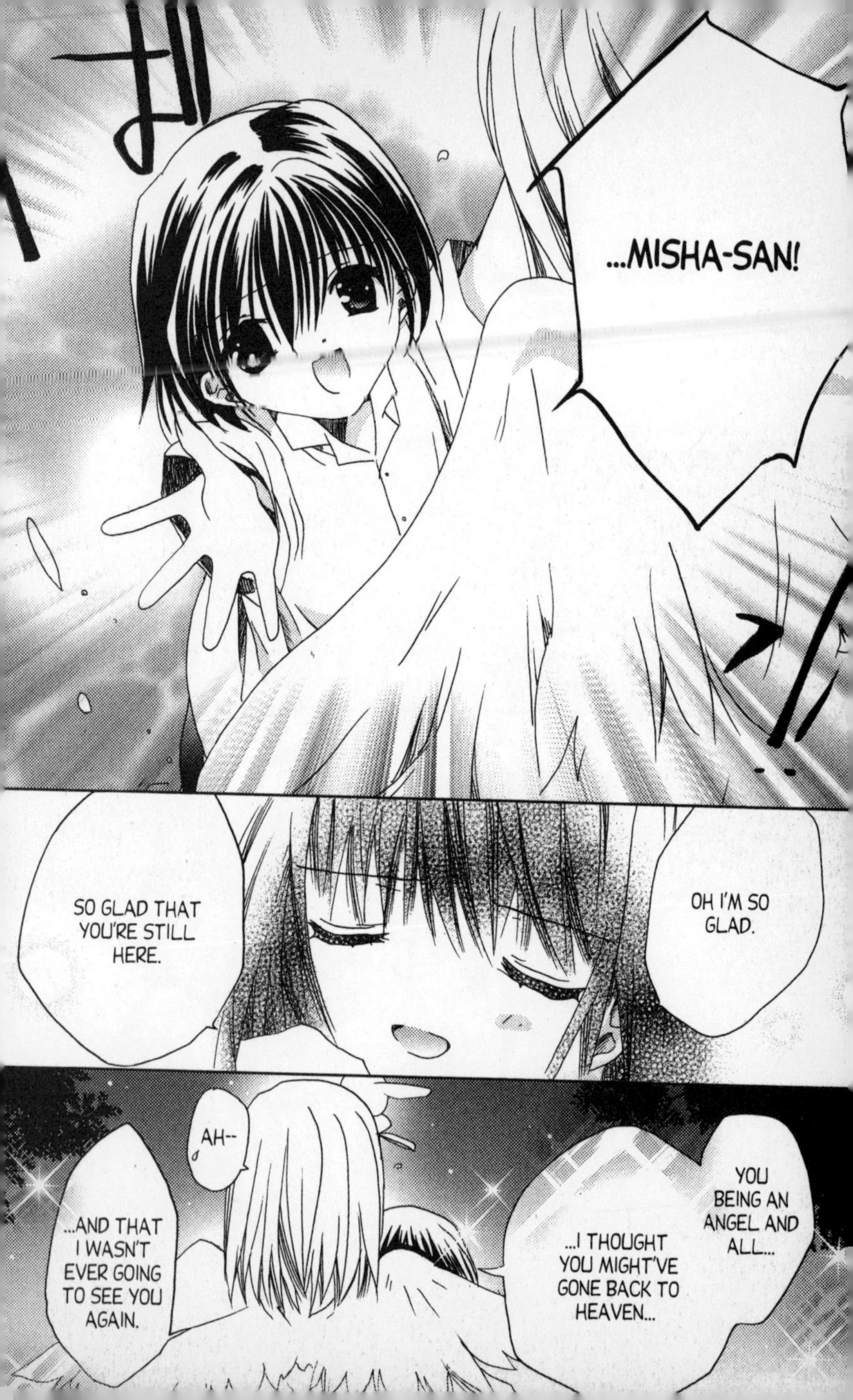
...MISHA-SAN!
OH I'M SO GLAD.
SO GLAD THAT YOU'RE STILL HERE.
YOU BEING AN ANGEL AND ALL...
...I THOUGHT YOU MIGHT'VE GONE BACK TO HEAVEN...
AH--
...AND THAT I WASN'T EVER GOING TO SEE YOU AGAIN.

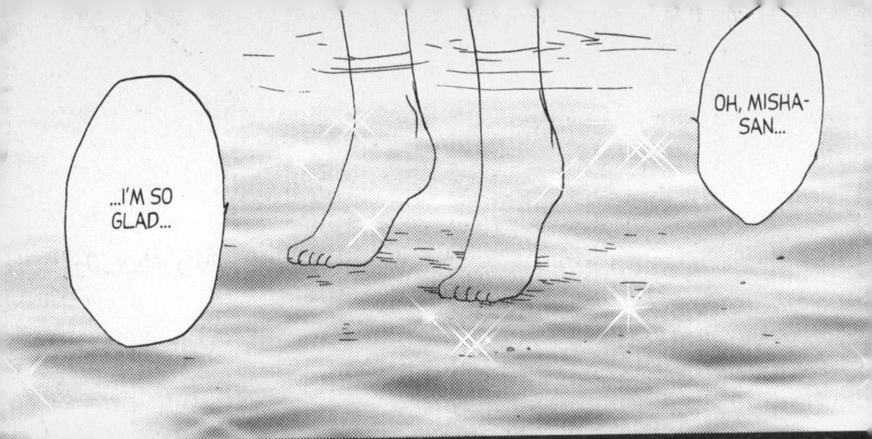
OH, MISHA-SAN...
...I'M SO GLAD...
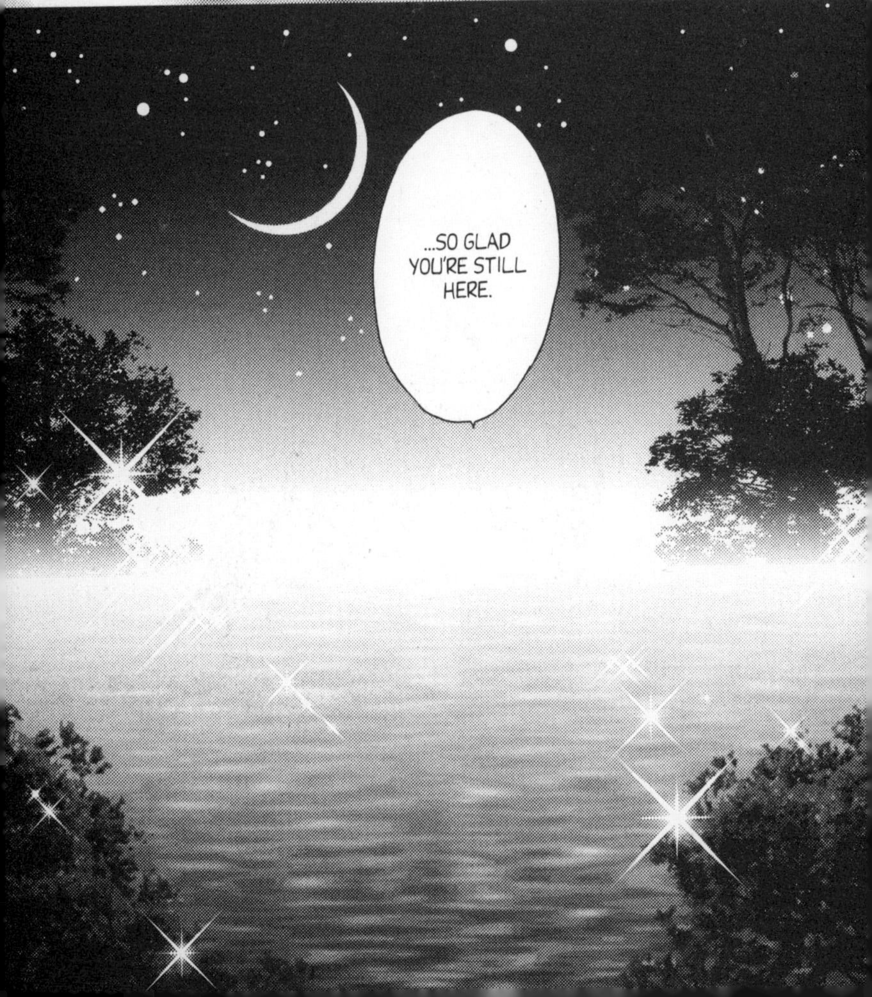
...SO GLAD YOU'RE STILL HERE.

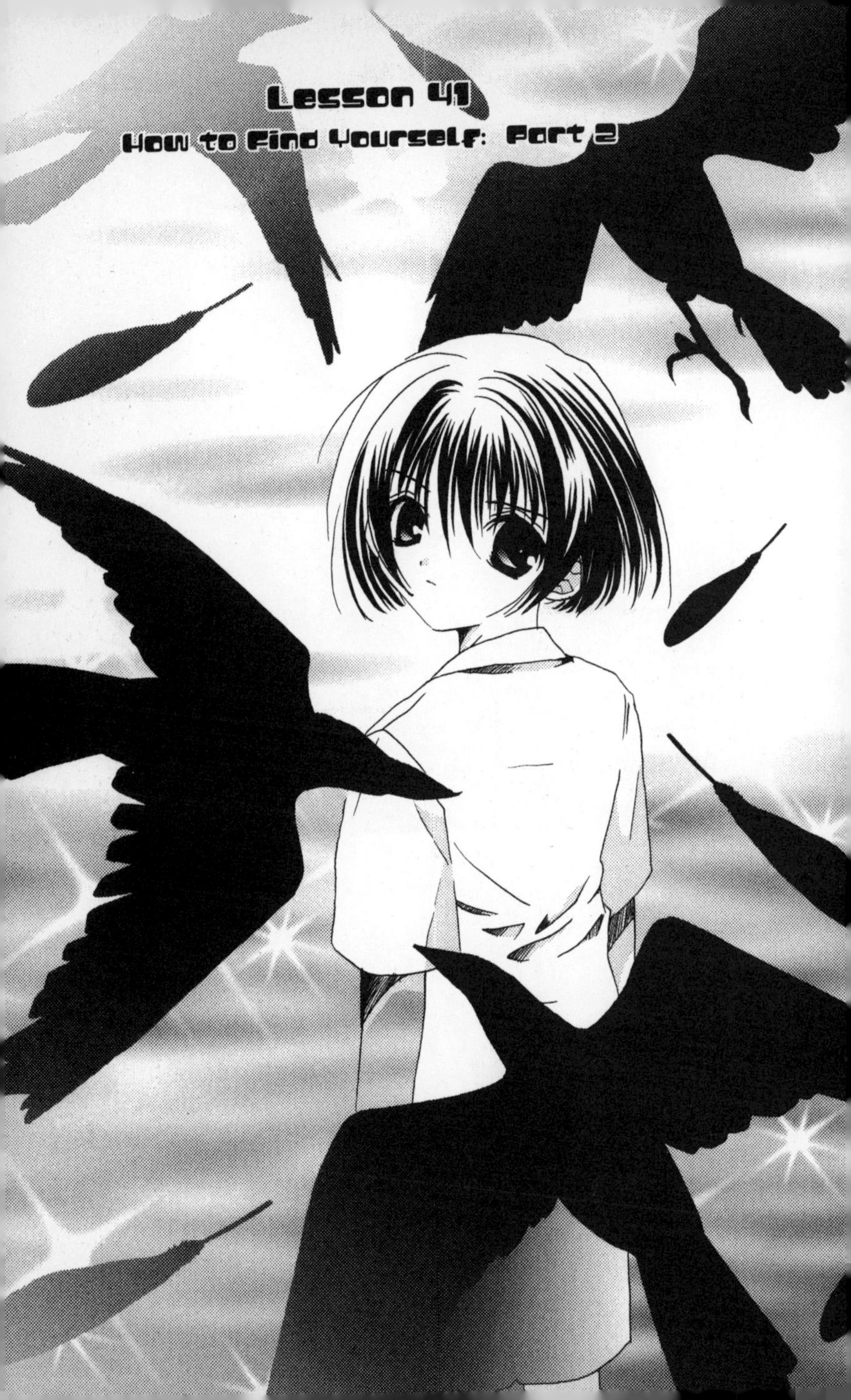
Lesson 41
How to Find Yourself: Part 2

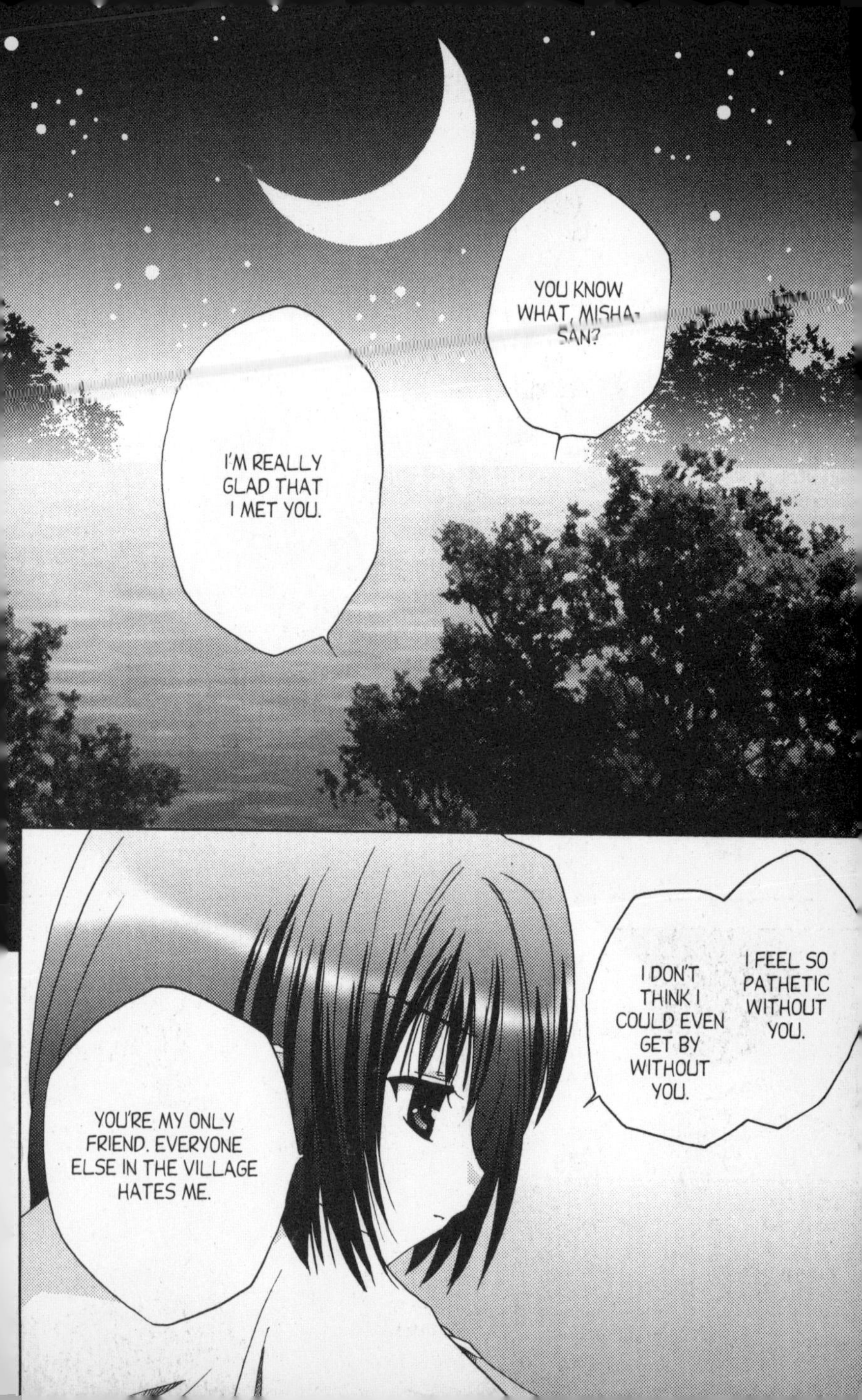
YOU KNOW WHAT, MISHA-SAN?
I'M REALLY GLAD THAT I MET YOU.
I FEEL SO PATHETIC WITHOUT YOU.
I DON'T THINK I COULD EVEN GET BY WITHOUT YOU.
YOU'RE MY ONLY FRIEND. EVERYONE ELSE IN THE VILLAGE HATES ME.

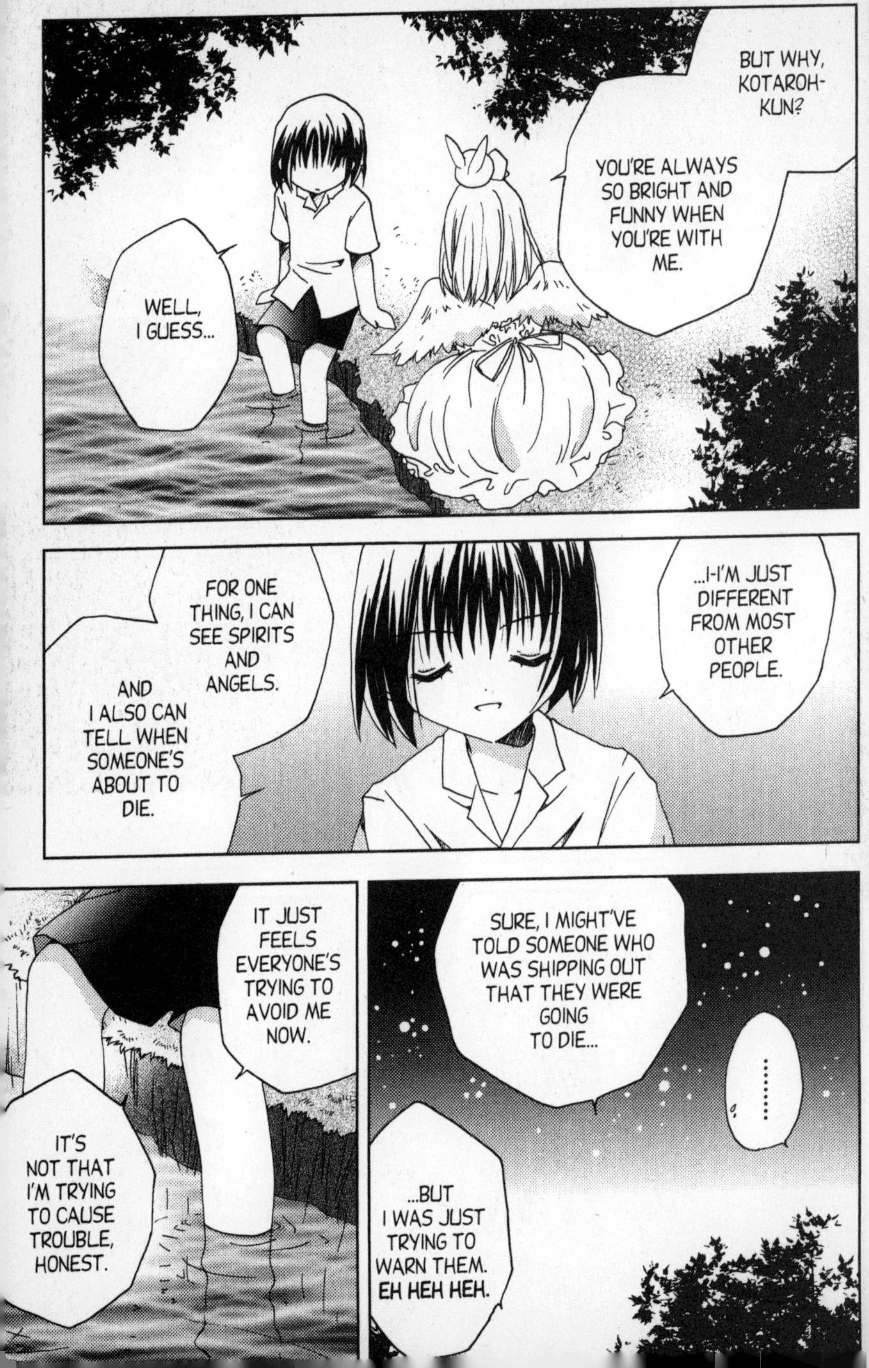
BUT WHY, KOTAROH-KUN?
YOU'RE ALWAYS SO BRIGHT AND FUNNY WHEN YOU'RE WITH ME.
WELL, I GUESS...
...I-I'M JUST DIFFERENT FROM MOST OTHER PEOPLE.
FOR ONE THING, I CAN SEE SPIRITS AND ANGELS.
AND I ALSO CAN TELL WHEN SOMEONE'S ABOUT TO DIE.
SURE, I MIGHT'VE TOLD SOMEONE WHO WAS SHIPPING OUT THAT THEY WERE GOING TO DIE...
......
...BUT I WAS JUST TRYING TO WARN THEM. EH HEH HEH.
IT JUST FEELS EVERYONE'S TRYING TO AVOID ME NOW.
IT'S NOT THAT I'M TRYING TO CAUSE TROUBLE, HONEST.

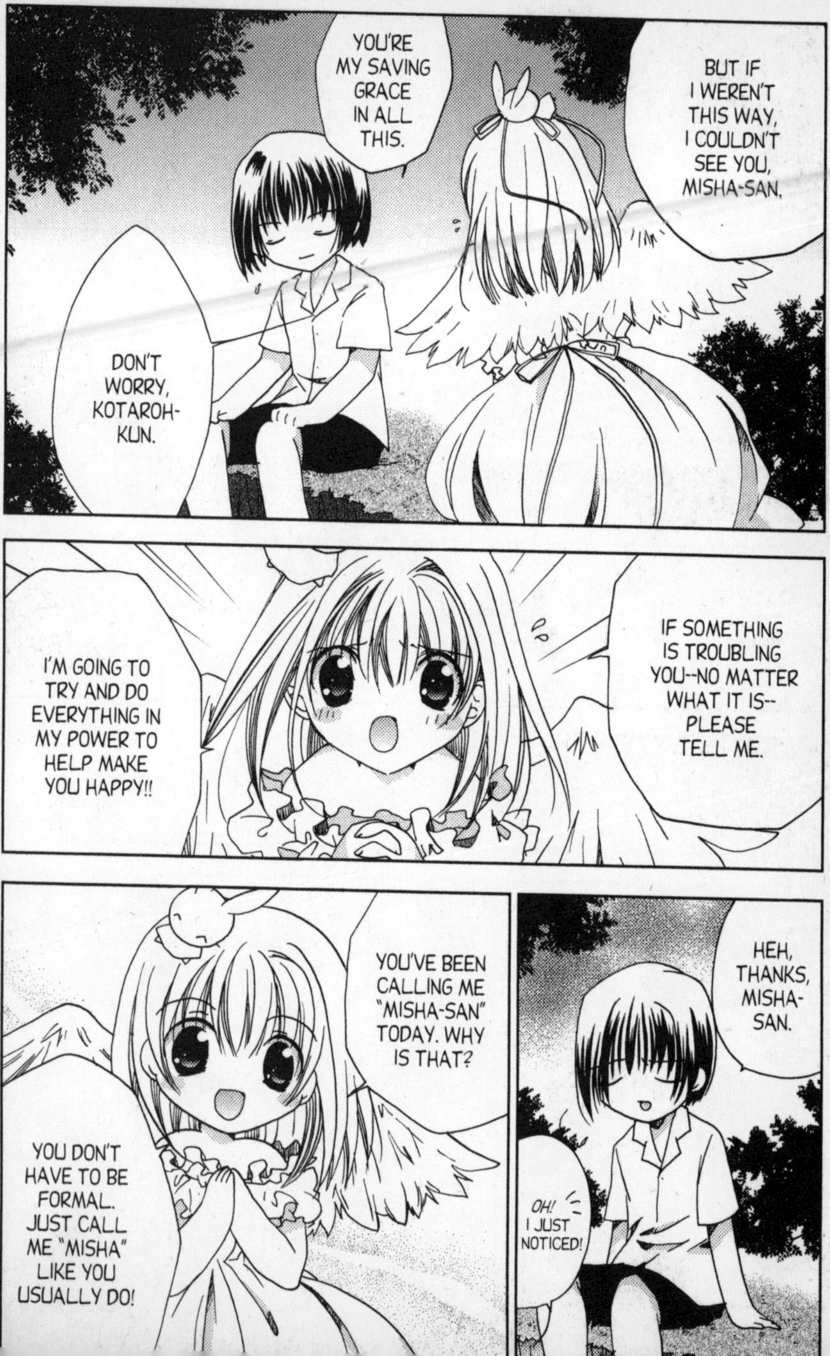
BUT IF I WEREN'T THIS WAY, I COULDN'T SEE YOU, MISHA-SAN.
YOU'RE MY SAVING GRACE IN ALL THIS.
DON'T WORRY, KOTAROH-KUN.
IF SOMETHING IS TROUBLING YOU--NO MATTER WHAT IT IS--PLEASE TELL ME.
I'M GOING TO TRY AND DO EVERYTHING IN MY POWER TO HELP MAKE YOU HAPPY!!
HEH, THANKS, MISHA-SAN.
OH! I JUST NOTICED!
YOU'VE BEEN CALLING ME "MISHA-SAN" TODAY. WHY IS THAT?
YOU DON'T HAVE TO BE FORMAL. JUST CALL ME "MISHA" LIKE YOU USUALLY DO!

DOOOHHHH!

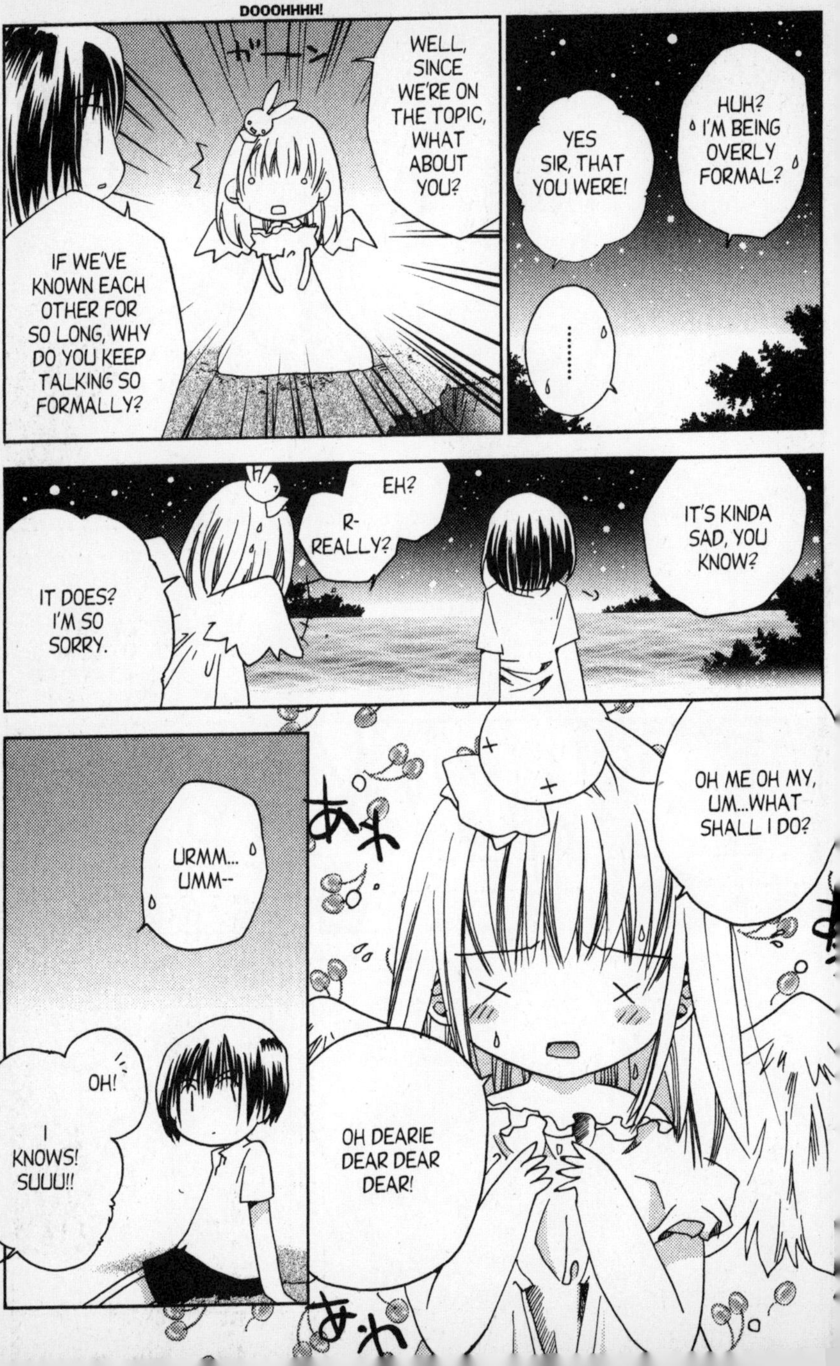
HUH? I'M BEING OVERLY FORMAL?
YES SIR, THAT YOU WERE!
......
ガーン
WELL, SINCE WE'RE ON THE TOPIC, WHAT ABOUT YOU?
IF WE'VE KNOWN EACH OTHER FOR SO LONG, WHY DO YOU KEEP TALKING SO FORMALLY?
IT'S KINDA SAD, YOU KNOW?
EH? R-REALLY?
IT DOES? I'M SO SORRY.
OH ME OH MY, UM...WHAT SHALL I DO?
あわ
OH DEARIE DEAR DEAR DEAR!
あわ
URMM... UMM--
OH!
I KNOWS! SUUU!!

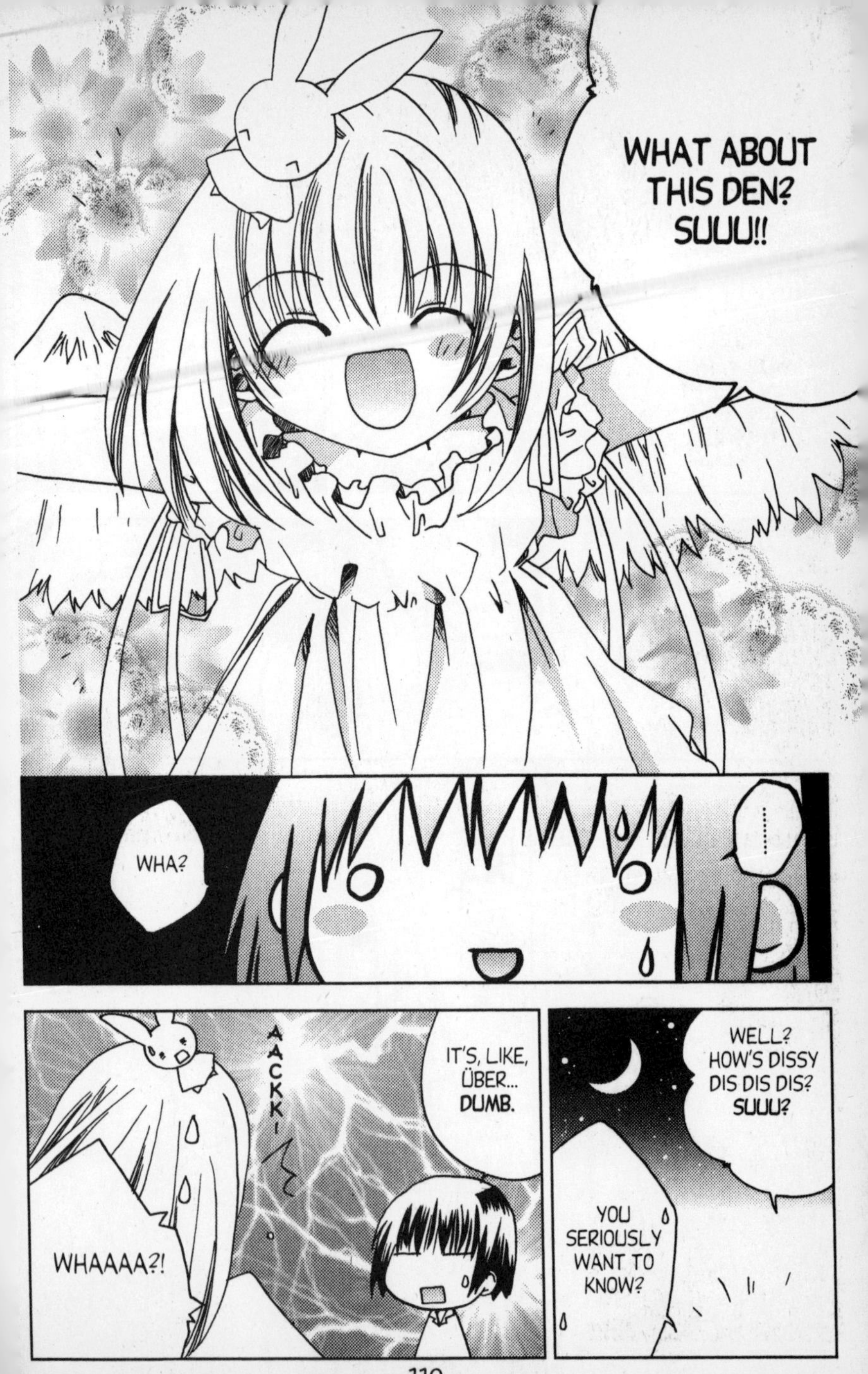
WHAT ABOUT THIS DEN? SUUU!!
......
WHA?
WELL? HOW'S DISSY DIS DIS DIS? SUUU?
YOU SERIOUSLY WANT TO KNOW?
IT'S, LIKE, ÜBER... **DUMB.**
AACKK!
WHAAAA?!

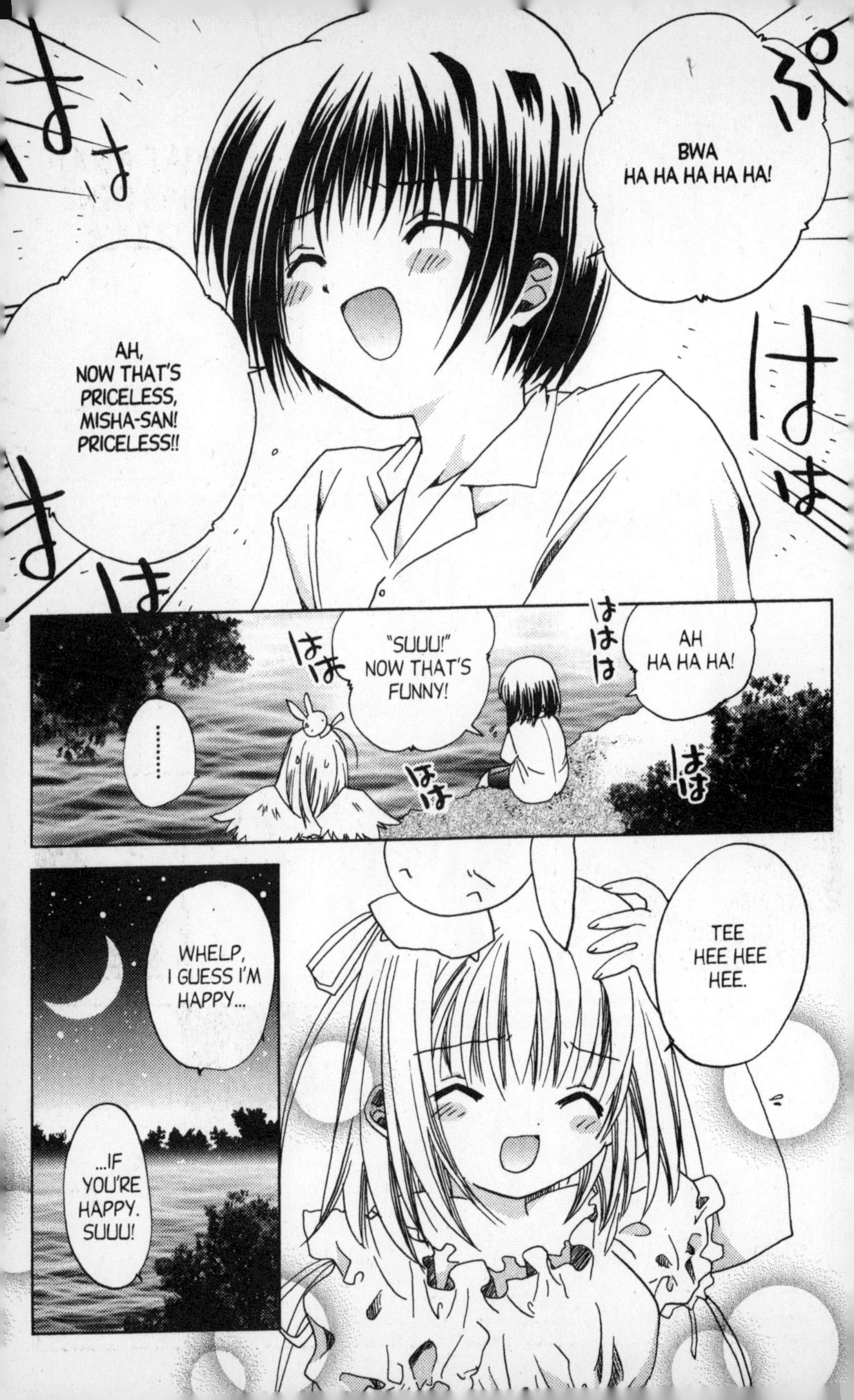
ぷ
BWA HA HA HA HA HA!
はは
AH, NOW THAT'S PRICELESS, MISHA-SAN! PRICELESS!!
ははは
AH HA HA HA!
ははは
"SUUU!" NOW THAT'S FUNNY!
はは
はは
......
TEE HEE HEE HEE.
WHELP, I GUESS I'M HAPPY...
...IF YOU'RE HAPPY. SUUU!

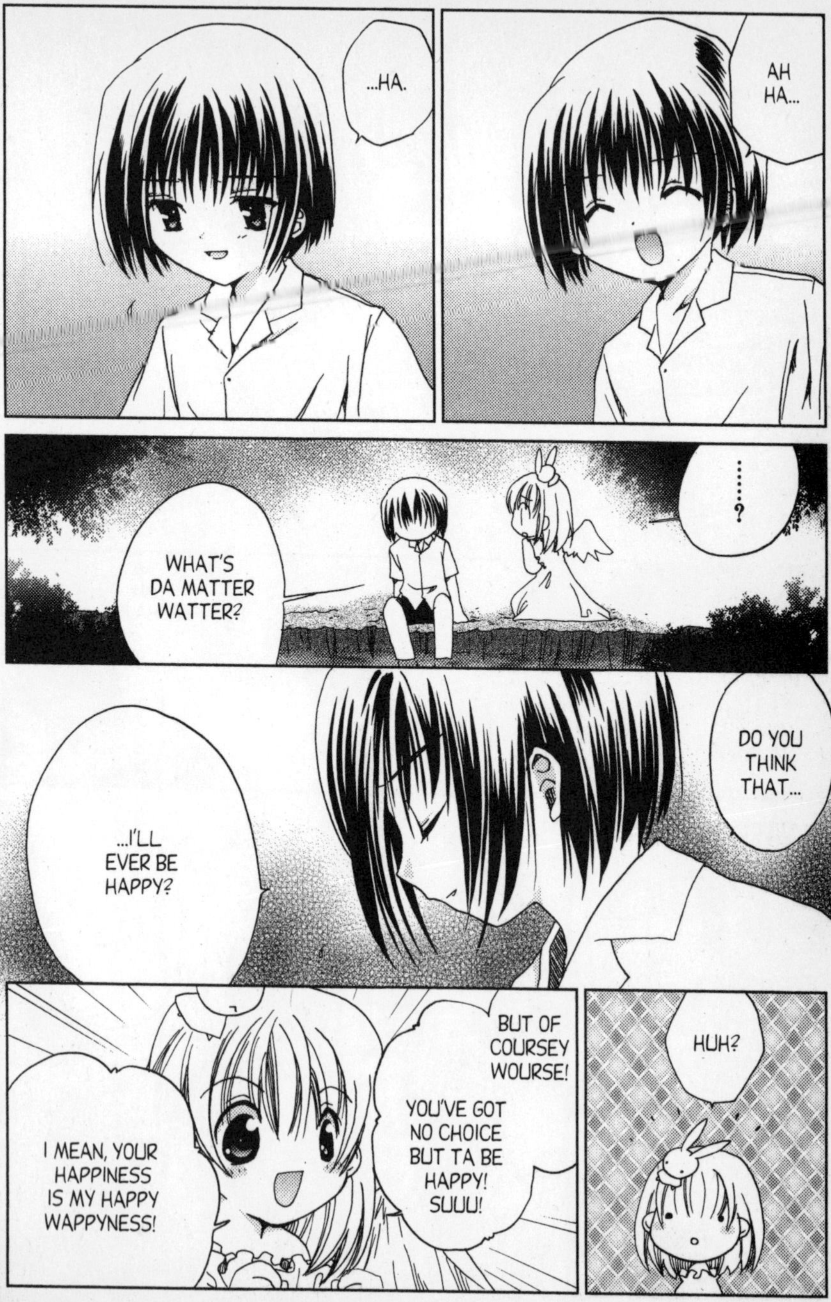
AH HA...
...HA.
......?
WHAT'S DA MATTER WATTER?
DO YOU THINK THAT...
...I'LL EVER BE HAPPY?
HUH?
BUT OF COURSEY WOURSE!
YOU'VE GOT NO CHOICE BUT TA BE HAPPY! SUUU!
I MEAN, YOUR HAPPINESS IS MY HAPPY WAPPYNESS!

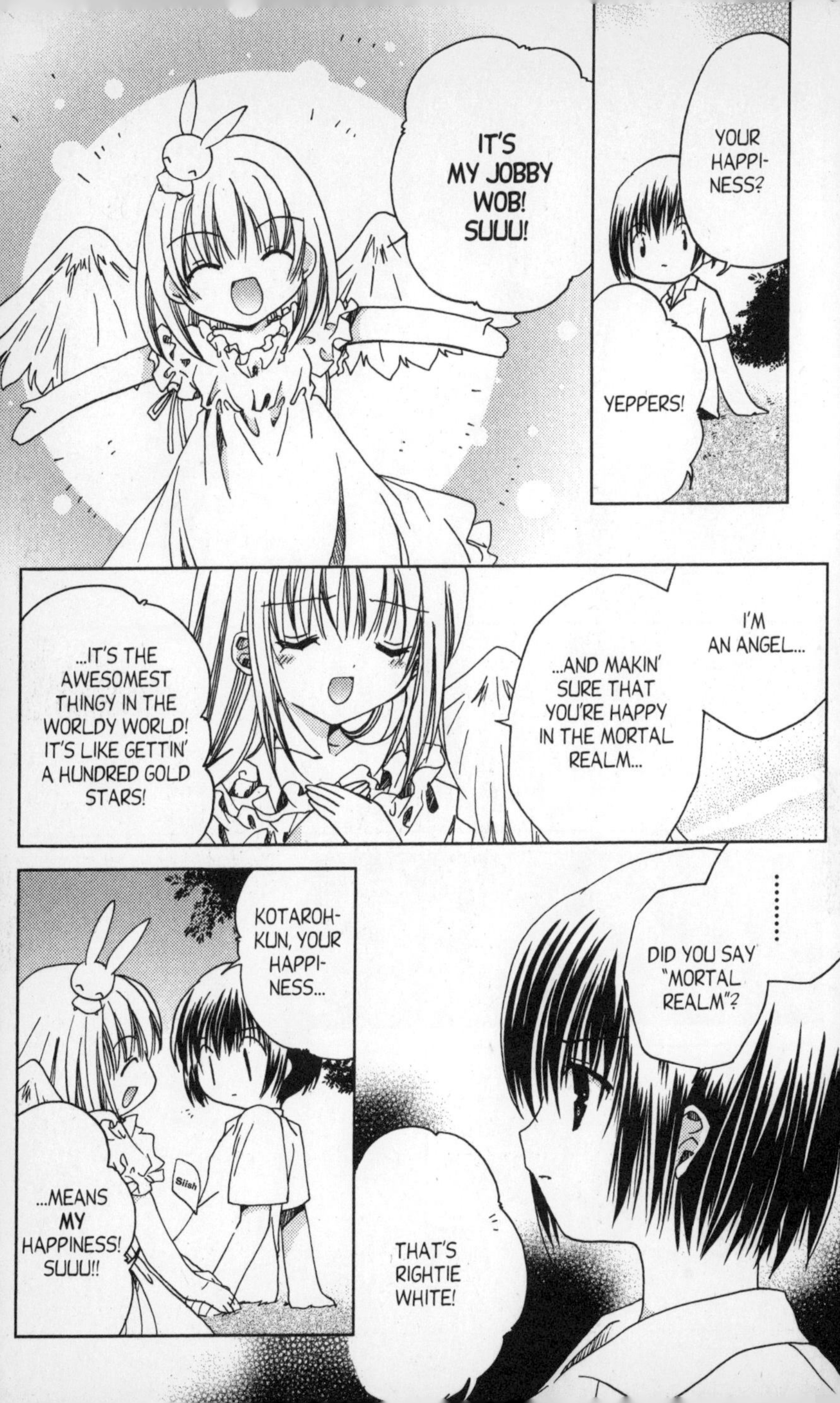
YOUR HAPPI-NESS?
YEPPERS!
IT'S MY JOBBY WOB! SUUU!
I'M AN ANGEL...
...AND MAKIN' SURE THAT YOU'RE HAPPY IN THE MORTAL REALM...
...IT'S THE AWESOMEST THINGY IN THE WORLDY WORLD! IT'S LIKE GETTIN' A HUNDRED GOLD STARS!
....
DID YOU SAY "MORTAL REALM"?
THAT'S RIGHTIE WHITE!
KOTAROH-KUN, YOUR HAPPI-NESS...
Siish
...MEANS **MY** HAPPINESS! SUUU!!

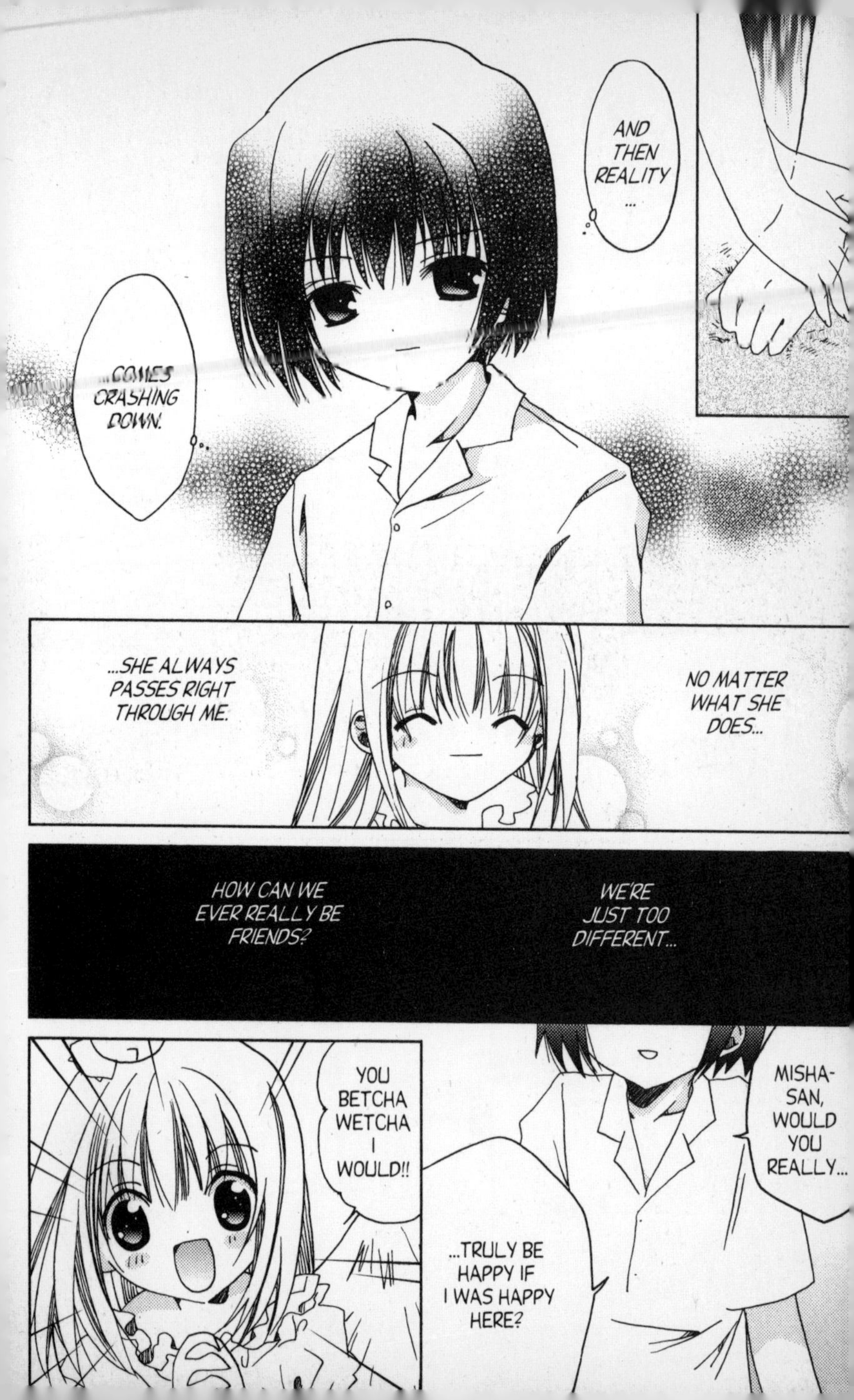
AND THEN REALITY ...
...COMES CRASHING DOWN.
NO MATTER WHAT SHE DOES...
...SHE ALWAYS PASSES RIGHT THROUGH ME.
WE'RE JUST TOO DIFFERENT...
HOW CAN WE EVER REALLY BE FRIENDS?
MISHA-SAN, WOULD YOU REALLY...
...TRULY BE HAPPY IF I WAS HAPPY HERE?
YOU BETCHA WETCHA I WOULD!!

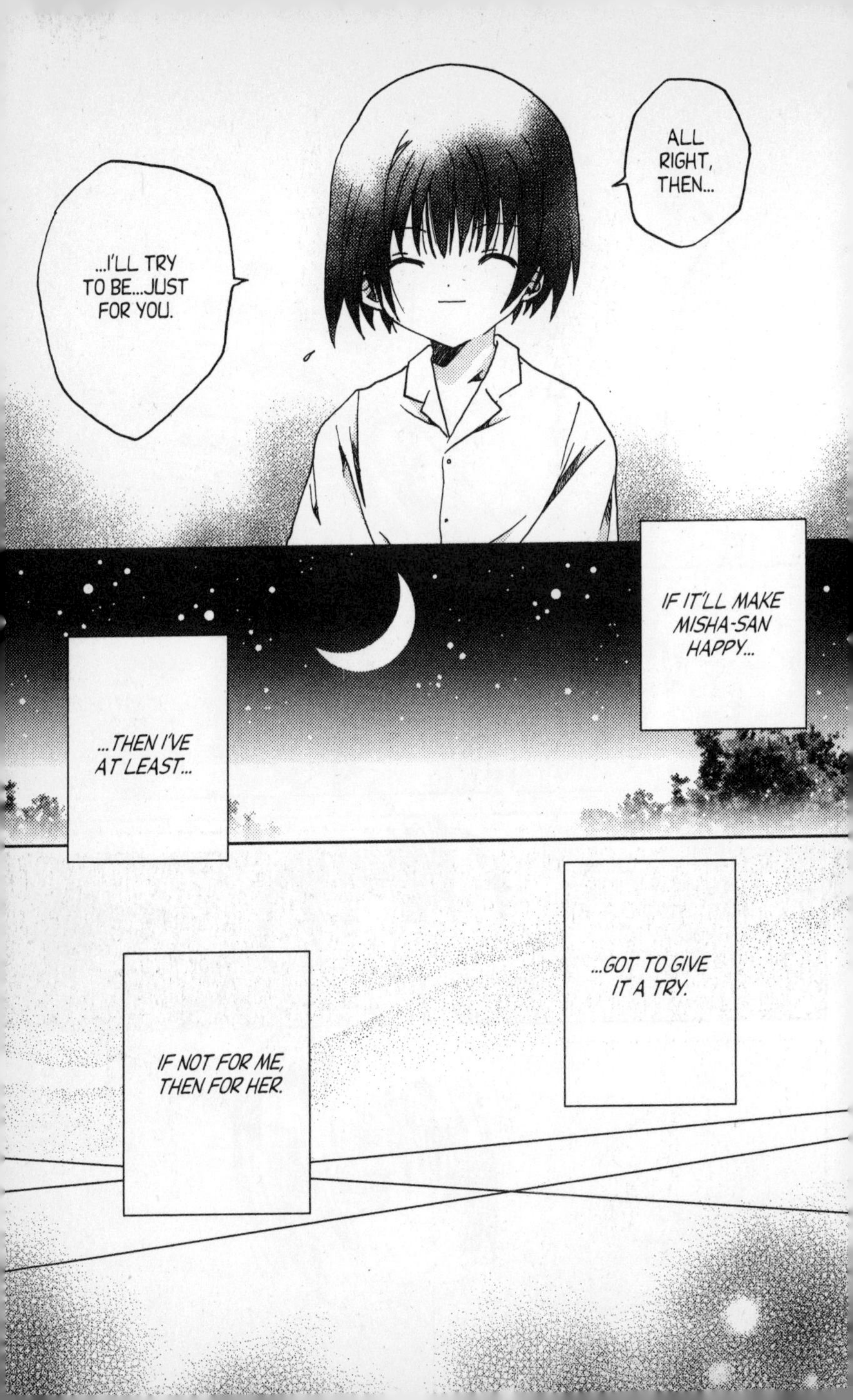
ALL RIGHT, THEN...
...I'LL TRY TO BE...JUST FOR YOU.
IF IT'LL MAKE MISHA-SAN HAPPY...
...THEN I'VE AT LEAST...
...GOT TO GIVE IT A TRY.
IF NOT FOR ME, THEN FOR HER.

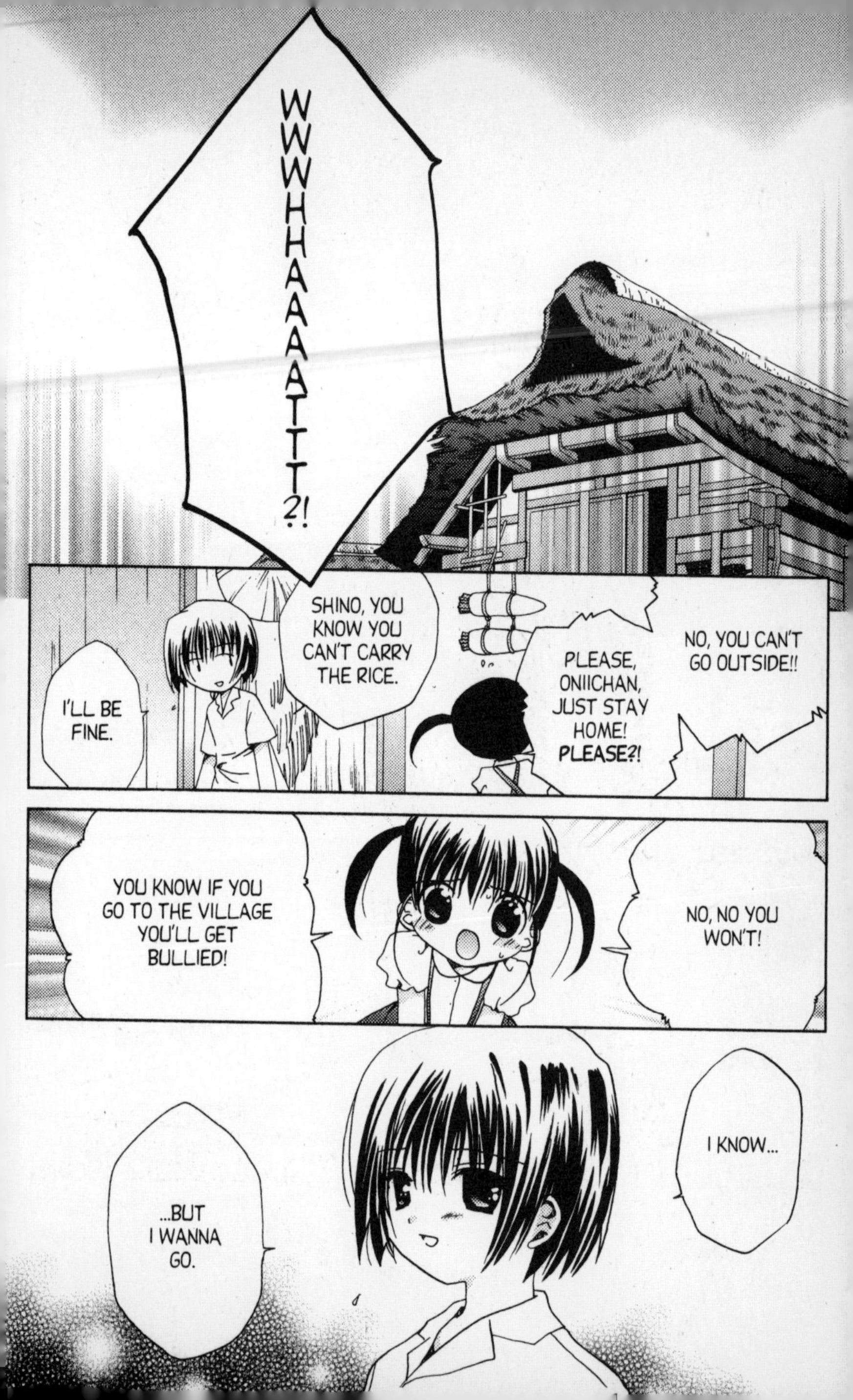
WWWHHAAAATTTT?!
NO, YOU CAN'T GO OUTSIDE!!
PLEASE, ONIICHAN, JUST STAY HOME! PLEASE?!
SHINO, YOU KNOW YOU CAN'T CARRY THE RICE.
I'LL BE FINE.
NO, NO YOU WON'T!
YOU KNOW IF YOU GO TO THE VILLAGE YOU'LL GET BULLIED!
I KNOW...
...BUT I WANNA GO.

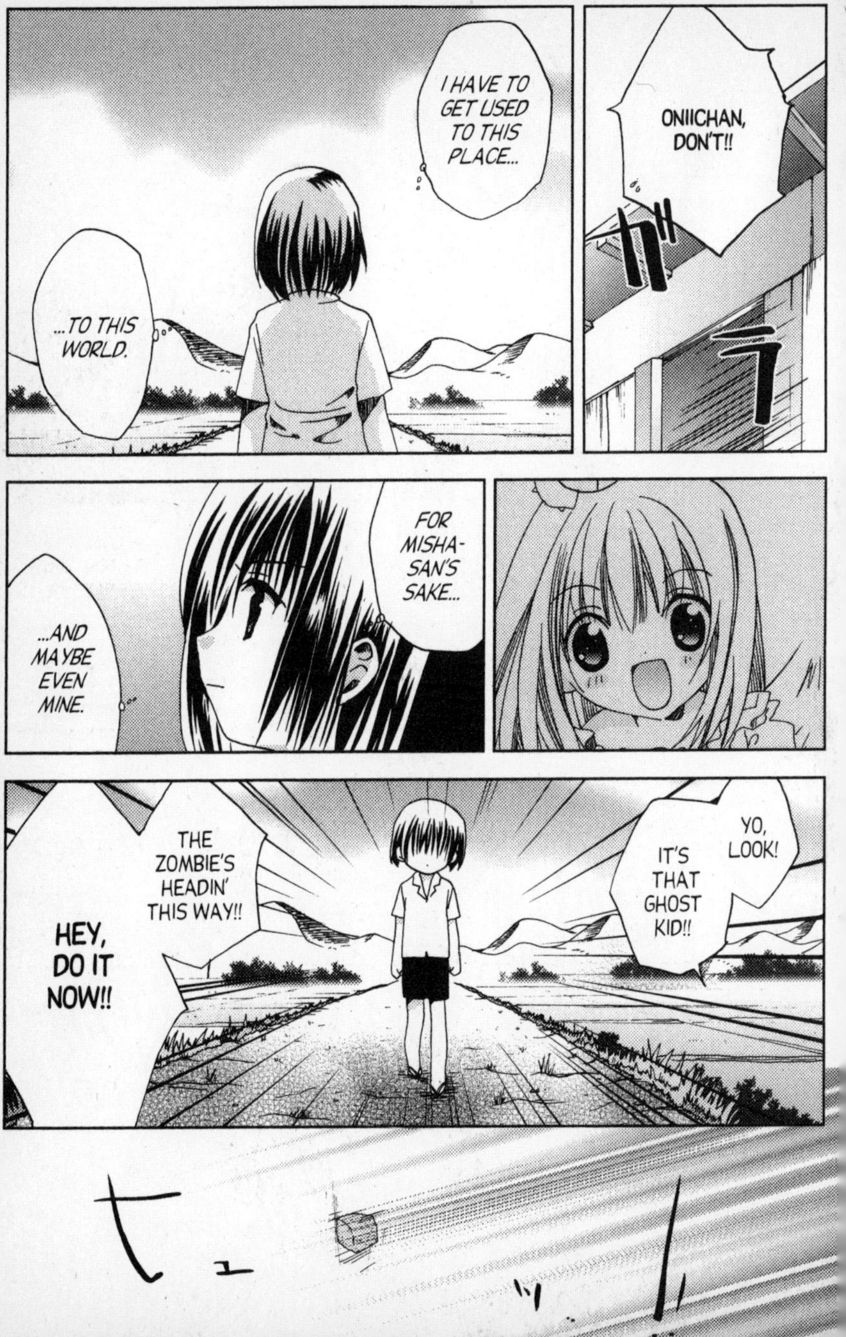
ONIICHAN, DON'T!!
I HAVE TO GET USED TO THIS PLACE...
...TO THIS WORLD.
FOR MISHA-SAN'S SAKE...
...AND MAYBE EVEN MINE.
YO, LOOK!
IT'S THAT GHOST KID!!
THE ZOMBIE'S HEADIN' THIS WAY!!
HEY, DO IT NOW!!

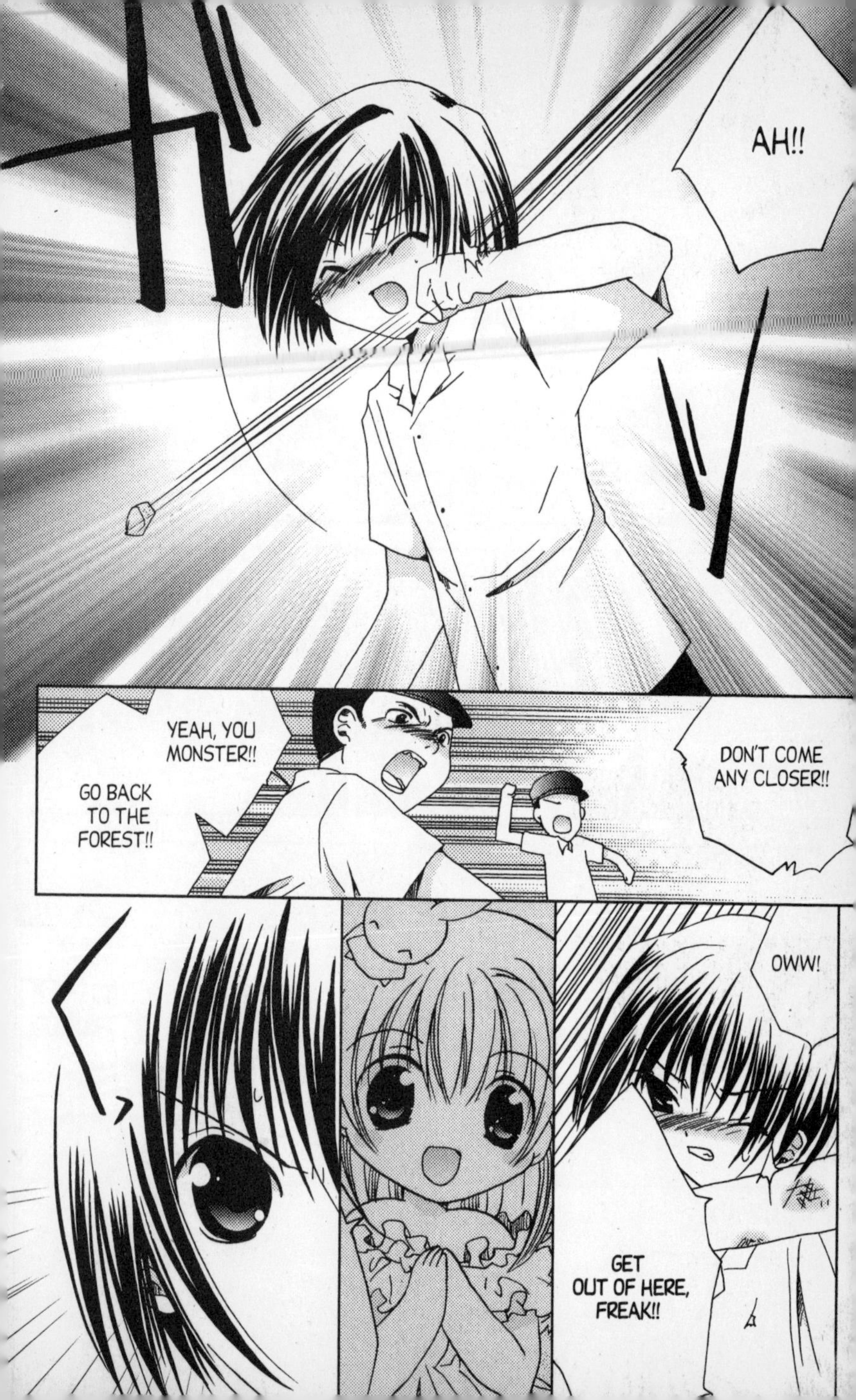
AH!!
DON'T COME ANY CLOSER!!
YEAH, YOU MONSTER!!
GO BACK TO THE FOREST!!
OWW!
GET OUT OF HERE, FREAK!!

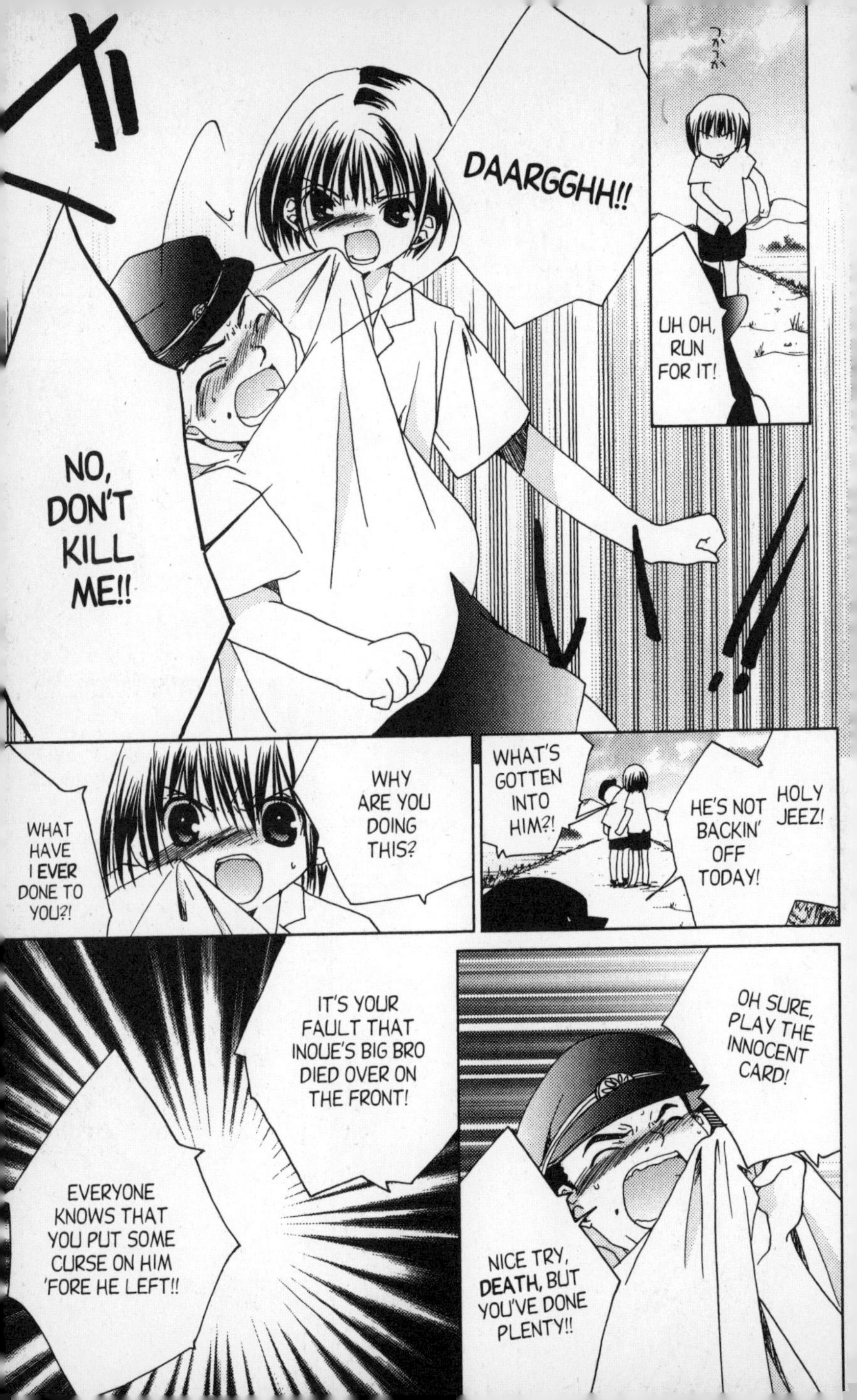
UH OH, RUN FOR IT!
DAARGGHH!!
NO, DON'T KILL ME!!
HOLY JEEZ!
HE'S NOT BACKIN' OFF TODAY!
WHAT'S GOTTEN INTO HIM?!
WHY ARE YOU DOING THIS?
WHAT HAVE I EVER DONE TO YOU?!
OH SURE, PLAY THE INNOCENT CARD!
NICE TRY, DEATH, BUT YOU'VE DONE PLENTY!!
IT'S YOUR FAULT THAT INOUE'S BIG BRO DIED OVER ON THE FRONT!
EVERYONE KNOWS THAT YOU PUT SOME CURSE ON HIM 'FORE HE LEFT!!

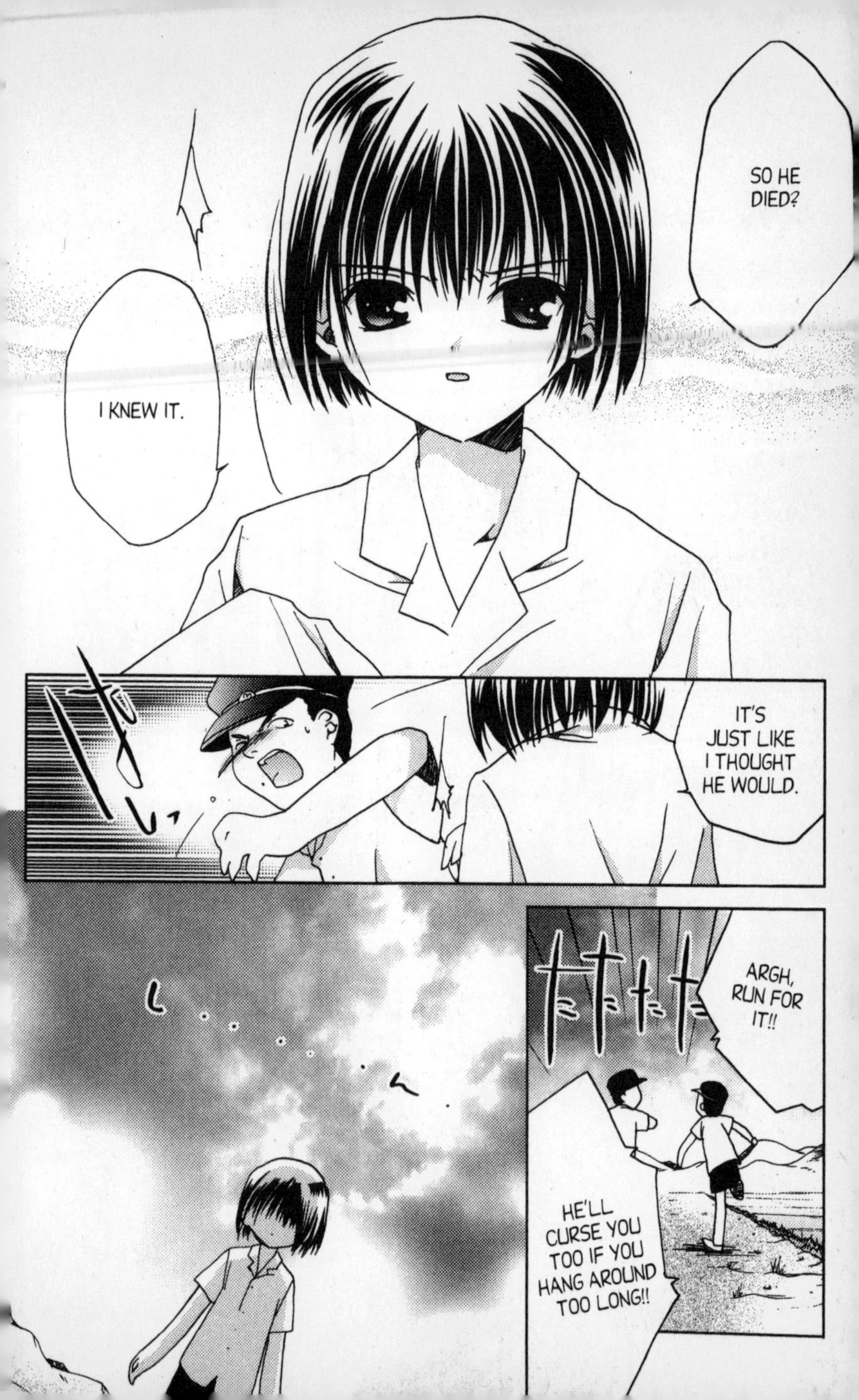

SO HE DIED?
I KNEW IT.
IT'S JUST LIKE I THOUGHT HE WOULD.
ARGH, RUN FOR IT!!
HE'LL CURSE YOU TOO IF YOU HANG AROUND TOO LONG!!

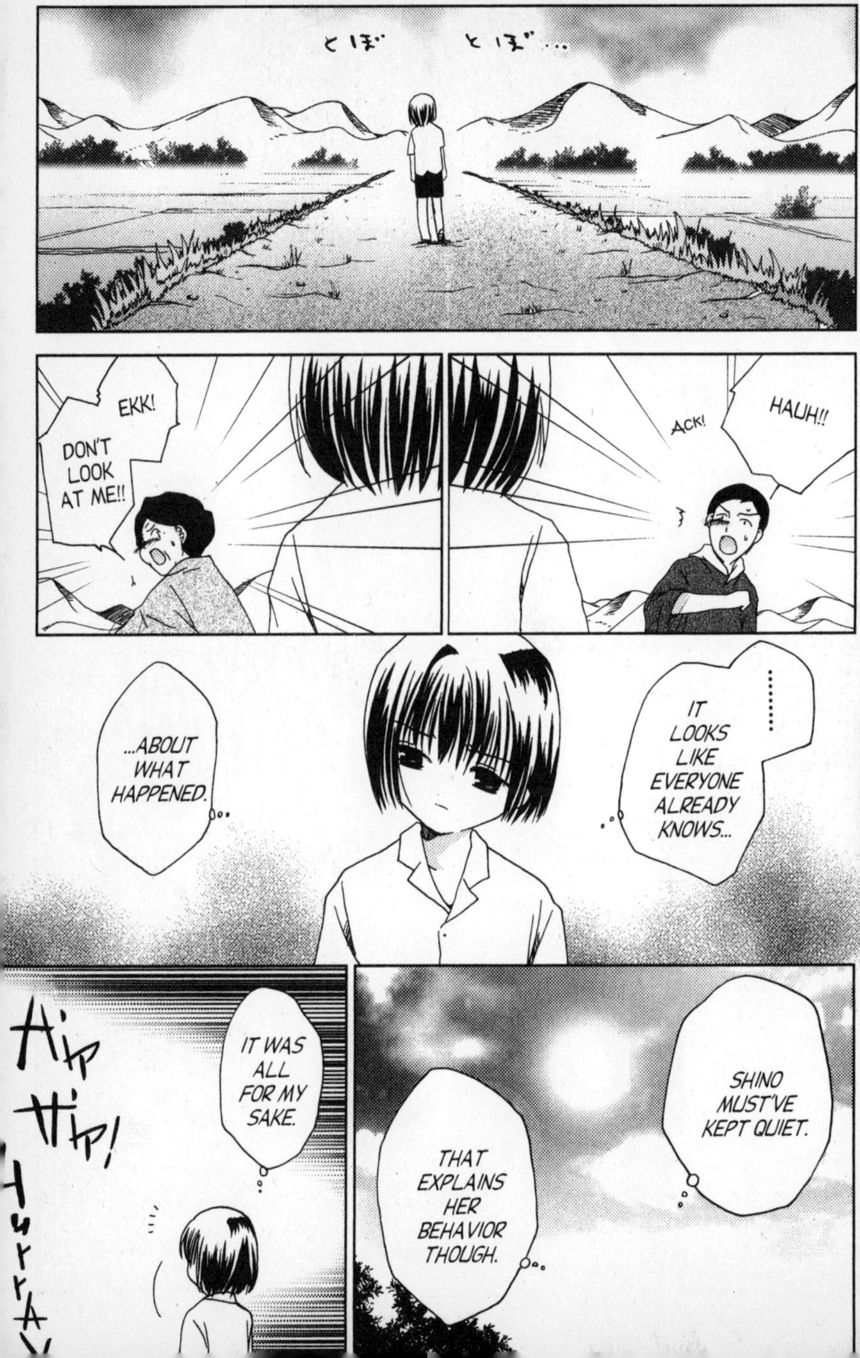
とぼ とぼ…
HAUH!!
ACK!
EKK!
DON'T LOOK AT ME!!
IT LOOKS LIKE EVERYONE ALREADY KNOWS...
......
...ABOUT WHAT HAPPENED.
SHINO MUST'VE KEPT QUIET.
THAT EXPLAINS HER BEHAVIOR THOUGH.
IT WAS ALL FOR MY SAKE.
Hip Hip!
Hurra

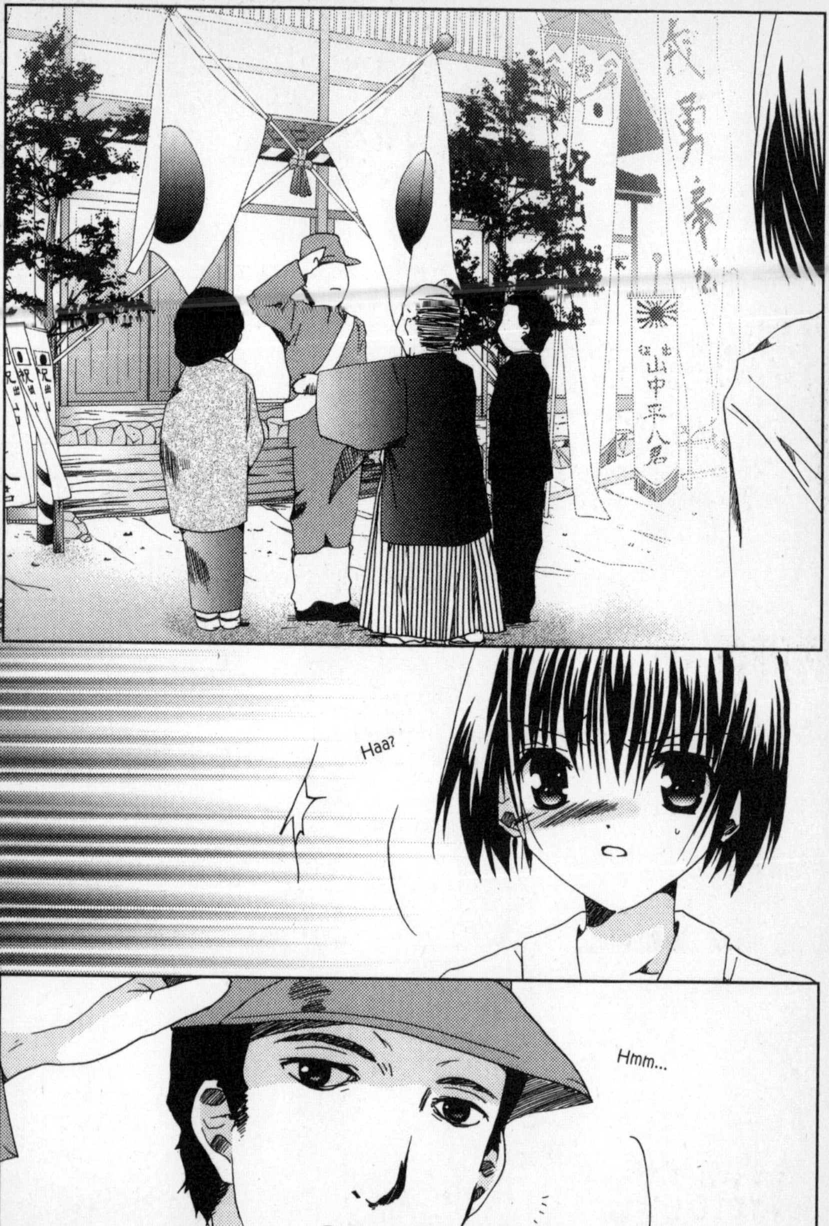
Haa?
Hmm...

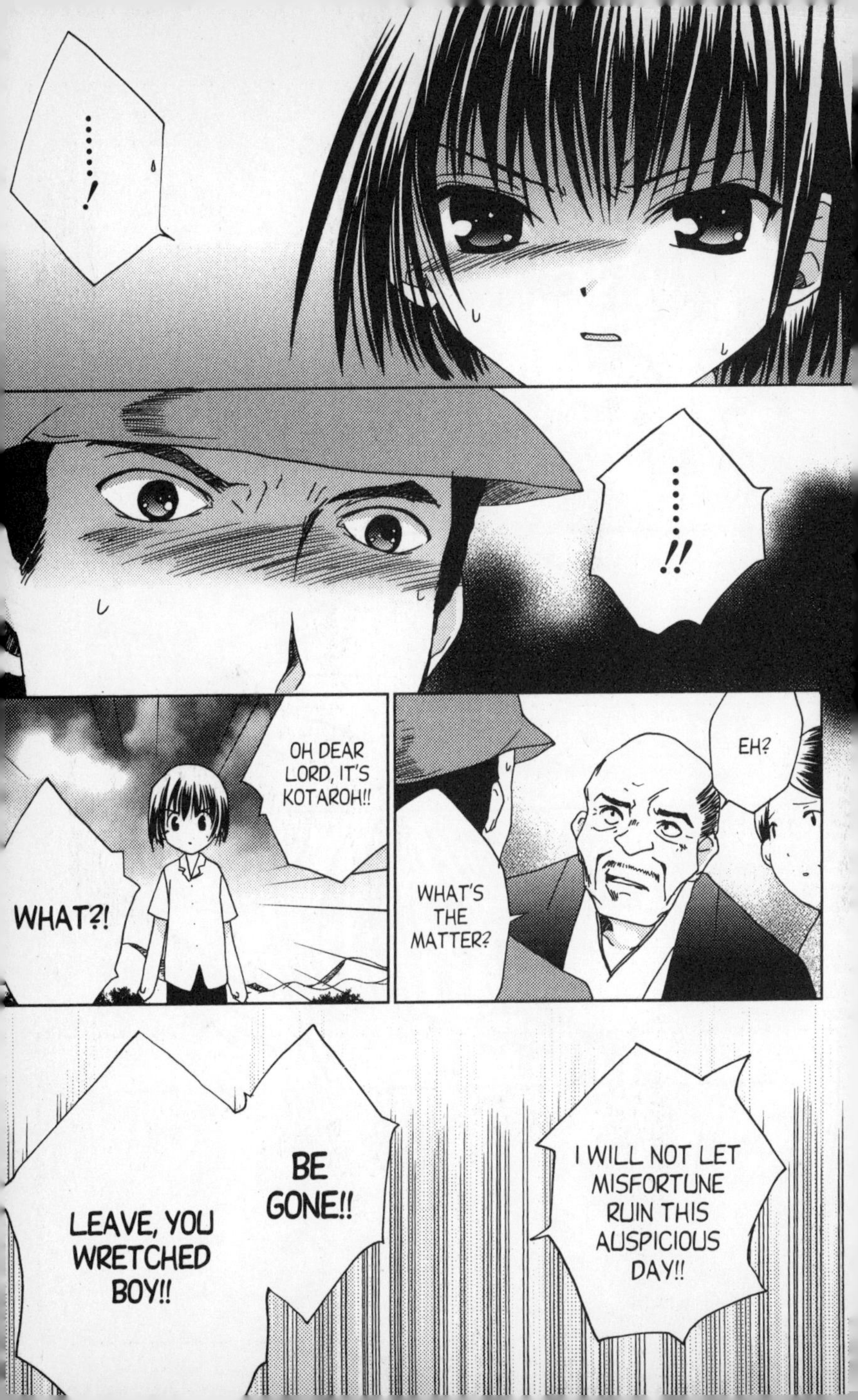
......!
......!!
EH?
WHAT'S THE MATTER?
OH DEAR LORD, IT'S KOTAROH!!
WHAT?!
I WILL NOT LET MISFORTUNE RUIN THIS AUSPICIOUS DAY!!
BE GONE!!
LEAVE, YOU WRETCHED BOY!!

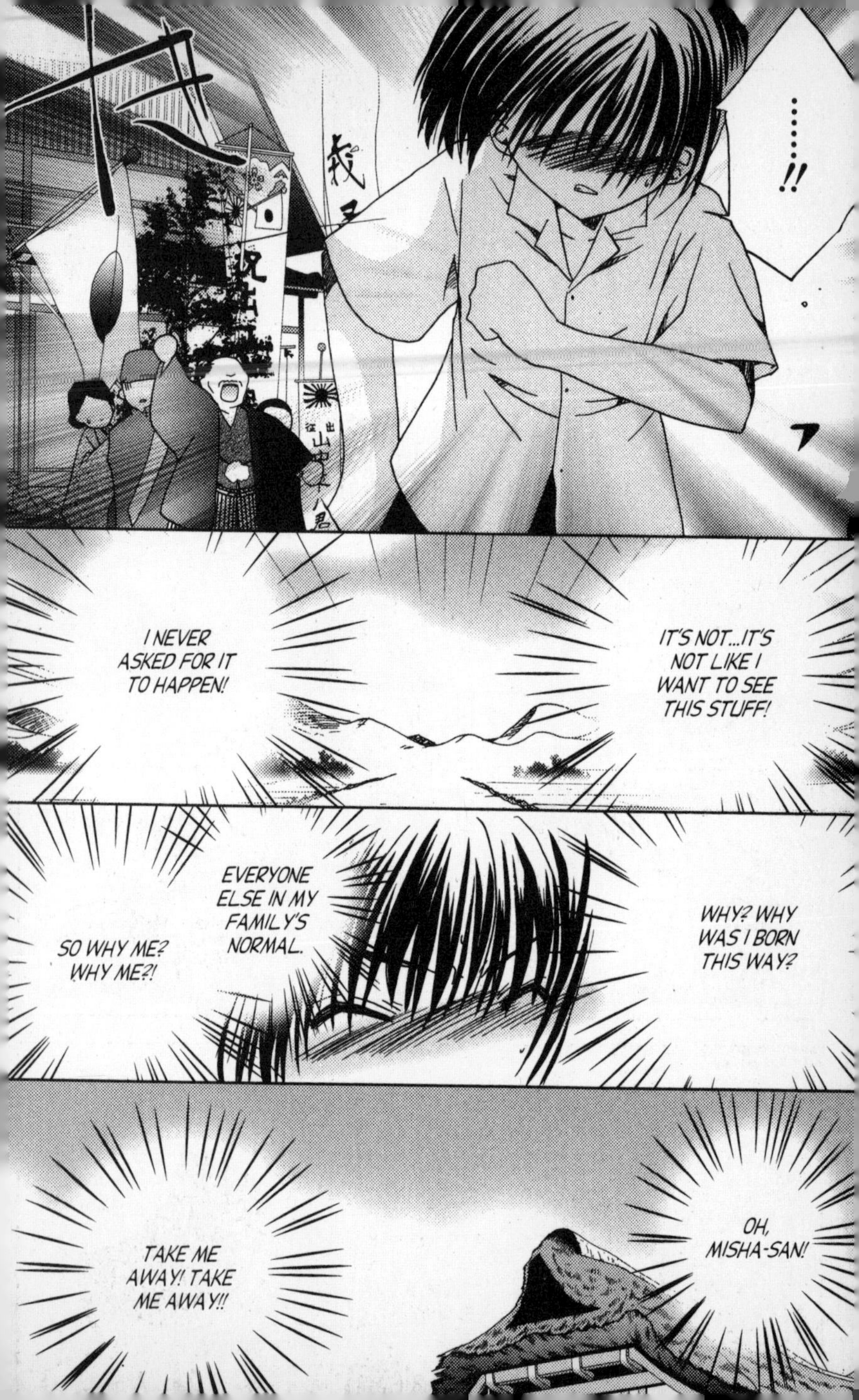
......!!
IT'S NOT...IT'S NOT LIKE I WANT TO SEE THIS STUFF!
I NEVER ASKED FOR IT TO HAPPEN!
WHY? WHY WAS I BORN THIS WAY?
EVERYONE ELSE IN MY FAMILY'S NORMAL.
SO WHY ME? WHY ME?!
OH, MISHA-SAN!
TAKE ME AWAY! TAKE ME AWAY!!

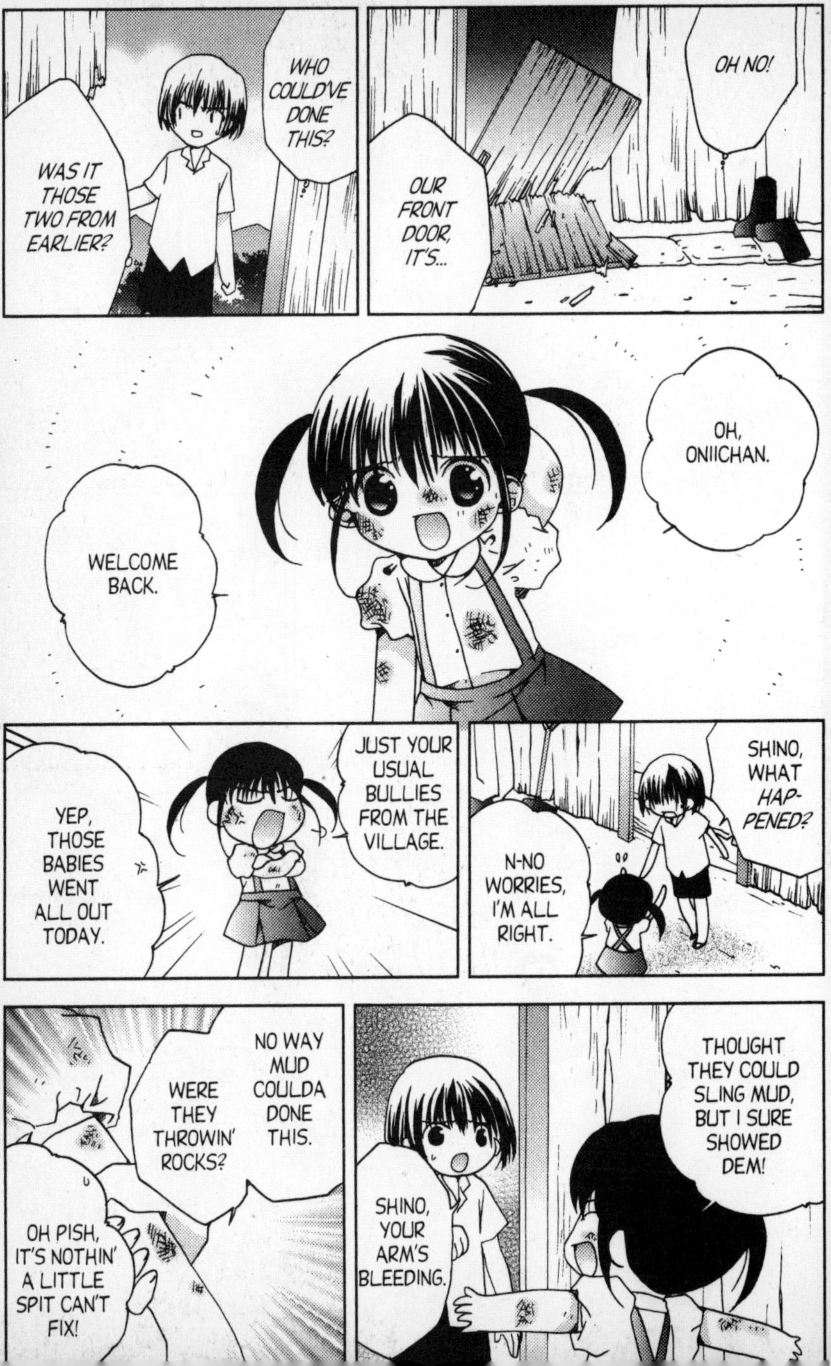
OH NO!
OUR FRONT DOOR, IT'S...
WHO COULD'VE DONE THIS?
WAS IT THOSE TWO FROM EARLIER?
OH, ONIICHAN.
WELCOME BACK.
SHINO, WHAT HAPPENED?
N-NO WORRIES, I'M ALL RIGHT.
JUST YOUR USUAL BULLIES FROM THE VILLAGE.
YEP, THOSE BABIES WENT ALL OUT TODAY.
THOUGHT THEY COULD SLING MUD, BUT I SURE SHOWED DEM!
SHINO, YOUR ARM'S BLEEDING.
NO WAY MUD COULDA DONE THIS.
WERE THEY THROWIN' ROCKS?
OH PISH, IT'S NOTHIN' A LITTLE SPIT CAN'T FIX!

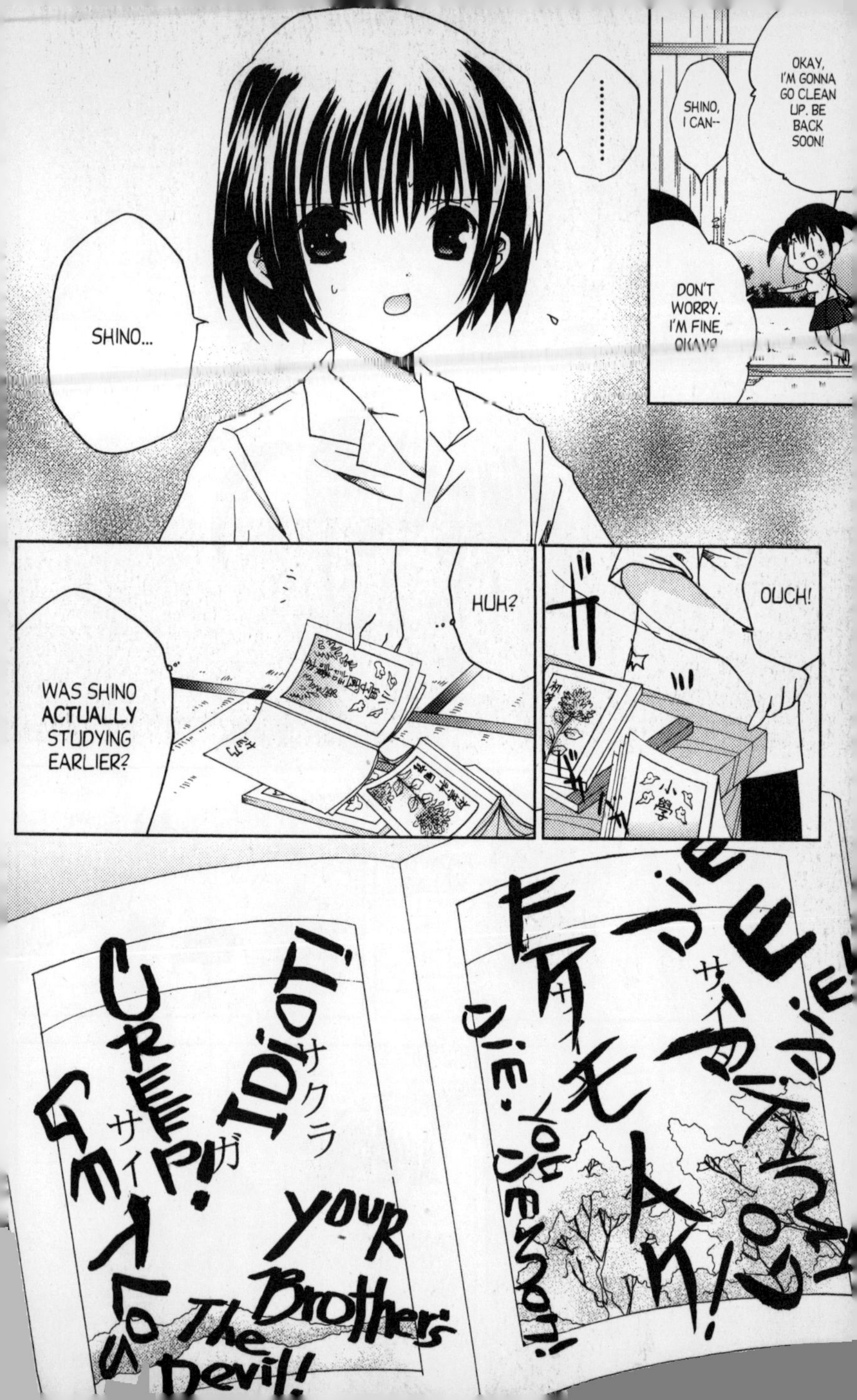
OKAY, I'M GONNA GO CLEAN UP. BE BACK SOON!
SHINO, I CAN--
DON'T WORRY. I'M FINE, OKAY?
......
SHINO...
OUCH!
HUH?
WAS SHINO ACTUALLY STUDYING EARLIER?
DIE, YOU DEMON!
IDIOT!
CREEP!
YOUR Brother's The Devil!

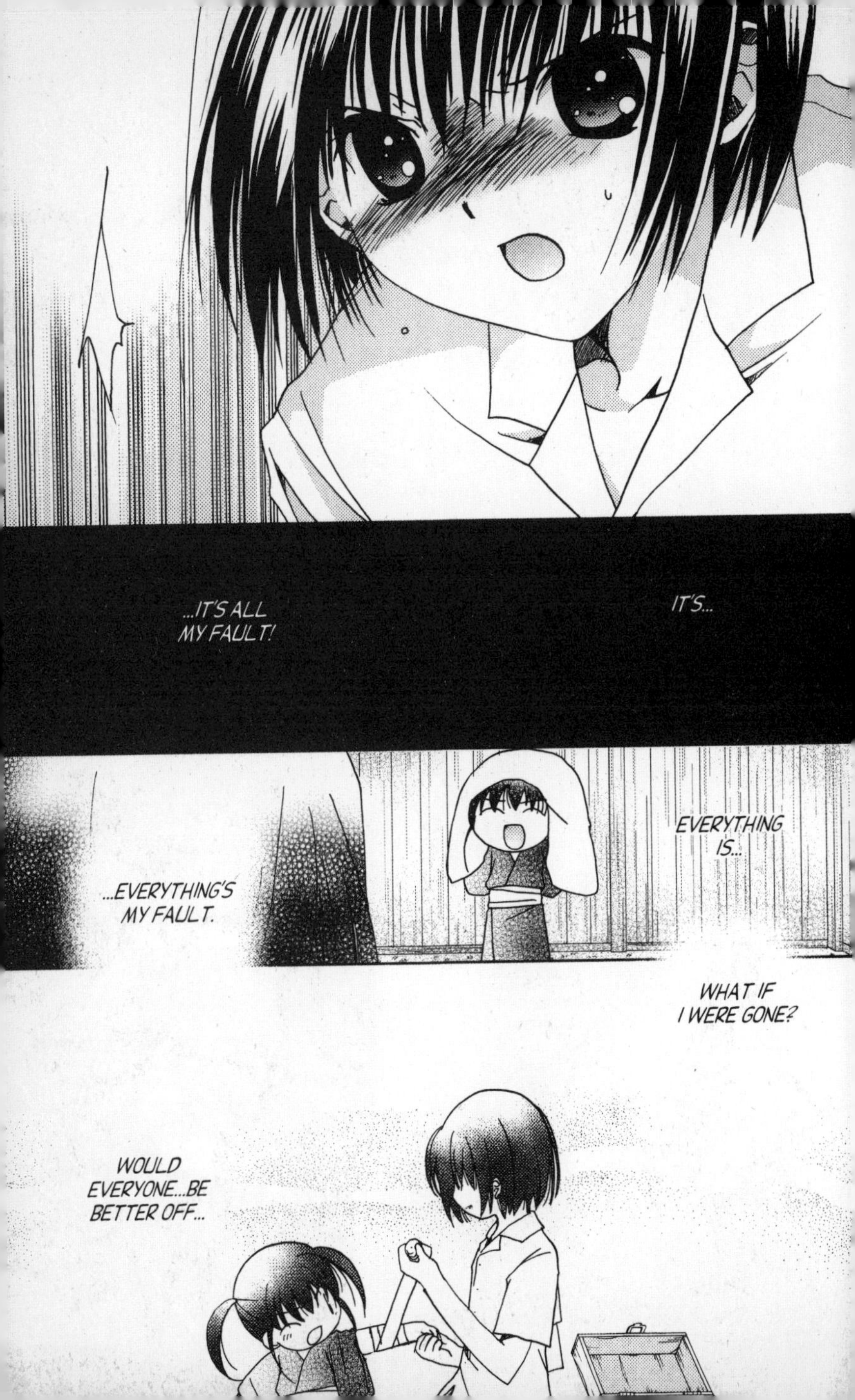
IT'S...
...IT'S ALL MY FAULT!
EVERYTHING IS...
...EVERYTHING'S MY FAULT.
WHAT IF I WERE GONE?
WOULD EVERYONE...BE BETTER OFF...

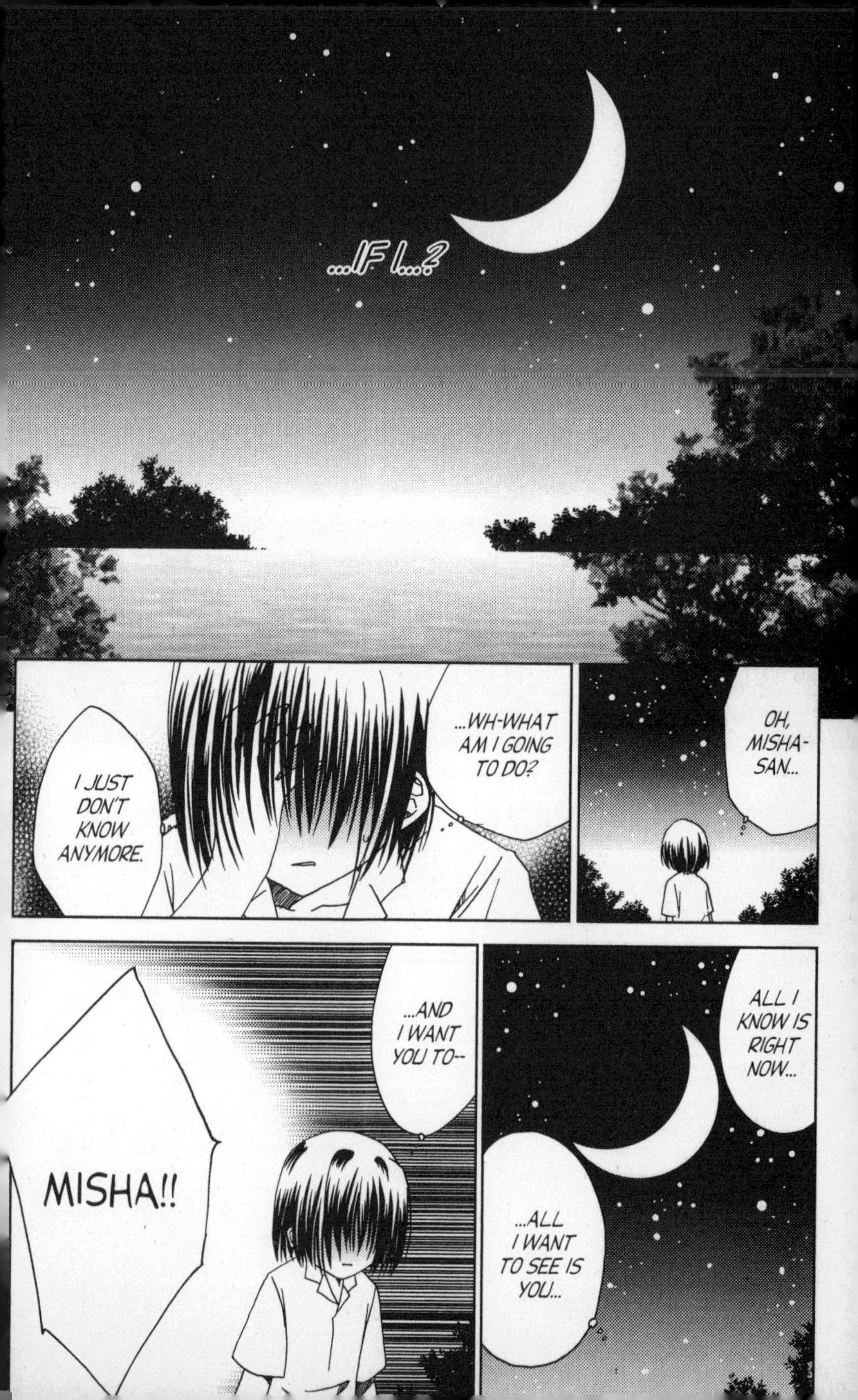
...IF I...?
OH, MISHA-SAN...
...WH-WHAT AM I GOING TO DO?
I JUST DON'T KNOW ANYMORE.
ALL I KNOW IS RIGHT NOW...
...ALL I WANT TO SEE IS YOU...
...AND I WANT YOU TO--
MISHA!!

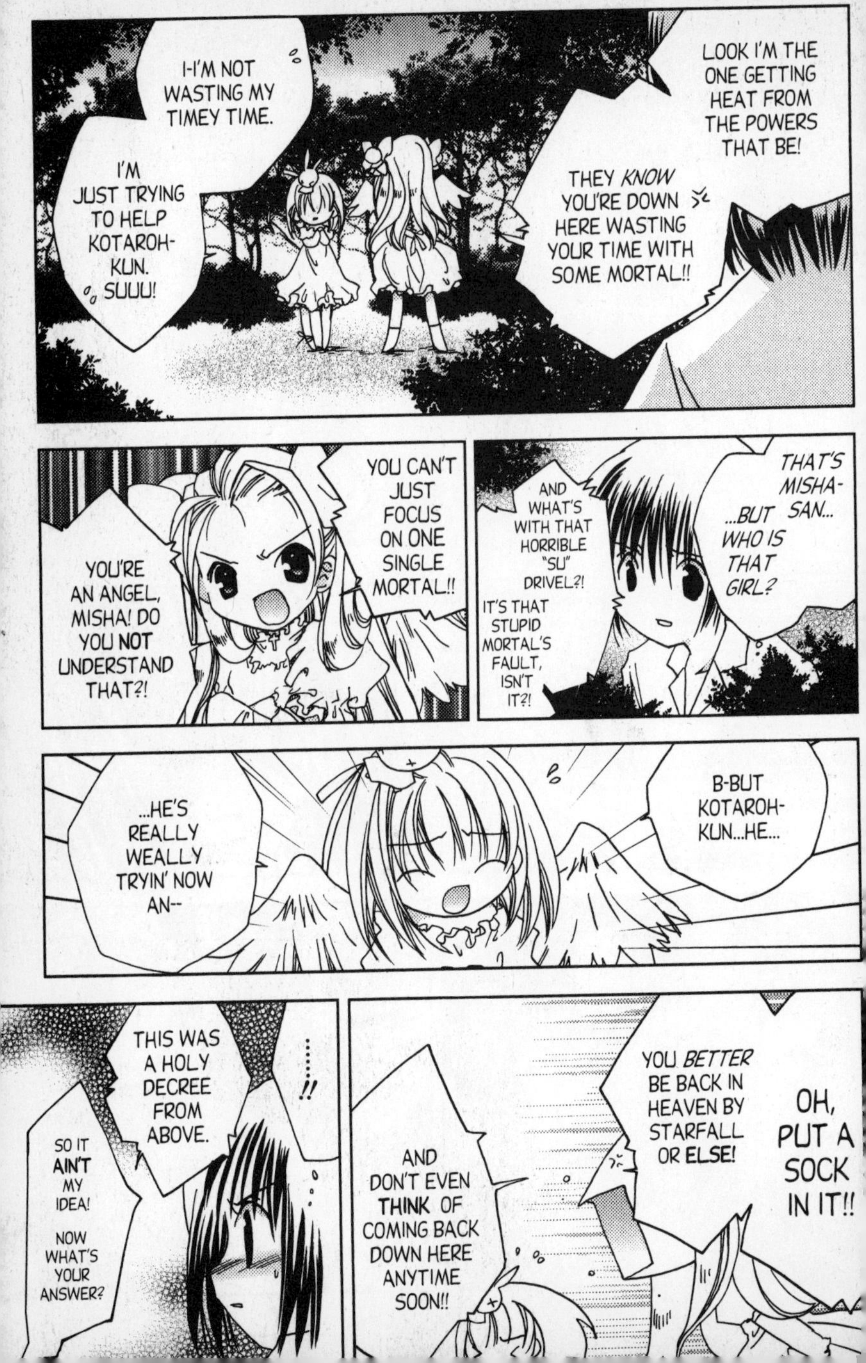

LOOK I'M THE ONE GETTING HEAT FROM THE POWERS THAT BE!
THEY *KNOW* YOU'RE DOWN HERE WASTING YOUR TIME WITH SOME MORTAL!!
I-I'M NOT WASTING MY TIMEY TIME.
I'M JUST TRYING TO HELP KOTAROH-KUN. SUUU!
THAT'S MISHA-SAN...
...BUT WHO IS THAT GIRL?
AND WHAT'S WITH THAT HORRIBLE "SU" DRIVEL?!
IT'S THAT STUPID MORTAL'S FAULT, ISN'T IT?!
YOU CAN'T JUST FOCUS ON ONE SINGLE MORTAL!!
YOU'RE AN ANGEL, MISHA! DO YOU **NOT** UNDERSTAND THAT?!
B-BUT KOTAROH-KUN...HE...
...HE'S REALLY WEALLY TRYIN' NOW AN--
OH, PUT A SOCK IN IT!!
YOU *BETTER* BE BACK IN HEAVEN BY STARFALL OR **ELSE**!
AND DON'T EVEN **THINK** OF COMING BACK DOWN HERE ANYTIME SOON!!
......!!
THIS WAS A HOLY DECREE FROM ABOVE.
SO IT **AIN'T** MY IDEA! NOW WHAT'S YOUR ANSWER?

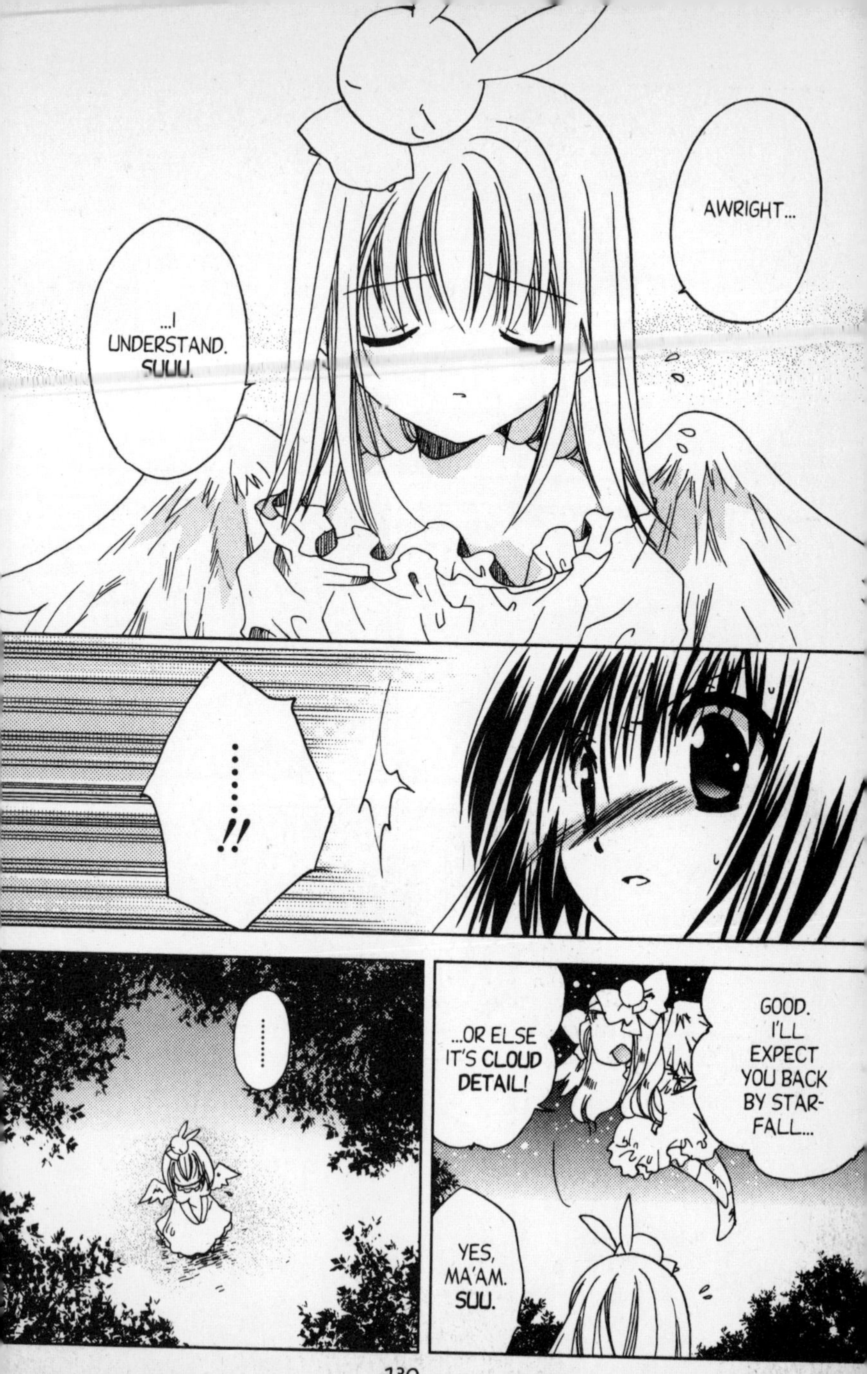
AWRIGHT...
...I UNDERSTAND. SUUU.
......!!
GOOD. I'LL EXPECT YOU BACK BY STAR-FALL...
...OR ELSE IT'S CLOUD DETAIL!
YES, MA'AM. SUU.
......

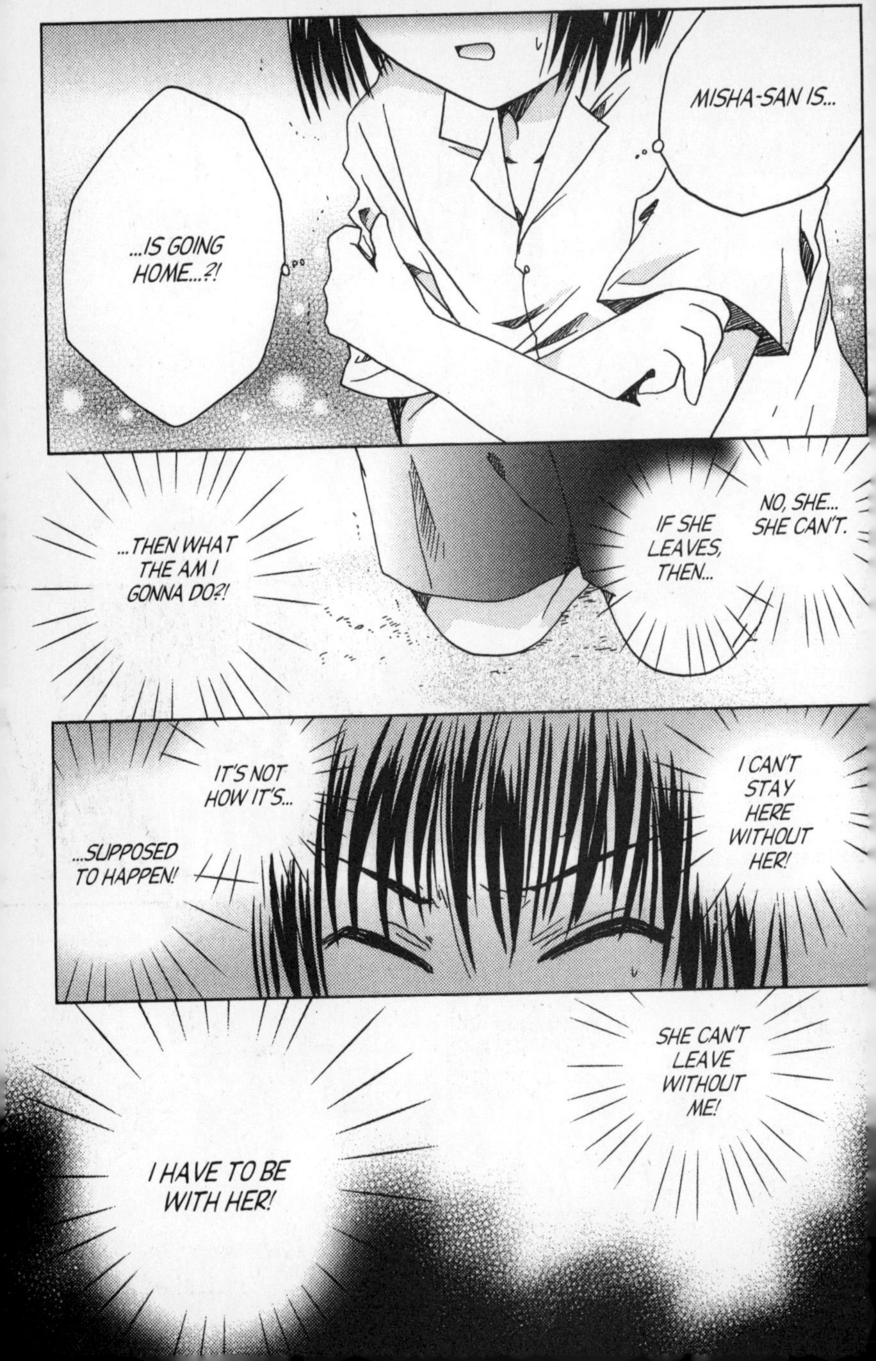
MISHA-SAN IS...
...IS GOING HOME...?!
NO, SHE... SHE CAN'T.
IF SHE LEAVES, THEN...
...THEN WHAT THE AM I GONNA DO?!
I CAN'T STAY HERE WITHOUT HER!
IT'S NOT HOW IT'S...
...SUPPOSED TO HAPPEN!
SHE CAN'T LEAVE WITHOUT ME!
I HAVE TO BE WITH HER!

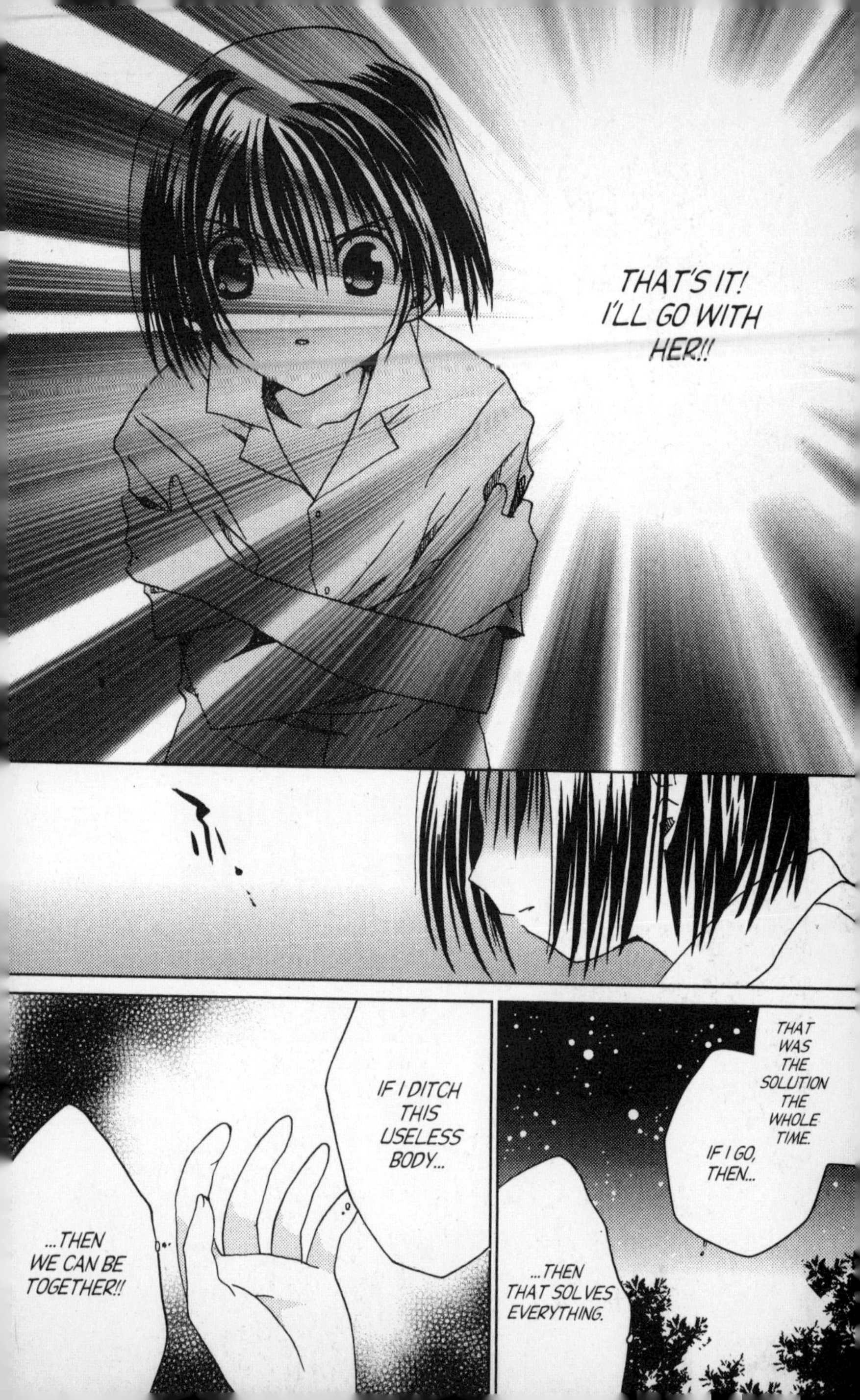
THAT'S IT! I'LL GO WITH HER!!
THAT WAS THE SOLUTION THE WHOLE TIME.
IF I GO, THEN...
...THEN THAT SOLVES EVERYTHING.
IF I DITCH THIS USELESS BODY...
...THEN WE CAN BE TOGETHER!!

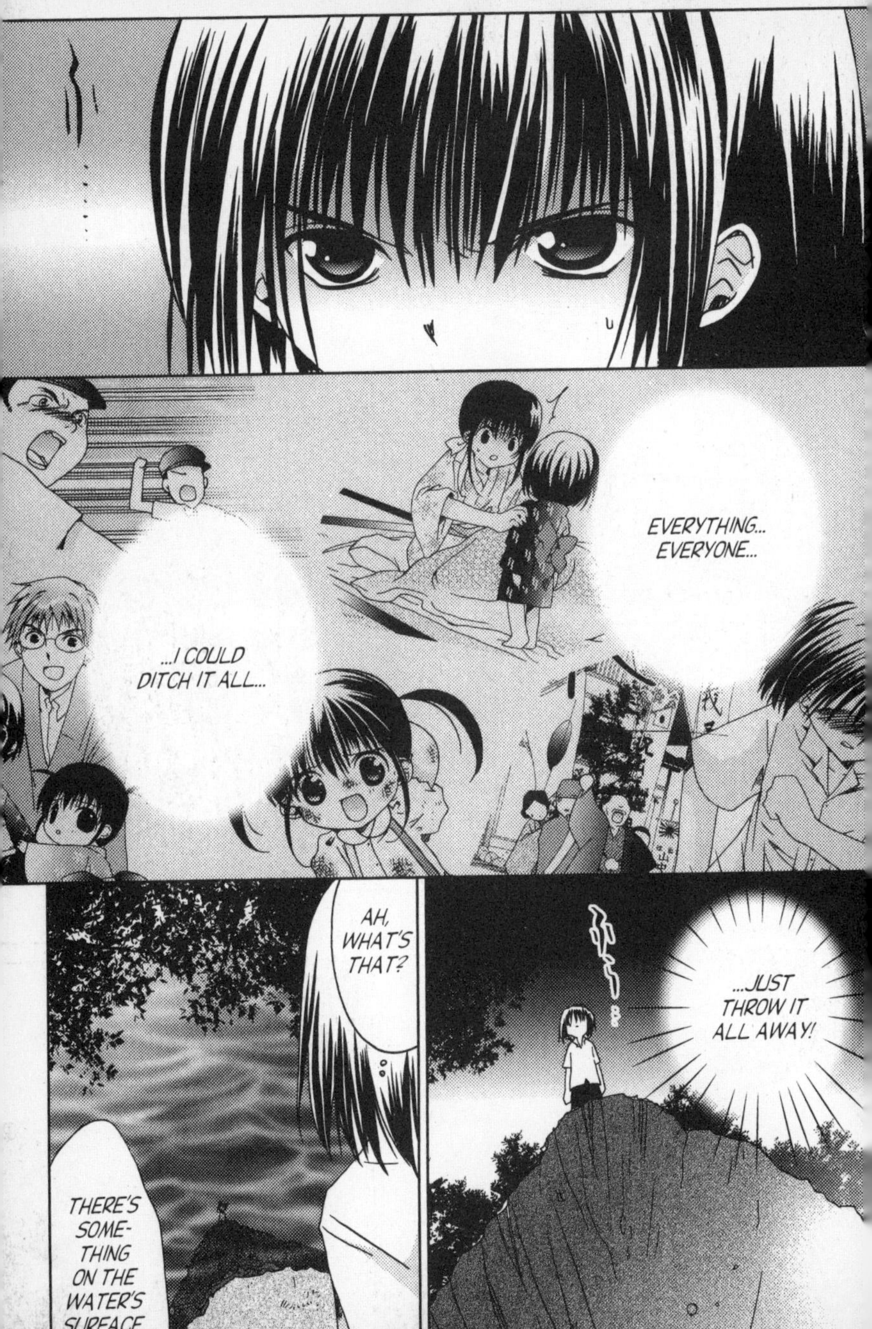
EVERYTHING... EVERYONE...
...I COULD DITCH IT ALL...
...JUST THROW IT ALL AWAY!
AH, WHAT'S THAT?
THERE'S SOME-THING ON THE WATER'S SURFACE.

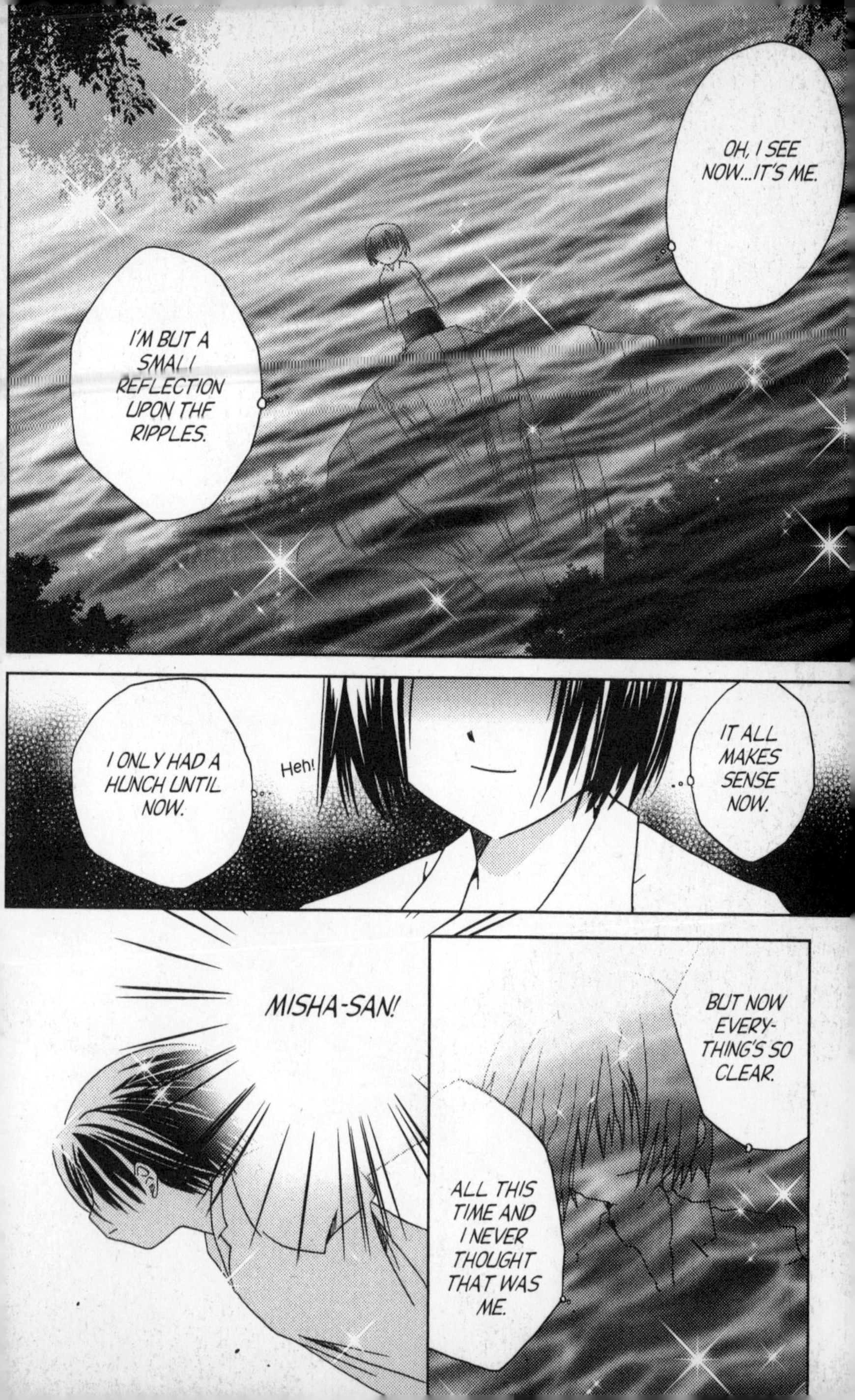
OH, I SEE NOW...IT'S ME.
I'M BUT A SMALL REFLECTION UPON THE RIPPLES.
IT ALL MAKES SENSE NOW.
Heh!
I ONLY HAD A HUNCH UNTIL NOW.
BUT NOW EVERYTHING'S SO CLEAR.
ALL THIS TIME AND I NEVER THOUGHT THAT WAS ME.
MISHA-SAN!

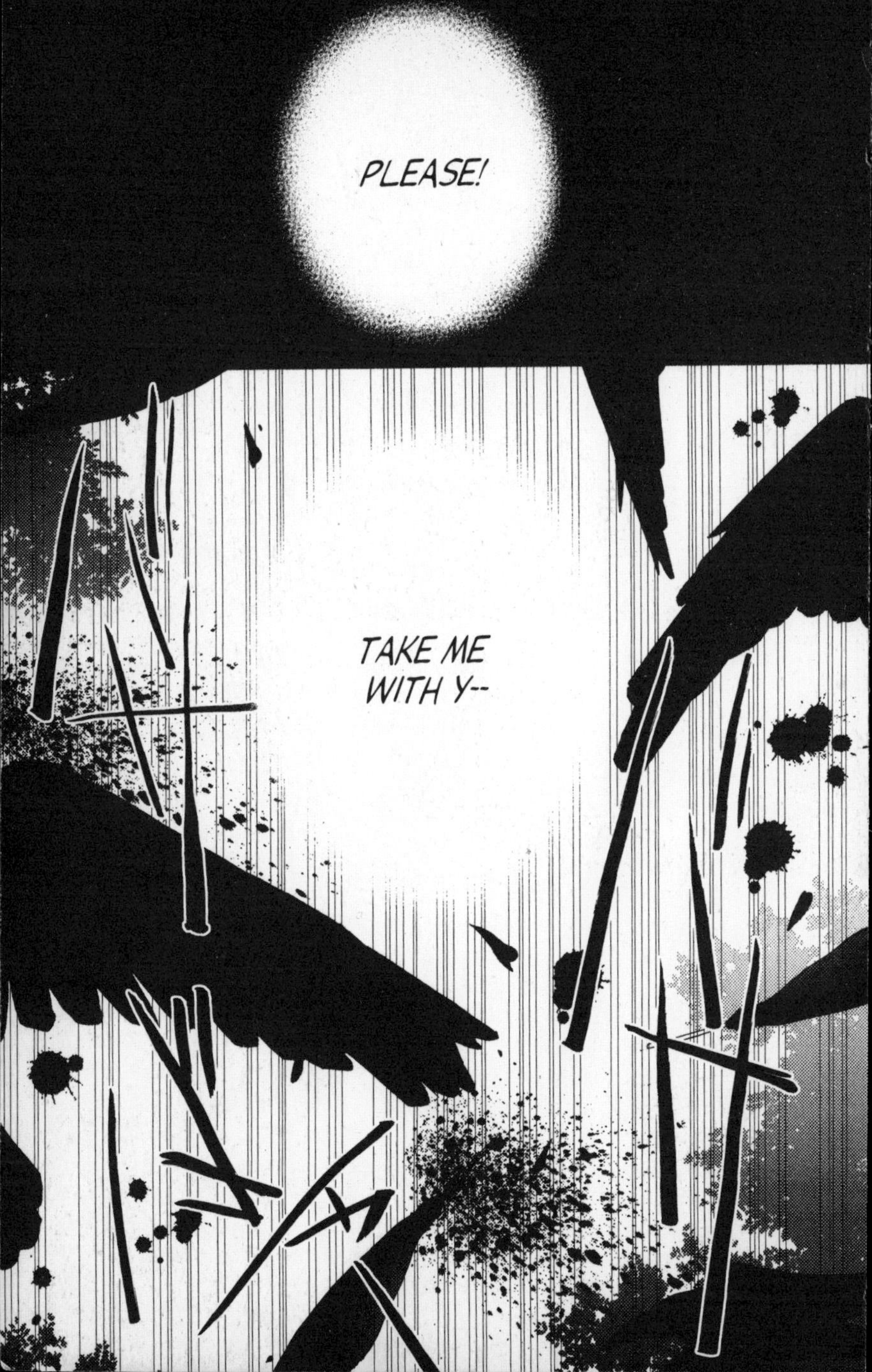
PLEASE!
TAKE ME WITH Y--

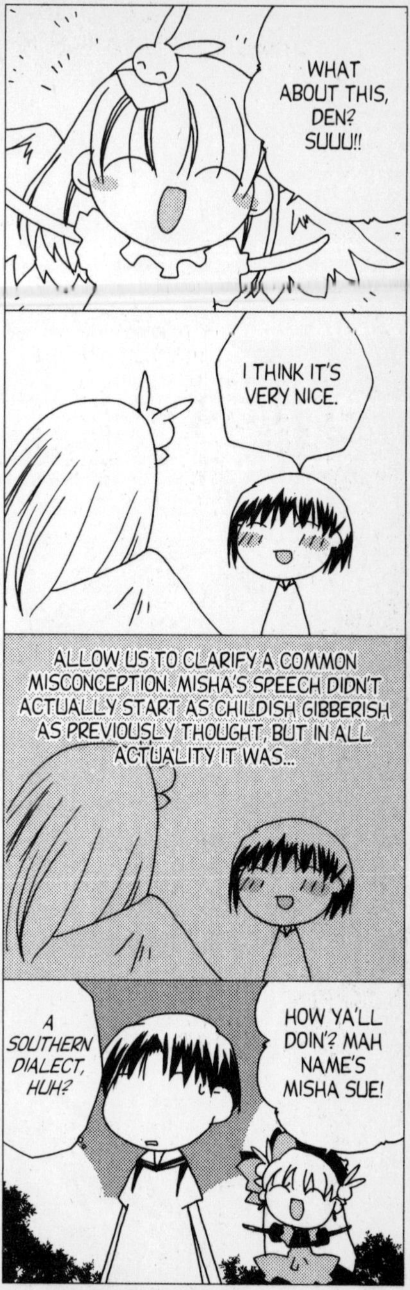
WHAT ABOUT THIS, DEN? SUUU!!
I THINK IT'S VERY NICE.
ALLOW US TO CLARIFY A COMMON MISCONCEPTION. MISHA'S SPEECH DIDN'T ACTUALLY START AS CHILDISH GIBBERISH AS PREVIOUSLY THOUGHT, BUT IN ALL ACTUALITY IT WAS...
HOW YA'LL DOIN'? MAH NAME'S MISHA SUE!
A SOUTHERN DIALECT, HUH?

Lesson 42
How to Find Yourself: Part 3

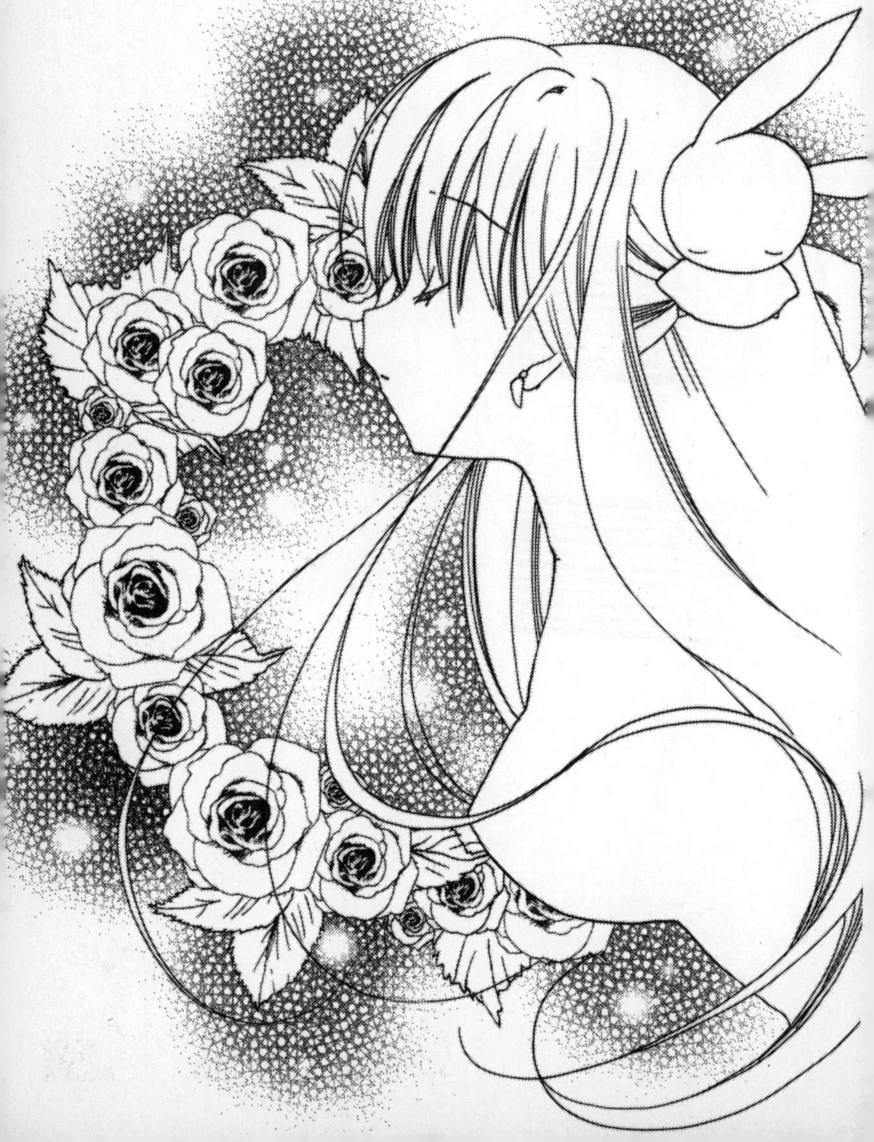

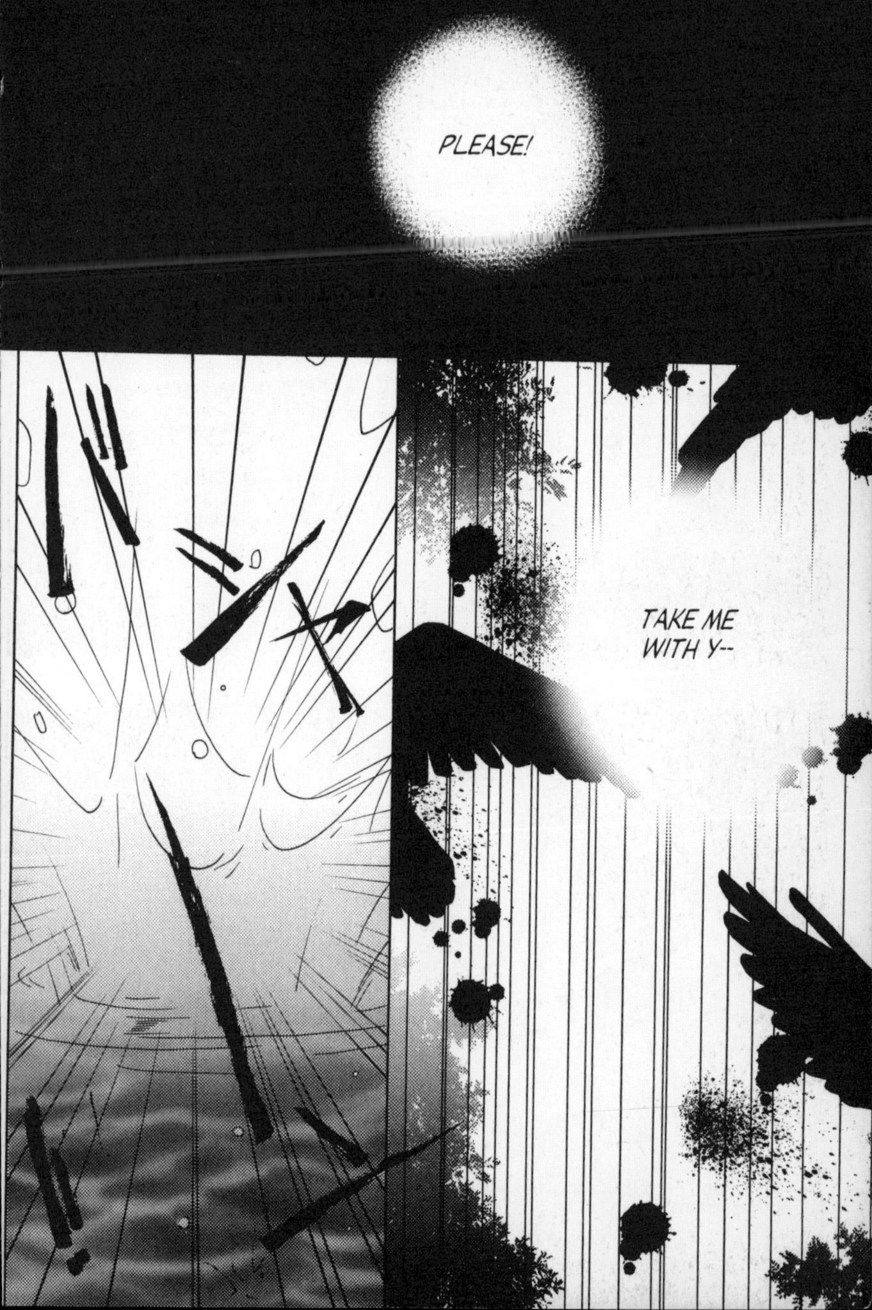
PLEASE!
TAKE ME WITH Y--

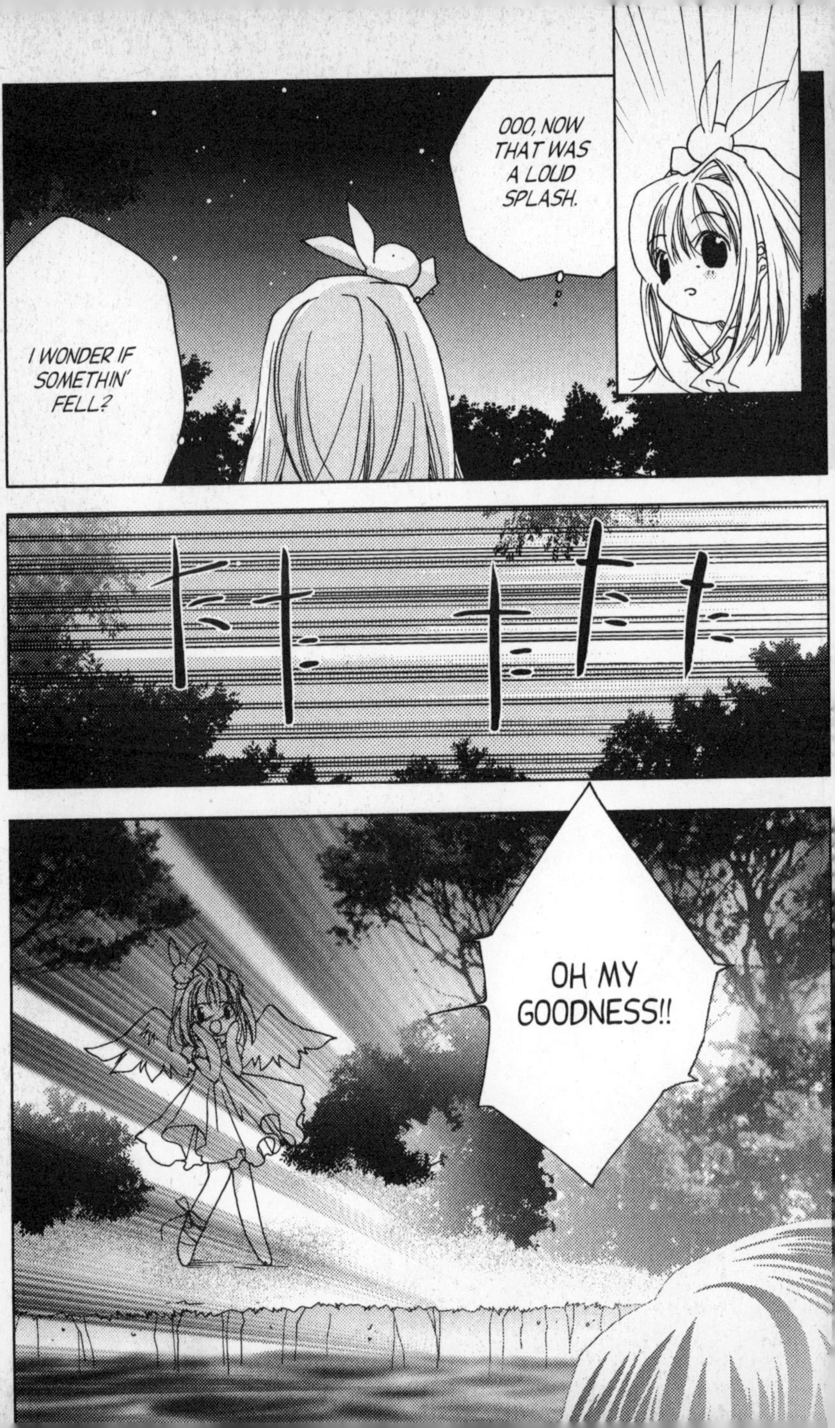
OOO, NOW THAT WAS A LOUD SPLASH.
I WONDER IF SOMETHIN' FELL?
OH MY GOODNESS!!

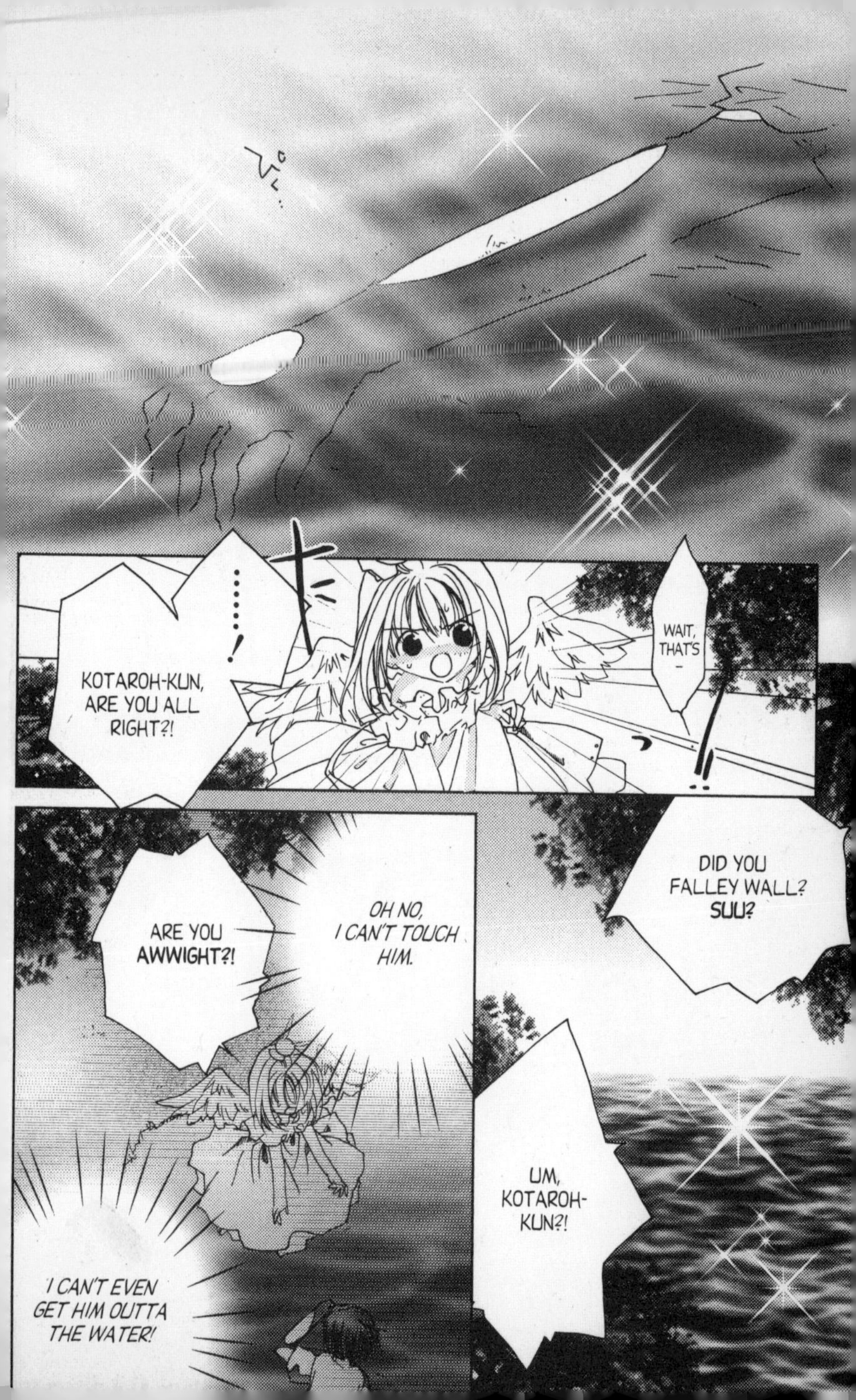
WAIT, THAT'S —
......!
KOTAROH-KUN, ARE YOU ALL RIGHT?!
DID YOU FALLEY WALL? SUU?
UM, KOTAROH-KUN?!
OH NO, I CAN'T TOUCH HIM.
ARE YOU AWWIGHT?!
I CAN'T EVEN GET HIM OUTTA THE WATER!

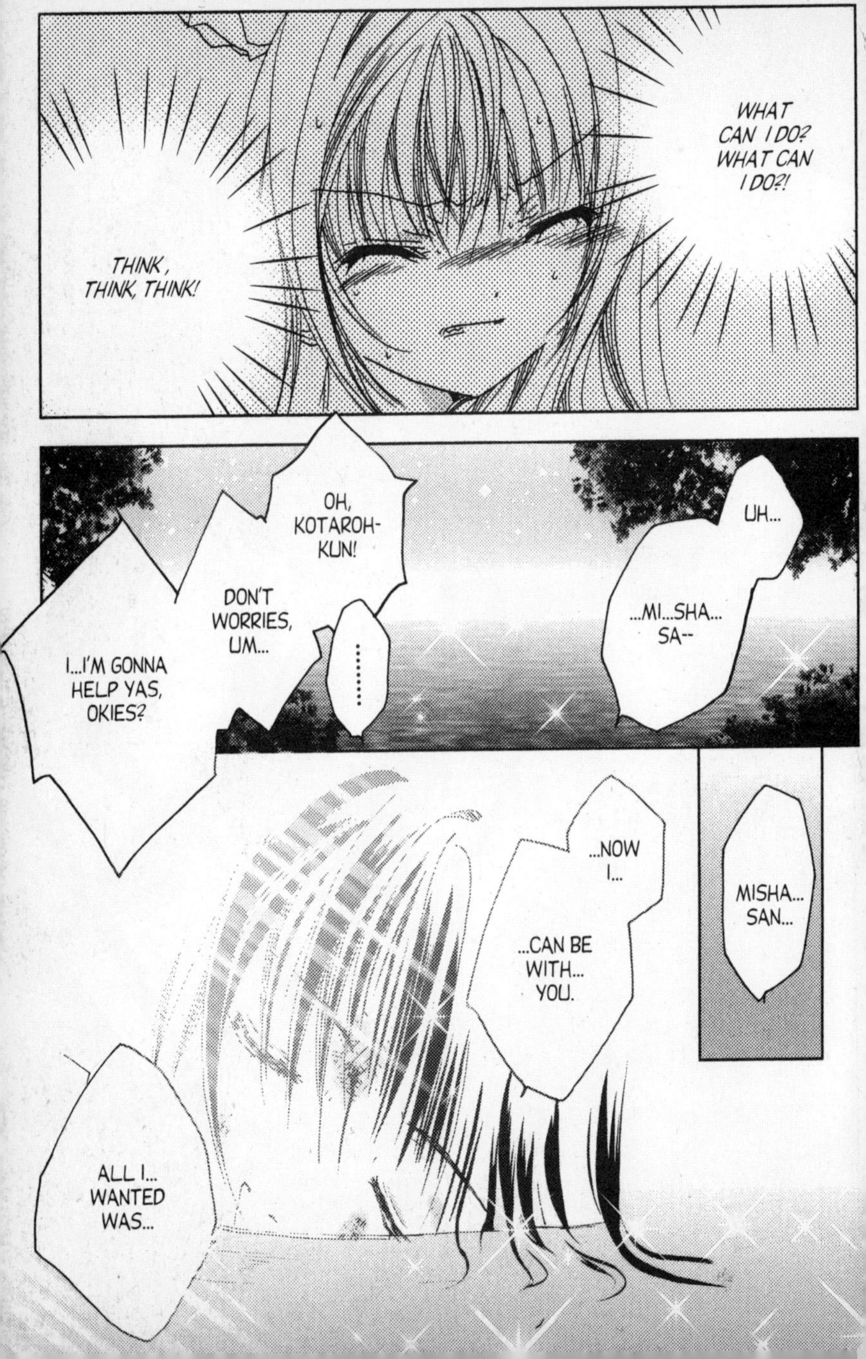
WHAT CAN I DO? WHAT CAN I DO?!
THINK, THINK, THINK!
UH...
...MI...SHA... SA--
....
OH, KOTAROH-KUN!
DON'T WORRIES, UM...
I...I'M GONNA HELP YAS, OKIES?
MISHA... SAN...
...NOW I...
...CAN BE WITH... YOU.
ALL I... WANTED WAS...

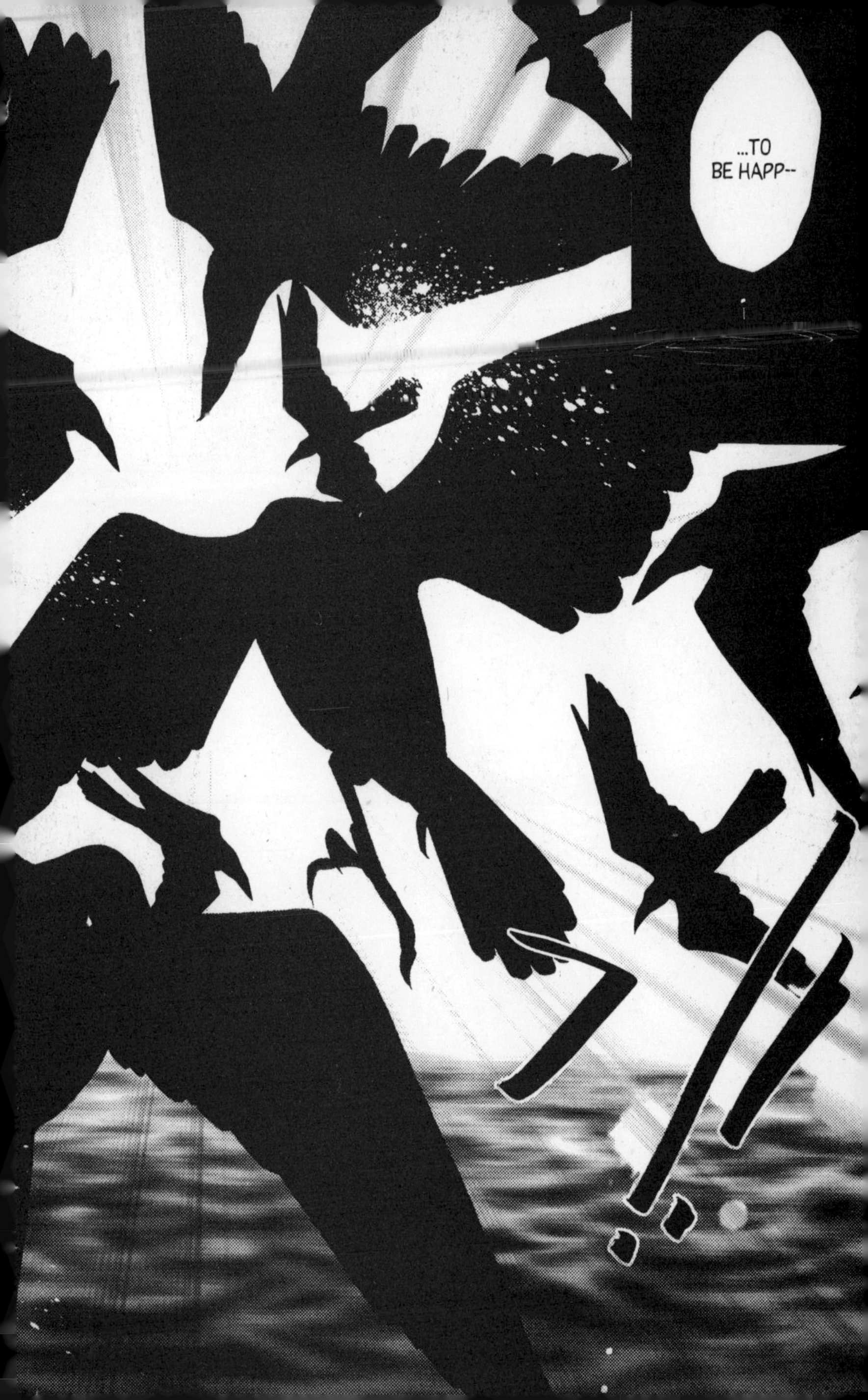
...TO
BE HAPP--

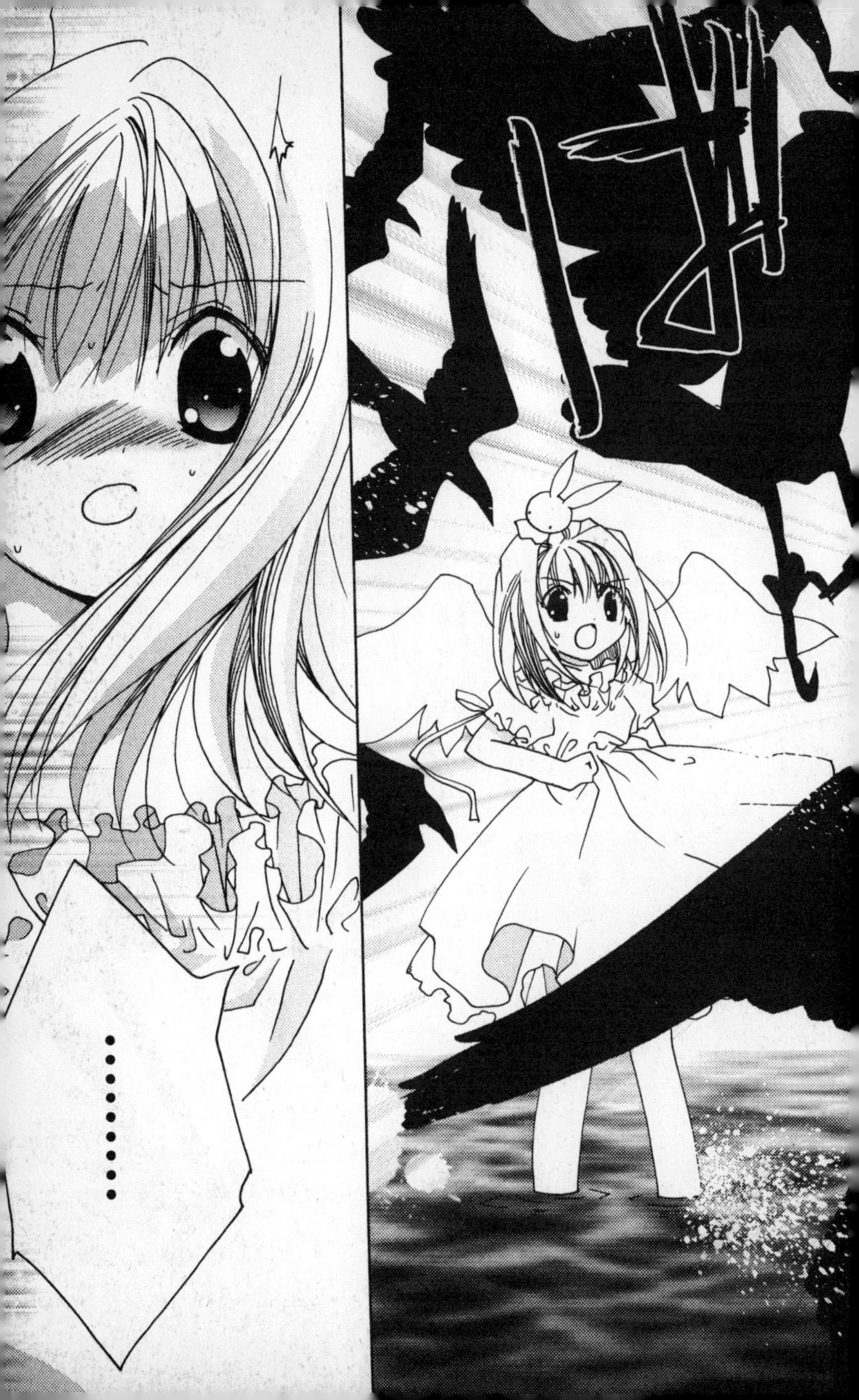
……

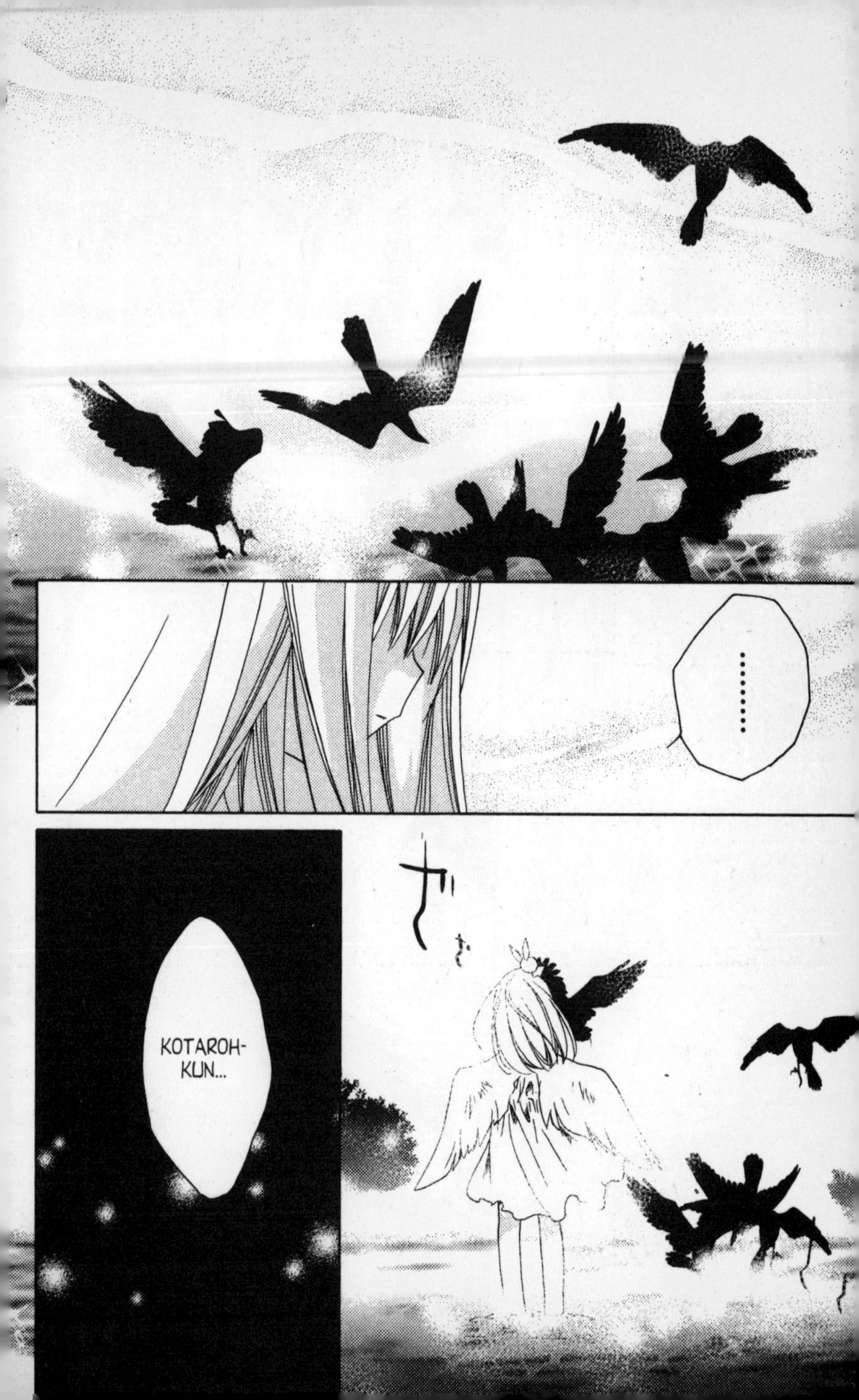
......
KOTAROH-KUN...

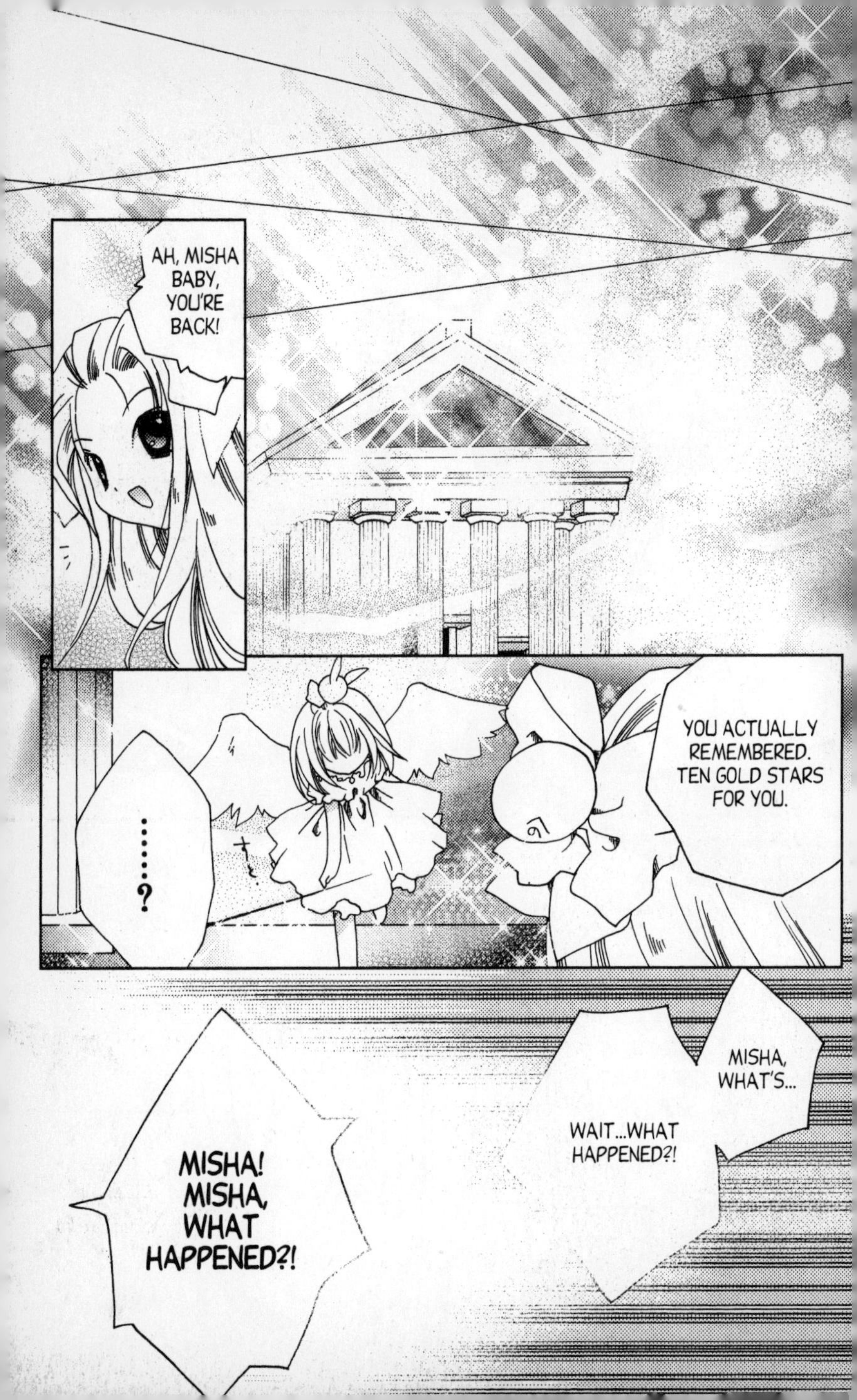
AH, MISHA BABY, YOU'RE BACK!
YOU ACTUALLY REMEMBERED. TEN GOLD STARS FOR YOU.
......?
MISHA, WHAT'S...
WAIT...WHAT HAPPENED?!
MISHA! MISHA, WHAT HAPPENED?!

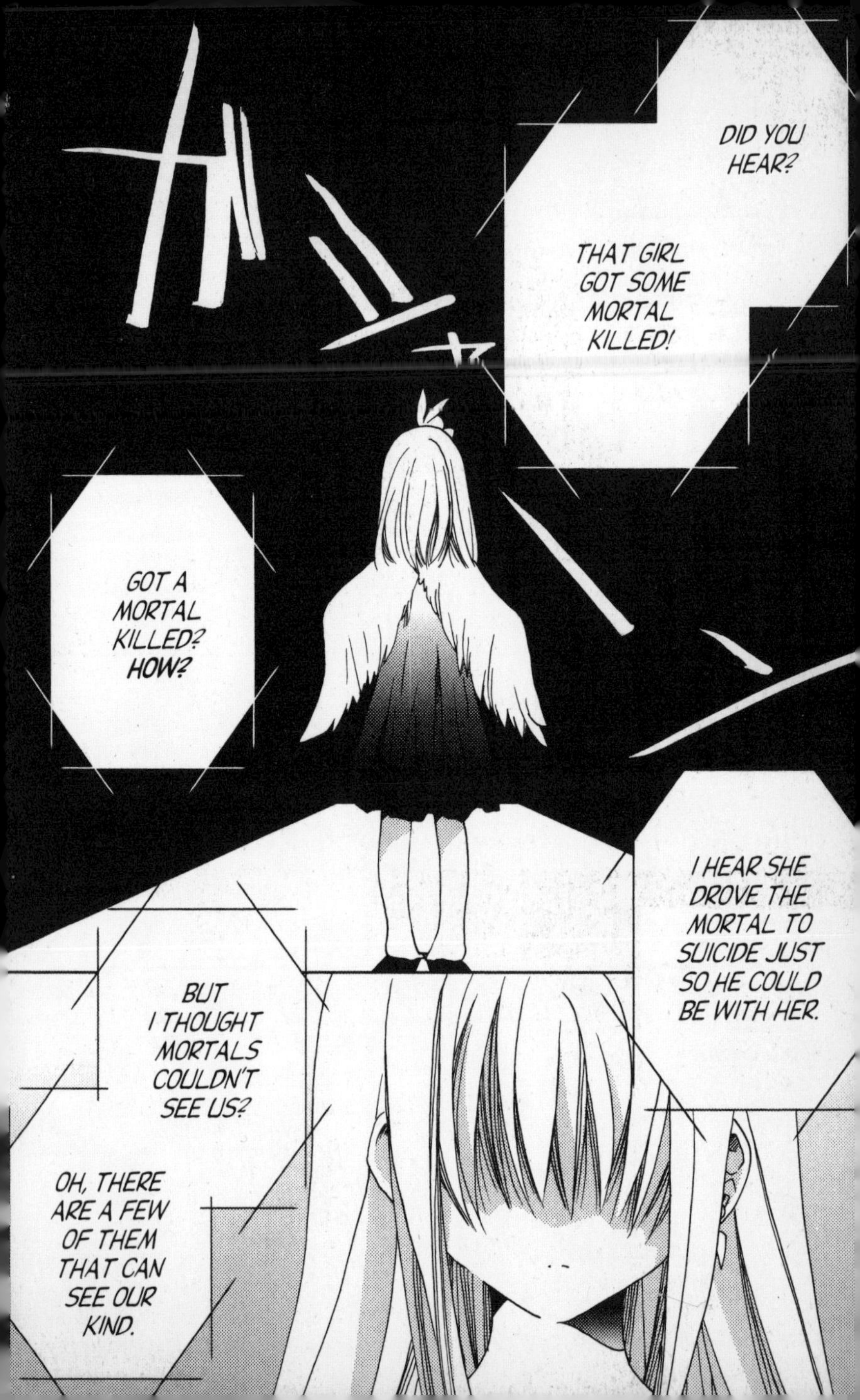
DID YOU HEAR?
THAT GIRL GOT SOME MORTAL KILLED!
GOT A MORTAL KILLED? HOW?
I HEAR SHE DROVE THE MORTAL TO SUICIDE JUST SO HE COULD BE WITH HER.
BUT I THOUGHT MORTALS COULDN'T SEE US?
OH, THERE ARE A FEW OF THEM THAT CAN SEE OUR KIND.

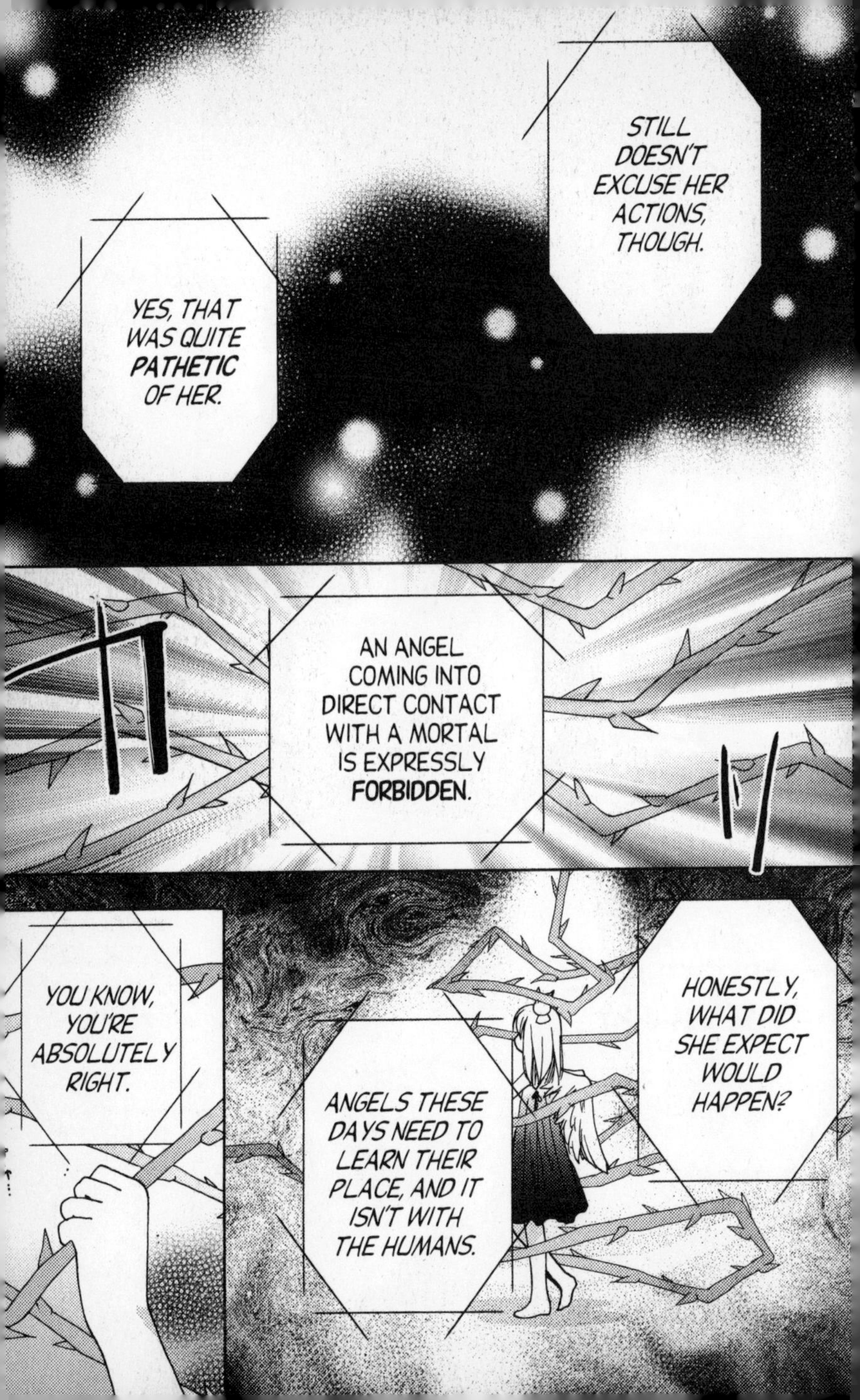
STILL DOESN'T EXCUSE HER ACTIONS, THOUGH.
YES, THAT WAS QUITE PATHETIC OF HER.
AN ANGEL COMING INTO DIRECT CONTACT WITH A MORTAL IS EXPRESSLY FORBIDDEN.
HONESTLY, WHAT DID SHE EXPECT WOULD HAPPEN?
ANGELS THESE DAYS NEED TO LEARN THEIR PLACE, AND IT ISN'T WITH THE HUMANS.
YOU KNOW, YOU'RE ABSOLUTELY RIGHT.

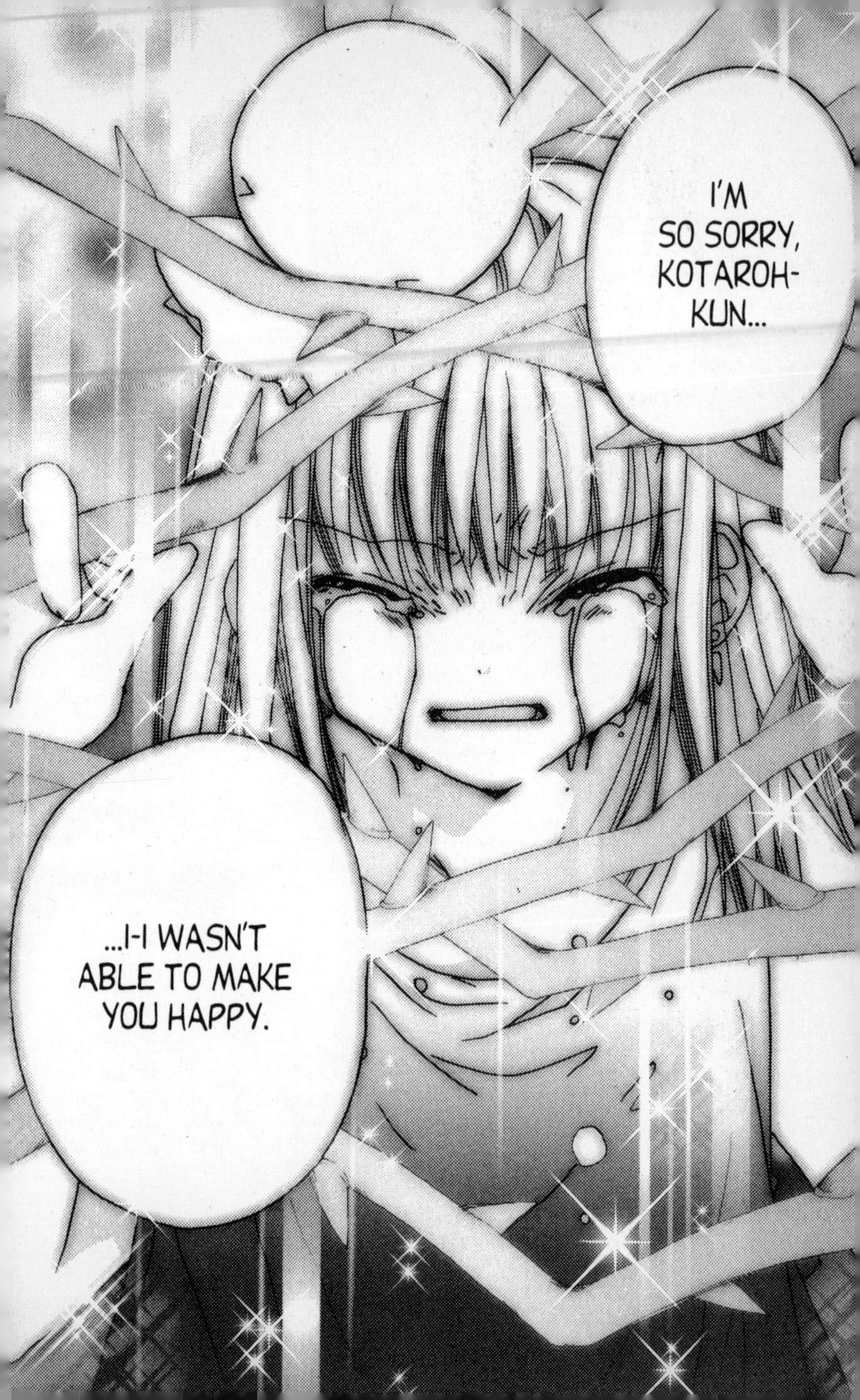
I'M SO SORRY, KOTAROH-KUN...
...I-I WASN'T ABLE TO MAKE YOU HAPPY.

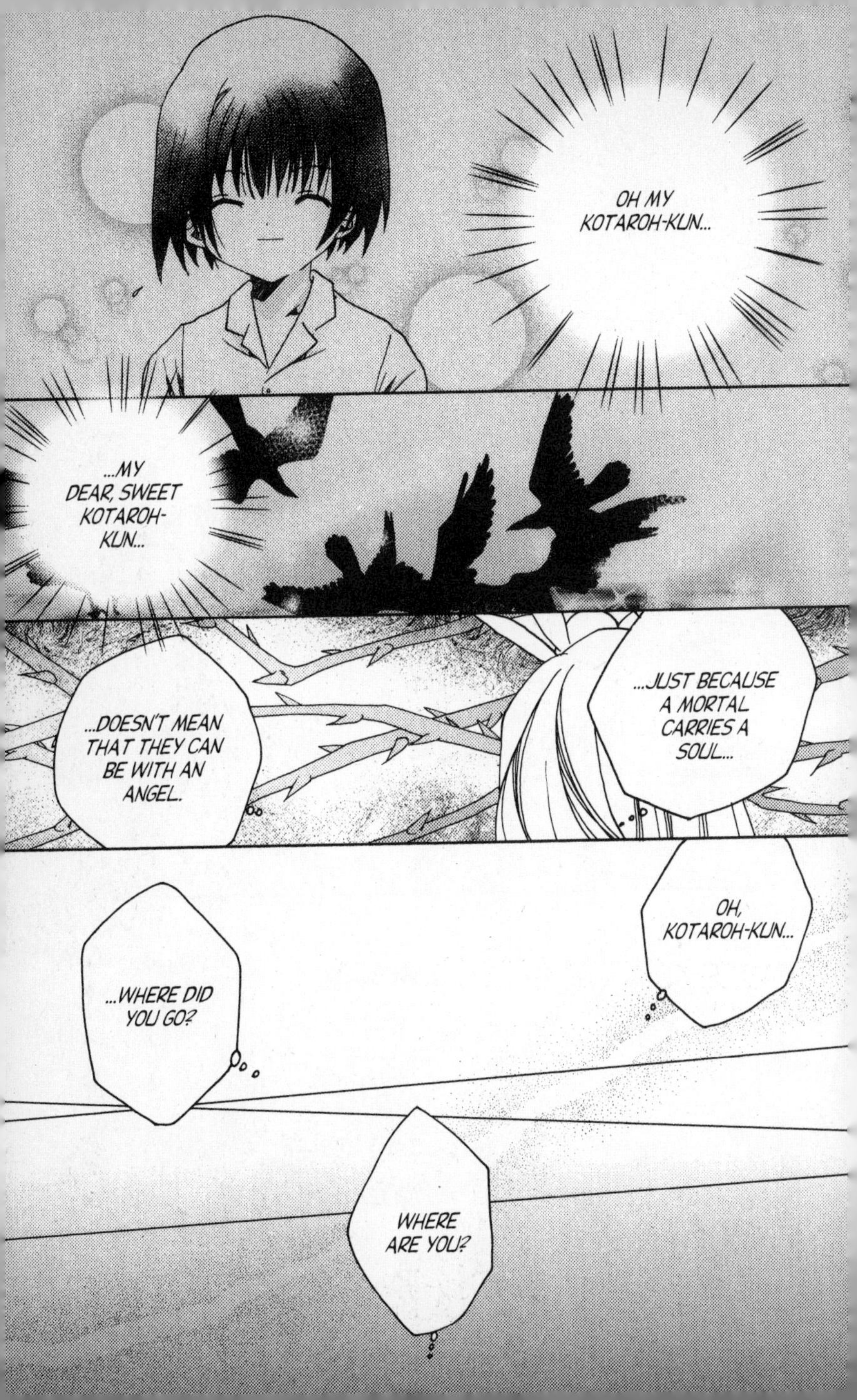
OH MY KOTAROH-KUN...
...MY DEAR, SWEET KOTAROH-KUN...
...JUST BECAUSE A MORTAL CARRIES A SOUL...
...DOESN'T MEAN THAT THEY CAN BE WITH AN ANGEL.
OH, KOTAROH-KUN...
...WHERE DID YOU GO?
WHERE ARE YOU?

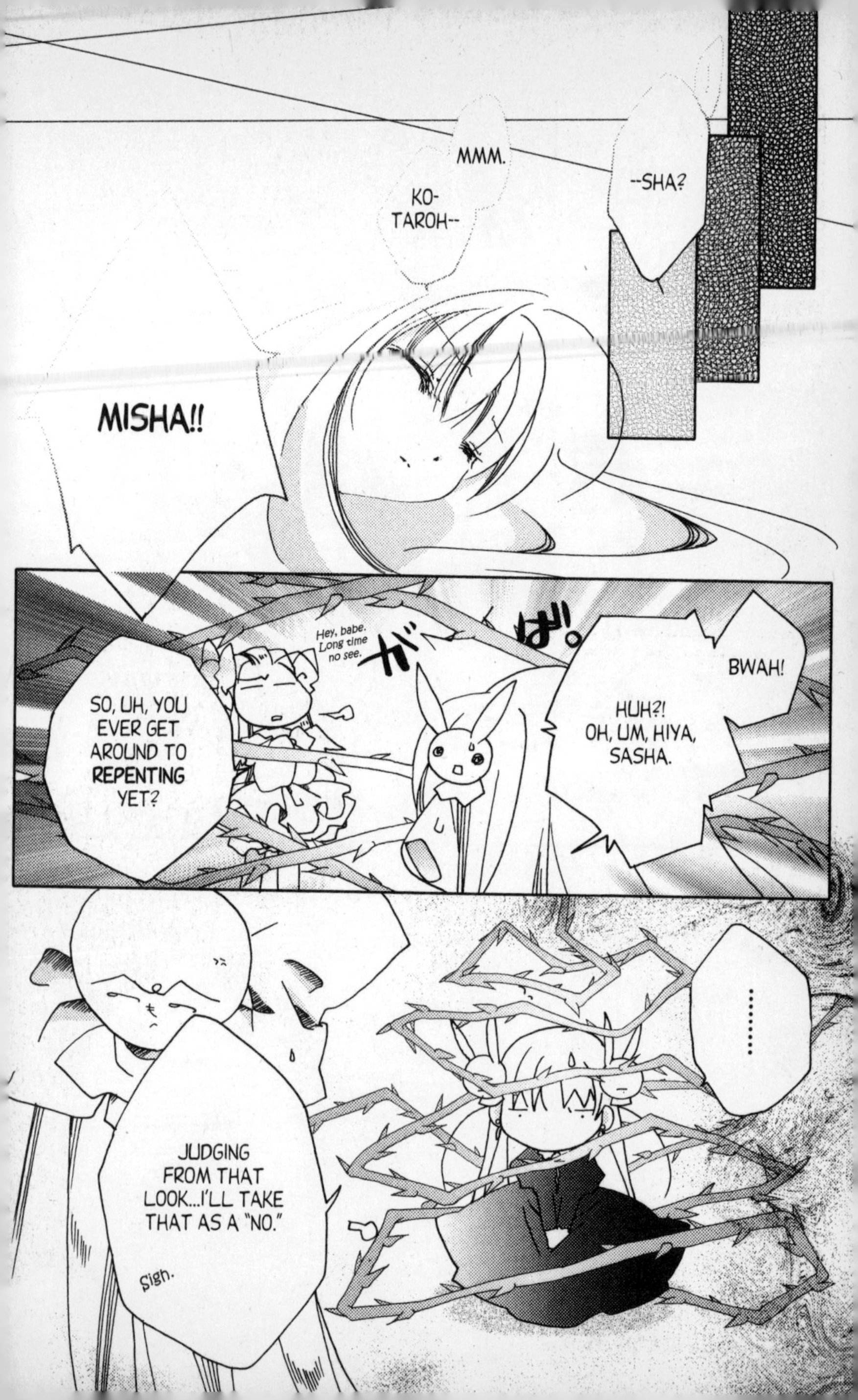
--SHA?
MMM.
KO-TAROH--
MISHA!!
BWAH!
HUH?! OH, UM, HIYA, SASHA.
が
Hey, babe. Long time no see.
SO, UH, YOU EVER GET AROUND TO REPENTING YET?
......
JUDGING FROM THAT LOOK...I'LL TAKE THAT AS A "NO."
Sigh.

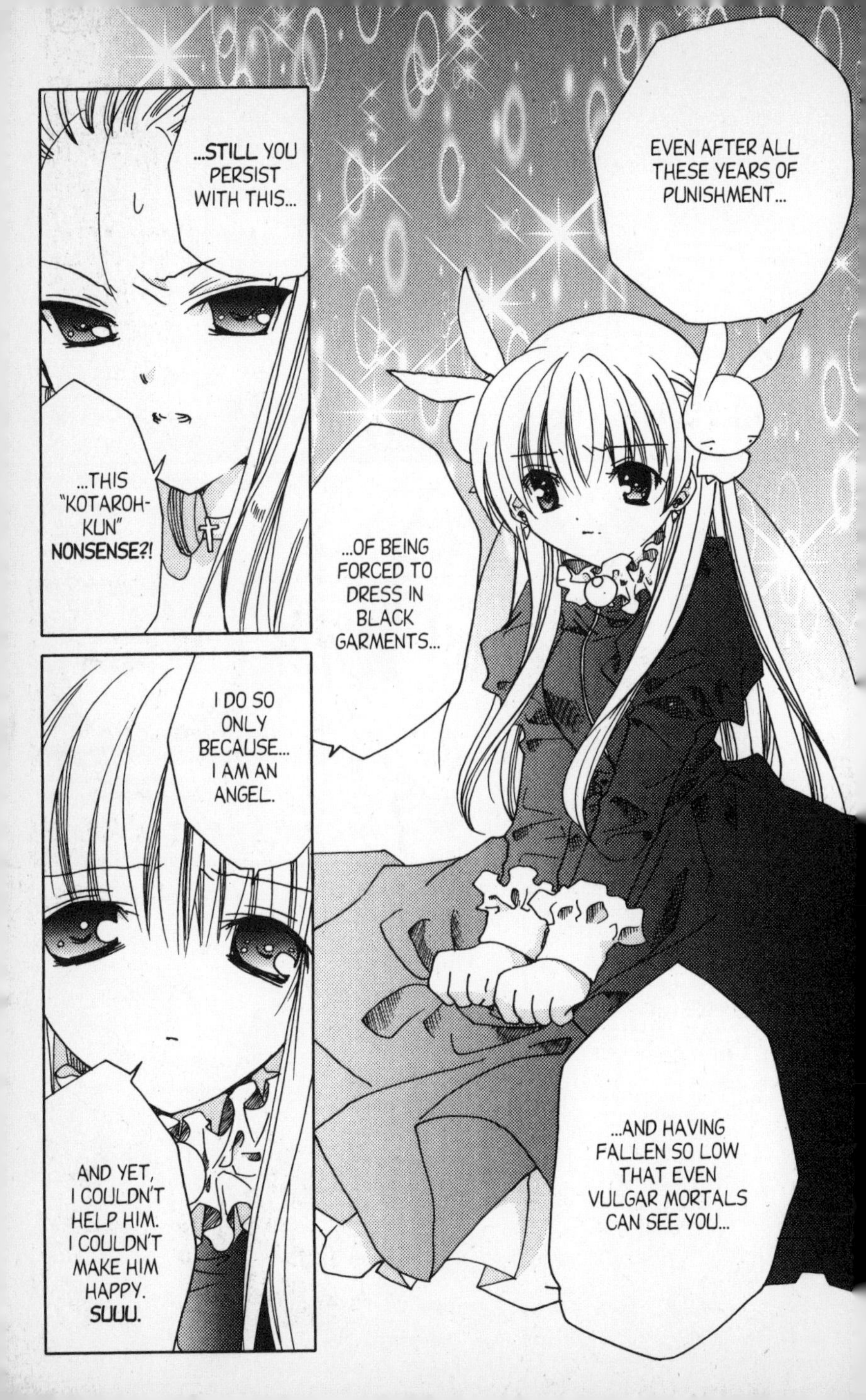
EVEN AFTER ALL THESE YEARS OF PUNISHMENT...
...OF BEING FORCED TO DRESS IN BLACK GARMENTS...
...AND HAVING FALLEN SO LOW THAT EVEN VULGAR MORTALS CAN SEE YOU...
...STILL YOU PERSIST WITH THIS...
...THIS "KOTAROH-KUN" NONSENSE?!
I DO SO ONLY BECAUSE... I AM AN ANGEL.
AND YET, I COULDN'T HELP HIM. I COULDN'T MAKE HIM HAPPY. SUUU.

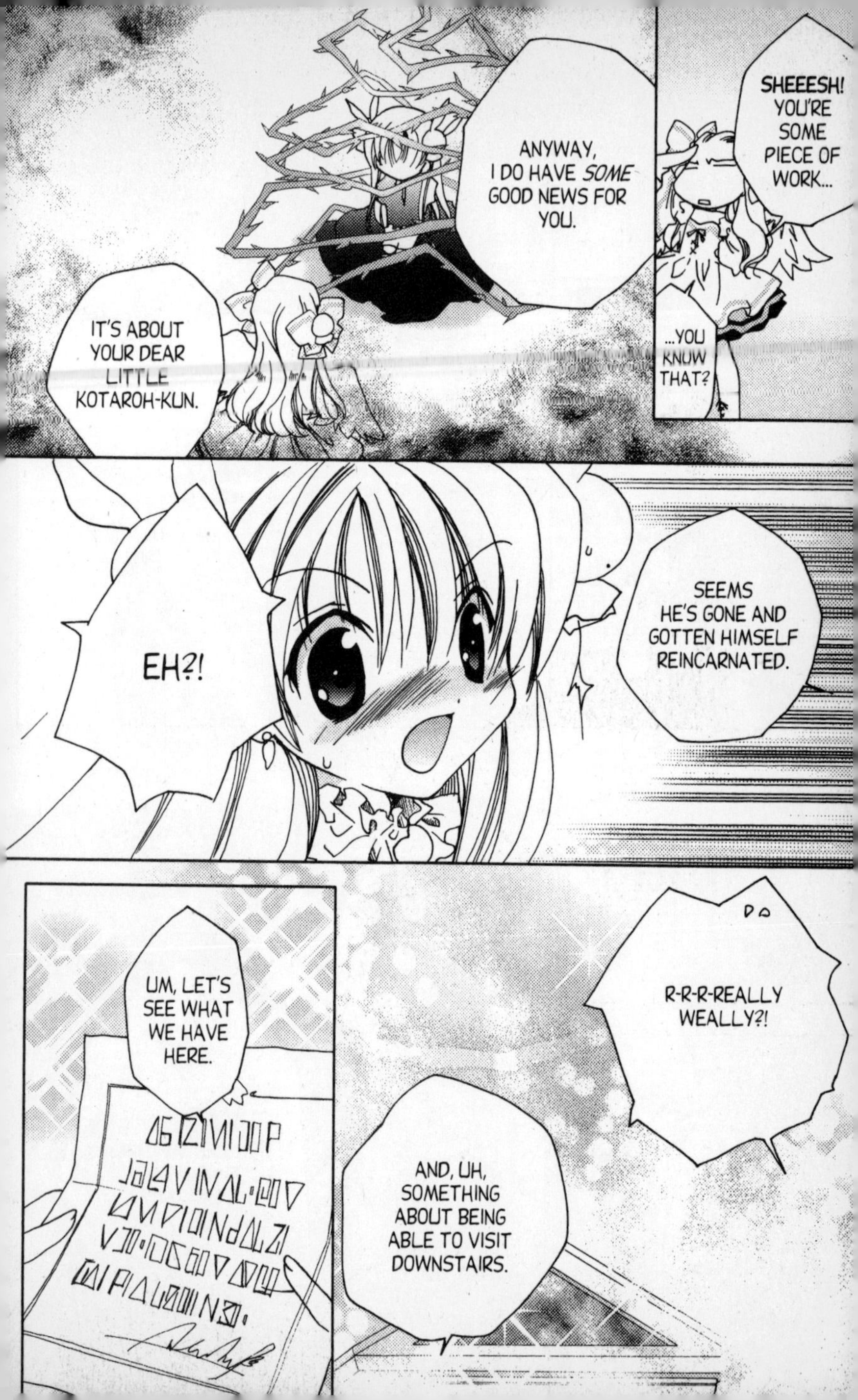
SHEEESH! YOU'RE SOME PIECE OF WORK...
...YOU KNOW THAT?
ANYWAY, I DO HAVE *SOME* GOOD NEWS FOR YOU.
IT'S ABOUT YOUR DEAR LITTLE KOTAROH-KUN.
SEEMS HE'S GONE AND GOTTEN HIMSELF REINCARNATED.
EH?!
R-R-R-REALLY WEALLY?!
UM, LET'S SEE WHAT WE HAVE HERE.
AND, UH, SOMETHING ABOUT BEING ABLE TO VISIT DOWNSTAIRS.

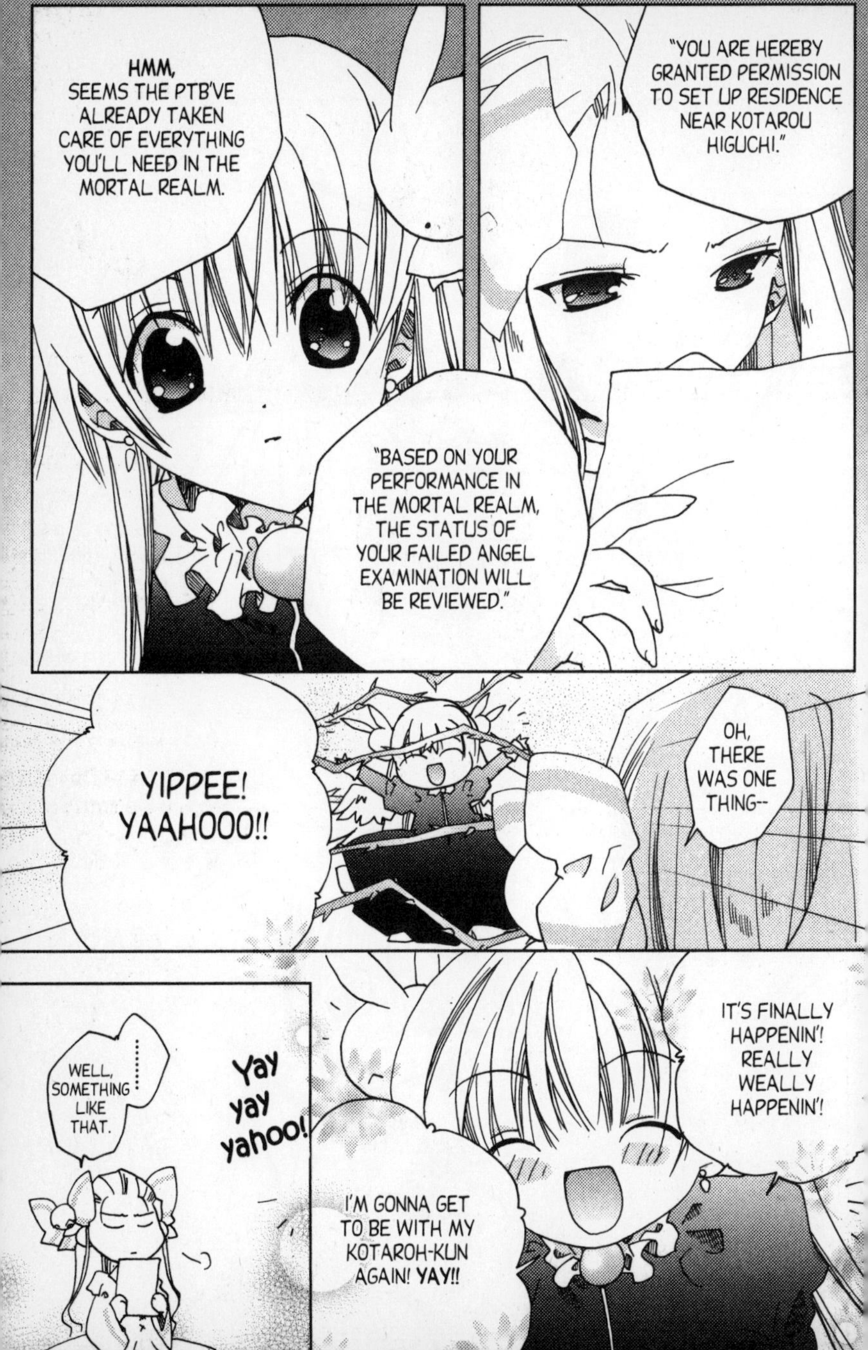
"YOU ARE HEREBY GRANTED PERMISSION TO SET UP RESIDENCE NEAR KOTAROU HIGUCHI."
HMM, SEEMS THE PTB'VE ALREADY TAKEN CARE OF EVERYTHING YOU'LL NEED IN THE MORTAL REALM.
"BASED ON YOUR PERFORMANCE IN THE MORTAL REALM, THE STATUS OF YOUR FAILED ANGEL EXAMINATION WILL BE REVIEWED."
OH, THERE WAS ONE THING--
YIPPEE! YAAHOOO!!
IT'S FINALLY HAPPENIN'! REALLY WEALLY HAPPENIN'!
I'M GONNA GET TO BE WITH MY KOTAROH-KUN AGAIN! YAY!!
Yay yay yahoo!
......
WELL, SOMETHING LIKE THAT.

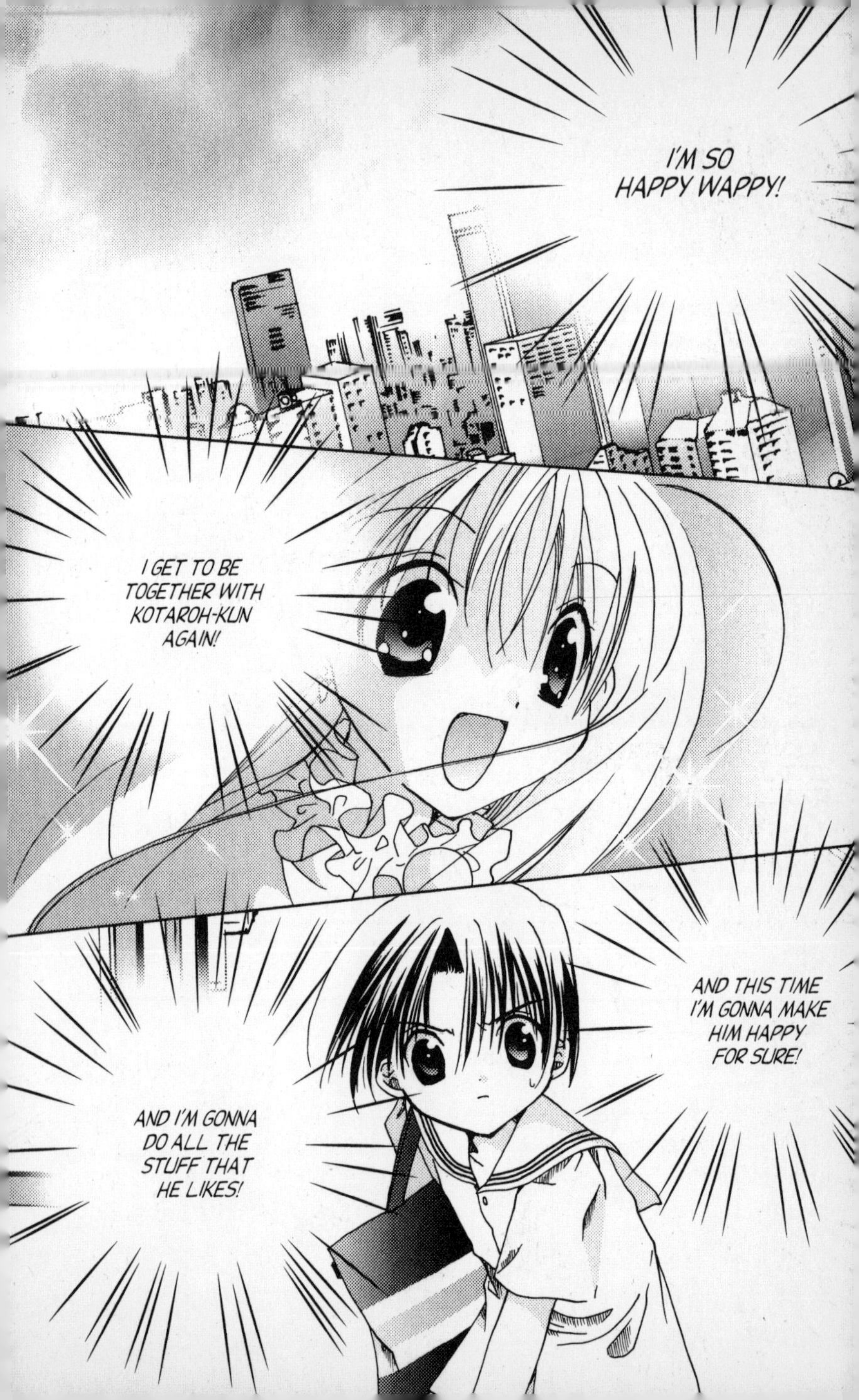
I'M SO HAPPY WAPPY!
I GET TO BE TOGETHER WITH KOTAROH-KUN AGAIN!
AND THIS TIME I'M GONNA MAKE HIM HAPPY FOR SURE!
AND I'M GONNA DO ALL THE STUFF THAT HE LIKES!

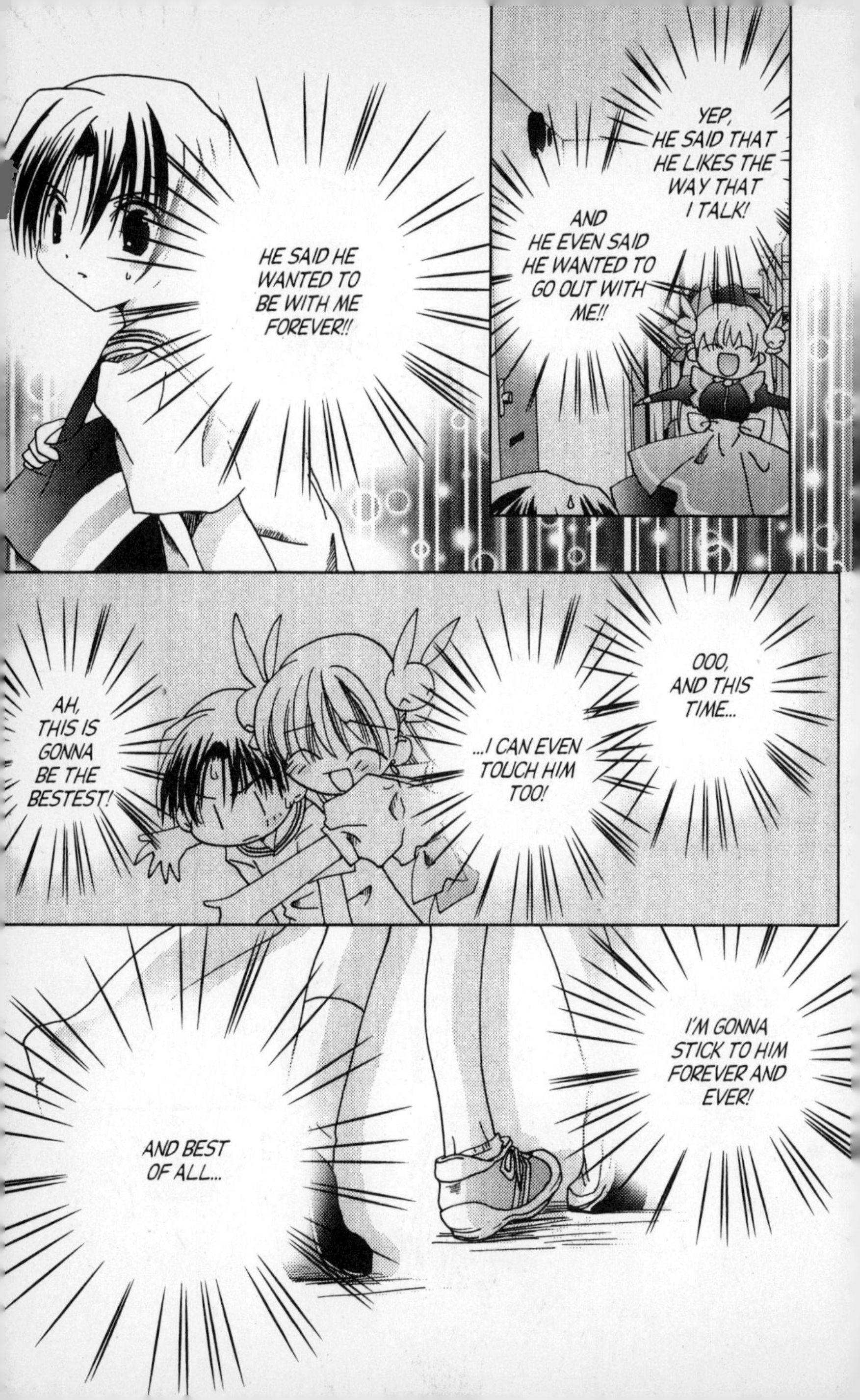
YEP, HE SAID THAT HE LIKES THE WAY THAT I TALK!
AND HE EVEN SAID HE WANTED TO GO OUT WITH ME!!
HE SAID HE WANTED TO BE WITH ME FOREVER!!
OOO, AND THIS TIME...
...I CAN EVEN TOUCH HIM TOO!
AH, THIS IS GONNA BE THE BESTEST!
I'M GONNA STICK TO HIM FOREVER AND EVER!
AND BEST OF ALL...

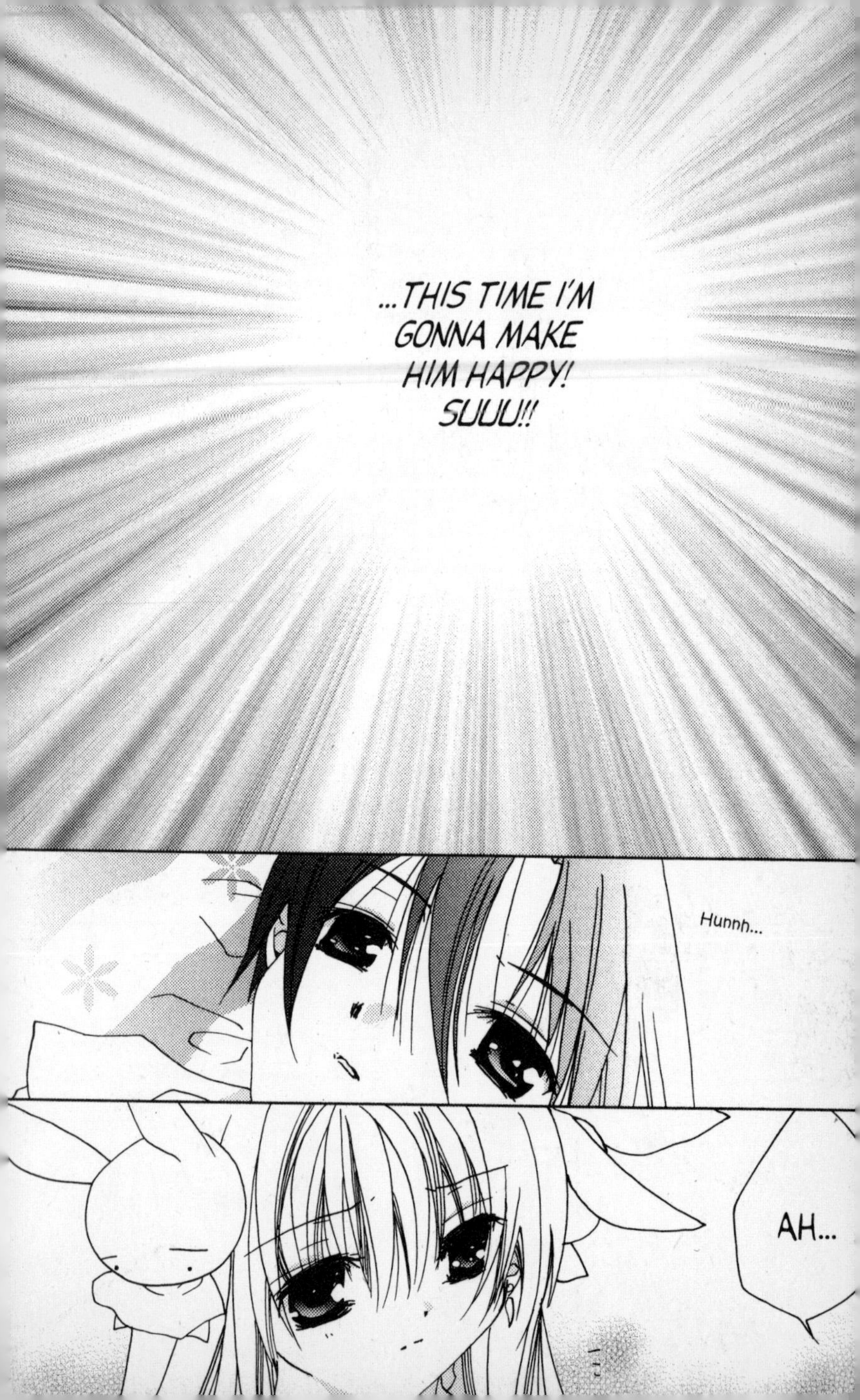
...THIS TIME I'M GONNA MAKE HIM HAPPY! SUUU!!
Hunnh...
AH...

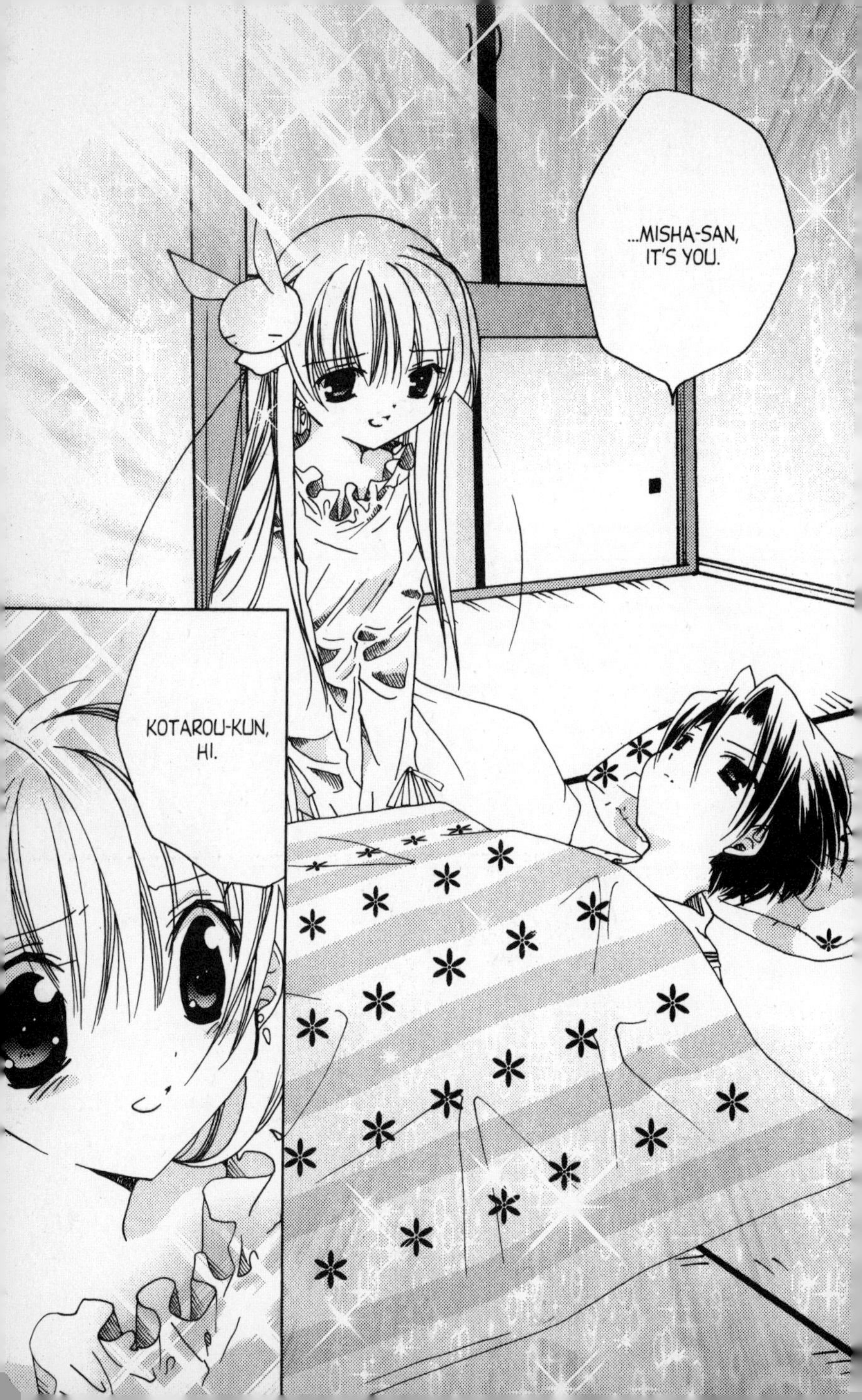
...MISHA-SAN, IT'S YOU.
KOTAROU-KUN, HI.

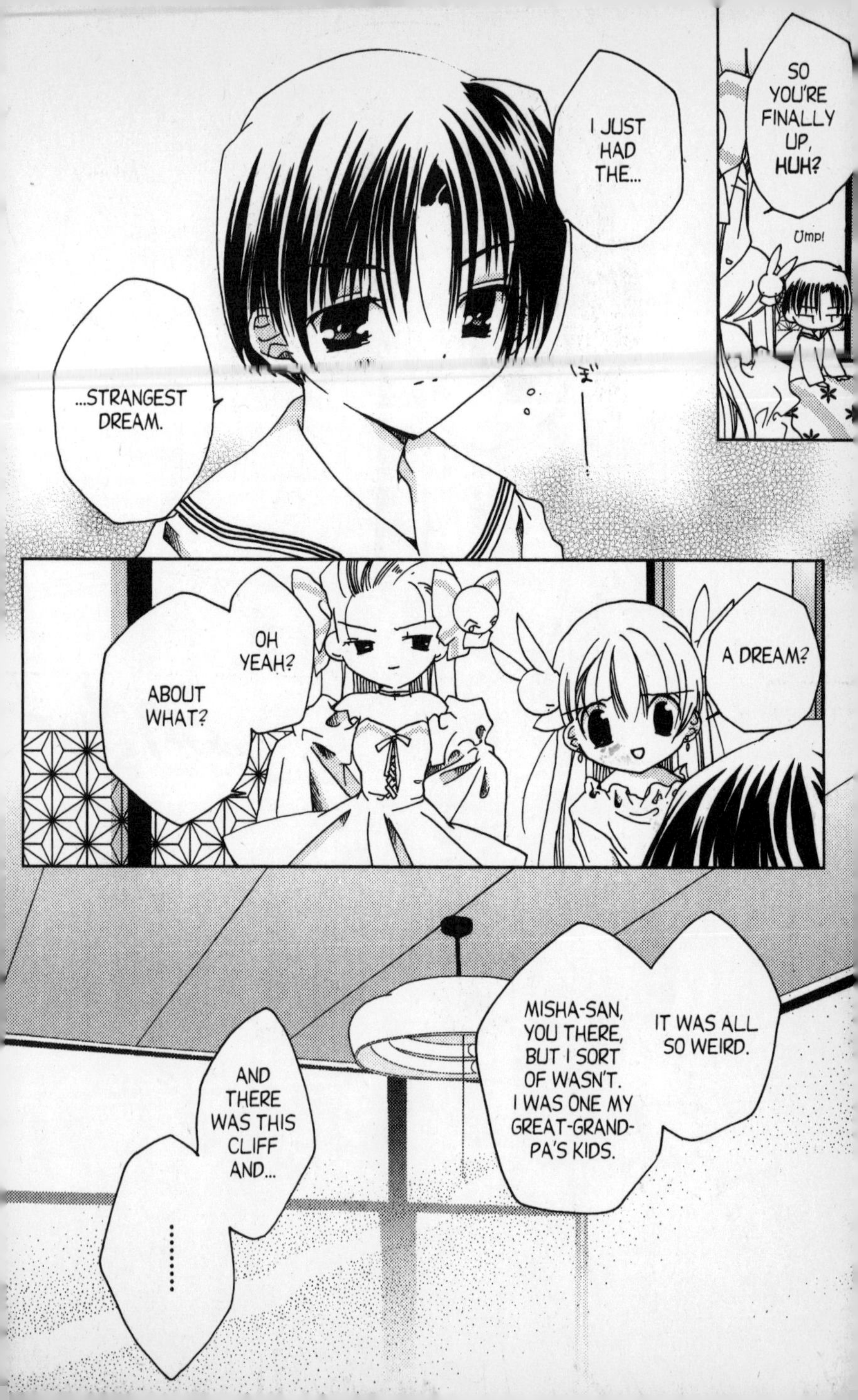
SO YOU'RE FINALLY UP, HUH?
Ump!
I JUST HAD THE...
...STRANGEST DREAM.
A DREAM?
OH YEAH?
ABOUT WHAT?
IT WAS ALL SO WEIRD.
MISHA-SAN, YOU THERE, BUT I SORT OF WASN'T. I WAS ONE MY GREAT-GRAND-PA'S KIDS.
AND THERE WAS THIS CLIFF AND...
......

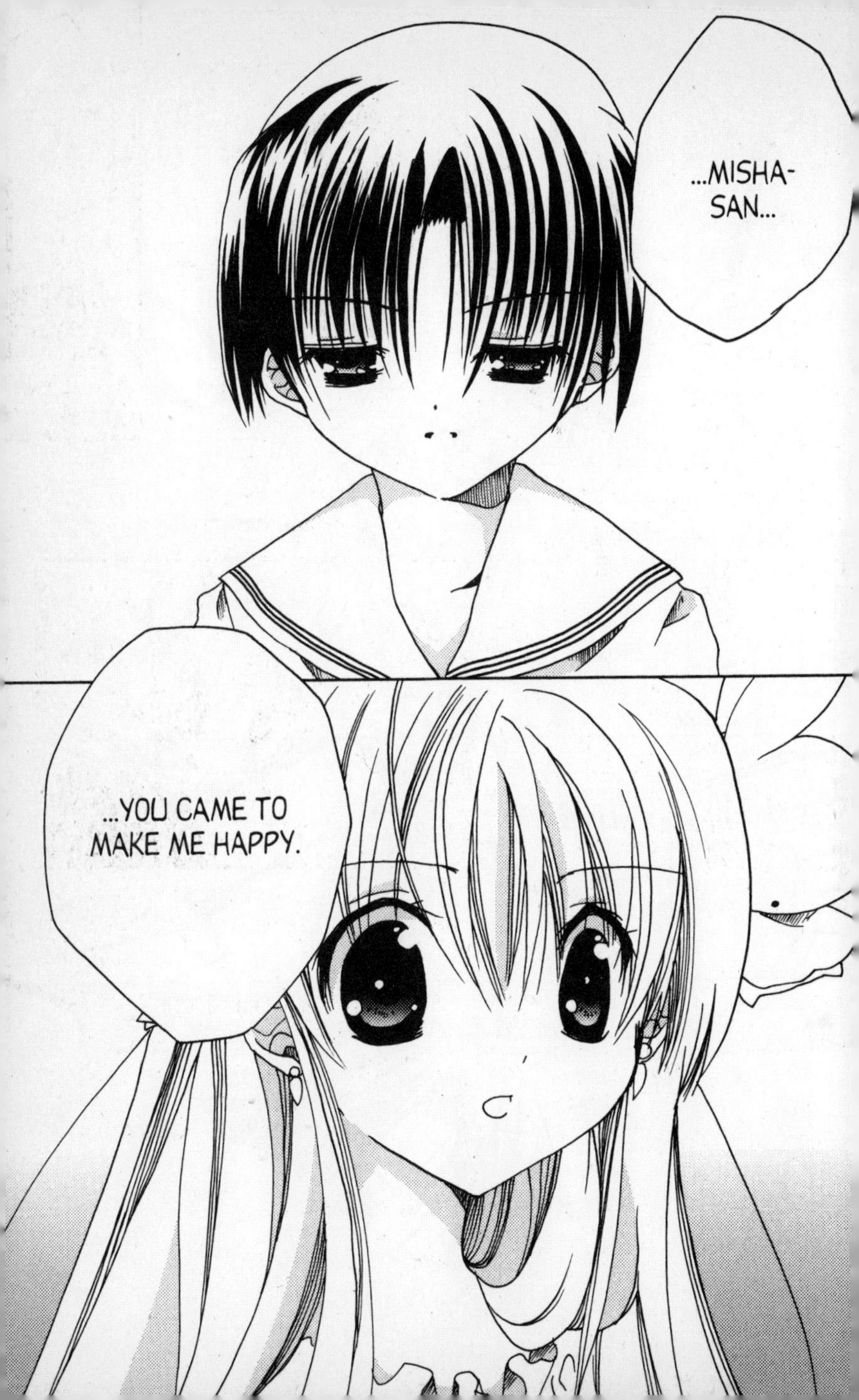
...MISHA-SAN...
...YOU CAME TO MAKE ME HAPPY.

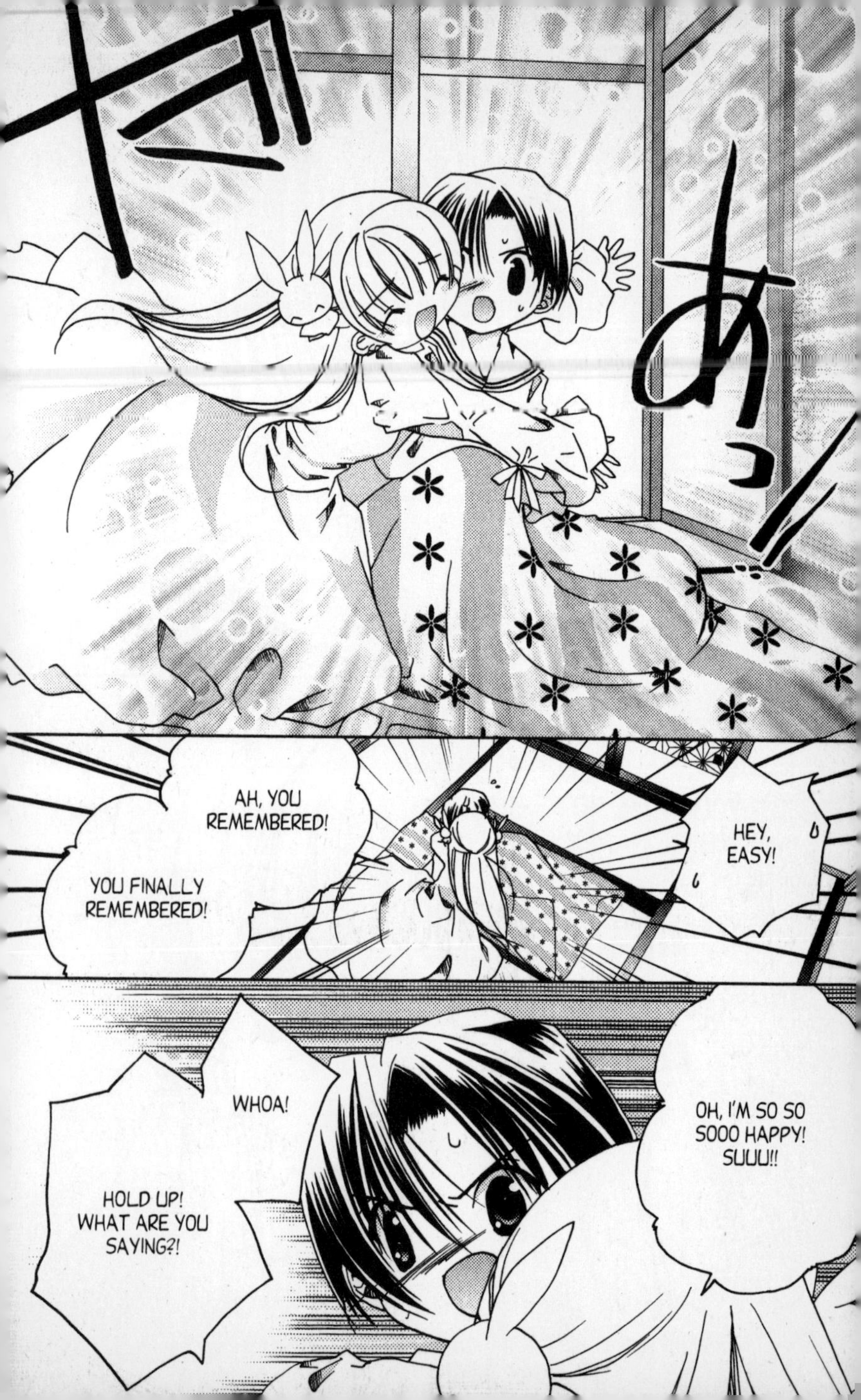
あっ
HEY, EASY!
AH, YOU REMEMBERED!
YOU FINALLY REMEMBERED!
OH, I'M SO SO SOOO HAPPY! SUUU!!
WHOA!
HOLD UP! WHAT ARE YOU SAYING?!

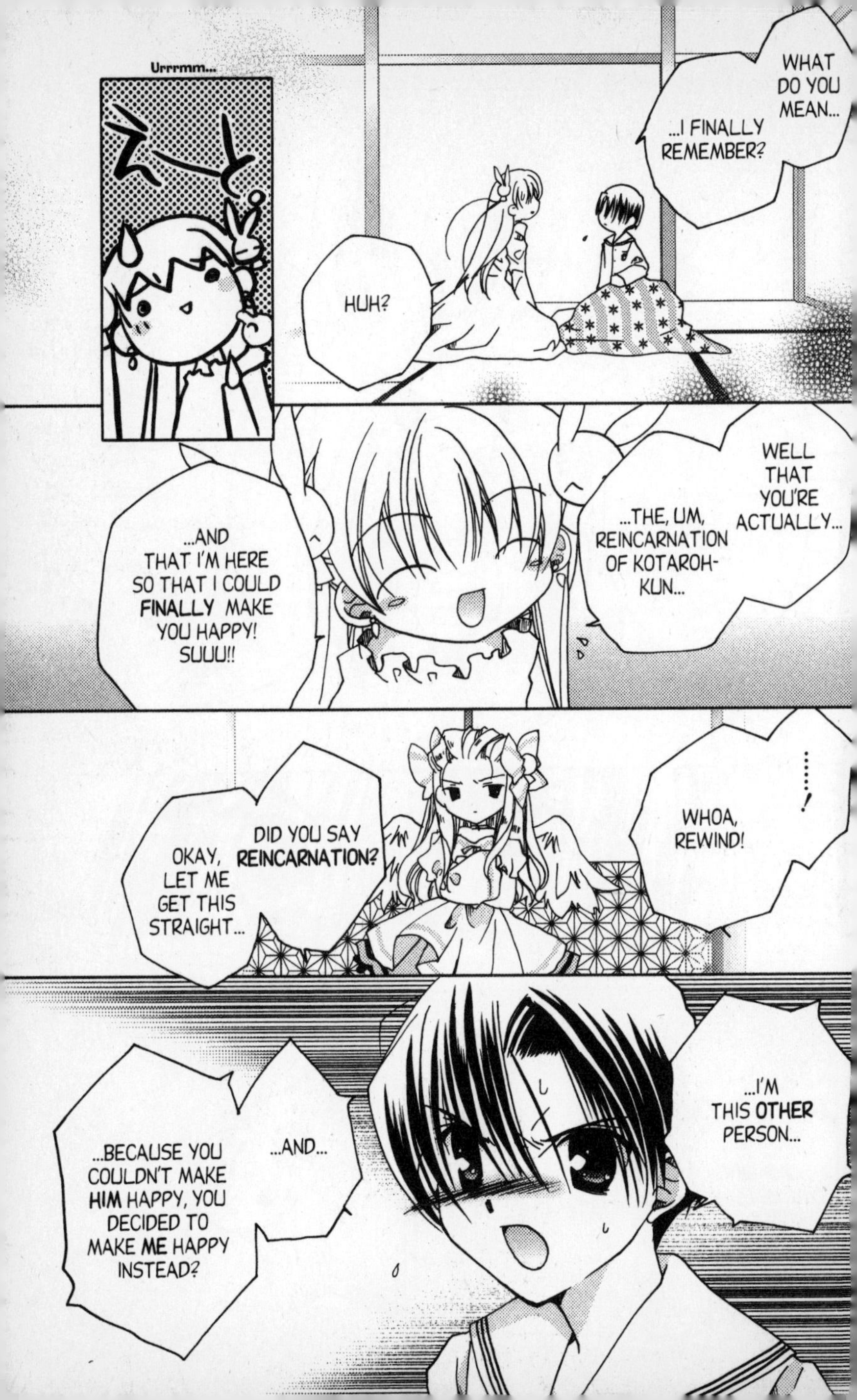

WHAT DO YOU MEAN...
...I FINALLY REMEMBER?
HUH?
Urrrmm...
えーと
WELL THAT YOU'RE ACTUALLY...
...THE, UM, REINCARNATION OF KOTAROH-KUN...
...AND THAT I'M HERE SO THAT I COULD FINALLY MAKE YOU HAPPY! SUUU!!
......!
WHOA, REWIND!
DID YOU SAY REINCARNATION?
OKAY, LET ME GET THIS STRAIGHT...
...I'M THIS OTHER PERSON...
...AND...
...BECAUSE YOU COULDN'T MAKE HIM HAPPY, YOU DECIDED TO MAKE ME HAPPY INSTEAD?

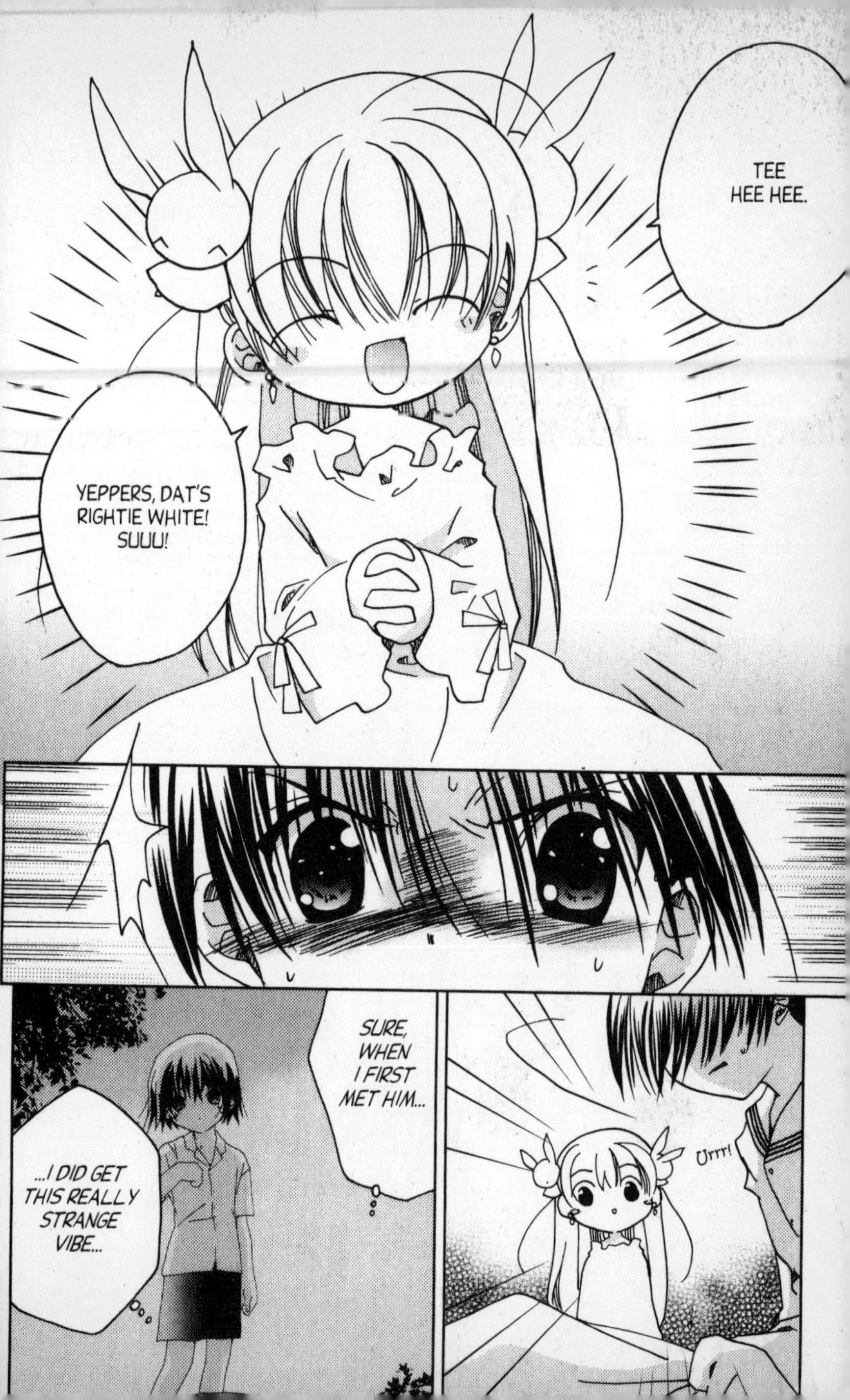
TEE HEE HEE.
YEPPERS, DAT'S RIGHTIE WHITE! SUUU!
Urrr!
SURE, WHEN I FIRST MET HIM...
...I DID GET THIS REALLY STRANGE VIBE...

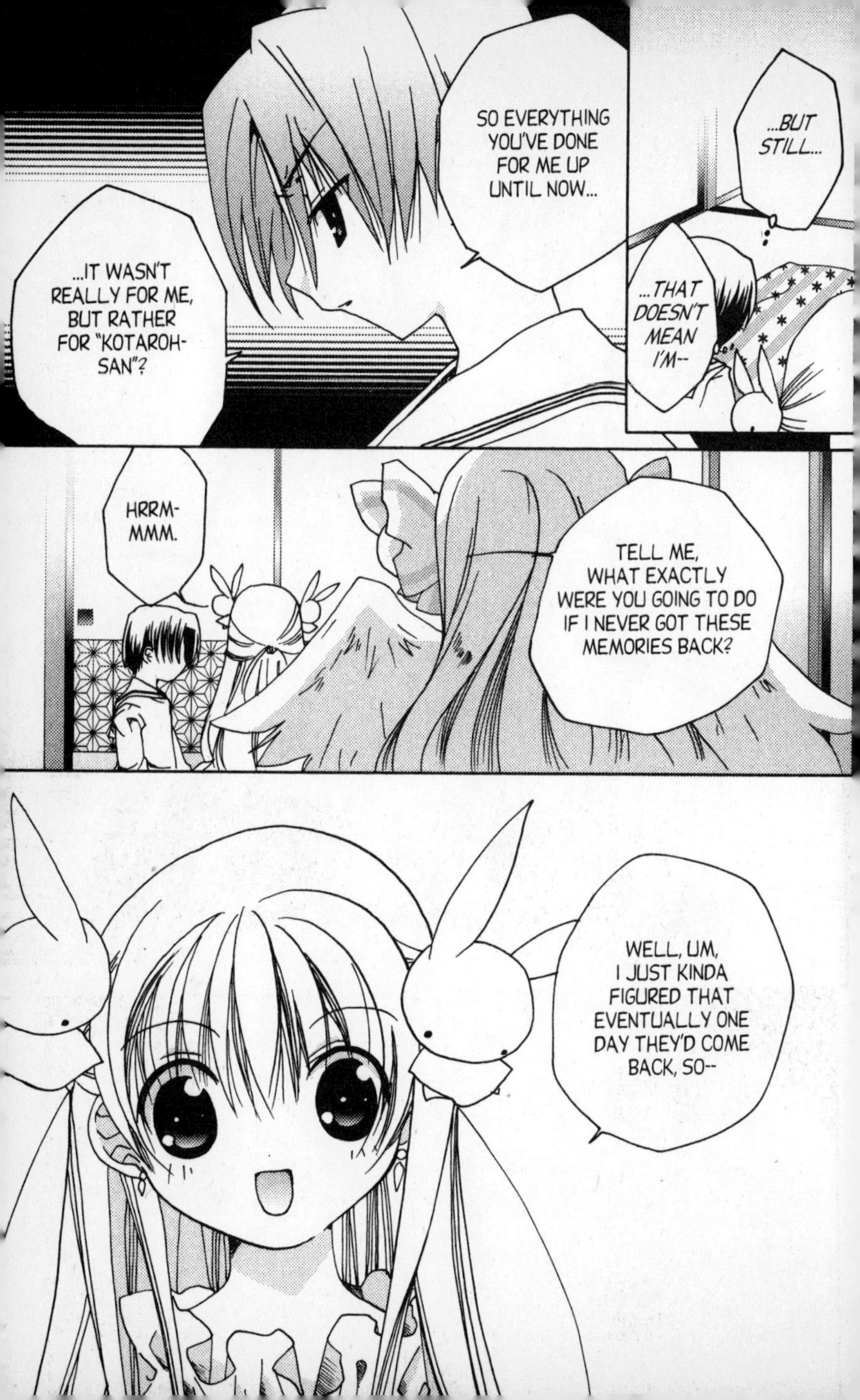
...BUT STILL...
...THAT DOESN'T MEAN I'M--
SO EVERYTHING YOU'VE DONE FOR ME UP UNTIL NOW...
...IT WASN'T REALLY FOR ME, BUT RATHER FOR "KOTAROH-SAN"?
TELL ME, WHAT EXACTLY WERE YOU GOING TO DO IF I NEVER GOT THESE MEMORIES BACK?
HRRM-MMM.
WELL, UM, I JUST KINDA FIGURED THAT EVENTUALLY ONE DAY THEY'D COME BACK, SO--

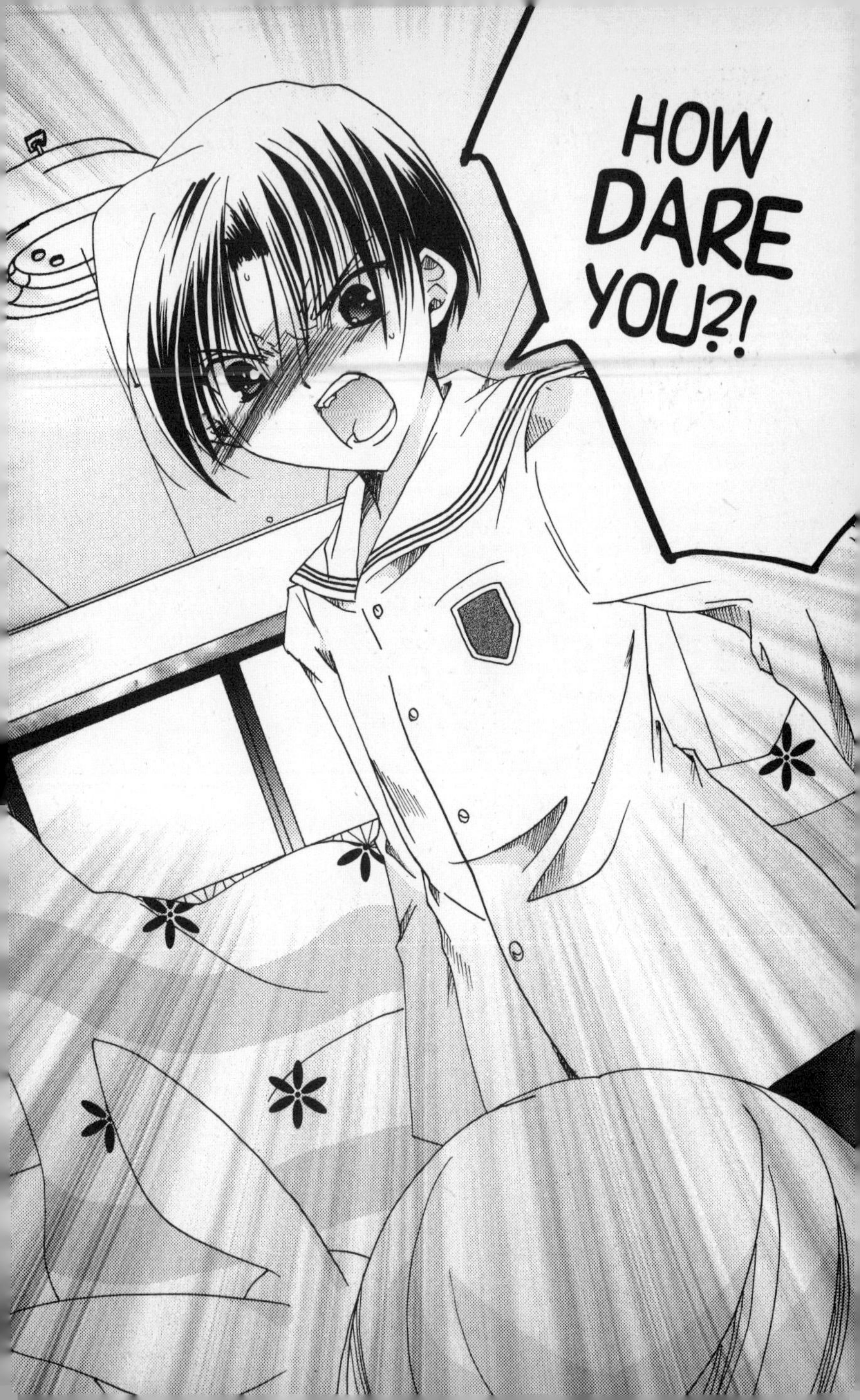
HOW DARE YOU?!

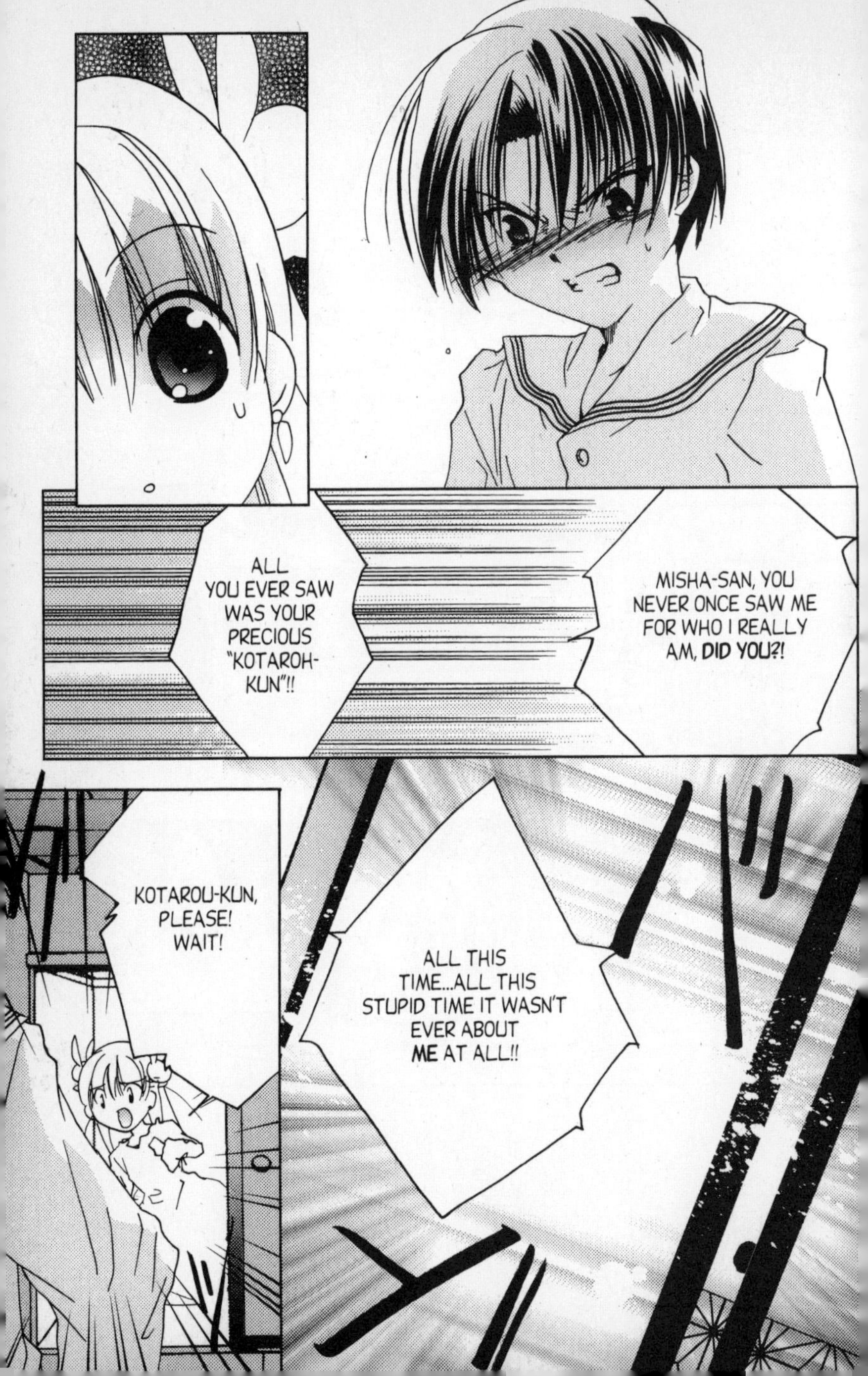
MISHA-SAN, YOU NEVER ONCE SAW ME FOR WHO I REALLY AM, **DID YOU?!**
ALL YOU EVER SAW WAS YOUR PRECIOUS "KOTAROH-KUN"!!
ALL THIS TIME...ALL THIS STUPID TIME IT WASN'T EVER ABOUT **ME** AT ALL!!
KOTAROU-KUN, PLEASE! WAIT!

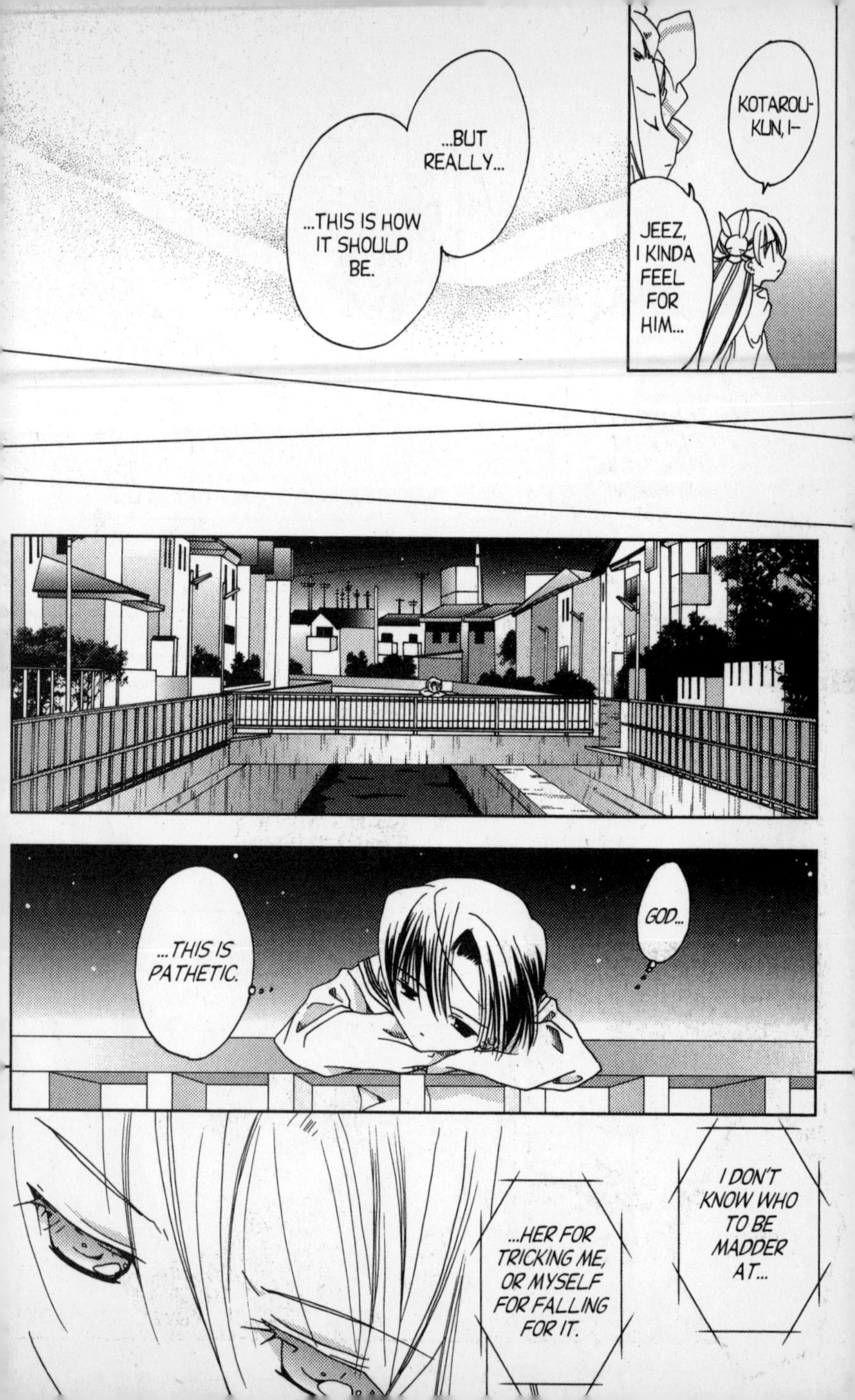
KOTAROU-KUN, I-
JEEZ, I KINDA FEEL FOR HIM...
...BUT REALLY...
...THIS IS HOW IT SHOULD BE.
GOD...
...THIS IS PATHETIC.
I DON'T KNOW WHO TO BE MADDER AT...
...HER FOR TRICKING ME, OR MYSELF FOR FALLING FOR IT.

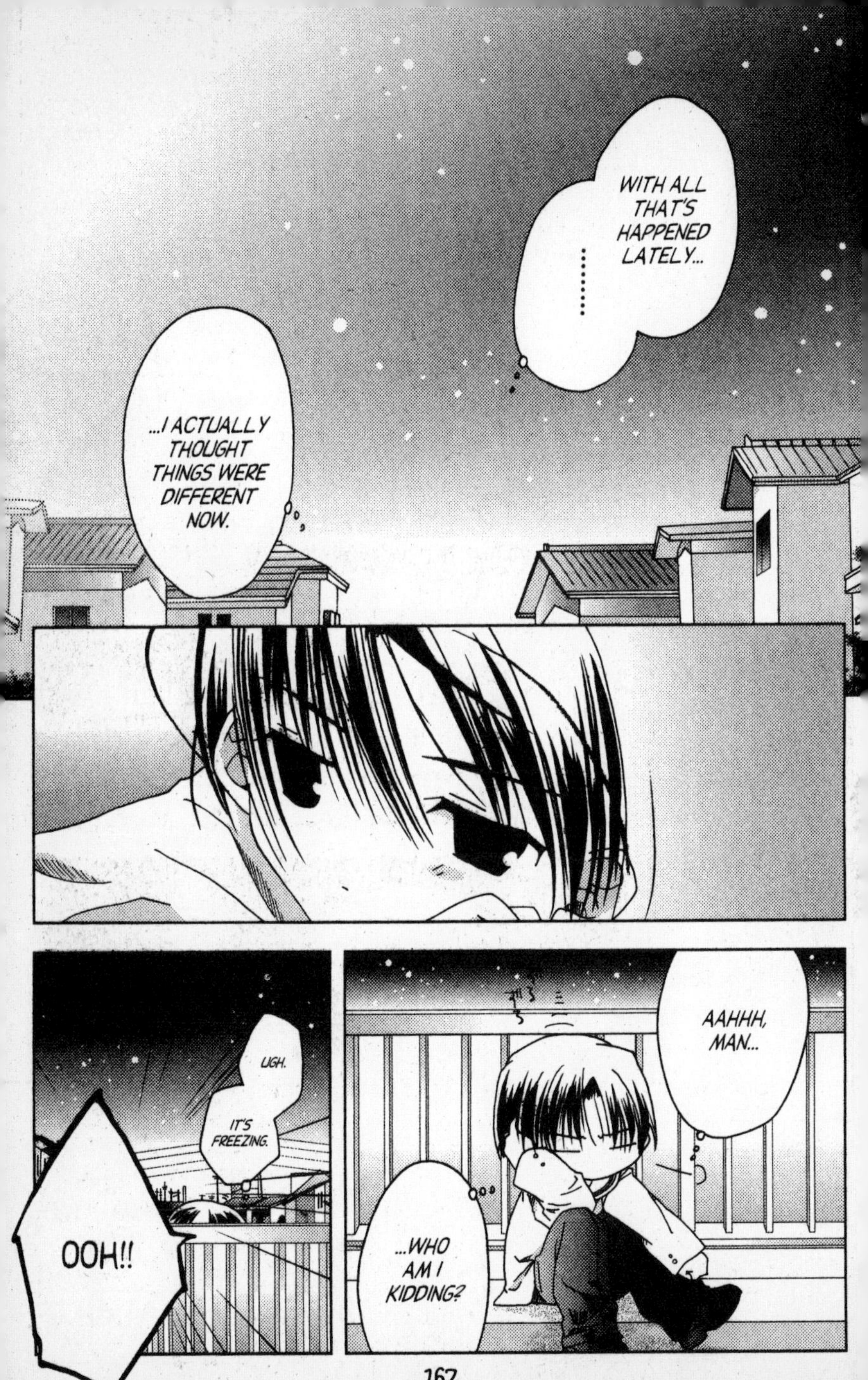
WITH ALL THAT'S HAPPENED LATELY...
......
...I ACTUALLY THOUGHT THINGS WERE DIFFERENT NOW.
AAHHH, MAN...
...WHO AM I KIDDING?
UGH.
IT'S FREEZING.
OOH!!

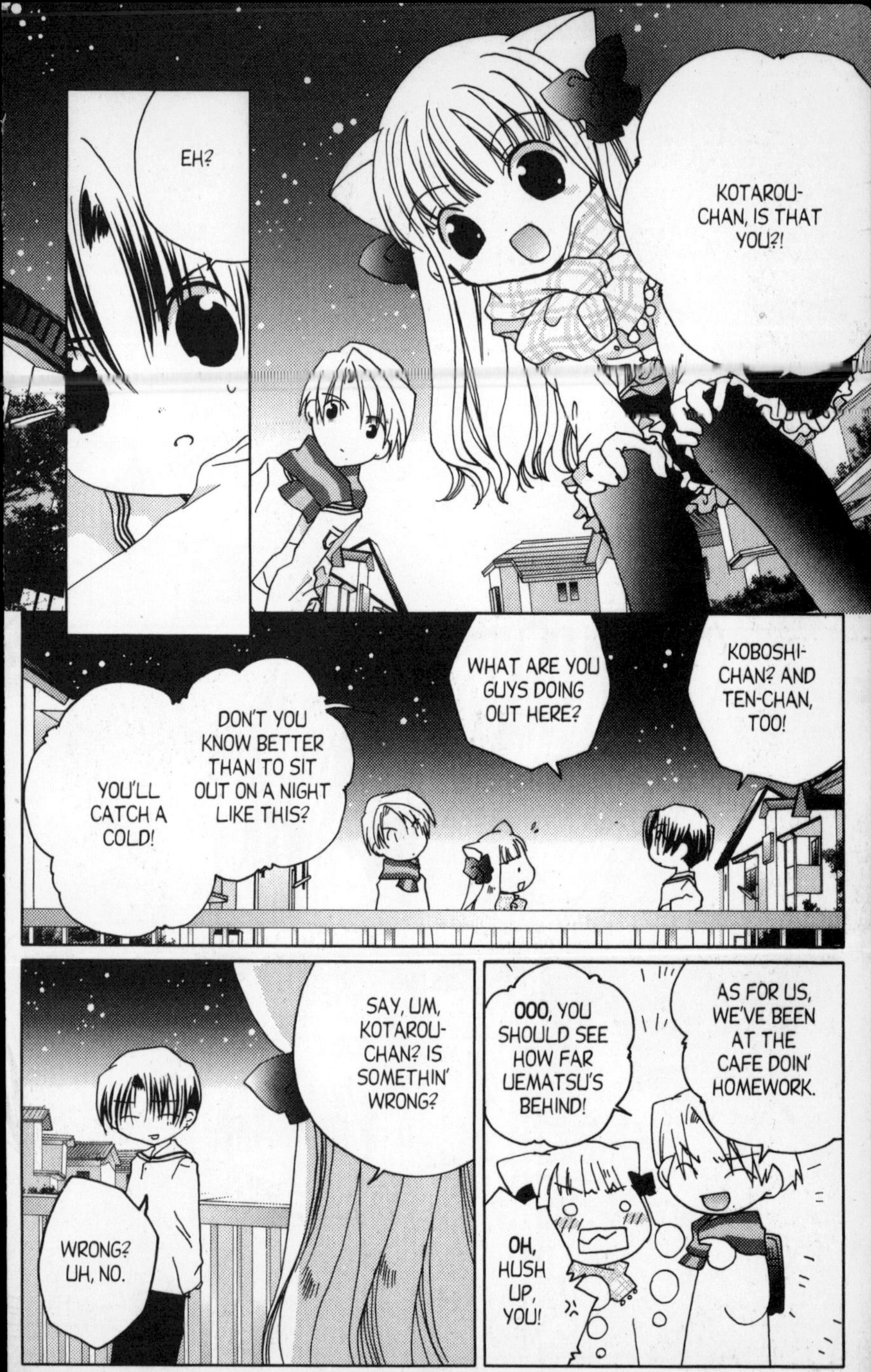
KOTAROU-CHAN, IS THAT YOU?!
EH?
KOBOSHI-CHAN? AND TEN-CHAN, TOO!
WHAT ARE YOU GUYS DOING OUT HERE?
DON'T YOU KNOW BETTER THAN TO SIT OUT ON A NIGHT LIKE THIS?
YOU'LL CATCH A COLD!
AS FOR US, WE'VE BEEN AT THE CAFE DOIN' HOMEWORK.
OOO, YOU SHOULD SEE HOW FAR UEMATSU'S BEHIND!
OH, HUSH UP, YOU!
SAY, UM, KOTAROU-CHAN? IS SOMETHIN' WRONG?
WRONG? UH, NO.

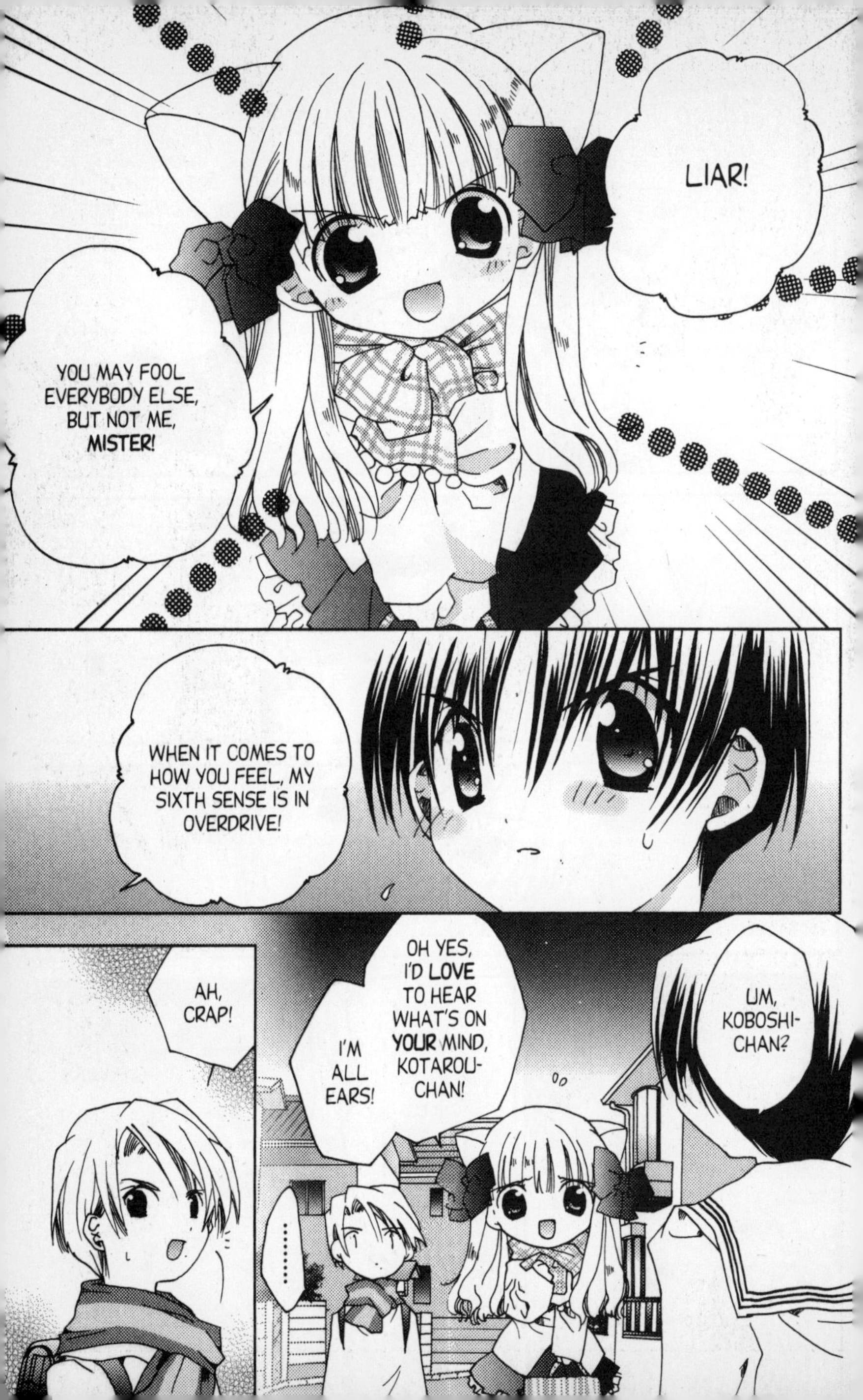
LIAR!
YOU MAY FOOL EVERYBODY ELSE, BUT NOT ME, MISTER!
WHEN IT COMES TO HOW YOU FEEL, MY SIXTH SENSE IS IN OVERDRIVE!
UM, KOBOSHI-CHAN?
OH YES, I'D LOVE TO HEAR WHAT'S ON YOUR MIND, KOTAROU-CHAN!
I'M ALL EARS!
......
AH, CRAP!

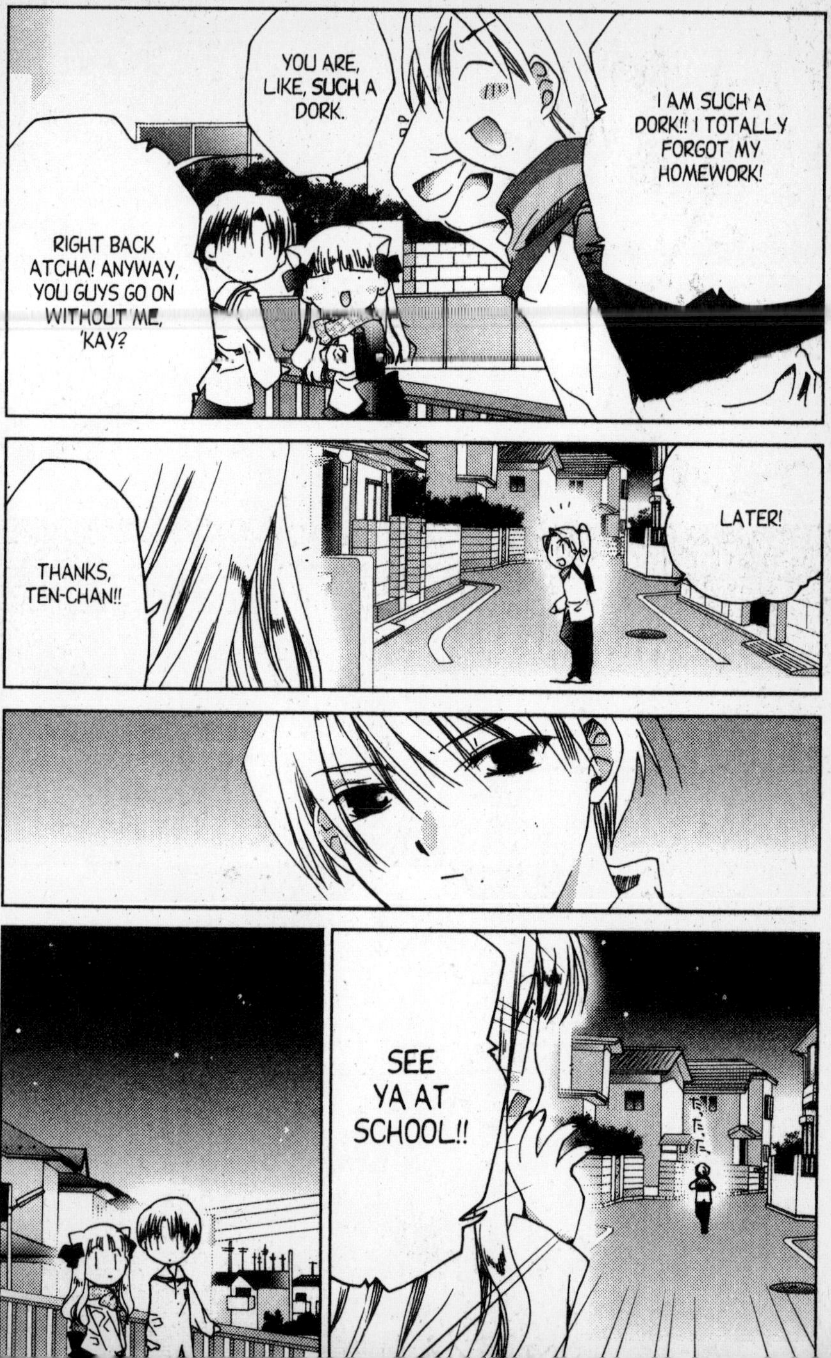
I AM SUCH A DORK!! I TOTALLY FORGOT MY HOMEWORK!
YOU ARE, LIKE, SUCH A DORK.
RIGHT BACK ATCHA! ANYWAY, YOU GUYS GO ON WITHOUT ME, 'KAY?
LATER!
THANKS, TEN-CHAN!!
SEE YA AT SCHOOL!!

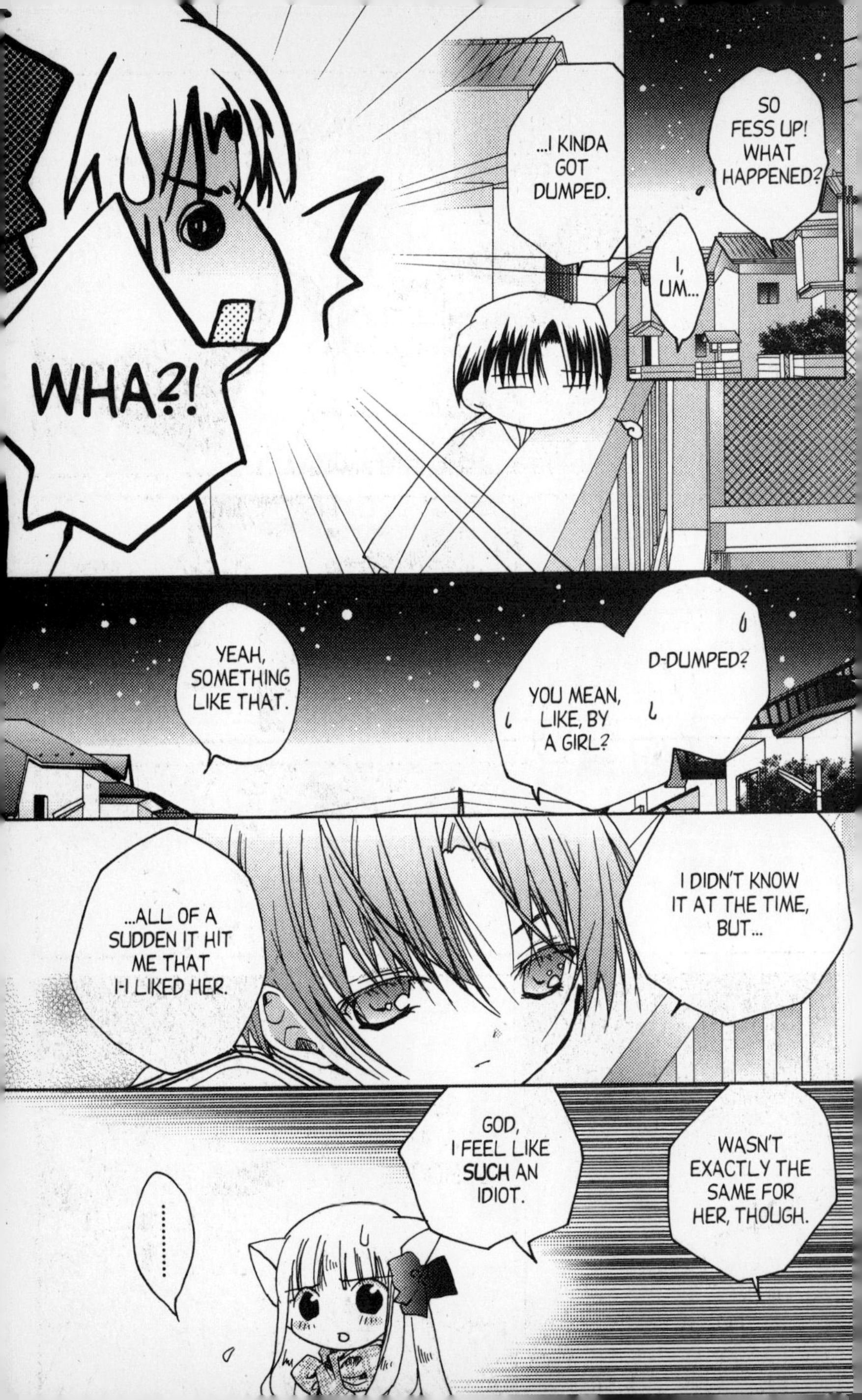
SO FESS UP! WHAT HAPPENED?
I, UM...
...I KINDA GOT DUMPED.
WHA?!
D-DUMPED? YOU MEAN, LIKE, BY A GIRL?
YEAH, SOMETHING LIKE THAT.
I DIDN'T KNOW IT AT THE TIME, BUT...
...ALL OF A SUDDEN IT HIT ME THAT I-I LIKED HER.
WASN'T EXACTLY THE SAME FOR HER, THOUGH.
GOD, I FEEL LIKE SUCH AN IDIOT.
......

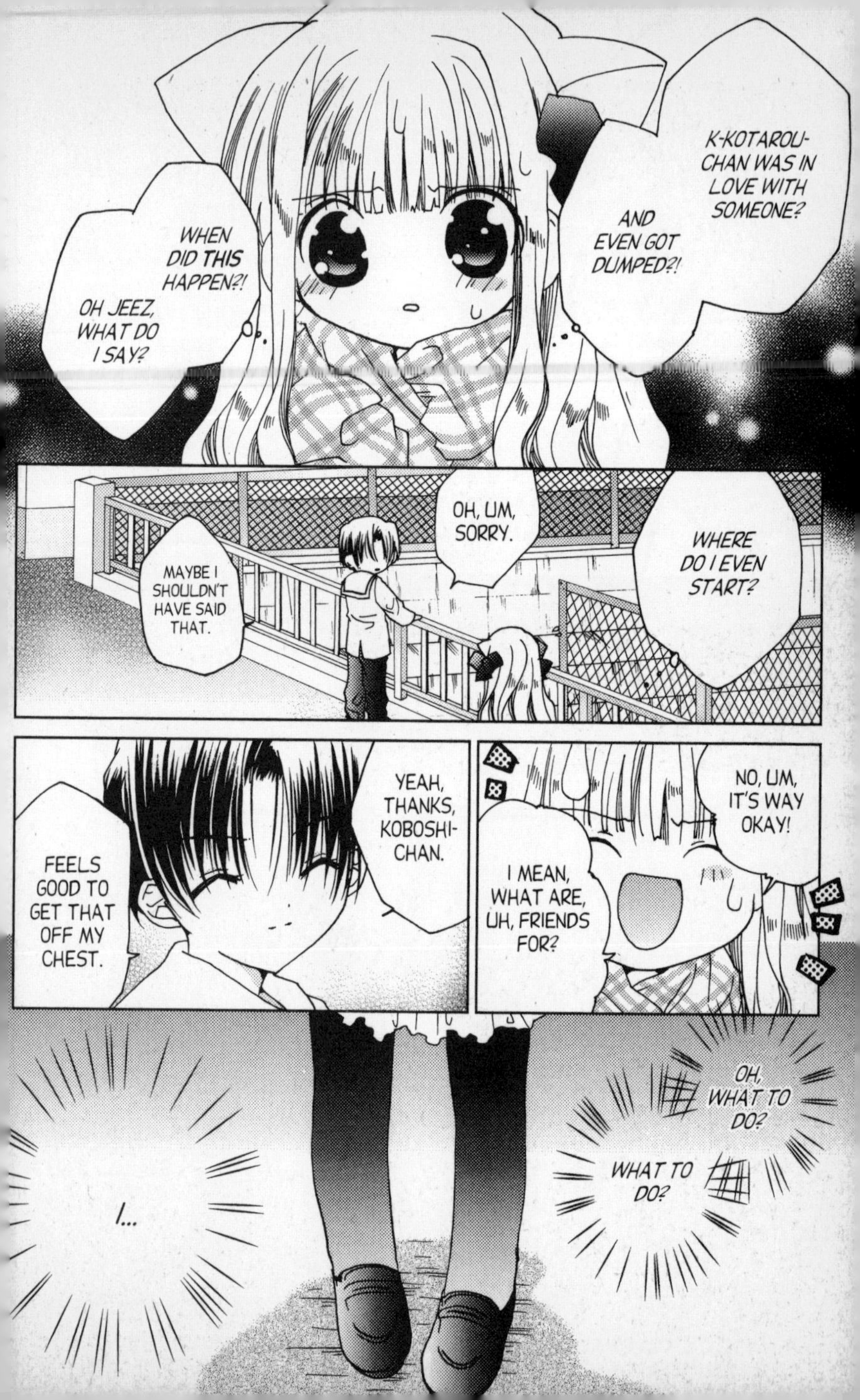
K-KOTAROU-CHAN WAS IN LOVE WITH SOMEONE?
AND EVEN GOT DUMPED?!
WHEN DID THIS HAPPEN?!
OH JEEZ, WHAT DO I SAY?
WHERE DO I EVEN START?
OH, UM, SORRY.
MAYBE I SHOULDN'T HAVE SAID THAT.
NO, UM, IT'S WAY OKAY!
I MEAN, WHAT ARE, UH, FRIENDS FOR?
YEAH, THANKS, KOBOSHI-CHAN.
FEELS GOOD TO GET THAT OFF MY CHEST.
OH, WHAT TO DO?
WHAT TO DO?
I...

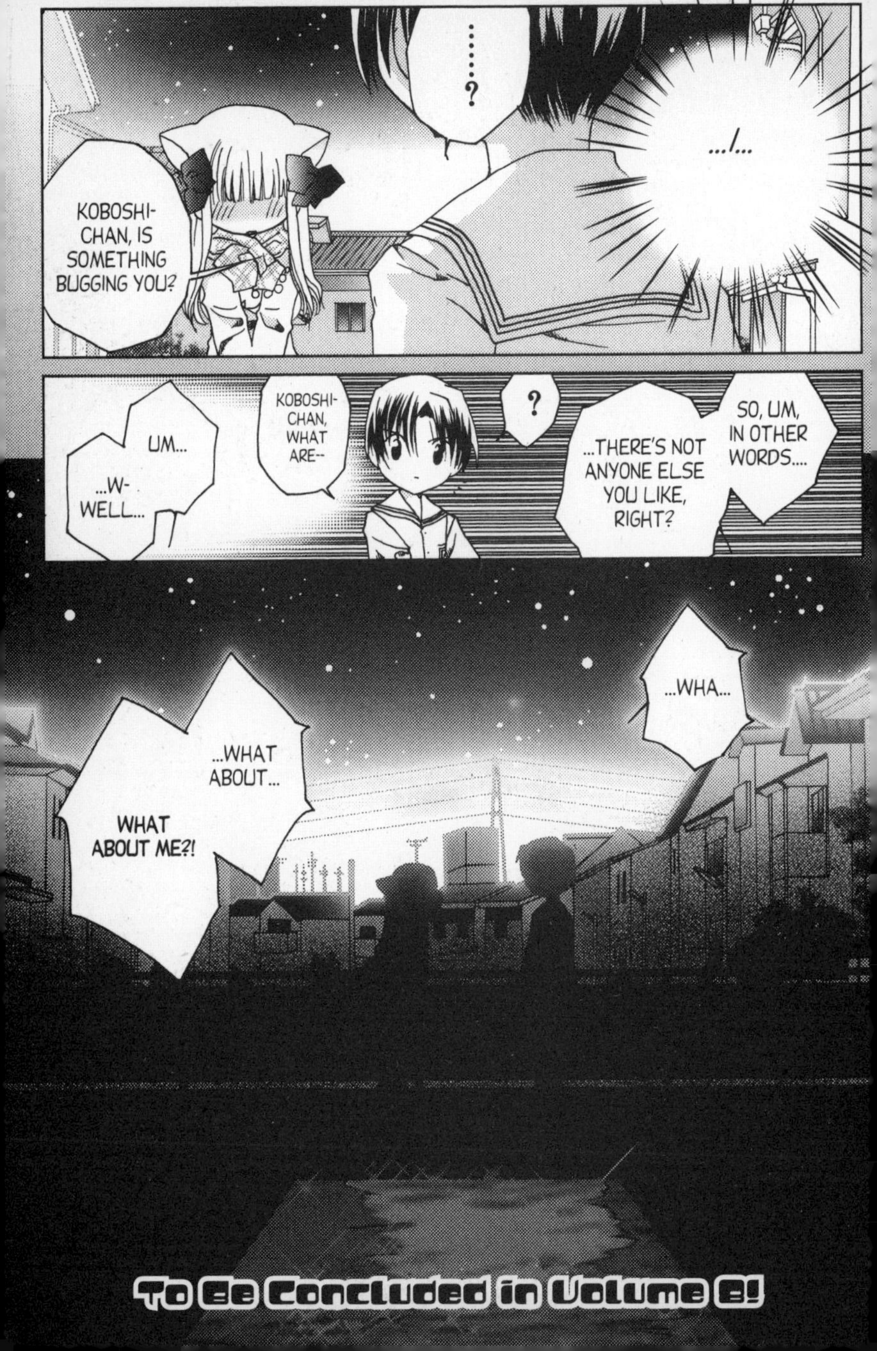
...!...
......?
KOBOSHI-CHAN, IS SOMETHING BUGGING YOU?
SO, UM, IN OTHER WORDS....
...THERE'S NOT ANYONE ELSE YOU LIKE, RIGHT?
?
KOBOSHI-CHAN, WHAT ARE--
UM...
...W-WELL...
...WHA...
...WHAT ABOUT...
WHAT ABOUT ME?!
To Be Concluded in Volume 8!

Urrrmm...

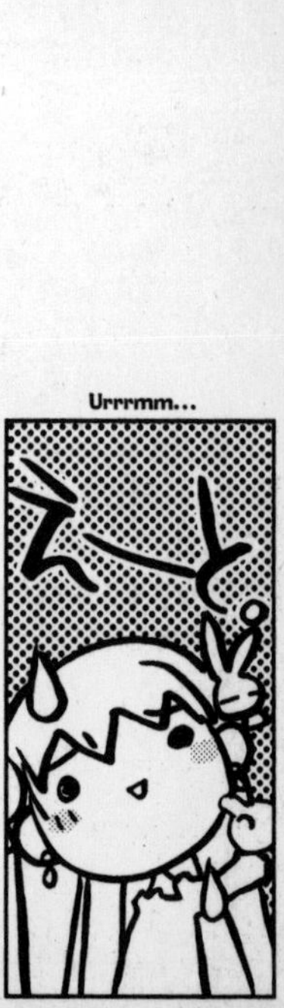
えーと

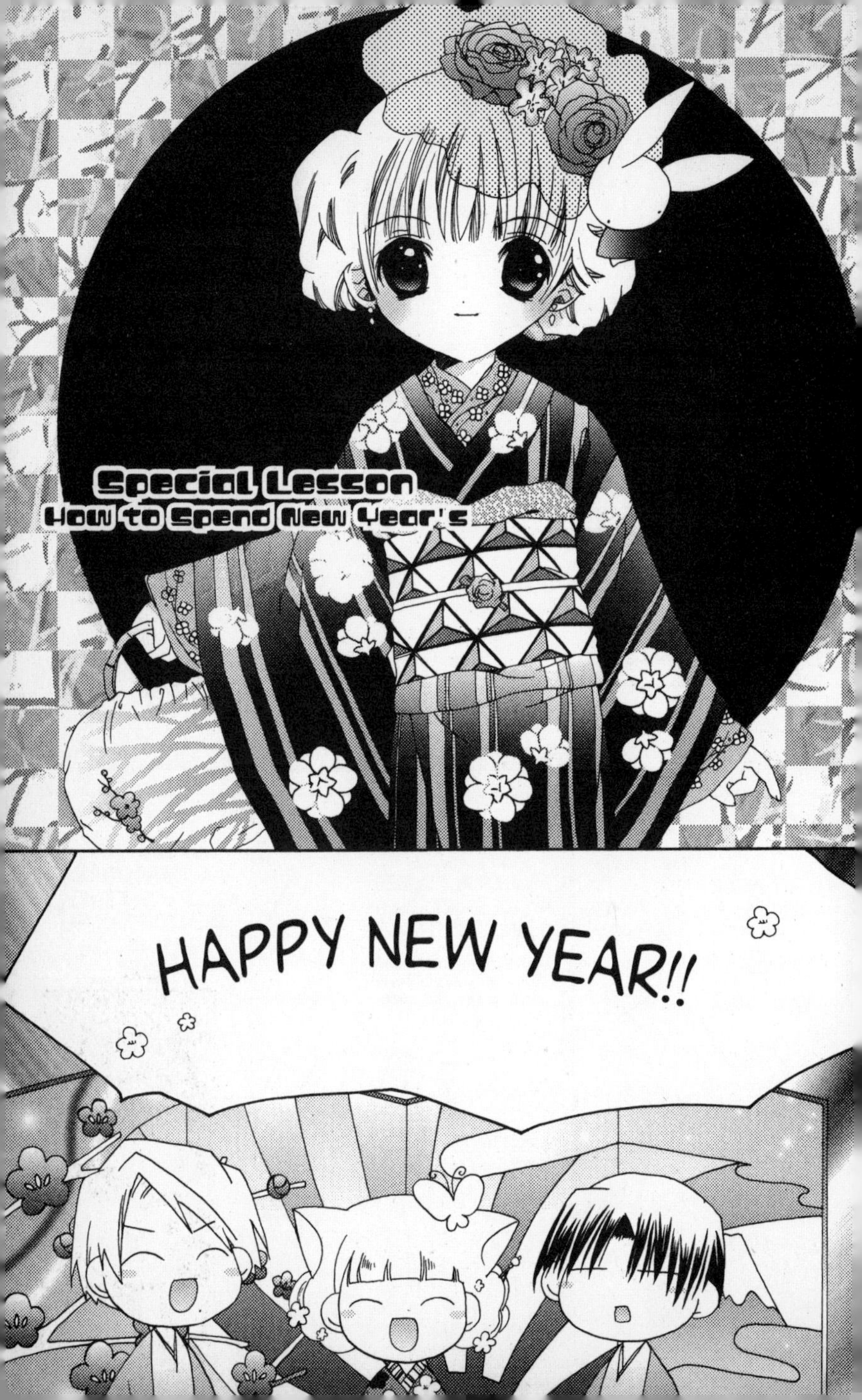
Special Lesson
How to Spend New Year's
HAPPY NEW YEAR!!

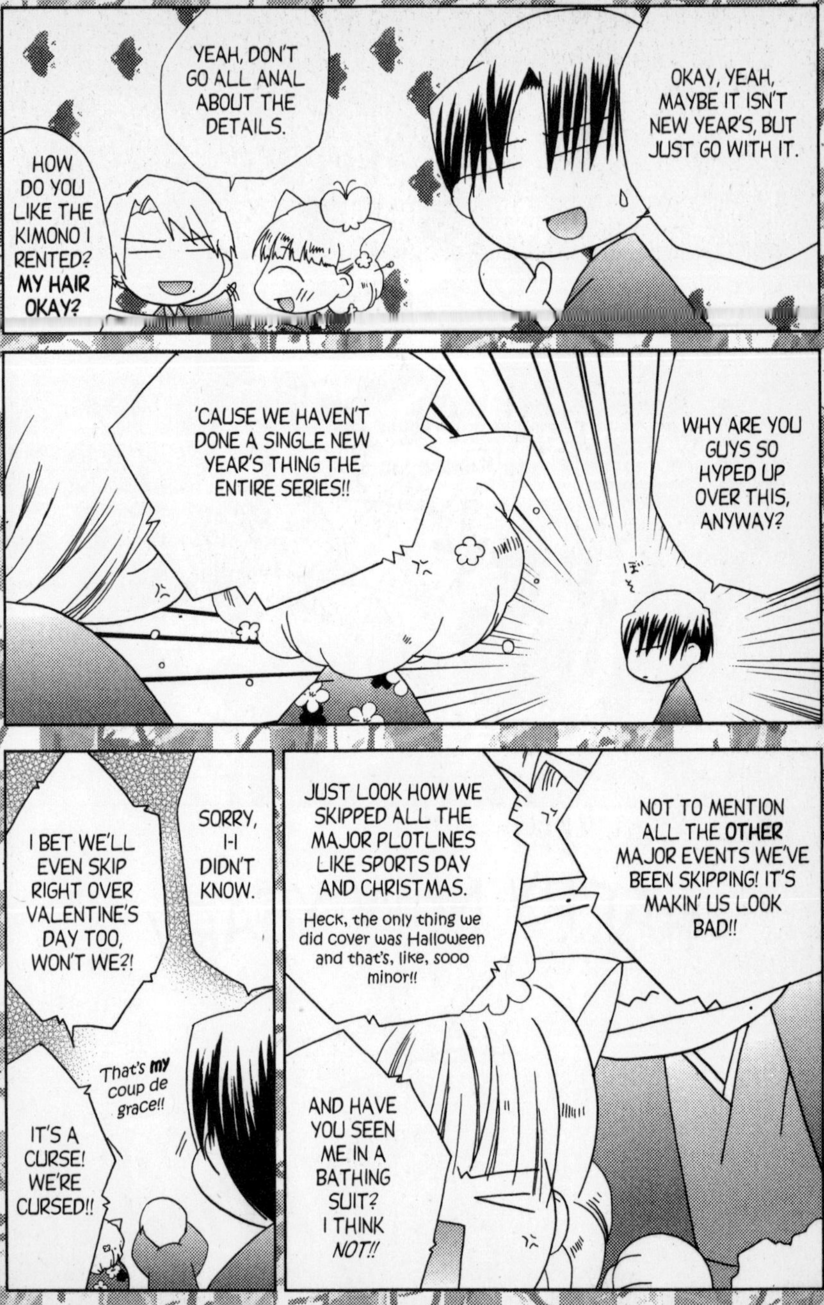
OKAY, YEAH, MAYBE IT ISN'T NEW YEAR'S, BUT JUST GO WITH IT.
YEAH, DON'T GO ALL ANAL ABOUT THE DETAILS.
HOW DO YOU LIKE THE KIMONO I RENTED? **MY HAIR OKAY?**
WHY ARE YOU GUYS SO HYPED UP OVER THIS, ANYWAY?
'CAUSE WE HAVEN'T DONE A SINGLE NEW YEAR'S THING THE ENTIRE SERIES!!
NOT TO MENTION ALL THE **OTHER** MAJOR EVENTS WE'VE BEEN SKIPPING! IT'S MAKIN' US LOOK BAD!!
JUST LOOK HOW WE SKIPPED ALL THE MAJOR PLOTLINES LIKE SPORTS DAY AND CHRISTMAS.
Heck, the only thing we did cover was Halloween and that's, like, sooo minor!!
AND HAVE YOU SEEN ME IN A BATHING SUIT? I THINK *NOT!!*
SORRY, I-I DIDN'T KNOW.
I BET WE'LL EVEN SKIP RIGHT OVER VALENTINE'S DAY TOO, WON'T WE?!
*That's **my** coup de grace!!*
IT'S A CURSE! WE'RE CURSED!!

And now we proudly present...

Our cheap attempt at a flashback that incorporates all the missed events.

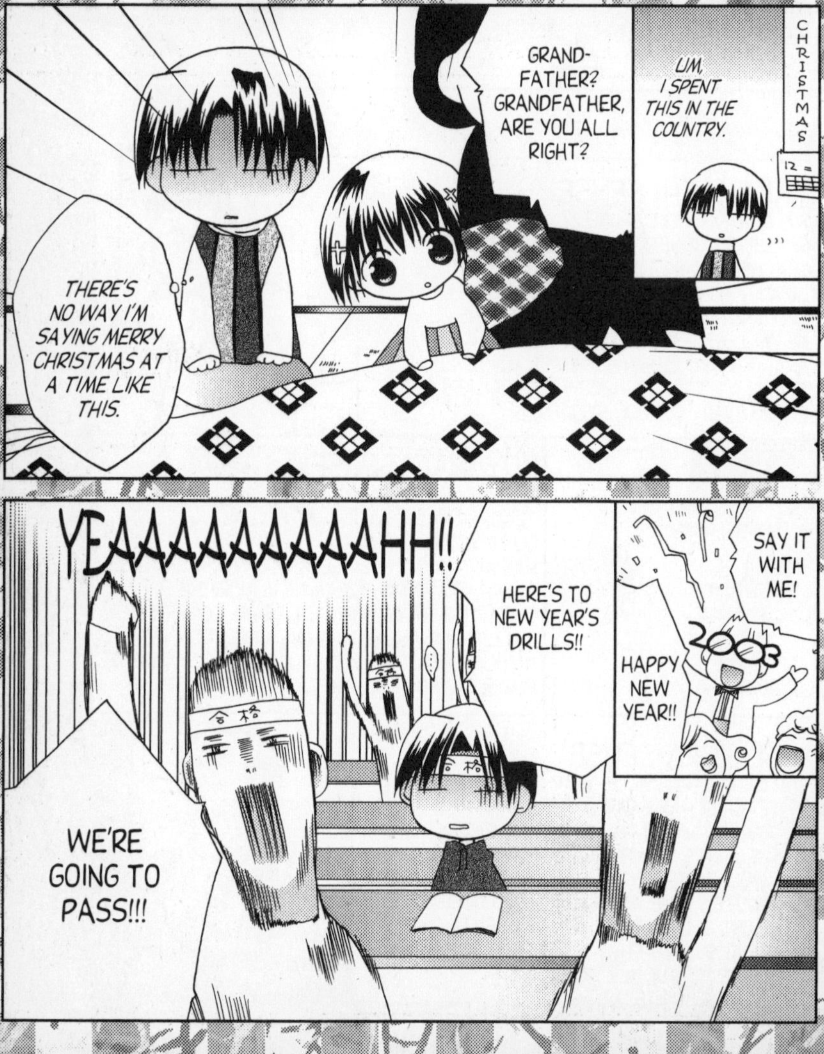
CHRISTMAS
UM, I SPENT THIS IN THE COUNTRY.
12
GRAND-FATHER? GRANDFATHER, ARE YOU ALL RIGHT?
THERE'S NO WAY I'M SAYING MERRY CHRISTMAS AT A TIME LIKE THIS.
SAY IT WITH ME!
2003
HAPPY NEW YEAR!!
HERE'S TO NEW YEAR'S DRILLS!!
YEAAAAAAAAAHH!!
WE'RE GOING TO PASS!!!

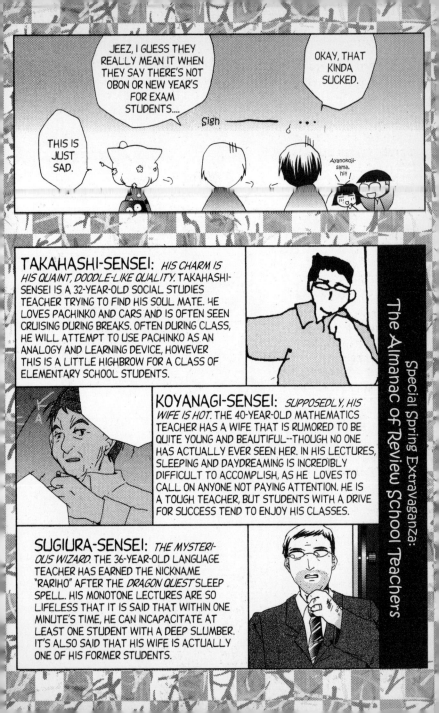

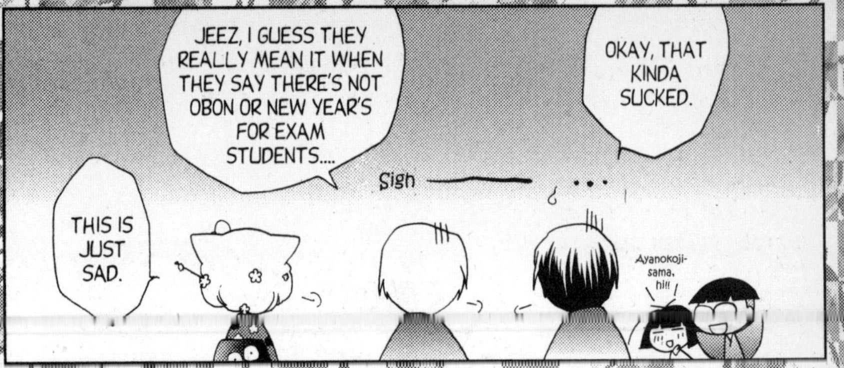
OKAY, THAT KINDA SUCKED.
JEEZ, I GUESS THEY REALLY MEAN IT WHEN THEY SAY THERE'S NOT OBON OR NEW YEAR'S FOR EXAM STUDENTS....
...
Ayanokoji-sama, hi!!
Sigh
THIS IS JUST SAD.

Special Spring ExtraVaganza: The Almanac of Review School Teachers

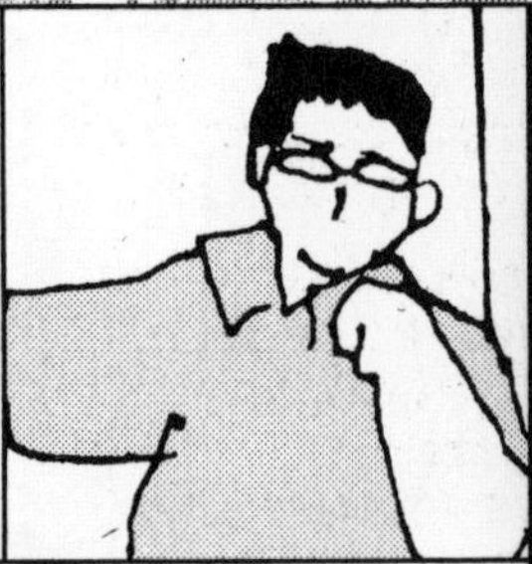

TAKAHASHI-SENSEI: *HIS CHARM IS HIS QUAINT, DOODLE-LIKE QUALITY.* TAKAHASHI-SENSEI IS A 32-YEAR-OLD SOCIAL STUDIES TEACHER TRYING TO FIND HIS SOUL MATE. HE LOVES PACHINKO AND CARS AND IS OFTEN SEEN CRUISING DURING BREAKS. OFTEN DURING CLASS, HE WILL ATTEMPT TO USE PACHINKO AS AN ANALOGY AND LEARNING DEVICE, HOWEVER THIS IS A LITTLE HIGHBROW FOR A CLASS OF ELEMENTARY SCHOOL STUDENTS.

KOYANAGI-SENSEI: *SUPPOSEDLY, HIS WIFE IS HOT.* THE 40-YEAR-OLD MATHEMATICS TEACHER HAS A WIFE THAT IS RUMORED TO BE QUITE YOUNG AND BEAUTIFUL--THOUGH NO ONE HAS ACTUALLY EVER SEEN HER. IN HIS LECTURES, SLEEPING AND DAYDREAMING IS INCREDIBLY DIFFICULT TO ACCOMPLISH, AS HE LOVES TO CALL ON ANYONE NOT PAYING ATTENTION. HE IS A TOUGH TEACHER, BUT STUDENTS WITH A DRIVE FOR SUCCESS TEND TO ENJOY HIS CLASSES.

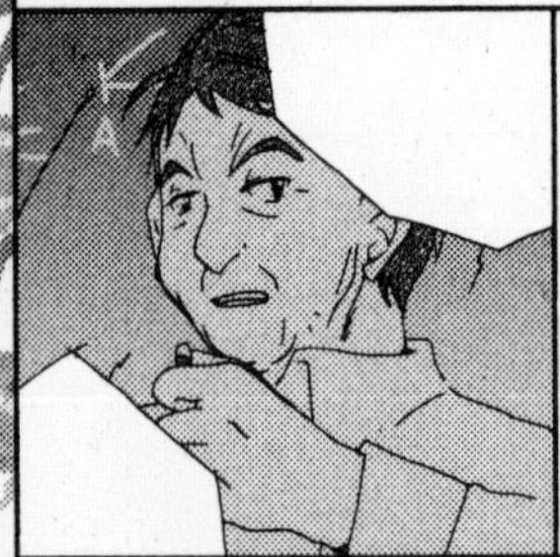

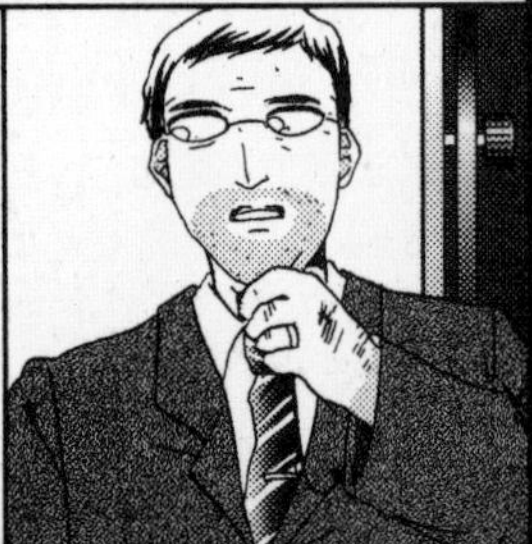

SUGIURA-SENSEI: *THE MYSTERIOUS WIZARD.* THE 36-YEAR-OLD LANGUAGE TEACHER HAS EARNED THE NICKNAME "RARIHO" AFTER THE *DRAGON QUEST* SLEEP SPELL. HIS MONOTONE LECTURES ARE SO LIFELESS THAT IT IS SAID THAT WITHIN ONE MINUTE'S TIME, HE CAN INCAPACITATE AT LEAST ONE STUDENT WITH A DEEP SLUMBER. IT'S ALSO SAID THAT HIS WIFE IS ACTUALLY ONE OF HIS FORMER STUDENTS.

Let's see...you just finished Volume 7 and wow-wee! Once again, thank you so very much for your support. I truly appreciate it.
-Koge-Donbo.

Currently in Pita-Ten, the season being featured is winter. Not just winter, but *midwinter*. Now, I'm sure that some of you inquiring minds out there have noticed, but...

That's right!! I bet you were thinking that their uniforms were a bit too thin and meager looking, right? I mean, it's winter and all they've got is a scarf.

To be quite honest, I had been mulling over the idea of "What coat should I draw for them? A double coat or should it be a short coat?" for quite some time, but all the while I was still trying to figure out the coat, the story kept advancing.
Dohhh. 6

So basically I ended up saying, "It's a little late to have them all in coats now." So I decided to have them trucking along with just a scarf.

Double doh! Anyhow, here is what I decided on for the coat.
→

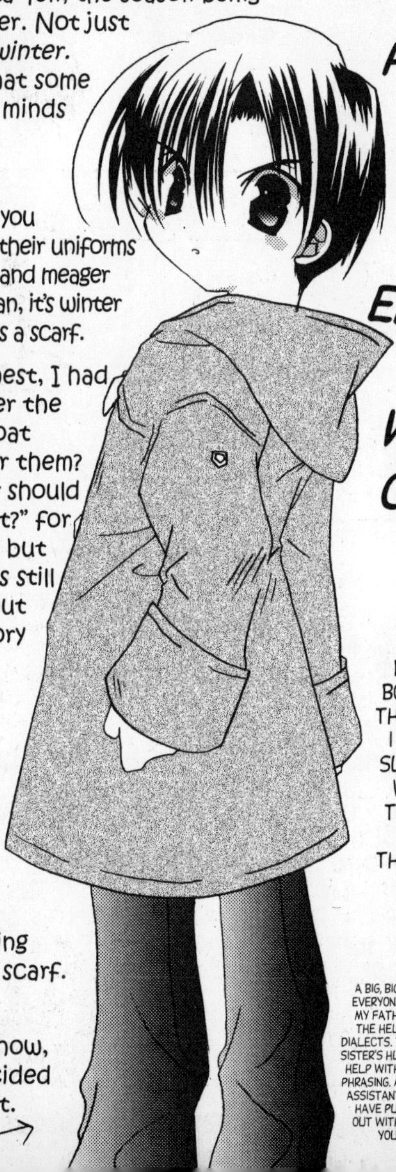

PRESENTING SEIEI ACADEMY'S MISAKI ELEMENTARY SCHOOL'S WINTER COAT!!!

BY THE WAY, THE NEXT BOOK, VOLUME 8, WILL BE THE FINAL BOOK. UWAAHH!! I FEEL SO SAD ALL OF A SUDDEN!! I HOPE YOU GUYS WILL CONTINUE TO SEE THIS SERIES THROUGH TO THE END AS WELL. THANK YOU SO VERY MUCH!
- KOGE-DONBO 2003.3.22

A BIG, BIG THANKS TO EVERYONE! KAIYU-SAN, MY FATHER, FOR ALL THE HELP WITH THE DIALECTS. TO MY EDITOR'S SISTER'S HUSBAND FOR HIS HELP WITH THE ENGLISH PHRASING. AND TO ALL MY ASSISTANTS, I COULDN'T HAVE PUT THIS BOOK OUT WITHOUT ALL OF YOUR HELP.

In the Last Volume of...

PITA-TEN

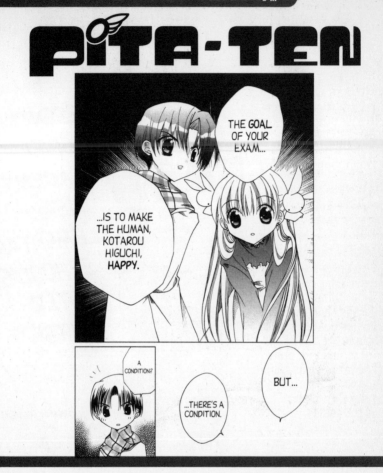

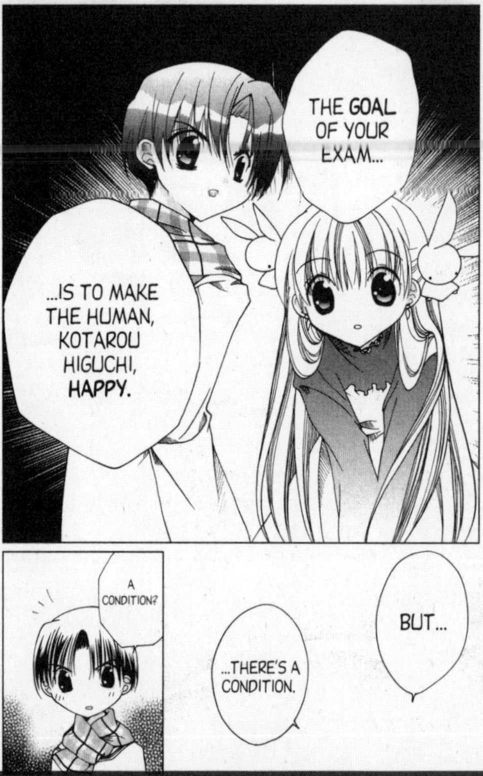
THE GOAL OF YOUR EXAM...
...IS TO MAKE THE HUMAN, KOTAROU HIGUCHI, HAPPY.
BUT...
...THERE'S A CONDITION.
A CONDITION?

Kotarou may finally have to move on! His relationship with Misha is in shambles and Shia is out of the picture...so who is left? Kotarou's long-time friend Koboshi, that's who! When she confesses her true feelings for him, will Takashi sit idly by? These matters of the heart may just have to wait for Kotarou's impending middle school entrance exam. Meanwhile, Misha is cramming for her Angelic Examination, but a hard truth is about to be revealed that could spell disaster. Futures will be decided and fates sealed with the outcome of these exams! Don't miss out on any of the tear-jerking drama in the final volume of Pita-Ten!

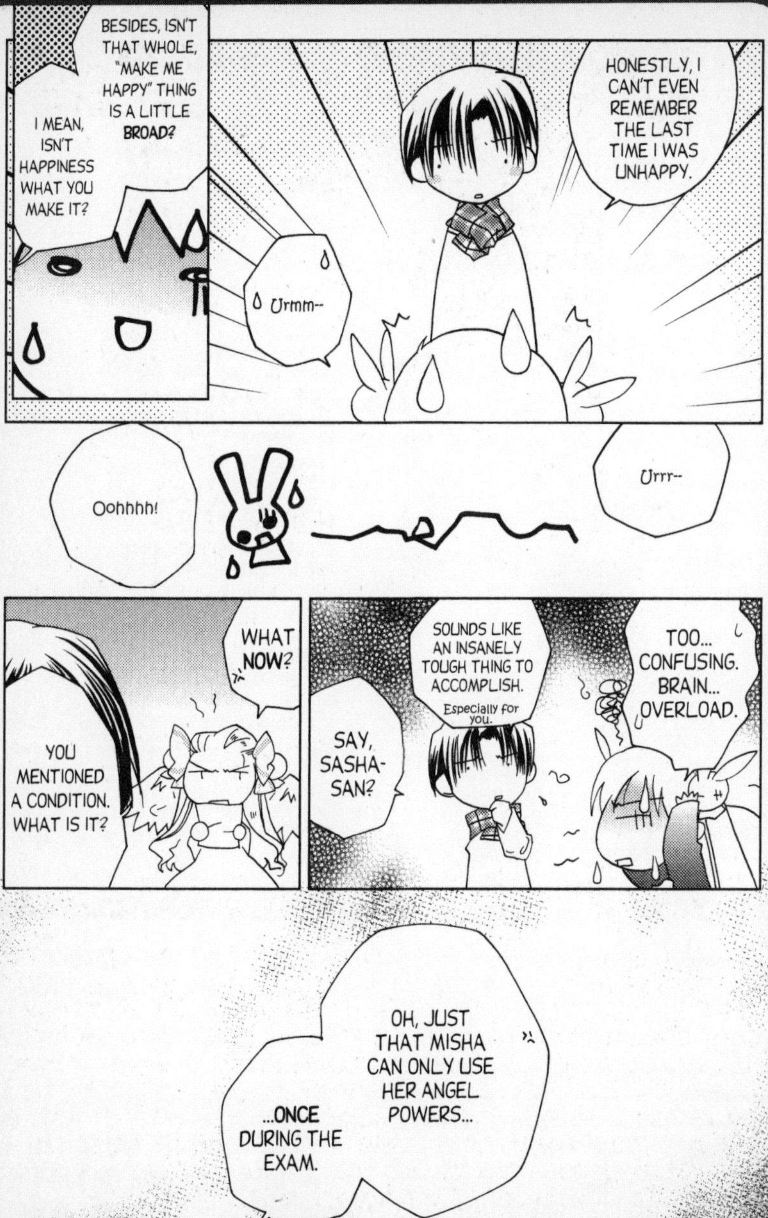
HONESTLY, I CAN'T EVEN REMEMBER THE LAST TIME I WAS UNHAPPY.
Urmm--
BESIDES, ISN'T THAT WHOLE, "MAKE ME HAPPY" THING IS A LITTLE BROAD?
I MEAN, ISN'T HAPPINESS WHAT YOU MAKE IT?
Urrr--
Oohhhh!
TOO... CONFUSING. BRAIN... OVERLOAD.
SOUNDS LIKE AN INSANELY TOUGH THING TO ACCOMPLISH.
Especially for you.
SAY, SASHA-SAN?
WHAT NOW?
YOU MENTIONED A CONDITION. WHAT IS IT?
OH, JUST THAT MISHA CAN ONLY USE HER ANGEL POWERS...
...ONCE DURING THE EXAM.

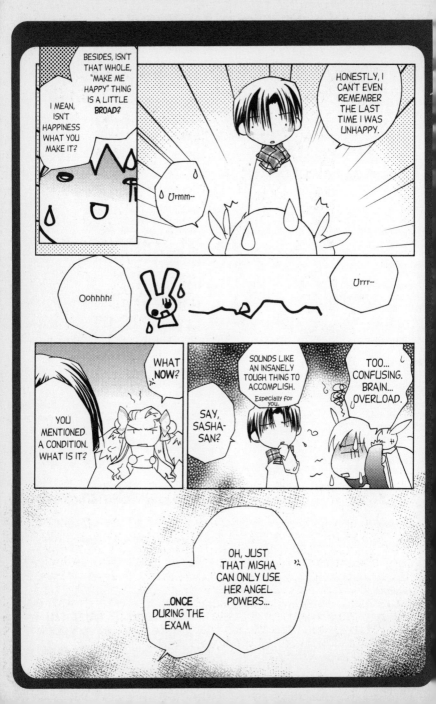

ALSO AVAILABLE FROM TOKYOPOP

You want it? We got it!
A full range of TOKYOPOP
products are available now at:
www.TOKYOPOP.com/shop

09.21.04T

ALSO AVAILABLE FROM TOKYOPOP®

MANGA

.HACK//LEGEND OF THE TWILIGHT
@LARGE
ABENOBASHI: MAGICAL SHOPPING ARCADE
A.I. LOVE YOU
AI YORI AOSHI
ALICHINO
ANGELIC LAYER
ARM OF KANNON
BABY BIRTH
BATTLE ROYALE
BATTLE VIXENS
BOYS BE...
BRAIN POWERED
BRIGADOON
B'TX
CANDIDATE FOR GODDESS, THE
CARDCAPTOR SAKURA
CARDCAPTOR SAKURA - MASTER OF THE CLOW
CHOBITS
CHRONICLES OF THE CURSED SWORD
CLAMP SCHOOL DETECTIVES
CLOVER
COMIC PARTY
CONFIDENTIAL CONFESSIONS
CORRECTOR YUI
COWBOY BEBOP
COWBOY BEBOP: SHOOTING STAR
CRAZY LOVE STORY
CRESCENT MOON
CROSS
CULDCEPT
CYBORG 009
D•N•ANGEL
DEARS
DEMON DIARY
DEMON ORORON, THE
DEUS VITAE
DIABOLO
DIGIMON
DIGIMON TAMERS
DIGIMON ZERO TWO
DOLL
DRAGON HUNTER
DRAGON KNIGHTS
DRAGON VOICE
DREAM SAGA
DUKLYON: CLAMP SCHOOL DEFENDERS
EERIE QUEERIE!
ERICA SAKURAZAWA: COLLECTED WORKS
ET CETERA
ETERNITY
EVIL'S RETURN
FAERIES' LANDING
FAKE
FLCL
FLOWER OF THE DEEP SLEEP
FORBIDDEN DANCE
FRUITS BASKET

G GUNDAM
GATEKEEPERS
GETBACKERS
GIRL GOT GAME
GRAVITATION
GTO
GUNDAM SEED ASTRAY
GUNDAM WING
GUNDAM WING: BATTLEFIELD OF PACIFISTS
GUNDAM WING: ENDLESS WALTZ
GUNDAM WING: THE LAST OUTPOST (G-UNIT)
HANDS OFF!
HAPPY MANIA
HARLEM BEAT
HYPER RUNE
I.N.V.U.
IMMORTAL RAIN
INITIAL D
INSTANT TEEN: JUST ADD NUTS
ISLAND
JING: KING OF BANDITS
JING: KING OF BANDITS - TWILIGHT TALES
JULINE
KARE KANO
KILL ME, KISS ME
KINDAICHI CASE FILES, THE
KING OF HELL
KODOCHA: SANA'S STAGE
LAMENT OF THE LAMB
LEGAL DRUG
LEGEND OF CHUN HYANG, THE
LES BIJOUX
LOVE HINA
LOVE OR MONEY
LUPIN III
LUPIN III: WORLD'S MOST WANTED
MAGIC KNIGHT RAYEARTH I
MAGIC KNIGHT RAYEARTH II
MAHOROMATIC: AUTOMATIC MAIDEN
MAN OF MANY FACES
MARMALADE BOY
MARS
MARS: HORSE WITH NO NAME
MINK
MIRACLE GIRLS
MIYUKI-CHAN IN WONDERLAND
MODEL
MOURYOU KIDEN: LEGEND OF THE NYMPH
NECK AND NECK
ONE
ONE I LOVE, THE
PARADISE KISS
PARASYTE
PASSION FRUIT
PEACH FUZZ
PEACH GIRL
PEACH GIRL: CHANGE OF HEART
PET SHOP OF HORRORS
PITA-TEN
PLANET LADDER

09.21.0

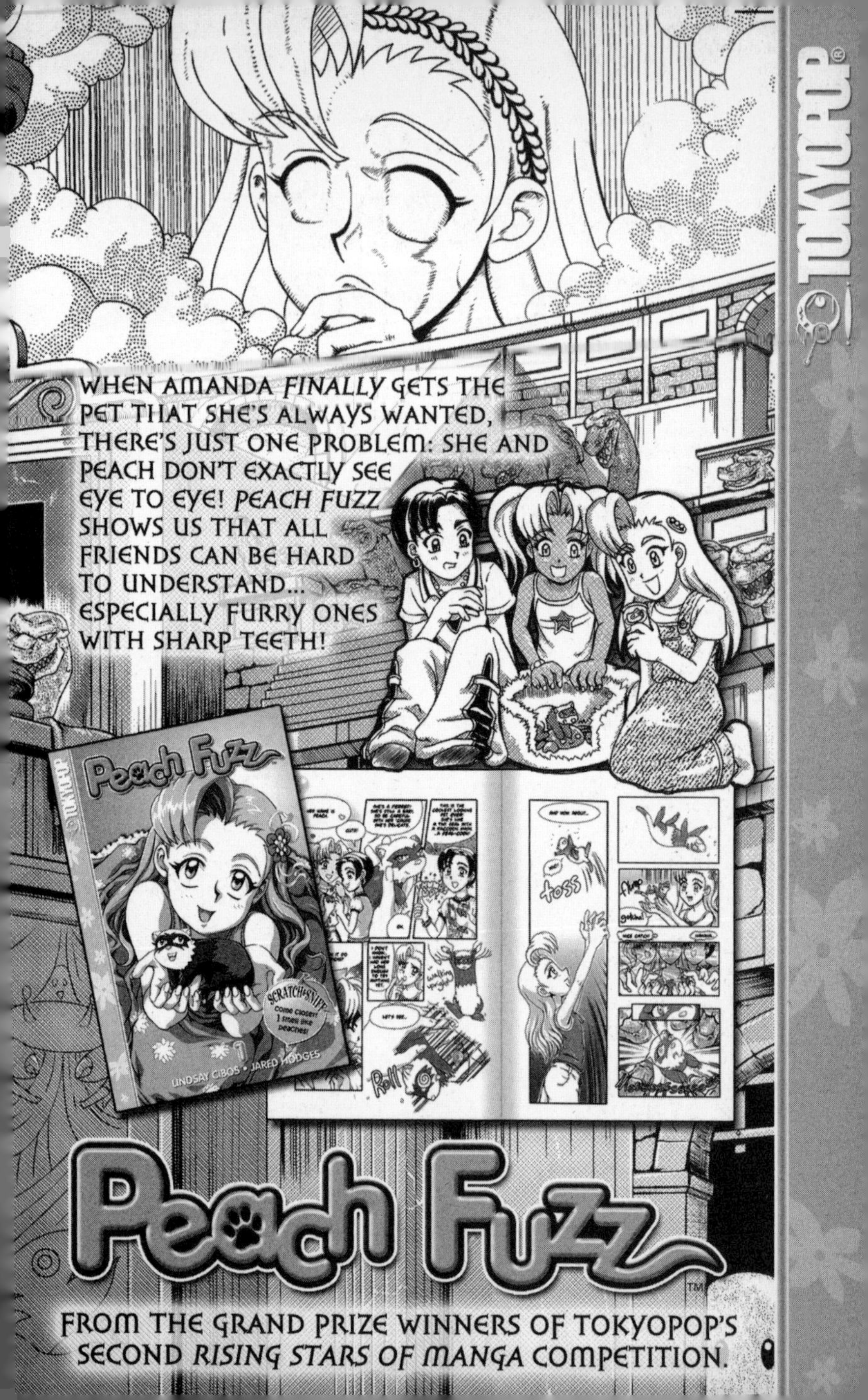
TOKYOPOP
WHEN AMANDA *FINALLY* GETS THE PET THAT SHE'S ALWAYS WANTED, THERE'S JUST ONE PROBLEM: SHE AND PEACH DON'T EXACTLY SEE EYE TO EYE! *PEACH FUZZ* SHOWS US THAT ALL FRIENDS CAN BE HARD TO UNDERSTAND... ESPECIALLY FURRY ONES WITH SHARP TEETH!
Peach Fuzz
SCRATCH & SNIFF
Come closer! I smell like peaches!
1
LINDSAY CIBOS • JARED HODGES
toss
Roll
Peach Fuzz™
FROM THE GRAND PRIZE WINNERS OF TOKYOPOP'S SECOND *RISING STARS OF MANGA* COMPETITION.

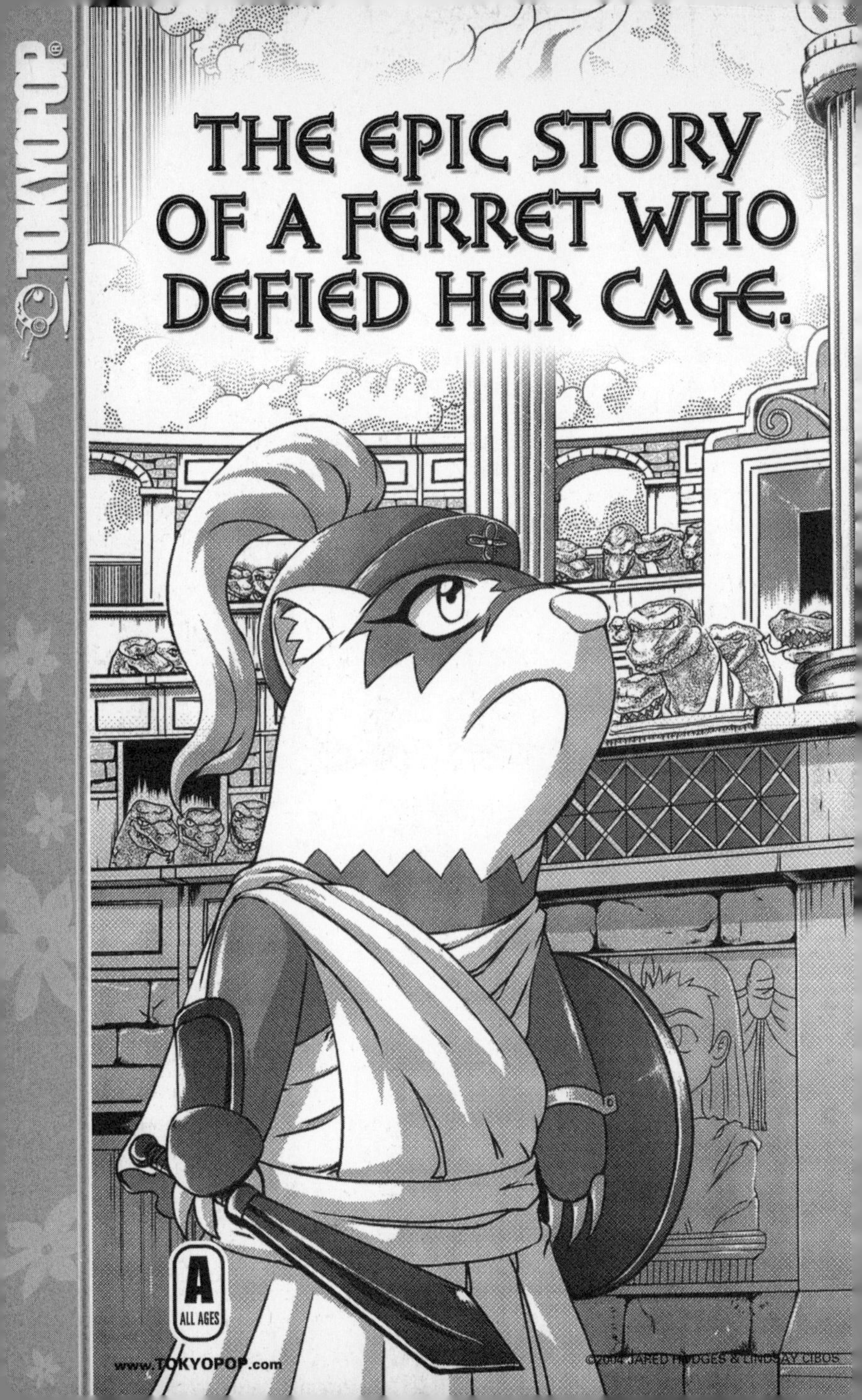
TOKYOPOP
THE EPIC STORY OF A FERRET WHO DEFIED HER CAGE.
A
ALL AGES
www.TOKYOPOP.com
©2004 JARED HODGES & LINDSAY CIBOS

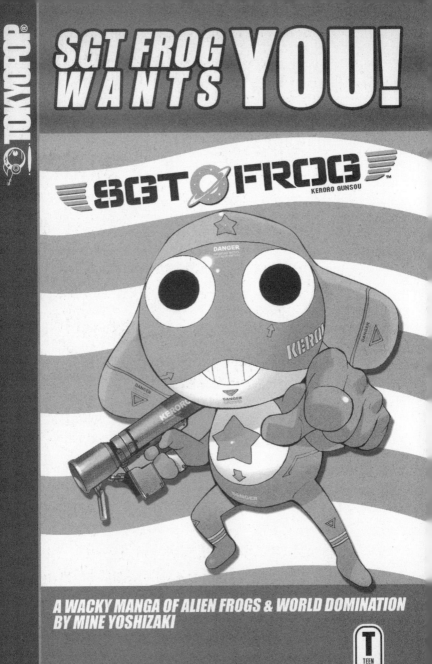

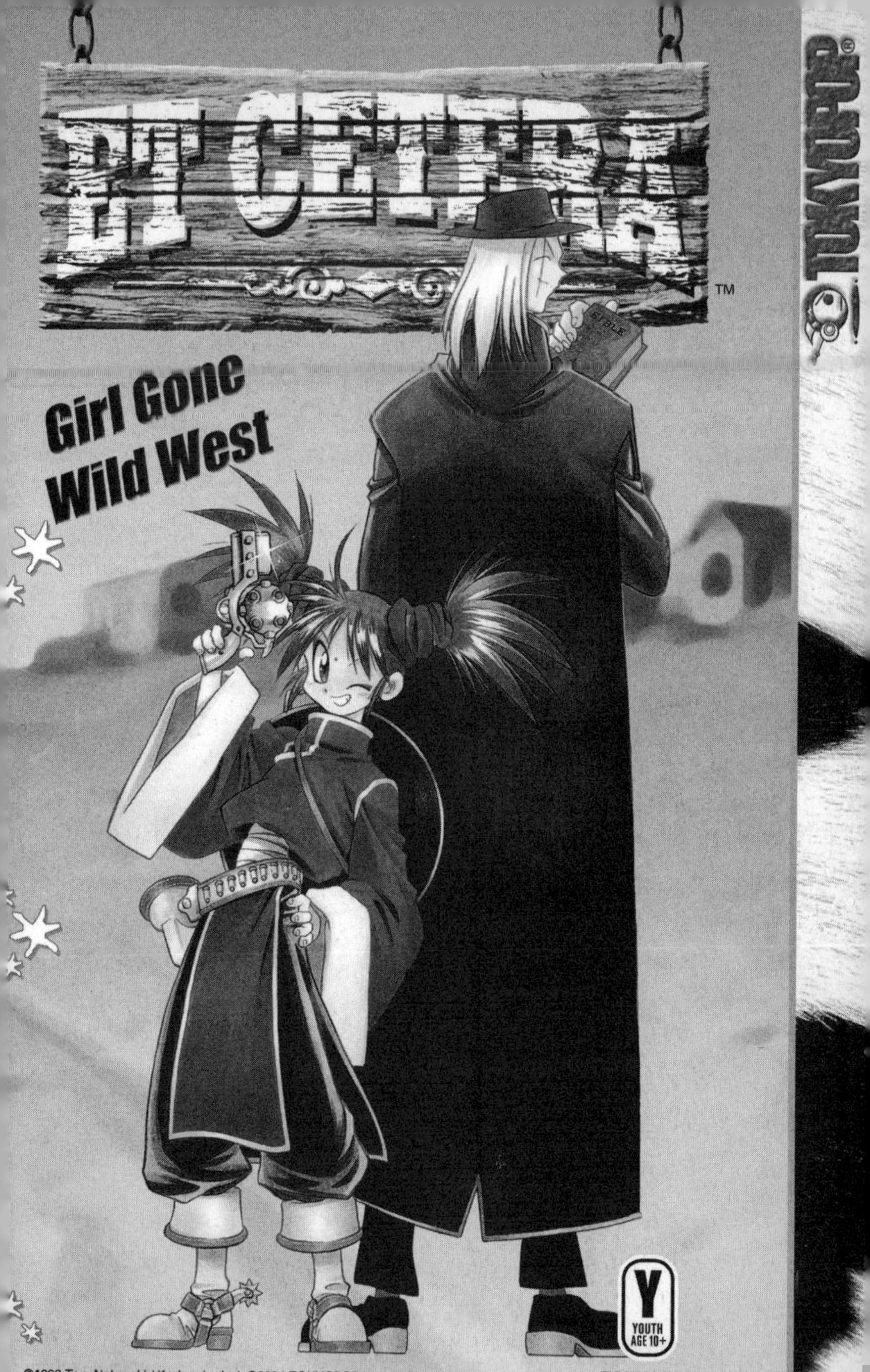
Et Cetera™
Girl Gone Wild West
BIBLE
Y
YOUTH AGE 10+
TOKYOPOP

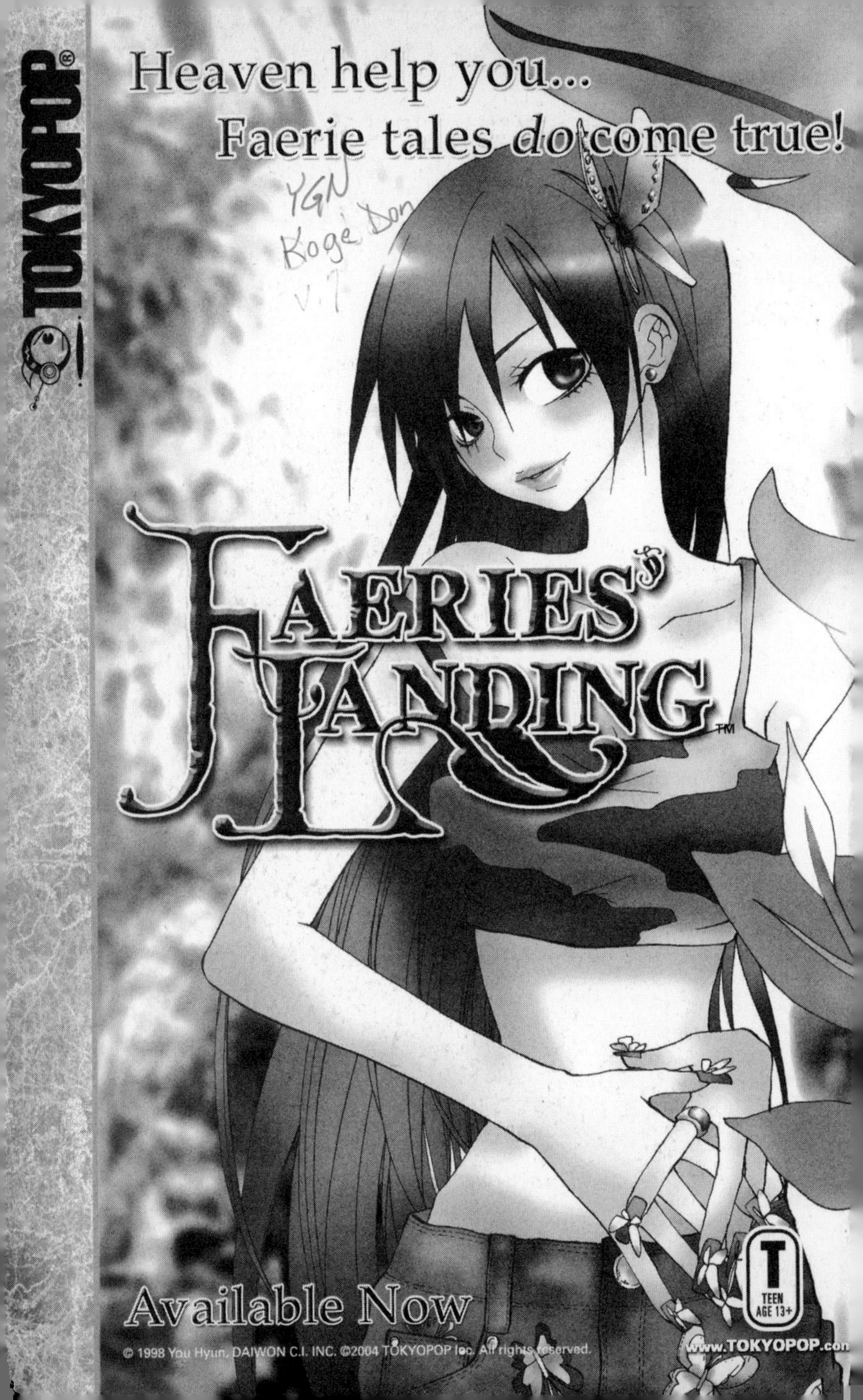

TOKYOPOP®
Heaven help you...
Faerie tales *do* come true!
FAERIES' LANDING™
Available Now
TEEN AGE 13+
© 1998 You Hyun, DAIWON C.I. INC. ©2004 TOKYOPOP Inc. All rights reserved.
www.TOKYOPOP.com

STOP!

This is the back of the book.
You wouldn't want to spoil a great ending!

This book is printed "manga-style," in the authentic Japanese right-to-left format. Since none of the artwork has been flipped or altered, readers get to experience the story just as the creator intended. You've been asking for it, so TOKYOPOP® delivered: authentic, hot-off-the-press, and far more fun!

DIRECTIONS

If this is your first time reading manga-style, here's a quick guide to help you understand how it works.

It's easy... just start in the top right panel and follow the numbers. Have fun, and look for more 100% authentic manga from TOKYOPOP®!